In the history of modern theatre Ibsen is one of the dominating figures. His conquest of the theatre over the past hundred years – first in Scandinavia, and then very quickly in Europe, North America and the wider world – makes him one of the most frequently performed playwrights in the world today.

The sixteen chapters of this *Companion*, contributed by a distinguished international team, explore Ibsen's life and work, providing an invaluable reference work for students of drama and of literature. In chronological terms they range from an account of Ibsen's earliest pieces, written during the 1850s when he was a young producer in Bergen, through the years of rich experimentation when he sought – in historical tragedy, in verse comedy, in dramatic poetry, in philosophical drama – to find his own style and dramatic idiom, to the mature 'Ibsenist' plays that made him famous towards the end of the nineteenth century.

Among the thematic topics explored here are Ibsen and comedy, Ibsen and the realistic problem play, and Ibsen and feminism. Another little-known aspect of his art – his achievement as a lyric poet – is given close attention. Two chapters account for the spread of Ibsen's influence on the international stage to the end of the nineteenth century and to the present; three related chapters, including an interview with John Barton and an essay by Arthur Miller, address the challenge that Ibsen's plays continue to present to theatre directors and to the practising dramatists of today, as well as to those who work in film and television.

A full chronology and a detailed list of works provide essential tools for the student and scholar. There are also extensive chapters on the changing nature of twentieth-century criticism of Ibsen and on those reference works essential to a fuller understanding of the dramatist.

James McFarlane is Emeritus Professor of European Literature at the University of East Anglia and Fellow of the Norwegian Academy of Science and Letters. Among his other works on Scandinavian subjects are the eight volumes of *The Oxford Ibsen*, the standard English text of the plays. From 1975–91 Professor McFarlane was editor of *Scandinavica: An International Journal of Scandinavian Studies*. He is also managing editor of Norvik Press.

D0071911

THE CAMBRIDGE
COMPANION TO
IBSEN

CAMBRIDGE COMPANIONS TO LITERATURE

THE CAMBRIDGE
COMPANION TO
IBSEN

EDITED BY

JAMES McFARLANE

Emeritus Professor of European Literature,
University of East Anglia, Norwich

CAMBRIDGE
UNIVERSITY PRESS

Published by the Press Syndicate of the University of Cambridge
The Pitt Building, Trumpington Street, Cambridge CB2 1RP
40 West 20th Street, New York, NY 10011–4211, USA
10 Stamford Road, Oakleigh, Melbourne 3166, Australia

First published 1994
Reprinted 1996, 1998

Printed in the United Kingdom at the University Press, Cambridge

A catalogue record for this book is available from the British Library

Library of Congress cataloguing in publication data

The Cambridge Companion to Ibsen / edited by James McFarlane.
p.   cm. (Cambridge Companions to Literature)
Includes bibliographical references and index.
ISBN 0 521 41166 1 (hardback) – ISBN 0 521 42321 X (paperback).
1. Ibsen, Henrik, 1828–1906 – Criticism and interpretation.
I. McFarlane, James Walter.   II. Series.
PT8895.C27 1994 839.8'226–dc20 93-7884 CIP

ISBN 0 521 41166 1 hardback
ISBN 0 521 42321 X paperback

CE

CONTENTS

ILLUSTRATIONS

CONTRIBUTORS

ASBJØRN AARSETH is Professor of Scandinavian Literature at the University of Bergen; from 1986 to 1990 he edited the scholarly journal *Edda*, and is the author of a range of books (in Norwegian) on literary theory and criticism, on theatrical history, and more specifically on Ibsen; among his English publications is *'Peer Gynt' and 'Ghosts': Texts and Performance* (1989).

JOHN BARTON was a Fellow of King's College, Cambridge from 1954 until 1960, in which year he joined the Royal Shakespeare Company, becoming Associate Director in 1964; alongside his many Shakespeare productions, he has also directed other classic writers of the European theatre, including productions of Ibsen both in England and in Norway (Bergen and Oslo).

ERROL DURBACH is Professor of Theatre Studies at the University of British Columbia, Vancouver; he edited the volume *Ibsen and the Theatre* (1980), and is the author of *Ibsen the Romantic* (1982) and *'A Doll's House': Ibsen's Myth of Transformation* (1991).

INGA-STINA EWBANK is Professor of English at the University of Leeds and the author of many critical studies in the field of English and Scandinavian literature, with special emphasis on Ibsen and Strindberg.

GAIL FINNEY is Professor of German and Comparative Literature at the University of California (Davis) and author of *The Counterfeit Idyll* (1984) and *Women in Modern Drama* (1989).

JANET GARTON is Senior Lecturer in Scandinavian Studies at the University of East Anglia; she has edited *Facets of European Modernism* (1985), and among her other publications are a critical study of *Jens Bjørneboe* (1985), *Norwegian Women's Writing 1850–1990* (1993), and many translations from the Norwegian.

BJØRN HEMMER has held chairs of literature at the Universities of Trondheim and Oslo, and is now Professor of Literature at Agder College, Kristiansand; he has written extensively (in Norwegian) on Ibsen, and is currently joint editor of the biennial *Contemporary Approaches to Ibsen*.

JAMES MCFARLANE is Emeritus Professor of European Literature at the University of East Anglia; he was General Editor of the eight-volume *Oxford Ibsen* (1960–77) and is the author of several books on Ibsen and other literary topics; his most recent publication is *Ibsen and Meaning* (1989).

FREDERICK J. MARKER and LISE-LONE MARKER both hold professorships at the University of Toronto, and together they have written extensively on many aspects of Scandinavian theatre; their publications include *The Scandinavian Theatre: A Short History* (1975), *Edward Gordon Craig and 'The Pretenders': A Production Revisited* (1981), three studies of Ingmar Bergman (1982, 1983 and 1992), and *Ibsen's Lively Art: A Performance Study of the Major Plays* (1989).

ARTHUR MILLER, dramatist.

JOHN NORTHAM is Fellow of Clare College, sometime University Lecturer in English, Cambridge, and Emeritus Professor of Modern and Comparative Drama, University of Bristol; his publications include *Ibsen's Dramatic Method: A Study of the Prose Dramas* (1953, 2nd edn 1971), *Ibsen: A Critical Study* (1973) and *Ibsen's Poems* (1986).

SANDRA SAARI is Professor of Literature in the College of Liberal Arts at Rochester Institute of Technology in Rochester, N.Y.; she has written and lectured on many aspects of Ibsen and is currently Secretary of the Ibsen Society of America and on the Editorial Board of *Contemporary Approaches to Ibsen*.

EGIL TÖRNQVIST is Professor of Scandinavian Studies at the University of Amsterdam; among his publications are studies of Strindberg, O'Neill and Bergman; his most recent work is *Transposing Drama: Studies in Representation* (1991).

SIMON WILLIAMS is Professor of Dramatic Art at the University of California (Santa Barbara); among his publications are *German Actors of the Eighteenth and Nineteenth Centuries* (1985) and *Shakespeare on the German Stage* (1990).

ROBIN YOUNG is Lecturer in English at the University College of Wales, Aberystwyth, and author of *Time's Disinherited Children: Childhood, Regression and Sacrifice in the plays of Henrik Ibsen* (1989).

PREFACE

References in this *Companion* to Ibsen's text in English translation are generally to *The Oxford Ibsen* 8 vols. (London, 1960–77). In order to keep the number of end-notes to a minimum, these references are wherever possible inserted into the body of the chapter in square brackets, using lower case italic roman numerals for the volume number, followed by the page number(s), thus: [*iv*, 623–7]. Where in order to give extra point to the critical argument – or for any other reason – a contributor has modified the Oxford text, this is indicated by the addition of an asterisk, thus: [*vi*, 256*]. If a different English edition has been used, full bibliographical details are given in the end-notes to the relevant chapter. Where the argument requires reference to Ibsen's Norwegian text, the edition used is the Centenary Edition: Henrik Ibsen, *Samlede Verker*, Hundreårsutgave, 22 vols. (Oslo, 1928–57); the form in such cases is volume number (roman numerals in upper case), followed by page number(s), thus: [XVI, 160].

The chapters on 'A century of Ibsen criticism' and on 'Works of reference', taken together, give the best general guide to further reading; additional bibliographical information may be found in the notes which follow the other chapters. Readers wishing to keep abreast of current developments in Ibsen criticism and scholarship will find the (now biennial) volumes of *Contemporary Approaches to Ibsen* (Oslo, 1966 ff.) especially useful.

CHRONOLOGY

1828   *20 March*   Born in Skien, the second son in a family of six children born to Knud Ibsen and his wife Marichen (née Altenburg); is baptized Henrik Johan.

1835   Financial problems force the family to move to a smaller house at Venstøp, a couple of miles outside Skien; here they live for the next eight years.

1843   *October*   The family moves back from Venstøp to Skien.
       27 December   Henrik leaves home to earn his living as an apothecary's apprentice in Grimstad, where he lives for the next six years.

1846   *9 October*   A maid in the house bears him an illegitimate son who is given the name Hans Jacob Henriksen.

1848–9   *Winter*   Writes his first play *Catiline*; it is submitted to, and rejected by, the Christiania Theatre.

1850   *12 April*   *Catiline* published privately under the pseudonym of Brynjolf Bjarme.
       28 April   Arrives in Christiania (later Oslo) to prepare for university entrance examination; is not successful (September).
       c. 19 May   Completes writing *The Burial Mound*, again under the pseudonym of Brynjolf Bjarme; is performed at the Christiania Theatre later in the year (26 September), the first ever performance of an Ibsen play.

1851   *January–September*   Contributes occasional critical articles and poems to periodicals.
       26 October   Arrives in Bergen to take up an appointment at the recently established Norwegian Theatre there; his contract stipulates that he is also 'to assist the Theatre as a dramatic author'.

1852   *15 April*   Leaves on an extended study tour of theatres in Hamburg, Copenhagen and Dresden, returning to Bergen at the beginning of August.

1853   *2 January*   His three-Act comedy *St John's Night* (the authorship of which he later repudiated) performed on the third anniversary of the founding of the Bergen theatre.

1854   *2 January*   A revised version of *The Burial Mound* performed in Bergen, with little success.

1855   *2 January*   *Lady Inger*, a historical drama in five Acts, performed at the theatre in Bergen.

      27 November   Reads a paper on 'Shakespeare and his influence upon Scandinavian literature' to a Bergen literary society; the text has seemingly not survived.

1856   *2 January*   *The Feast at Solhoug* performed in Bergen, followed on 13 March by a performance in Christiania.

      7 January   First meets Suzannah Thoresen, his future wife, at the house of her step-mother, Magdalene Thoresen, author and dramatist.

      March–April   Accompanies the theatre company on a short guest season in Trondheim.

      Summer   Goes on a walking tour of Western Norway, from Bergen to Hardanger and back via Voss.

1857   *2 January*   *Olaf Liljekrans* performed at the Bergen Theatre.

      April   His five-year contract with the Bergen Theatre expires, and is renewed for another year.

      9 July   Writes from Christiania asking to be released from his Bergen appointment in order to accept a post at the Norwegian Theatre in Christiania.

      3 September   Takes up his new post in Christiania.

1858   A group of friends form a literary association called 'The Learned Holland', with meetings at the house of Paul Botten-Hansen, the University librarian.

      5 March   The Royal Theatre, Copenhagen, rejects *The Vikings at Helgeland* because of its 'crudeness'.

      25 April   *The Vikings at Helgeland* is published as a supplement to a journal.

      18 June   Marries Suzannah Thoresen.

      24 November   First performance of *The Vikings* at the Christiania Norwegian Theatre, produced by the author.

1859   *January*   The poem 'On the Heights' is published in a journal.

      23 December   His son, Sigurd, is born – the only child of his marriage.

1860   *Winter*   Ibsen under attack in the press and from the Board of the theatre for alleged lack of enterprise; these attacks continue over several months.

1862   The poem 'Terje Vigen' printed as the New Year supplement to a journal.

24 May   Awarded a small travel grant to collect folksongs and folktales in Western Norway.

1 June   The Norwegian Theatre in Christiania goes bankrupt and Ibsen loses his job; for the next two years he has no regular income.

31 December   *Love's Comedy* printed as a New Year supplement in a journal.

1863   *1 January*   Appointed literary adviser, on a temporary basis, to a reorganized Christiania Theatre.

27 May   Awarded a small government grant to allow him a year's stay, mainly in Rome, 'to study art, art history and literature'.

July–August   Period of intense work on *The Pretenders*; eventually published in October.

1864   *17 January*   *The Pretenders* first performed in Christiania, produced by the author.

5 April   Leaves Christiania for Copenhagen and the South.

4 May   Witnesses German victory parade in Berlin following Dano-Prussian War; then by train to Italy, via Vienna and Trieste to Venice, where he stays six weeks.

Summer   Spends several weeks in Rome; then for two months to Genzano, returning to Rome in early September; his wife and child join him in Rome.

mid-July   Begins intense period of work on his 'dramatic poem' *Brand*.

1865   *Summer*   Completes *Brand* in Ariccia.

1866   *15 March*   *Brand* published in Copenhagen, and is well received by the public in Scandinavia.

12 May   He is awarded an annual government grant to enable him to devote himself to his writing; his economic circumstances are greatly improved.

June–September   Moves to Frascati for the summer.

1867   Completes *Peer Gynt* at Cacamicciola on the island of Ischia, and later at Sorrento; it is published on 14 November in Copenhagen.

October–November   Returns to Rome from Sorrento via Pompeii and Naples.

1868   *mid-May*   Leaves Rome and travels for five weeks (with short stays at Florence, Bologna, Venice and Bolzano) before settling down for the summer in Berchtesgaden; leaves at the end of

August for Munich, before eventually taking up permanent residence in Dresden (An der Frauenkirche 6) with his wife and son at
the beginning of October.

1869   *8 June*   Moves house to Königsbrücker Strasse 33.

end-July   Visits Stockholm and stays there until end-September;
is decorated by the King with the Vasa Order; receives invitation
to spend two months in Egypt as Norway's representative at the
opening of the Suez Canal.

30 September   *The League of Youth* published.

October–December   Travels widely in Egypt, to Nubia and the
Red Sea, and sails through the newly opened Canal in mid-
November, returning to Dresden via Paris in mid-December.

1870   *19 July*   Leaves Dresden for Copenhagen via Lübeck; stays there
until end-September, and returns to Dresden early October.

1871   *January–February*   Prepares a selection of his poems for publication.

13 February   Hears that he has been honoured by Denmark with
the Order of Dannebrog.

3 May   His selected *Poems* published in an edition of 5,000
copies.

June   Begins work in earnest on *Emperor and Galilean*, which
occupies him until May 1873.

1872   Edmund Gosse publishes an article on the *Poems* in the *Spectator*,
the first critical discussion of Ibsen in England, and follows this
with further articles in *Spectator*, *Academy*, *Fortnightly Review*
and *Fraser's Magazine* over the next two years.

15 July   Leaves for Berchtesgaden for the summer, returning to
Dresden at the beginning of September; his new address is Wet-
tiner Strasse 22.

1873   Serves on the jury of the International Art Exhibition in Vienna
between 15 June and 1 August.

July   Decorated by Norway with the Knight's Order of St Olaf
on the occasion of the coronation of Oscar II.

August   Revises *Lady Inger* for a new edition.

16 October   *Emperor and Galilean* published.

1874   *23 January*   Invites Edvard Grieg to compose incidental music to
Peer Gynt.

19 July   Arrives on a visit to Christiania, returning to Dresden in
mid-September.

10 September   Is honoured by a torchlight procession by Christiania students.

1875   *?13 April* Moves from Dresden to Munich, taking up residence in his new home at Schönfeld Strasse 17 at the beginning of May; Munich is his permanent residence for the next three years.

?8 August Leaves for Kitzbühel, in the Tyrol, for the summer, returning to Munich on 1 October.

1876   *February* First full-length translation of a work by Ibsen into English: *The Emperor and the Galilean* by Catherine Ray.

24 February First performance of *Peer Gynt*, with Grieg's music, at the Christiania Theatre.

3 June Ibsen attends a performance of *The Pretenders* in Berlin by the Meiningen players.

5 August Leaves with his wife and son for Gossensass in the Tyrol, and returns to Munich at the end of September.

1877   *1 May* Moves house to Schellingstrasse 20; associates with the Munich literary circle, the Society of Crocodiles, and especially with Paul Heyse.

5 September Receives an honorary doctorate from the University of Uppsala, Sweden.

11 October *Pillars of Society* published.

1878   *?10 August* Leaves Munich with his wife and son for Gossensass, and moves on to Rome at the beginning of October with the intention of spending the winter 'south of the Alps'.

1879   *July* Moves to Amalfi for the summer months; pays brief visit to Sorrento before returning to Munich in mid-October: Amalienstrasse 50a.

4 December *A Doll's House* published.

1880   *August–September* Spends some weeks in Berchtesgaden on vacation before returning to Munich end-September.

2 November Leaves Munich to winter in Rome, where his son Sigurd is to complete his law studies, and is mainly resident in Rome for the next five years.

15 December 'Quicksands', an adaptation of *Pillars of Society*, played at the Gaiety Theatre, London – the first performance of any Ibsen play on the English stage.

1881   *28 June* The Ibsen family leaves Rome for Sorrento, where Ibsen works on the composition of *Ghosts*; they return to Rome 5 November.

12 December *Ghosts* published.

1882   'The Child Wife', an adaptation of *A Doll's House*, played at the Grand Opera House, Milwaukee – the first performance in English of any Ibsen play in North America.

July   Moves to Gossensass for the summer, eventually returning to Rome 24 November.

28 November   An Enemy of the People published.

1883   *Summer*   Spends from beginning of July until early October in Gossensass, then about three weeks in Bolzano, returning to Rome end October.

1884   *30 June*   Leaves Rome for Gossensass for the summer, where he works on the final revision of *The Wild Duck*; returns via Bolzano to Rome 13 November.

11 November   The Wild Duck published.

1885   *June–September*   Extended visit to Norway; stays a month in Trondheim, two months in Molde; leaves 5 September, travelling via Bergen, Christiania and Copenhagen to Germany.

October   Takes up residence again in Munich, Maximilianstrasse 32, and is resident in Munich for the next six years.

1886   *23 November   Rosmersholm* published.

22 December   Ibsen attends a production of *Ghosts* at Meiningen as the guest of the Duke of Saxe-Meiningen.

1887   *Summer*   From early July until mid-October stays in Denmark (mainly in Frederikshavn and Sæby) and in Sweden.

1888   *28 November   The Lady from the Sea* published.

1889   *3–15 March*   Ibsen attends performances of his plays in Berlin and Weimar, and is fêted.

7 June   A Doll's House performed at the Novelty Theatre, London – the first substantial production in England.

Summer   Leaves at the beginning of July for Gossensass, accompanied by his wife; makes the acquaintance of Emilie Bardach and Helene Raff on holiday there; returns to Munich beginning October.

29 September   Die Freie Bühne in Berlin selects *Ghosts* as its opening play.

1890   First collected edition of Ibsen's dramas in English begins publication under the editorship of William Archer.

29 May   André Antoine presents *Ghosts* at the Théâtre Libre in Paris.

December   Hedda Gabler published.

1891   *13 March*   J. T. Grein's Independent Theatre performs *Ghosts* in London, and raises a storm of criticism.

July–October   Leaves for a summer holiday in Norway; takes an extended cruise to the North Cape and back, returning to Christiania on 7 August. Decides to take up residence there. Makes the acquaintance of Hildur Andersen.

9 October   Attends lecture in Christiania by Knut Hamsun, who severely criticizes Ibsen's dramas.

21 October   Moves into rented accommodation in Victoria Terrasse, Christiania (now Oslo).

1892   *11 October*   His son Sigurd marries the poet Bjørnstjerne Bjørnson's daughter Bergliot.

12 December   *The Master Builder* published.

1893   *11 July*   His first grandchild born.

1894   *December*   *Little Eyolf* published.

1895   *July*   Moves from Victoria Terrasse to Arbiens gate 1, on the corner with Drammensveien.

1896   *12 December*   *John Gabriel Borkman* published.

1898   *20 March*   The world sends its congratulations to Ibsen on his seventieth birthday; publication begun of his collected works in Norwegian and in German; he receives many honours and decorations.

1899   *19 December*   *When We Dead Awaken* published.

1900   Ibsen suffers his first stroke, which puts a stop to any further writing; suffers a second stroke the following year.

1906   *23 May*   Dies.

These are arranged alphabetically by English title. The main date given is for publication except where explicitly stated otherwise.

Brand 1866 *Brand*
   First perf. Stockholm 24 Mar. 1885; other early perfs. include Christiania, Bergen and Trondheim (all 1895), Paris (1895) Copenhagen (1895) and Berlin (1898); first English perf. London 11 Nov. 1912. Trans. into English 1891, 1894 and ff.; into German (1872, 1874, 1876, 1882 and ff.); French (1895), Swedish (1870), Dutch (1893), Finnish (1896), Russian (1897), etc.

Burial Mound, The 1850 *Kjæmpehøjen*
(also known as The Warrior's Barrow)
   First ver. perf. Christiania 26 Sep. 1850; publ. 1909; revised version perf. Bergen 2 Jan. 1854 (publ. Bergen in periodical form 1854). Unpublished English trans. perf. 30 May 1912 by the Ibsen Club at the Clavier Hall, London. Trans. into English 1921, and 1970 (both versions); also German (1898).

Catiline 1850 *Catilina*
   First perf. Stockholm 1881; other perfs. include Oslo (1935) and London (1936). Trans. into English 1878 (Act I with a summary of Acts II and III), 1921 and ff.; into German (1896).

Doll's House, A 1879 *Et dukkehjem*
   First perf. Copenhagen 21 Dec. 1879; other early perfs. include Stockholm, Christiania and Bergen (1880), Munich and many other German cities (1880), Vienna (1881), Milwaukee (1882) and Louisville, Kentucky (1883); a free adaptation entitled 'Breaking a Butterfly' perf. 3 Mar. 1884 in London; first substantial London perf. 7 Jun. 1889. First

translated into English (under the title of *Nora*) 1880; other early English translations 1882, 1889, and ff. Other trans. include German (1880, 1890, 1891, 1892 and ff.), Swedish (1880), Finnish (1880), Polish (1882), Russian (1883, 1891, 1896, and ff.), Italian (1894), Dutch (1887, 1893, and ff.), Serbo-Croat (1891), Spanish (1894), Portuguese (1894), Hungarian (1894), Catalan (1903), etc.

Emperor and Galilean   1873   *Kejser og Galilæer*
First perf. Leipzig 27 Feb. 1896, then Berlin 1898; first half only perf. Christiania 1903. Trans. into English (1876), later revised 1890; other trans. include German (1888, in two different versions), French (1895), Italian (1902), Spanish (1903), etc.

Enemy of the People, An   1882   *En folkefiende*
(also known as An Enemy of Society)
First perf. Christiania 13 Jan. 1883, and later that same year in Bergen, Gothenburg, Stockholm and Copenhagen; other early perfs. include Berlin (1887), Bern (1888), Vienna (1890), and Paris (1893); first London production 14 Jun. 1893, which subsequently went on tour to America.

Feast at Solhoug, The   1856   *Gildet paa Solhoug*
First perf. Bergen 2 Jan. 1856, publ. 19 Mar. 1856, and subsequently perf. Christiania 13 Mar. 1856; other early perfs. include Stockholm (1857), Copenhagen (1861), Vienna (1891) and Munich (1897). Trans. into English (1908, 1970), and German (1888, 1898, and ff.).

Ghosts   1881   *Gengangere*
First perf. Chicago (in Norwegian) 20 May 1882, subsequently in Helsingborg, Copenhagen, Stockholm and Christiania (all 1883, though not at the leading theatres), Augsburg (1886), Berlin (1887) and Paris (1890); first English perf. London 13 Mar. 1891. Trans. into English (1885, 1888, and ff.), and into German (1884, 1890, 1893, 1899, and ff.), French (1889), Russian (1891, 1896), Czech (1891), Polish (1891), Italian (1892), Catalan (1894), Portuguese (1895), etc.

Hedda Gabler   1890   *Hedda Gabler*
First perf. Munich 31 Jan. 1891, with perfs. in the immediately following weeks in Berlin, Helsingfors, Stockholm, Copenhagen and Christiania; first English perf. London 20 Apr. 1891. Trans. into English (1891 in two different versions), into German (1891 in three different

versions), French (1892), Dutch (1891), Russian (1891), Italian (1893), Spanish (1894), Portuguese (1895), etc.

John Gabriel Borkman   1896   *John Gabriel Borkman*

A public reading in Norwegian for copyright purposes took place at the Avenue Theatre, London, 14 Dec. 1896; first perf. proper in Helsinki 10 Jan. 1897; Copenhagen, Christiania and Stockholm (as well as a number of provincial towns in Norway) all saw perfs. that same month, as did Frankfurt and Berlin; the first London perf. was on 3 May 1897 at the Strand Theatre, and the Criterion Independent Theatre in New York put it on in Nov. 1897. Trans. into English, German, French and Russian (all in 1897).

Lady from the Sea, The   1888   *Fruen fra havet*

First perfs. Christiania and Weimar, both 12 Feb. 1889, with further perfs. later that same year in Copenhagen, Helsingfors, Stockholm and Berlin; first London perf. 11 May 1891. Trans. into English (1890 in two different versions, 1891), and into German (1888, 1889, 1894 and ff.), French (1892), Swedish (1888), Russian (1891, 1896), Italian (1894), Finnish (1910), etc.

Lady Inger   1855   *Fru Inger til Østeraad*
            1874 [2nd rev. edn *Fru Inger til Østråt*]

First perf. 2 Jan. 1855 Bergen, publ. 1857; other early perfs. include Trondheim (1857), Christiania (1859), Stockholm (1877), Berlin (1878); a perf. in English was given by the Stage Society in London 28 Jan. 1906. Trans. into English (1890, 1970), into German (1877, 1891), Russian (1896), French (1903).

League of Youth, The   1869   *De unges Forbund*

(also known as The Young Men's League)

First perf. in Christiania 18 Oct. 1869, and subsequently in Stockholm (1869), Copenhagen (1870), Bergen (1877) and Berlin (1891); first English perf. 25 Feb. 1900 at Vaudeville Theatre, London. Trans. into English in 1890 (in two different versions), and into German (1872, 1881), French (1893), Czech (1891), Italian (1894), Russian (1896), Spanish (1903), etc.

Little Eyolf   1894   *Lille Eyolf*

On 3 Dec. 1894 there was a public reading for copyright purposes at the Haymarket Theatre, London; the first perf. proper was 12 Jan.

1895 in Berlin, followed by Christiania (15 Jan. 1895); by May 1895 there had been perfs., in Bergen, Vienna, Milan, Copenhagen, Stockholm and Paris; first English perf. was 23 Nov. at the Avenue Theatre, London. Trans. into English 1895, and into German (1895), French (1895), Dutch (1895), Russian (1895), Italian (1897), etc.

Love's Comedy   1862   *Kjærlighedens Komedie*
First perf. Christiania 24 Nov. 1873, and subsequently in Gothenburg (1889), Stockholm (1889), Berlin (1896), Paris (1897) and Copenhagen (1898); first English perf. in Manchester (Gaiety) 22 Feb. 1909. Trans. into English 1900, and into German (1889), French (1896), Russian (1896), Finnish (1905), Dutch (1908), etc.

Master Builder, The   1892   *Bygmester Solness*
Matinée reading of the play in Norwegian at the Haymarket Theatre, London, on 7 Dec. 1892; first genuine perfs. on 19 Jan. 1893 (Berlin and Trondheim), followed by Christiania and Copenhagen in Mar. 1893; performed in Chicago in Feb. 1893 (in Norwegian) and Mar. 1893 (in English); first London perf. 20 Feb. 1893 at Trafalgar Square Theatre.

Olaf Liljekrans   perf. 1857, publ. 1902   *Olaf Liljekrans*
First perf. Bergen 2 Jan. 1857; perf. in English at the Rehearsal Theatre, London, 18 Jun. 1911. Trans. into German (1898) and English (New York, 1921, and London, 1970).

Peer Gynt   1867   *Peer Gynt*
First perf. Christiania 24 Feb. 1876, and subsequently in Copenhagen (1886), Gothenburg (1892), Stockholm (1895), Bergen and Trondheim (1895), and Paris (1896). Experimental perfs. in London in Feb. and Apr. 1911 (Rehearsal Theatre) and 27 Apr. 1913 (Ibsen Studio); first substantial London perf. 6 Mar. 1922 at the Old Vic.

Pillars of Society   1877   *Samfundets støtter*
(also known as Pillars of the Community)
First perf. Copenhagen 18 Nov. 1877, and subsequently in Christiania 6 Nov. 1878 (in Swedish trans.) and 7 Mar. 1879, Stockholm (1877) and Gothenburg (1878). In Berlin in Jan. and Feb. 1878 it was performed in no fewer than five different theatres in three different translations. An adapted version ('Quicksands') perf. London Dec. 1880; first substantial London perf. 17 July 1889 at the Opéra Comique. First trans. into English (excerpts) 1878, and 1888; also into German (1878, in three

different versions, 1891 and 1897), French (1893), Czech (1879), Finnish (1884), Italian (1892 and 1897), Dutch (1893 and 1906), Russian (1896), Spanish (1903), etc.

Poems   1871   *Digte*
Trans. into English in 1902 and 1912 (both selected) and 1986 (in full); and into German (1881, 1886, and ff.).

Pretenders, The   1863   *Kongs-Emnerne*
Publ. 31 Oct. 1863 with '1864' on title page. First perf. Christiania 17 Jan. 1864, and subsequently in Copenhagen (1871), Berlin (1876), Stockholm (1879) and Vienna (1891); first London perf. (Haymarket) 13 Feb. 1913. Trans. into English 1890, and also into German (1872), Finnish (1884), French (1893), Italian (1895), Russian (1896), Dutch (1910), Welsh (1951), etc.

Rosmersholm   1886   *Rosmersholm*
First perf. Bergen 17 Jan. 1887, and later that year in Christiania, Berlin, Gothenburg, Stockholm and Helsinki; other perfs. include Zurich (1888), Paris (1893) and Vienna (1893); first English perf. London (Vaudeville Theatre) 23 Feb. 1891. Trans. into English 1889 and 1891, and into German (1887, in two different versions, 1890, 1893), Dutch (1892), French (1893), Italian (1894), Czech (1898), Polish (1898), Russian (1904), etc.

St John's Night   perf. 1853, publ. posth. 1909   *Sancthansnatten*
(also known as Midsummer Eve)
First perf. Bergen 2 Jan. 1853; one English performance recorded (London, Chelsea) 1 May 1921.

Vikings at Helgeland, The   1858   *Hærmændene paa Helgeland*
First perf. Christiania 24 Nov. 1858; other perfs. include Copenhagen (1875), Stockholm (1875), Munich, Dresden and Vienna (all 1876), and Moscow (1892); first London perf. 1903.

When We Dead Awaken   1899   *Når vi døde vågner*
Public readings for copyright purposes in advance of the real première were held in London (16 Dec. 1899), Christiania (11 Jan. 1900) and Berlin (26 Jan. 1900); the first perf. proper was in Stuttgart (26 Jan. 1900), followed by perfs. in the month of Feb. in Copenhagen, Christiania, Stockholm, Helsingfors, Frankfurt and Leipzig; by the end of the

year there had been perfs. in Berlin and a number of other German cities, as well as in Zurich, Milan and Moscow; there was a perf. (in Danish) in Chicago Feb. 1900; the first London perf. was on 26 Jan. 1903 (Imperial Theatre).

Wild Duck, The 1884 *Vildanden*

First perf. Bergen 9 Jan. 1885, and within weeks in Christiania, Helsinki, Stockholm and Copenhagen; other perfs. include Berlin (1888), Bern (1889), Dresden (1889), Vienna (1891) and Paris (1891); first English perf. in London (Royalty Theatre) 5 May 1894. Trans. into English 1890, and also into German (1887, in two versions, 1890, 1894, 1900 and ff.), Swedish (1885), Russian (1892), French (1893), Italian (1894), etc.

I

ASBJØRN AARSETH

Ibsen's dramatic apprenticeship

In retrospect the 1840s appear relatively undramatic in Norwegian literary history. Writers were mostly cultivating collective memories and giving written form to folk tales and popular ballads and in other ways working on the construction of a national mythology, in historical studies as well as in poetry. There was no permanent theatre established in the country, although several towns by this time had more or less appropriate theatre buildings where itinerant theatre companies, mostly Danish, could perform vaudevilles and plays according to the popular taste of the small bourgeois audiences.

Theatrical activity in Norway was nothing more than a pale reflection of a Danish tradition which seemed to be losing the vigour it had enjoyed in the early decades of the century. Under such circumstances it was understandable that practically nobody in Norway was giving much attention to the art of writing for the theatre. In Grimstad the young assistant pharmacist Henrik Ibsen had no chance to acquaint himself with the standards and techniques of professional theatrical performance, but he must have been an avid reader of classical and contemporary literature. His reading in those early years included dramatic works by Shakespeare, Schiller, Ludvig Holberg and Adam Oehlenschläger, and his literary talent and ambitions were clearly recognized by his few intimate friends. At this point it was not Ibsen's primary intention to earn his living as a writer. In his spare time he was busy preparing himself for the entrance examination to the University of Christiania, where he hoped to be accepted as a student of medicine.

The academic curriculum included a selection of Latin texts by Cicero, Caesar, Sallust, Ovid and others. Among the characters Ibsen came across in his reading was a nobleman of the first century BC, Lucius Catilina, one of the unsuccessful rebels of the Roman republic. He is an outstanding target of Cicero's polemical rhetoric (*In Catilinam*), and his story is told with much the same lack of sympathy by Sallust (*Bellum Catilinae*).

Together with the conspiracy of Brutus, that of Catiline seems to have been particularly attractive to writers of tragedy. The English Renaissance stage saw three plays on this subject, of which Ben Jonson's *Catiline His Conspiracy* (1611) is the only one available to posterity. In his preface to the first edition of *Die Räuber*, his first play (1782), Schiller refers to the tragic potential of a Brutus or a Catiline. Even in Ibsen's own time the subject was not unknown. Together with Auguste Maquet, Alexandre Dumas the elder published *Catilina*, a five-Act drama, in Paris in 1848, and in 1855 Ferdinand Kürnberger published his *Catilina*, also in five Acts, in Hamburg.

There is no firm evidence that Ibsen knew any of the versions published prior to his own, which was written in the winter of 1848–9 and published in the spring of 1850 under the pseudonym of Brynjolf Bjarme. The ghost of Sulla appears in the third Act while in Ben Jonson's play the same ghost gives the opening expository monologue, but this does not necessarily indicate a debt. Ben Jonson's ghost may be seen as an inheritance from Seneca's tragedies, while Ibsen probably borrowed the device from Shakespeare's *Julius Caesar*, also in the Senecan tradition.

Ibsen's main source for his first drama was no doubt Sallust. A comparison of the two texts reveals a certain parallel already in the openings. Sallust begins with a reflection on the double nature of man:

> It behooves all men who wish to excel the other animals to strive with might and main not to pass through life unheralded, like the beasts, which Nature has fashioned grovelling and slaves to the belly. All our power, on the contrary, lies in both mind and body; we employ the mind to rule, the body rather to serve; the one we have in common with the Gods, the other with the brutes. Therefore I find it becoming, in seeking renown, that we should employ the resources of the intellect rather than those of brute strength.[1]

The author is here concerned with the justification of his own historiographical project rather than with the character of Catiline, but Ibsen seems to have ignored this distinction. That the young Ibsen himself was preoccupied with the prospect of oblivion and more or less desperately clinging to his occasional glimpses of literary creativity as a way to renown, we know from the poem 'Resignation', written in 1847 when he was nineteen years old. Reading Sallust must have struck a chord in the aspiring poet. He had no difficulty in investing his own as yet unspecified ambitions in the ethically rather dubious character of Catiline. Here was a man in deep personal crisis, despising himself for his aimless life, ready to risk anything for some historical achievement:

> I must! I must! Deep down within my soul
> a voice commands, and I will do its bidding;
> I feel I have the courage and the strength

to lead a better, nobler life than this.
One endless round of dissipated pleasures!
No, they can never still my inner urge! [. . .]
Yet still at times, as at this moment now,
A secret dream will smoulder in my breast!
Ah, as I gaze upon that city, proud
and lofty Rome . . . and the depravity
and rottenness in which it long lies steeped
stand out in sharp relief before my soul . . .
at once an inner voice cries out aloud:
'Wake, Catiline, awake and be a man!'   [i, 39*]

In Ibsen's dramatic presentation the centre of interest is not so much the political conflict of Catiline versus the leaders of the Roman republic as the moral conflict within the character himself. The two opposing sides of his psyche are represented by two women fighting to get the upper hand. The structure of the plot verges on allegory. On the one side there is his loving wife Aurelia, urging him to settle down in some peaceful rural province with the promise of a harmonious existence enjoying the fruits of the earth. On the other side there is the vestal Furia, secretly scheming for revenge, appealing to his desire to play a role in history by means of organizing the many dissatisfied elements in an uprising aimed at the overthrow of the corrupt establishment in Rome.

The constellation of the hero between two women, one the embodiment of unselfish love and the other representing heedless and destructive ambition, was to become a basic pattern in several of Ibsen's later plays. This device of personifying a grave emotional and moral dilemma in the hero's turbulent mind is practically fully fledged from the start, a remarkable indication of something which for lack of a better word we may call dramatic instinct. The erotic triangle is certainly a commonplace in nineteenth-century drama, but the particular function developed for it on the Ibsen stage exceeds the ordinary measure of complication and brings out a tragic dimension in the situation of the character in question. The playwright also reveals a considerable talent for variation each time the tragic triangle appears in a new guise. Among the more striking examples from the later prose dramas are Rosmer between his late wife and Rebecca West in *Rosmersholm*, Borkman between Ella and Gunhild in *John Gabriel Borkman*, and Rubek between Maja and Irene in *When We Dead Awaken*.

Another promising quality in Ibsen's first drama is the way he succeeds in creating a Romantic hero, a man who in his magnanimity is doomed to failure for reasons that are located partly in his own character, partly in the circumstances which have given him such ill-behaved and undependable followers. Catiline regrets the decline of ancient Roman virtues, but he is no virtuous Roman himself. He is attracted to Furia, the vestal virgin, but when she finds out that he is the man who seduced her younger sister and caused her death, her love turns into hatred and thirst for revenge.

The mixture of a frivolous lasciviousness, a greed for power and a certain highmindedness and generosity in dealing with the less noble characters who want him as their leader, may seem rather excessive for a theatre audience accustomed to a much less complex kind of hero. It is perhaps not surprising that the play was not accepted by the management of the Christiania Theatre in 1849. The reason given was not that the play was poorly written, but that the resources of the theatre were insufficient for such a task. The first performance of *Catiline* did not take place until 1881, in Stockholm.

A revised edition of the play was published in Copenhagen in 1875. It was prefaced with a short survey of the conditions under which it had been written, and the now famous dramatist, re-reading his first attempt, found that it contained qualities of which he had no need to be ashamed: 'Much of what my later writings have been about – the clash of ability and aspirations, of will and possibility, at once the tragedy and the comedy of mankind and of the individual – is already adumbrated here' [*i*, 112].

Neither the refusal by the theatre nor the lack of critical acclaim at the appearance in print of the first version of *Catiline* managed to curb the literary ambitions of the twenty-two-year-old student who had arrived in Christiania in 1850. Both his play and some of his poems met with sympathetic interest among his fellow students, and he was elected editor of the handwritten student society paper.

Ibsen clearly had noticed that the revolutionary fever which had spread so quickly among young intellectuals in Europe in 1848 and 1849, and which was part of his own incentive in Grimstad for writing about the Roman rebel, was no longer in vogue. The nationalist trend from the Forties was once more setting the tone in Norwegian art and literature. This was the spiritual context of his second effort to reach the stage, *The Burial Mound*, a dramatic poem in one Act, presented to the Christiania Theatre in the Summer of 1850. Ibsen still preferred to hide behind the pseudonym of Brynjolf Bjarme, indicating that he was not sure of himself yet. This minor play was accepted, and the first performance of an Ibsen drama took place on 26 September that year.

The Burial Mound is the product of a young writer trying hard to comply with what he considers to be the popular taste of the day. The central character of Gandalf, a Viking chief from Norway leading his men in a raid on the peaceful coast of Normandy, is a rather idealized figure, as indeed are most of the others too. The plot may be seen as a study in the construction of dramatic *peripeteia* and *discovery*, devices cultivated by playwrights since the golden age of Greek tragedy, and analysed in Aristotle's *Poetics*.[2]

There are a number of turning points and some surprising revelations in the one-Act play. The peaceful home of old Bernard and his foster-daughter Blanka is invaded by the rude Vikings, seeking revenge for the presumed death of Gandalf's father some years earlier. Gandalf has sworn by his native gods that since his father's death is not avenged, he will kill every person he comes across on the former battlefield, or else take his own life. The mound is believed to be his father's grave. Blanka's exercise of Christian virtues impresses Gandalf, and he decides not to kill anybody. Bernard is captured, and confesses to being the slayer of the old Norwegian chief. Gandalf feels bound by his oath and makes preparations for his own death. Witnessing the distress of Gandalf and Blanka, who are in love but must part, Bernard reveals that he is none other but Gandalf's father Audun, who was wounded and left behind by the returning Vikings. After being nursed back to life by the gentle Blanka, he had decided to change his identity, burying his Viking sword and armour in the mound and settling as a Christian recluse. This revelation unties the knot, and the two lovers can be happily married on the spot, under the pious hands of old Audun: 'Eternal blessing be upon this pact/Combining Nordic strength with Southern mercy' [*i*, 150].

The Viking age, ending in the triumph of Christianity over the ruthless tenets and practices of the ancient Norse religion, offered a historical theme which had been successfully explored and exploited by the Danish poet and dramatist Adam Oehlenschläger, who died in the same year as Ibsen's work reached the stage for the first time. Compared to the dramatic form of the old master, Ibsen's treatment of the religious conflict is full of improbabilities and curious coincidences. His verses were praised for their lyrical qualities, however, and he was considered a promising young writer by the theatre people in Christiania.

In 1850 the famous violinist Ole Bull had founded a permanent theatre in Bergen, his home town. The actors hired were native speakers, not Danish as at the Christiania Theatre. The national profile of the new enterprise was made clear also by its name, the Norwegian Theatre. In 1851 Ole Bull approached Henrik Ibsen in Christiania and offered him a post combining the duties of stage instructor with those of resident author at his theatre. He was to assist the artistic director in the production of the plays, arrange the settings, suggest costume designs, even supervise the dialogue, while the artistic director was in charge of the interpretation. As an author he was expected to write one play every year to be presented on the anniversary of the theatre's founding, starting on 2 January 1853.

Ibsen accepted the post, and he was to stay in Bergen from the autumn of 1851 to the summer of 1857, with the exception of part of the year 1852 which he spent in Copenhagen and Dresden, studying stage technique with a grant from the theatre's directorate. The all-round theatre experience he acquired during these years seems to have had a decisive formative effect on Ibsen's career. Initially he did not see himself exclusively as a writer for the theatre. He wrote poetry, he painted, he tried prose fiction, he published several critical reviews and articles. Later he also collected works in the oral tradition; and at one point in 1858 he considered the possibility of an academic career, applying for a scholarship to qualify himself for the first chair to be announced in Scandinavian literature at the University of Christiania. The application, however, was soon withdrawn.

The stay in Denmark and Germany, Ibsen's first visit abroad, which lasted more than three months, no doubt also meant a lot to the twenty-four-year-old apprentice. He met actors, instructors, critics and outstanding writers such as Hans Christian Andersen and J. L. Heiberg. He saw performances of different kinds of drama, four plays by Shakespeare and a number of plays by Holberg, Oehlenschläger, Heiberg and Henrik Hertz. Earlier that year Hermann Hettner's *Das moderne Drama. Aesthetische Untersuchungen* had been published in Brunswick. The author, a thirty-year-old professor at the University of Jena, opens his preface by expressing the wish that his book would fall into the hands of young dramatists. It is highly probable that this widely discussed book did fall into the hands of the young Norwegian, either in Copenhagen or in Dresden, and that it influenced his ideas about the nature of modern drama.

That year Ibsen wrote *St John's Night*, a fairy-tale comedy, to meet his obligation for the anniversary of the theatre, and the following year he revised *The Burial Mound* for the corresponding occasion on 2 January 1854. A more substantial contribution, and one with which he was rather pleased himself, was the new drama he completed for the 1855 anniversary, *Lady Inger*.

Hettner's book expressed a strong belief in the potential of historical drama on the modern stage. It is clear, he writes, that 'the seriousness of the age calls for the field of history'.[3] It is not sufficient to compose history and fiction in some gaudy mixture; the true historical drama is complete truth and complete poetry at the same time. To select characters and events from national history for dramatic presentation does not exempt the author from observing the principles and conditions of psychological drama, according to this German critic. Whether historical or fictitious, the plot must evolve in accordance with internal necessity and character logic. Hettner also strongly recommended the selection of historical events which would have potential significance for a contemporary audience. History should be regarded as a living presence, not as a dead thing of the past.

In *Lady Inger* Ibsen tried, but with rather limited success, to realize a concept of national historical tragedy. A couple of Danish historians had just published accounts of the events in Norway in the 1520s, an age when the decimated Norwegian nobility showed themselves more than ever to be lacking in strength and leadership, thus opening the country for Danish rule. Ibsen chose to focus on a female representative of the nobility, Lady Inger, a widow residing at Østraat on the Trondheim Fjord with her daughter Eline. He did not follow the sources available to him very closely, but took the liberty of investing his character with a complex mixture of national feelings and personal ambitions that the historical Ingerd Ottisdotter most likely did not entertain. The idea probably was that an anti-Danish sentiment might correspond nicely to the ideological features of Norway in the 1850s, thus colouring the events of the past to meet the needs of the present.

In this respect Hettner's recommendation can be said to have been obeyed, but his advice about avoiding coincidence in the development of the action was thoroughly ignored. *Lady Inger* is pre-eminently a study in the effects of chance encounters in an action which lacks any rigorous structure. During one dark night in 1528, at a time when the political and dynastic situation of Scandinavia was extremely confused, the Great Hall of Østraat receives a series of visitors representing Norwegian, Danish and Swedish interests. The half-expected and half-unexpected events on this dark occasion kindle a spark of secret hope in Lady Inger. As a young woman she bore an illegitimate son to the Swedish Count Sten Sture. In the light of the information available to her regarding the situation in the three countries, she now sees a promising future for her son, who is unknown to her since he was brought up in Sweden. Through her secret arrangements he is to become King of Norway as well as Sweden. A young Swedish visitor, whom she thinks stands in her son's way, is assassinated on her command. The play ends when she realizes that the man killed was in fact her son.

The plot is highly complex, with many cases of mistaken identity resulting from the extreme secretiveness with which the various visitors set about their missions, with some of them handing over information to the wrong person, and with nobody ultimately achieving their objective. The influence from the French tradition of *la pièce bien faite* is certainly noticeable; in October 1854 the theatre had performed a historical play by Eugène Scribe, *Les Contes de la Reine de Navarre*. Ibsen himself, who on several occasions expressed reservations regarding the Scribean art of dramatic intrigue, thought that *Lady Inger* was his best play from the Bergen years. It was his first attempt to write a complete play in prose, and the dialogue reveals considerable understanding regarding the construction of a dramatic scene, although frequent asides are used to inform the audience of the state of things, an element which is felt to be more artificial in a prose play than it seems to be in a dramatic poem.

The performance of *Lady Inger* was no success, and the author had problems in finding a publisher for it. Finally it was printed as a serial in a Christiania newspaper in the summer of 1857. A second revised and corrected edition was published in Copenhagen in 1874.

Most of the plays Ibsen composed in the 1850s were based on historical and literary sources. Norwegian history, Icelandic sagas (in Danish translation) as well as folk tales and ballads all stimulated his imagination. In 1853 a collection of Norwegian popular ballads was edited by M. B. Landstad. Inspired by the ballad rhythm as well as the medieval setting and love conflicts of this collection, Ibsen wrote a lyric drama, *The Feast at Solhoug*, for the 1856 anniversary. It is a three-Act play, alternating between verse and prose, with the plot built around the homecoming of an outlawed minstrel, creating erotic conflict because he is secretly loved by two sisters. The sisters, Margit and Signe, are vaguely reminiscent of the characters of Furia and Aurelia, but the young minstrel, Gudmund Alfson, is not like Catiline; he is of a forthright, gentle disposition, courting Signe since Margit in his absence has married an older man. Margit's character is more complex; she is ready to poison her husband in order to clear the way for a union with Gudmund.

The feast is an occasion for popular entertainment, and a lot of songs and tales are performed or merely hinted at in the various scenes, colouring the development of the plot with the appropriate sentiments of love, chivalry, enchantment and bravery. This strain of vaudeville and folklore helps to create an atmosphere of genuine peasant culture, so much adored by the townspeople of that age of National Romanticism. The play is not purely idyllic, however. Signe is also the object of the reckless and threatening sheriff, and Margit's rather slow-witted husband is killed by him in the skirmish off-stage. In spite of this episode, the ending is a happy one. The King's messenger arrives like a *deus ex machina*, announcing the annulment of the hero's outlawry, and the future of Gudmund and Signe is assured, while Margit announces her intention of joining a convent.

With its pleasant balance of lyric and drama but without any deeper personal commitment *The Feast at Solhoug* hit the mark of popular taste in Bergen, and shortly afterwards also in Christiania and Trondheim. It was the first stage success of the twenty-eight-year-old playwright; it was also the first play by Ibsen to be performed abroad – in 1857 at the Royal Dramatic Theatre in Stockholm. One of the critics in Christiania suggested that it was an imitation of an earlier Danish Romantic tragedy by Henrik Hertz, *Svend Dyring's House* (1837). This allegation was repeated by several critics, and Ibsen became increasingly annoyed by it. His play has the popular ballad atmosphere and the mixture of verse and prose in common with the Danish tragedy, but both plot and characters are much more closely related to the mythical world of the ballads in the latter case.

The notion that Ibsen was significantly influenced by Hertz's work was strongly resisted by Ibsen's first biographer, the Finnish scholar Valfrid Vasenius, as well as by Ibsen himself in a lengthy preface to the second edition in 1883 of *The Feast at Solhoug* [i, 369–74]. The author explains how his play grew out of his own experiences and preoccupations at the time. The story of Margit, torn between her wealthy but unattractive husband and the charming outlaw, developed as a transformation of a similar relationship in the saga drama he was planning in those years but which he hesitated to complete.

One of the reasons for this hesitation seems to have been his preoccupation at this time with the theory of drama and its relationship to the other main genres. He published an article in a Christiania newspaper in May 1857, 'On the Heroic Ballad and its Significance for Literature' [i, 672–84]. Following the aesthetic authorities of the age, J. L. Heiberg and G. W. F. Hegel, Ibsen states that drama is a higher synthesis of lyric and epic poetry. Since the saga presents its material in a form which is purely epic, the dramatist who wants to make use of this material will have to introduce a lyric element which would be alien to the world of the saga. However,

> in the heroic ballad on the other hand there are lyric elements present, admittedly in a different form from drama, but present nevertheless – and the dramatist who draws his material from the ballads does not have to subject his material to the kind of transformation necessary when it is drawn from the saga. This represents a very considerable advantage, permitting the poet to give in his work a more accurate and more intimate reflection of the period and of the events he is dealing with; and he is thereby enabled (if he is otherwise capable) to present his heroes to the beholder in the way in which they are already familiar from folk poetry direct. [i, 676]

This was the concept on which Ibsen had based *The Feast at Solhoug*; and the success which this play had enjoyed made him feel confident that it would work a second time. 'The Grouse in Justedal' was the title of a play he had been working on as early as in 1850. The story was based on a legend about a young girl who alone had survived the Black Death in the remote valley of Justedal. He had planned four Acts, but gave it up after an Act and a half was completed. In 1856 he returned to this epic material and combined it with one of the ballads of Landstad's collection. The result was a three-Act play, *Olaf Liljekrans*, Ibsen's last contribution under the contract with the Bergen Theatre, presented on 2 January 1857.

We may assume that this combination of narrative and ballad was intended as a dramatic synthesis according to the formula Ibsen had found in the writings of J. L. Heiberg. The play is a composite of two entangled love stories. A wedding is agreed between Olaf Liljekrans, son of Lady Kirsten, and Ingeborg, daughter of the rich Arne of Guldvik. Since the agreement is worked out by the parents and based on property considerations and not on love, it is by its very nature vulnerable. Almost as in the ballad, Olaf has come under the spell, figuratively if not literally, of the beautiful, innocent Alfhild, a girl who lives in a remote mountain valley with her father, an old minstrel and fiddler. Ingeborg loves Hemming, her father's page. The plot is constructed in a typical romantic way with a series of complications temporarily preventing the happiness of the two couples, and with true love triumphing in the end.

An important theme undermining the pastoral aspect of the play is the clash of Alfhild's natural innocence with the greed and moral corruption dominating the society to which she is introduced through her liaison with Olaf. A target for satire is also offered by Ingeborg and Hemming, whose expectations of a comfortable life-style turn out to be incompatible with a simple cottage existence in the mountain wilderness to which they have fled.

The dialogue is similar to that of *The Feast at Solhoug*, with a mixture of prose and verse. Occasionally ballad-style fragments are introduced as a lyric expression of the mood. Asides are as frequent as in any of the plays from this early period. Misunderstandings and unexpected reversals abound, and the play clearly belongs to the tradition of *la pièce bien faite*. The author of *Olaf Liljekrans* is still very much an apprentice trying to please his audience; but his audiences did not conspicuously appreciate the play. It is one of Ibsen's weakest works, and he decided not to try to find a publisher for it. His recent interest in dramatic theory clearly brought him no guarantee of success as a dramatist.

In the spring of 1857 Ibsen had completed the term of five years he had agreed to serve the Bergen Theatre. He did sign a contract for another term, but shortly thereafter received a better offer from the new Norwegian Theatre in Christiania and was permitted to leave Bergen. By this time he had achieved a certain reputation in the country at large as an ambitious but as yet not wholly accomplished playwright.

NOTES

1 Quoted from J. C. Rolfe's translation in *Sallust*, The Loeb Classical Library, 116 (London, 1965) p. 3.
2 There is no evidence to suggest, however, that Ibsen actually read Aristotle.
3 Hermann Hettner, *Das moderne Drama. Aesthetische Untersuchungen* (Brunswick, 1852) p. 9.

2

BJØRN HEMMER

Ibsen and historical drama

In 1873 – close to the mid-point of half a century of creative authorship – Ibsen published the drama which he himself regarded as his 'hovedværk', his 'main work' or masterpiece: *Emperor and Galilean*. It was not to be a historical drama of the merely traditional kind. Ibsen's choice of subtitle – 'a world-historic drama' – betrayed his ambitions.

It was a vast historical canvas which he then unfolded, much broader than that of any of his earlier dramas. Years of painstaking labour, including the close study of historical sources, went into this evocation of characters and events from a distant past: the Roman Empire of the fourth century AD and the last twelve years of the life of Julian the Apostate.

Ibsen himself admitted in his correspondence [*iv*, 603–9][1] that the historical material he had been grappling with was enormous, and that he realized that he had sacrificed years of his life to this mammoth work, a 'double' drama in ten Acts. To call forth this historical epoch had been 'a Herculean task'. Nevertheless he was persuaded that he had succeeded in re-creating these historical characters in 'realistic' form. This had however not been his main concern: his perspective of history here had been – to use Nietzsche's terminology – neither antiquarian nor monumental. The prime purpose of historical material, he averred in 1873 in a letter to a friend, was to carry a universally valid significance:

> The play treats of the struggle between two irreconcilable powers in the life of the world, something which will in all ages repeat itself, and because of this universality I call the book 'a world-historic play'. Moreover, there is to be found in the character of Julian, as indeed in most of what I have written in my more mature years, more personal inner experience than I care to admit to the public. But at the same time it is a completely and wholly realistic piece of writing. I have seen the characters before my eyes in the light of the age . . .
>
> [*iv*, 604]

The symbolic function of history thus takes pride of place for Ibsen. That historical drama might also serve a didactic purpose was an idea with which

Ibsen had long been familiar. He had himself used history – and particularly *national* history – in this very way.

Emperor and Galilean nevertheless was to mark Ibsen's definitive farewell to historical drama; thereafter, historical perspectives were to be replaced by contemporary perspectives. Even before the 1870s there had been clear signs of an impending change in his authorship; but Ibsen had very obviously felt the need for that distancing which a *historical* perspective gives. In a piece he wrote in 1862 about the theatre he conceded that there were certain tendencies in the age which pointed to a more realistic description of everyday reality; but he saw this trend as nevertheless presenting problems for an author: 'Certainly it takes a more powerful vision to glimpse things which are poetically or artistically usable amid all the turmoil of the chance events one is caught up in than it does to detect them, for example, in a past age which stands at some distance, is complete and is, so to say, in perspective.' [xv, 301].

Ibsen thus finally gave up historical drama at a time when he could look back on very nearly a quarter of a century of literary endeavour. Time after time he had turned to the past for material for his plays. What had motivated him was more than just the need for a distanced perspective. The young Ibsen began his career within a tradition of late Romanticism, in which historical drama still enjoyed great prestige. Shakespeare, Schiller and Adam Oehlenschläger (1779–1850) – the dominant figure of Danish Romanticism – were the most important literary models in this genre.

In 1807 Oehlenschläger had awarded *national* historical drama a very special status: 'The most sublime thing which a writer can bring to the theatre is without doubt some historical exploit. Since every nation has had its own exploits, it follows that every nation ought also to have its own particular form of national drama. This special national quality is the noblest blossom of poetry.'[2] The situation in the Norwegian theatre and for Norwegian writers about the year 1850 was that there was still no national tradition on which to build. The task of creating a genuinely Norwegian drama had only just begun. But the age was clearly aware that any growth in national consciousness would need to find its base in *history*.

Ibsen's first drama *Catiline* (1850) actually had no connection with a programme of this kind. As also in the case of *Emperor and Galilean*, it is the symbolic function of history which forms the prime consideration, both in relation to what is universally valid and to what is personally experienced. In his 'Author's Note' of 1850 to the drama, the youthful dramatist wrote that he had taken certain liberties with history, letting it serve 'to clothe the underlying idea running through the play' [i, 108]. There was also in this play a conflict between two forces: that in existence as such and that in the inner life of the individual.

Ibsen's historical drama is thus chronologically framed by two works built on Roman history. Between these two works one finds a succession of dramas where the material and the perspectives are essentially national. This served to reinforce the didactic function of history. Ibsen had many motives for addressing himself to his own country's past. For eleven years he was in the employment of theatres which had nationalistic objectives. From as early as 1851 therefore he was under an obligation to work 'in the national interest'.

It was a task he approached with certain strong inner convictions. He wanted to act in the service of the people and to help what (in a poem) he called 'Young Norway' to an awareness of itself. Political independence had been largely achieved by Norway's recently won constitution of 1814. Later came the struggle in the cultural field to build up a distinctively Norwegian 'identity', the very 'edifice of the nation'. In this period of National Romanticism, the justification and driving force resided in what one Norwegian historian has called 'the almost mystically determined notions of *folk individuality*'. This was also Ibsen's point of departure. In 1859 he wrote:

> The significance of nationality for the entire cultural life and development of the people has gained much in clarity and understanding in the last fifteen to twenty years. Particularly in recent years it has been increasingly borne in on the general consciousness that political freedom alone does not by any means make a people free in spirit and in truth . . . [xv, 224]

A people must be awakened to a consciousness of itself, Ibsen continued, of its history, its traditions, its language and its collective destiny in good times and ill: all those things which assert that 'in the truest sense of the word we comprise a nation'. It is here that Ibsen sees the great mission for art, and for himself. The theatre is to be a mirror for 'the people's self-examination', that it might recognize itself. A writer should therefore work within that area of tension between the old and the new: 'If the new is to appeal to the people, it must also in a certain sense be old; it must not be *invented*, but *rediscovered*' [i, 672]. The historical image created on stage by a dramatist must succeed in getting a vibrant response from the 'fundamental note' within the public's deeper nature.

But Ibsen was for long years uncertain of how he might succeed in creating a genuine national drama of this kind. He was, as was said above, clear in his own mind that national identity must be based in history. But *what* of the past could be used? Ibsen was well aware of the many pitfalls of historical drama. In 1857 he wrote: 'There is probably no form in literature which has as many difficulties to overcome as historical tragedy in order to be accepted by the public with lively interest and affection' [xv, 160]. It was an insight he had gained both from his own practical work as a man of the theatre and as a writer, and from theory. In the course of a study tour which he undertook in 1852, he happened upon a recently published monograph in German on the art of drama: Hermann Hettner's *Das moderne Drama*. Hettner is emphatically of the view that historical material must be given a contemporary relevance if the dramatist is to win the acclaim of his people. The aim is not to create some reflective image of history on stage, though the writer must always respect the inner truth of past events; rather Hettner maintains (arguing on the basis of *Hamlet*) that the drama must pre-eminently hold up a mirror to its own age – and it is this which must guide the dramatist in his choice of material. His conclusion is categorical: 'Historical drama must draw its strength from the very heart's blood of its own times and yet at the same time it must strike with assurance the distinctive note of the historical hero. This is and remains the eternal law of this form of art.'[3]

Ibsen's articles on the art of the theatre show that he had taken Hettner's main point: that interest and respect for history must be combined with a clear poetic vision of what is stirring in contemporary life. Many academic historians of the age were interested in national history precisely insofar as it related to the needs of contemporary society. Norway had been under foreign domination since the late Middle Ages. The young historians of the 1850s and 1860s were engaged in demonstrating the element of continuity in the life of the people, the organic connection between the then and the now. Both Ibsen and his contemporary, the poet Bjørnstjerne Bjørnson (1832–1910), gave close attention to the work of these historians. In 1861, Bjørnson expressed his belief that it was wholly necessary for Norwegians to have 'that pride in their ancestors which every people fighting for its national identity must have'.[4]

This battle for Norwegian-ness, for the individuality of the people, might be said to have something of the character of modern myth-making. James McFarlane rightly calls this phenomenon 'the Norwegian Myth'.[5] What is interesting historically is that this myth played a very real part as a driving force in the cultural aspirations of the age in creating a sense of national unity and independence. Behind it lay a collective dream of a national renaissance.

Such is the background against which one must view Ibsen's endeavours in the field of historical drama. Quite early in life he had already gained valuable insights into the nature of drama by virtue of his practical work in the theatre; and he also had a theoretical basis on which he could work. Nevertheless, with the benefit of hindsight, it is striking to see how uncertain his progress was in these years. One gains the impression that it was his relationship to historical material, to the past, which was the problem. He made many and various attempts to come to productive terms with past ages. Undoubtedly, he was most successful with a work like *Lady Inger* (1854) where he based himself on actual history. Admittedly he took considerable liberties with the facts of history. On this point he was clear in his own mind, and his views were not unlike Hettner's: 'We have in fact no right to demand the actual facts of history from genuine historical tragedy, but rather its possibilities; not the evident persons and characters, but the spirit and mind of the age' [xv, 160].

But in order to capture the spirit and the mind of a past age, it was Ibsen's view – in the best traditions of Romanticism – that the *literature* of the past offered the best evidence of what people had thought and felt. Many of these dramas were therefore constructed not from historical but from literary sources. *The Feast at Solhoug* (1856) takes its background from the author's studies of the folk-ballad tradition. *The Vikings at Helgeland* (1858) is based on his intensive study of saga literature. In a letter to the Royal Theatre, Copenhagen (8 February 1858) Ibsen admitted that this drama lacked any actual foundation in history; the characters were invented, structured on *literary* models from the Icelandic sagas and the *Volsungasaga*. His intention, he declared, had been 'to give a picture of the life of the saga age in general'.[6]

Doubtless it is more correct to say that, in *The Vikings at Helgeland*, Ibsen has presented an image of the characters of saga *literature*, such as he saw them. The pronounced intertextual nature of the drama results occasionally in the literary models becoming distressingly obvious. Ibsen's 'nationalistic' project was, in part at least, to stimulate 'ancestral pride' by giving his historical account a certain monumentality. At the same time, he attempted to create a psychological tragedy with Hjørdis in the main role. As Ibsen scholars have often indicated, she is an early Hedda Gabler, demonically destructive in her confined and constricted emotional life. Sigurd, the idealized hero, stands between Hjørdis and Gunnar – *his* brother-in-law and *her* husband. He is also bound by his loyalty to the woman to whom he is married but whom he does not love: the fair and gentle Dagny. It is the combative and heathen Hjørdis he is in love with, despite his revelation at the very end of his life that his ideals lie more with the new and gentler Christian age. This epochal conflict, which Ibsen doubtless inherited from Oehlenschläger, remains as an inadequately resolved element in the final phase of the drama.

The Vikings at Helgeland has something of the 'coldness' which Ibsen himself had declared was typical of the sagas: 'The saga is a great, cold epic, closed and complete within itself, essentially objective, and remote from all lyricism. It is in this cold, epic light that the saga age stands for us; it is in their magnificent sculptural beauty that its figures parade before us' [i, 675]. It would be difficult to claim that *The Vikings at Helgeland* mirrored anything of Ibsen's own age. It is a pastiche of the past, 'that damned imitation', as Bjørnson called it.

The constructive line of development in Ibsen's work in historical drama runs from *Lady Inger* to *The Pretenders* (1863). Both are nationalistic historical dramas, based on historical source material and on the lives of actual historical characters. Moreover, in both cases the dramatist sought inspiration and took his material from one of the major historians of the day: P. A. Munch (1810–63). In a commemorative speech he delivered in Rome in 1865, Ibsen paid tribute to Munch as 'a builder of the nation'. Scholarship and art are the twin pillars which support the nation's edifice, he claimed; and he distinguished – as he had done previously – between the political and the cultural independence of a people. Only the latter can secure the liberty and the future of a people, and it is this that gives the artist and the intellectual a special status: 'The man who promotes the cultural life of the nation has every right to hold his head high' [xv, 391].

Doubtless these ideas had also been in Ibsen's mind some years earlier when he was writing *The Pretenders*. The course of his own career had compelled him to ponder his own role in this notion of nation building. At the same time, the state of the country and its future continued to claim his attention. In *The Pretenders*, history – with its conflicts and its individual destinies – has both a symbolic and a didactic function. The drama was meant to act as a mirror to the age and the society in which it was written; but at the same time it reflects something of the writer himself. The drama has its background in a profound personal crisis. His own efforts to create a national dramatic tradition had met with strong opposition; the theatre in which he was employed had itself recently gone bankrupt; and he had had to endure much personal criticism and suspicion. It is little short of a miracle that he was able, at such a time of crisis, to gird himself once more to continue 'that activity whose aim it is to support and enhance our inner national life'.

In the whole of Norwegian literature there is no work where the concept of nationality is so brilliantly illuminated: not so much the notion of the *political* unity of the state but rather the idea of the people's own *sense* of solidarity and of shared identity. This is the vision which is Haakon Haakonsen's 'kongstanke', his great 'kingly thought' – the one which his rival, Duke Skule, eventually steals because he doubts whether he is himself called to kingship: 'Norway was a *kingdom*. It shall become a *people*. The men of Trondelag fought the men from Viken; the men of Agder fought the men of Hordaland, and the men of Haalogaland the men from Sogn. From now on all shall be one and know themselves and realize they are one!' [*ii*, 283].

Ibsen drew on two main sources for the historical material in *The Pretenders*: Sturla Tordsson's *Håkon Håkonsson's Saga* (1265) and P. A. Munch's *The History of the Norwegian People* (1857). It is interesting to see how Ibsen used his sources. He treats the historical facts with a fair degree of liberty, concentrating the time scale, re-casting the sequence of events, adding and omitting detail. But on important points he totally respects the facts of history; indeed, he frequently quotes directly and in detail from his sources. He took over what he felt he could use, but otherwise he invented on the basis of history's 'possibilities'. As in *Catiline*, the historical elements serve in the first instance to clothe the ideas which run through the drama. The same applies to the psychological make-up of the characters. In a letter written in 1870, Ibsen reveals something of the purely personal background which led to his writing the play: 'The fact that everybody was against me, the fact that I no longer had anyone standing by, of whom I could say that he had faith in me – all this ... could not help but create a mood in me which found its release in *The Pretenders*' [*ii*, 368]. These feelings are manifested most clearly in the drama through the person of Skule, in his despairing plea that surely one person must believe in him and in his right to the throne of Norway: 'But I must ... I must have one person who can believe in me. Just one!' [*ii*, 301]. It is a cry for help from a man who no longer has faith either in himself or in his life's mission. Whether Ibsen's own personal crisis went as deep as this is not easy to determine. But it is probable that his isolation prompted moments of anguished doubt, moments when he put to himself the question which Skule puts to the skald Jatgejr: 'Do you always feel quite certain that you are a *bard*?' [*ii*, 300]. Nevertheless, the biographical background has only limited relevance to the drama as a whole. *The Pretenders* is first and foremost the account of a political power struggle at national level, in which differing historical and value judgements are in conflict.

The Pretenders is indisputably the most important example of historical drama in Norwegian literature. It belongs to that category of national historical drama where the protagonists tend to belong to the uppermost levels of society. In consequence of their central role in the country's history, any account of their lives will also convey something of the political and ideological conflicts of their society. In this way, national historical drama acquires a clear double perspective: the one individual and psychological, the other national and political. What happens in any one of these arenas also has its consequences in the other.

This is clearly evident in *The Pretenders*. The three central characters, Haakon, Skule and Bishop Nicholas, respectively represent the monarchy, the aristocracy and the church – three traditional rivals for power. In the drama Haakon is presented as the only one of the three with a clear vision of the needs of the nation; he means to serve his country by bringing to an end the devastating internal factions. This is his 'kingly thought' and his mission. Opposing him are positioned Skule and Nicholas, both of them driven by an inner urge to power. They cannot bear to have anyone in authority over them; this makes for the narrowness of their perspective. But this urge for power becomes for them the path to impotence and a barren existence. Not until his life is nearing its end does Skule succeed in releasing himself from common cause with the Bishop – at which point he realizes that Haakon's great 'kingly thought' does give *him* the right to rule over land and people. It no longer matters whether Haakon had any right by birth to the throne or not: 'Greet King Haakon from me; say that even in my dying hour I do not know whether he is the rightful king by birth, but I know for certain he is the one whom God has chosen' [*ii*, 339]. Finally Skule goes to his death to preserve Haakon's 'kingly thought'. He had stolen it, tried to live for it, but only by his death is he able to serve it.

The two perspectives – the individually psychological and the nationalistic – are clearly evident in the way the two main antagonists are presented. They have totally different views of the needs of the country. This is conspicuously demonstrated in the scene where Haakon tells Skule of his vision of Norway's future, of a time when the various regions will stand united, and when the people will feel that they are as one. Skule's vision is the complete contrary; he believes that Haakon's policies will ultimately endanger the monarchy: 'Group must stand opposed to group, claim against claim, district against district, if the king is to have power in his hands. Every district, every clan, must either need the king or fear him. Remove all conflict, and in that moment you rob yourself of power' [*ii*, 283]. The political outlook of the man of experience here conflicts with the idealism of youth which is intent on pursuing a new policy, on creating new historical conditions. Skule believes that Haakon's national assembly is unworkable because history has no record of any such thing. Haakon replies that Skule can only tell the old story all over again; time has moved on without his having realized it. Haakon alone has the ability to think 'unhistorically' – something which Nietzsche recognized as equally necessary for the health of a people and of its culture as the ability to think 'historically'.

On the psychological level, it is evident that the two men are presented in a way wholly consistent with the ideas they respectively propound: Haakon is confident and integrated, unshakable in his faith in his own historical mission; Skule is inwardly split, forever lacking confidence in himself and his right to play that role in the nation's affairs which he aspires to. Nicholas too is presented as a split and contentious character, a symbol of the eternal repetitiveness of civil war, its 'perpetuum mobile'. He represents the principle of evil in the life of both Skule and the nation.

The Pretenders is thus both a period drama and a drama of ideas. Behind the human conflicts one sees the fateful play of the country's destiny and that of its people. It recalls something which Ibsen had already commented on in a review he had written in 1857: 'It is not the overt conflict of ideas which is unfolded to our gaze (and which never occurs in real life either); what we see are the human conflicts, and interwoven with these, deeply embedded, are the conflicting ideas, vanquished or victorious' [xv, 163–4].

But *The Pretenders* is also a drama which belongs to a romantic tradition, where the individual is presented as one who is chosen, someone who is the bearer of a mission. Within this perspective, the nationalistic and the historical elements recede into the background and yield to the psychological and the metaphysical. In this respect the drama acquires a more generalized significance, not merely an 'autobiographical' dimension, even though (as was said above) it echoes a profound personal crisis in Ibsen's life at this point. There are good reasons to assume that both Skule and Haakon embody aspects of Ibsen's own problems as a writer, his doubts and his belief in his mission and his personal role in the life of the nation. There is no doubt that Haakon embodies the ideal of the writer; he is the complete personality who, in good times as in bad, follows the path he knows he must, and sees his life in the light of a high-minded and selfless purpose. This gives him the strength that Skule lacks. Skule is a tragic character who, though greatly gifted, lacks what would mark him out for the task he yearns to accomplish. *The Pretenders* is thus a drama about the nature of mission, about the enigmatic processes of being chosen, and about the individual's impotence when it comes to determining his own mission. He – along with Nicholas – has experienced that inner rebelliousness which, in *Emperor and Galilean*, leads Julian on to apostasy. The Skule-type figure is also an embodiment of that kind of inwardly divided personality which Ibsen was to return to time and time again. Only in the final phase of his life does

Skule emerge as a whole personality. Only then is he able to see his life in the light of the drama's dominant idea.

As drawn by Ibsen, Bishop Nicholas represents the force of evil in history – an interpretation which does not accord with that of the historical sources used by the dramatist. (In reality, the historical Nicholas attempted to reconcile the warring factions.) The Bishop plays a major role in the less time-bound nationalistic perspective which the drama also encompasses. *The Pretenders* was to give contemporary society a reminder of the need for national unity and for strength in critical situations. It was essential for Norway at this time to stand united in the face of Swedish pressure for a revision of the constitutional problems facing the two countries. This was what Ibsen probably intended that his countrymen should see reflected in the play. It was not merely a matter of heightening the people's conscious-ness of their own history, but also of highlighting those inner and outer forces which formed a constant threat. In the contemporary situation, the Nicholas syndrome represented a very real threat for the Norwegian people. This could be the reason for the Bishop being given such a major and *special* place in the drama. His long monologue, spoken in the guise of a ghost returned from the dead, breaks with all historical fiction; and its intro-duction is in many ways a discordant – and perhaps ill-advised – element in the play.

With *The Pretenders* Ibsen's dramatic apprenticeship reached its defini-tive close. It is a rich work which opens windows to things both historical and contemporary, both individual and national – and to the author himself. Henceforth there could be no doubt about Ibsen's rightful place among Norway's leading writers. What is astonishing is that after completing this major work of national historical drama he should then abandon this literary genre for ever. The reason is to be sought only partly in the fact that he thereafter distanced himself from the daily life of his country and its people by entering upon a twenty-seven-year self-imposed exile from Norway; it was also that the impact of events destroyed any faith he might have held in the Norwegians' right to lay claim to their own proud history. His dream of linking past and present, of creating some kind of national renaissance, was devastatingly destroyed. He woke to the realization that he had been held captive in a nationalistic myth.

The repudiation came in 1864 when the Norwegians failed to keep their promise to come to the aid of the Danes in their war against the Prussians. For Ibsen, this betokened not only a defeat for Scandinavianism; more specifically, it dealt a fatal blow to his faith in the power of nationalism and thereby to everything that had served him as the basis for his own literary activity. History had served as guarantor for the high ideals which he (along with many others) had cherished in respect of the people's potential, both present and future. Contemporary events were evidence that this was a delusion. Ibsen further concluded that this must also necessarily have consequences for literature. His letters of this time declare that the Norwegians must now strike out their past history, and writers must find a new foundation on which to base their work:

> *Back home* [i.e. in Norway] *I am afraid that from now on literature will have to take a new path*; there is at the present time no valid need or intrinsic necessity to go calling up the memory of our historic past; the things that have occurred there in the last two or three years – or, more correctly, those things that have not occurred – show pretty clearly that between the present generation of Norwegians and our mighty past, there is no closer connection than that between the Greek pirates of our day and the Ancients with their courage and faith and will, and with gods in their ranks.   [*ii*, 368; my italics]

For Ibsen, national history thereby lost its monumental and didactic function. In the period immediately after leaving Norway, he was clearly uncertain which direction his writing should take. Many plans were considered, but there was no advance. In 1864, whilst still resident in Rome, he had renewed thoughts of seeking the subject matter for his work in past history. His encounter with Italy had lent actuality to Roman history, and he began to show an interest in Julian the Apostate, the revolutionary and dreamer; but for the time being this plan was put aside. First, Ibsen had to settle his account with contemporary Norway and its many blemishes. He was to write three more plays before returning, in the early 1870s, to the history of the Emperor who took up battle with the Galilean.

Brand (1866), *Peer Gynt* (1867) and *The League of Youth* (1869) all embody attacks on certain phenomena in contemporary Norway – and may well be interpreted as bitter criticism of the Norwegian national character. But what is also clear is that, whilst at work on these plays, Ibsen distanced himself from matters collectively nationalistic and became more occupied with people as individuals, with Kierkegaard's 'hin Enkelte'.

What he had recently seen happening in Norway was put into strong relief for him by recent events in Italy, where in the struggle for liberty and independence under Garibaldi's leadership the individual had shown a great sense of dedication and self-sacrifice. In a letter written in 1865, Ibsen wrote that there was something here which the Italians had taught him: that it was essential 'to possess a whole soul'. Thus national problems became more generalized and were relocated on an individual plane: it was on the individual that demands were properly made. Here Ibsen found what he himself called 'firm ground beneath one's feet' – and a new basis for his writing.

Now it was no longer a question of a nation's renaissance but an *individual*'s renaissance. It is in this period that the dream of 'the new Adam' makes its appearance in Ibsen's work: most evidently in *Brand* initially, then later in *Emperor and Galilean*.

Ibsen's severe strictures on his compatriots had given him a public reputation as a writer who was both critical and negative. Whilst still at work on what he was to designate his 'masterpiece', Ibsen wrote to his publisher that his new drama would contain 'the positive philosophy' which the critics had long demanded of him [*iv*, 603]. Doubtless what was uppermost in his mind was the proclamation of 'The Third Empire', the goal for humankind's future development. Later – in a speech in Stockholm in 1887 [*iv*, 607–8] – he returned to this phrase as indicating the objectives and the optimism he associated with cultural development in general. 'The Third Empire' (an expression which, as 'The Third Reich', came to have quite different associations for a later generation) represents in Ibsen's thinking the future, the desire for greater individual freedom: *Utopia*. But dialectically linked to this dream there is a dark and menacing sub-current ever-present in his drama, a deep pessimism in respect of humanity's potential: *Dystopia*.

During the composition of *Emperor and Galilean* he repeatedly declared that world history was nothing more than one enormous shipwreck, and that mankind was altogether on the wrong track. He felt he was living in a chaotic, 'obscurantist' age [XVI, 374]. It was in this situation, where utopian and dystopian perspectives alternate, that Ibsen once again turned to confront history. He obviously felt the need for some clarifying perspective of distance – and for the symbolic function of history. In 1872 he wrote to Edmund Gosse:

> What I am putting into this book is a part of my own inner life; what I describe are things I have myself experienced in different forms, and the historical theme I have chosen also has a closer connection with the currents of our own age than one might at first think. This I regard as an essential demand to be made of any modern treatment of material so remote, if as a work of literature it is to be able to arouse any interest.   [*iv*, 603]

A little later he again wrote to Gosse that on this occasion he had kept strictly to history, but that there was nevertheless much 'self-anatomy' in the drama [*iv*, 604]. It is not difficult to see that Ibsen was holding fast to his youthful conception of the demands which were properly to be made of historical drama. Hermann Hettner's theories still held their validity for him. It should also be added that Hettner in large measure based himself on others' views of this genre, including those of Friedrich Hebbel and (indirectly through him) of G. W. F. Hegel. The former in particular had placed great emphasis on the notion that drama would always have special relevance to periods of transition and conflict in history. He had also maintained that the theatre should hold up a mirror to the dramatist's own age, and that the historical elements should serve primarily as a means of clothing the dramatist's ideas. A writer is always part of his own age, he had stressed.

Influences from Hegel on Ibsen also played their part. *Emperor and Galilean* is based on Hegelian notions of historical development, and on what constitutes the essence of a tragic conflict as it manifests itself in literature. Indeed Ibsen himself indicated that *Emperor and Galilean* had been written very much under the influence of German culture, and he stressed the dominant role of Hegel in the intellectual life of the 1870s.

There can be no doubt that Ibsen sensed that the years during which he was working on *Emperor and Galilean* constituted a period of extreme change, epoch-making in its nature. He called it 'a fight to the death between two epochs', where the conflict focused on the very meaning of existence. Now for the first time the authority of the church was severely shaken: the ideals of liberal humanism challenged those of traditional Christianity. Many people, including Ibsen, were ready to adopt a more dialectical and dynamically evolutionary way of thought, and value judgements became increasingly confused. When Ibsen sought to voice his hope that, despite all, the development of mankind was moving in the direction of some positive goal, he linked that hope to such concepts as 'liberation' and 'change' and 'The Third Empire'.

In *Emperor and Galilean* there is a struggle between Greek and Christian beliefs – between a world-orientated and a heaven-orientated view of existence. In this respect Ibsen was right when he characterized his drama to his publisher in the words: 'My play treats of both heaven and earth' [*iv*, 604]. Nevertheless there are reasons for thinking that the dramatist's point of departure lay in close personal experience. It is striking to see how often he emphasized his own engagement in the conflict which Julian undergoes – in a drama which is simultaneously 'world-historic' and individual. Not only does it seek to call to account a religion which by its inherent decadence and its life-denying nature had come to seem negative; it also acknowledges the fascination which Christianity had exercised over men's minds and so captivated them that they never fought completely free of it. Julian expresses this ambivalence thus:

> When my spirit, bemused by beauty, thirsted for the traditions and images of the lost world of the Greeks, I was paralysed by the Christian command: 'Seek only the one thing needful!' When I felt sweet desires and longings of the flesh, the Prince of Self-denial would trike terror into me with this: 'Die unto

this life, and live in the life beyond!' All human emotions have been forbidden since that day the seer of Galilee began to rule the world. With him, to live is to die. To love and to hate are to sin. But has he changed man's flesh and blood? Is man not still earth-bound as before? With every healthy fibre of our being we revolt against it. . . . And yet we are told to *will* against our own will! Thou shalt, thou shalt, thou shalt! [*iv*, 309]

In this conversation with Maximos the Mystic, Julian continues:

You cannot understand it, because you have never been in the power of this god-man. It is more than a doctrine he has spread over the world; it is magic which makes your soul captive. Once you have come under his spell, I don't think you can ever really escape.

MAXIMOS   Because you haven't really the *will* to do so.

JULIAN   How can I will what is impossible?

MAXIMOS   Is it worth willing what is possible?

JULIAN   Academic twaddle! You cannot fill me up with that any more. And yet . . .; oh no, no, Maximus! But you cannot understand our position. We are like vines transplanted to a strange new soil; . . . plant us back again and we should shrivel up; but in the new soil we do not thrive.

MAXIMOS   We? And who do you call we?

JULIAN   All those who stand in fear of the revelation. [*iv*, 310]

Julian therefore sees himself as representative of all those who are languishing under the regime of the Galilean because they yearn for a freer and more joyful life. He argues for this worldly life – as Emperor as well as an individual. At the same time he rebels against that power which, to judge by all the signs, seemingly wishes to use him for its own purposes. Constantly he is confronted by some inscrutable metaphysical power, a 'necessity', which threatens his individual liberty. Towards the end of his life, both he and Maximos acknowledge that 'the World Will' has controlled all things: 'To *will* is to *have to will*' [*iv*, 458]. Ibsen himself admitted that working on the character of Julian and tracing his destiny had in some sense made a fatalist of him; nevertheless, he claimed, it is still possible to conceive of this drama as being a kind of 'banner' [*iv*, 603].

Emperor and Galilean is the Janus face of Ibsen. On the one side the drama refers back to his earlier metaphysical and mission-inspired authorship; on the other it points forward to his realistic dramas with their focus on individual emancipation. *Emperor and Galilean* addresses an age of conflict and an act of individual rebellion fifteen hundred years ago in time. Within the historical and 'realistic' framework of Julian's life, Ibsen had necessarily to represent Christianity as victorious. Julian's attempt to revert to a world which carried the stamp of pre-Christian, pagan 'ideals' had to be shown as an aberration. These were 'the facts of history', and Ibsen had to yield to them. In the 1870s, the result of a related clash of philosophies was not given in advance.

Ibsen's dilemma seems to have been that in this situation he sympathized with those who rebelled, but at the same time he reacted against the one-sidedness evinced by both parties to the conflict. One-sidedness is symptomatic of a lack of insight into the dialectic of the historical process. It is conceivable that here Ibsen was incorporating a cautious warning to his contemporaries, attempting to be constructive, 'positive'. At all events history here acquired a didactic function to supplement the more obviously symbolic one.

Ibsen clearly seems to wish to indicate a third way – somewhat in line with Hegel's dialectical mode of thought. Both the antagonistic forces are to some extent right, though only in part; it is no use overlooking the historical and cultural justification of Christendom – and try to transplant the 'vines' in the old soil. They must have their roots in both the first and the second 'empires'. This is the perception, the Utopia, which Maximos endeavours to communicate to Julian, but which *he* does not succeed in coming to terms with. The right soil for that higher stage in the development of mankind is not yet there. And it is this that Maximos finally admits. Both he and the Christians are taken aback by the recognition that Julian has been a blind tool, has used his illusory 'freedom' only to achieve precisely what he did *not* wish: the consolidation of that power he wished to vanquish.

Again Ibsen had returned to the tragedy of the rebel and to the inscrutable and terrifying power that lies in being chosen to serve as an instrument in the development of historical necessity. Julian's career had been one of negation; it was in essence the tragedy of Duke Skule anew. Each was described by Ibsen as being like 'God's stepchild on earth'.

It could well be therefore that *Emperor and Galilean* contains Ibsen's reflections upon – and indeed his positive evaluation of – the role of the negator, the spirit of denial, within the historical and cultural process. There must be those who break with the status quo and who distance themselves from it if any kind of developmental progress is to occur. But Ibsen knew personally the cost of such an action: it brought with it the chill of isolation and loneliness. During a visit to Norway in 1874, in a speech which he gave to a group of students, he referred to such conditions as these, and adduced Julian's fate as an image of something he himself feared – namely, to be remembered merely 'with respectful acknowledgement by cold clear minds, whilst his opponents were lodged in warm, living human hearts, rich in love' [*iv*, 606].

One returns to the point made earlier: that *Emperor and Galilean* marked

Ibsen's definitive break with historical drama. He thus finished where he began – in Roman history. And he did it by describing a great world empire deep in crisis. But this crisis relates first and foremost to Ibsen's own time, and the presence of things *contemporary* had progressively become more evident in his work. After *Emperor and Galilean* he abandoned the distanced perspectives of history and entered the conflict-ridden reality of his own age, into 'all the turmoil of the chance events one is caught up in', as he had expressed it in 1862.

Ibsen let Julian approach his death with a message which spoke of a longing for a good and happy life, an earthly life of beauty and joy and sun. *That* dream – Utopia – lives on in Ibsen's contemporary works, reinforced by the consciousness of an ever-threatening defeat.

NOTES

1 Letter to Ludvig Daae, 23 February 1873.
2 Adam Oehlenschläger, 'Fortale' in *Nordiske Digte* (Copenhagen, 1807), p. xviii.
3 Hermann Hettner, *Das moderne Drama. Aesthetische Untersuchungen* (Brunswick, 1852), pp. 48–9 and pp. 59–60.
4 Bjørnstjerne Bjørnson, *Gro-tid* (Christiania, 1912), vol. I, p. 255.
5 James McFarlane, *Ibsen and Meaning* (Norwich, 1989), p. 104.
6 See *Henrik Ibsen. Brev 1845–1905*, ed. Øyvind Anker (Oslo, 1979), p. 83.

Other sources relevant to this chapter include

Lukács, Georg, 'Historical Novel and Historical Drama', in *The Historical Novel* (Harmondsworth, 1969), pp. 101–201.
Mjöberg, Jöran, *Drömmen om sagatiden* I-II (Stockholm, 1967).
Senelick, Laurence (ed.), *National Theatre in Northern and Eastern Europe, 1746–1900* (Cambridge, 1991), pp. 133–68.

3

JOHN NORTHAM

Dramatic and non-dramatic poetry

Brand is a work that has invited terms of discontinuity. It was Ibsen's response to what Halvdan Koht called the volcanic events of the year 1864, an eruption of bitterness over the death of his National-Romantic illusions about a modern Scandinavian brotherhood to match the heroic past. Georg Brandes, Ibsen's Danish critic and ally, referred to 'a shocking, yes overwhelming, impression of having come face to face with a strong and indignant genius, before whose penetrating gaze weakness feels constrained to lower its eyes'. Bjørn Hemmer has identified it as a milestone in Scandinavian literature, leading away from the current aesthetic and idealistic tendency into new fields, committed and contemporary; *Brand* became, and has remained, the most powerful drama of ideas in the whole of Scandinavian literature. And it is primarily by the ideas that criticism has been at once inspired and divided.

Brand has been taken to be a Christian and an anti-Christian work; the enactment of a specifically theological debate between Old and New Testament concepts of divinity; the story of an individual fighting an existential battle to define his own religious identity; a celebration and an exposé of idealism, secular or religious. It has been derived, for approval or blame, from different philosophical systems – Kierkegaard, Hegel, Nietzsche – and related to mythic patterns of universal extent. Brand has been seen as both a vindication of Romanticism and its indictment; or, more recently, as the victim of psychological or socio-psychological conditioning. The ambivalence concentrates, finally, on the meaning of the last scene; does it imply Brand's acceptance or rejection, and in what terms?

Ibsen himself might be thought to have restricted the scope of critical response by some direct and unambiguous statements of his own. His letter of 26 June 1869 to Georg Brandes states unequivocally enough that his play has been misunderstood as a religious play: he could as easily have constructed his syllogism about a sculptor or politician as about a priest. As for Kierkegaard it was, he wrote to Peter Hansen on 8 October 1870, a great mistake to suppose that he had depicted the life and career of Kierkegaard: 'That Brand is a clergyman is really immaterial. The demand of All or Nothing is made in all domains of life.' Ibsen's own approbation of his character was clearly enough expressed in the famous: 'Brand is myself in my best moments.' And yet the work itself resists simplification, even from that authoritative source; ambivalence is its essential feature. And it is useful to remember an implied ambiguity of a different kind, in Ibsen's description of *Brand* as a 'dramatic poem' – neither a poem nor a drama, but a drawing together of the two separate strands of Ibsen's output to date.

By the 1860s Ibsen's poetry had outstripped his plays in one important respect: the conventions of the drama had with one exception tied him, from considerations of grandeur, to the past, even where his preoccupations were with the present; in his poetry he had developed ways of confronting directly the age that he lived in. *Love's Comedy*, Ibsen's one important attempt to achieve the same in dramatic form, might be thought to have attained modernity but not much genuine sense of magnitude – Ibsen insisted that *Brand* was not to be such another performance. By contrast the narrative poem, of which Ibsen had long been master had, in 'On the Heights' and 'Terje Vigen', been transformed into what might be called the moral epic, its length used for extensive exploration of the fundamental moral dilemmas lurking behind the apparent trivia of the modern world. *Brand* started life as just such another narrative, the so-called 'Epic Brand' that was germinating as Ibsen left Norway for Italy in 1864.

Ibsen was not short of models or material for his intended Epic; the evangelical Pastor Lammers who came to the Skien district in 1849 was one; a friend, Christopher Bruun, a man of religion and iron principle who visited Ibsen in Italy while he was writing the poem, was another. Two Danish writers, both much admired and followed by Ibsen, Frederik Paludan-Müller and J. L. Heiberg, provided literary precedents of form though not of tone or substance with *Adam Homo* and *A Soul after Death* respectively. And there is no mistaking the Epic's origin in Ibsen's own bitter moral disgust at Norway–Sweden's recent abandonment of Denmark to German aggression. And yet, despite these models, materials and motivations, what ensued for Ibsen was, as he reported to Bjørnstjerne Bjørnson in September 1865, a year of agonizing frustration terminated suddenly in July 1865, when he abandoned the 212 eight-line stanzas that he had written and, with a new and remarkable fluency, composed in three months what was to become the dramatic poem *Brand*.

It was in Rome, during the famous visit to St Peter's in July 1865, that Ibsen suddenly perceived, as he put it, 'a strong and clear form for what I had to say'. The significance of the event has been variously explained.

Halvard Lie has suggested that it may have been the 'Dies Irae' heard there that provided Ibsen with a model both for the unusual metre he adopted for *Brand* and for its striking solemnity of tone:

> Dies irae, dies illa
> Solvet saeclum in favilla

Daniel Haakonsen has proposed that Ibsen was stimulated to reproduce the architectural audacity and symmetry of the building itself in the structure of his dramatic poem. Bjørn Hemmer has attributed Ibsen's change of form to a radical change in content: the Epic was abandoned for the dramatic poem because what he had to say had changed since he first embarked on it – from a negative and narrowly national satire to a more expansive and positive exploration of a universal dilemma. Different though they are, all three suggestions usefully hold together the two elements of Ibsen's revelation: form and content.

The Epic declares both from the start, in the first of its five surviving sections, a prologue addressed to the poet's 'accomplices'. The utter contempt for Norway that Ibsen expressed in a letter to Bjørnson of 16 September 1864, declining to share such hope for the future as Bjørnson might care to entertain, is clearly what informs his writing at the time – in the second stanza, for random example (my translation):

> The plague already rife. A corpse I see;
> as vast as Ymer's carcass, there it stretches
> and spreads a pestilence on firth and lea,
> infecting both the mighty and the wretches.
> Use Norway's flags to make the corpse's shroud!
> To-day's youth, help! and drown it in the waters!
> Where Earl met Jomsburg's men in battle loud
> the giant corpse best finds its burial quarters.   [*iii*, 37*]¹

The mythical–historical components familiar from Ibsen's earlier National-Romantic poems are evoked, but only to scorn the present. The heavy eight-line, five-foot iambic stanza imposes a daunting uniformity of movement and tone, precluding anything like the free development of emotion or event; the poem proceeds by exposition and explanation rather than inviting discovery through the interplay of characters left to define themselves in action and speech. Characters are stiffly emblematic at their first introduction and largely continue so. The young Brand comes from the North; turns his back on the sun; is pale, intense, dark; unhappy in his family; a priest-to-be. Einar comes from the South; faces the sun; is fair, robust, sparkling with joy; happy in his family; an artist-to-be. Such schematic obviousness and explicitness combine to cast an obsessive authorial censoriousness over the work. The Epic breaks off in the middle of Brand's sermon, the mood and vision little developed or changed from what they were 212 stanzas earlier. But as Ibsen began work on *Brand* his own views had changed considerably.

A letter of this later date, the one written in September 1865 to Bjørnson (above), announces Ibsen's abandonment of the narrowly and exclusively aesthetic outlook embodied in 'On the Heights': another (to his publisher Frederik Hegel in March 1866) announced that the purpose of the piece was to awaken his countrymen from their torpor and to make them recognize where the great issues were leading; an application to the King in April 1866 asserts it was to force them to 'think big'; to Bjørnson again, in March 1866, Ibsen described his own exultation and crusader-like courage during the writing of the piece. Finally, of course, there is the ultimate validation – 'Brand is myself in my best moments' – of October 1870. The negative censoriousness in which the Epic was conceived and largely confined had given way to a positive mood of committed and purposeful confrontation with modern life; and what now had to be said required a different form.

A brief snatch from the first scene of *Brand* makes clear some of the differences between Epic and dramatic poem:

> PEASANT Look, priest, however smart and such,
> a man can only do so much.
> Turn back; don't be so set on strife!
> We've only got the one bare life; –
> lose that, and what's there left behind?
> Seven miles, the nearest farm is, mind,
> with fog that hangs so thick you'll find,
> you'll need to cut it with a knife.
>
> BRAND Well, if it's thick we shan't fall prey
> to will-of-the-wisps and go astray.
>
> PEASANT There's ice-tarns though all round us here;
> and tarns like that are things to fear.
>
> BRAND We'll get across.
>
> PEASANT   Walk water? Hoo!
> That's easy said, just so much talking!
>
> BRAND One showed the way – where faith is true
> a man can cross dry-shod by walking.
>
> PEASANT Yes, long ago; but now he'd drop
> straight to the bottom, neck and crop ...   [*iii*, 78*]

This is manifestly a confrontation opposing strength to weakness but not in emblematic terms; and we are left to discover, not told, its significance. The four-foot iambic line (reproduced here in English as closely as possible) with endings freely varying between masculine and feminine, flexible rhyme-schemes, mobile caesuras, and shared occasionally between speakers, moves easily and is clearly intended to approximate to the conversational cut-and-thrust of personal interaction and the human diversity involved. The peasant's lack of spirit is offset by the burden of his responsibilities, Brand's strength by the harshness and violence of his words and actions. The setting, too, plays an active, not an emblematic role, intervening in the plot to test character in action. Its imagined vastness and extremity become metaphors of the man who seems confidently at home in it, magnifying his stature, yet some of its violent bleakness is transferred to him too. The actions and the speeches are prosaic enough but they nonetheless help set the prime theme of the work: the disparities of will, its courage and ruthlessness, the pain and the needful guidance it provides. The dramatic component of the dramatic poem allows Ibsen to address the essential condition of Norway without rigidly authorial denunciation; he works instead by a sharply life-like representation of the living contradictions involved.

There is, however, another metre in the piece beside the iambic, and it works not only to local but to structural effect. Since the distinction is often obscured in translation the feature is worth some attention here. Those who know Åse Lervik's classic study *Ibsens verskunst i Brand* will recognize the broad stimulus behind much that follows.

Lervik points out that only about two-thirds of the work is written in the iambic metre of that first scene; one-third is in four-foot trochaic lines. These are not scattered amongst the iambics but grouped for complete scenes or episodes; and these in turn are not evenly but tactically deployed as the work progresses. The differences between the two metres may seem slight and narrowly technical – a trochee is merely an iambus reversed, a stressed followed by an unstressed syllable – but an example shows what substantial contribution they can make.

In the course of Act I Brand encounters examples of the human frailties he is sworn to destroy: feebleness of will in the peasants, frivolousness in the artist Einar and Agnes, and wildness in Gerd. None of these encounters challenges him significantly, and the iambic line serves well enough to register them. But towards the end of the Act the metre changes abruptly and to great effect. Brand, standing alone after his latest iambic confrontation with Einar and Agnes, looks down on his boyhood home:

> Widow's farm. My infancy [...]
> That's the burden pressing in,
> weight of standing close in kin
> to a spirit concentrated
> on things earthly, isolated.

> Every goal of any scale
> trembles as behind a veil.
> All my courage, strength abated,
> heart and soul lose pith and sap;
> to home's nearness now awoken
> I feel alien by that token, –
> waking bound and shorn and broken,
> Samson in the harlot's lap ...   [*iii*, 95*]

The tone is clearly different from that of iambic passages. The opening of each line with the stressed syllable of the first trochee conveys in itself a kind of forthrightness; but many of the lines end on a stressed syllable too, where Brand clips off the final unstressed syllable. The resultant three-and-a-half-foot line, stressed at start and finish, has a very taut, intense character, suggestive of something like deep, concentrated self-communing. By contrast the iambic line varies its ending by adding an unstressed syllable, thus becoming a four-and-a-half foot line that begins and ends on an unstressed syllable. It seems more conversational, more easy-going. The variations intensify the differences between the basic metres. And Ibsen ensures that the differences should register by making sustained use of a metre once introduced.

In Act II the deployment of metres begins to take on a more structural function. There is the same initial establishing of the iambic mode of public discourse, followed by an abrupt change to Brand's trochaic musings over the deathbed repentance he has just witnessed:

> That was dying. Cleansed and lightened
> of each stain and dread of harm;
> now, his face impressive, calm,
> there he lies relieved and brightened ...   [*iii*, 109*]

But in this instance Brand shares the trochaic metre with Agnes, and on terms of equality. For Agnes is deep in the same sort of inner communion as Brand, defining her vision of a life-mission:

> And I see, no, sense him rather,
> raised up there on high, Our Father,
> feel Him looking from above
> full of grief and full of love,
> bright and mild as morning's morrow,
> grieved, though, unto death with sorrow ...   [*iii*, 114*]

She, with her vision of light and love, speaks as Brand's spiritual equal, if not his superior, for he is moved to adopt her vision in place of his own; but again it is the verse that helps us to discover his incompatibility of mind. He starts in something like her voice, in full, feminine-ended trochees, but by the end he has transposed her loving vision into imagery and movement identifiably his own, hard and bellicose:

> Let the world then go its way
> under song or thraldom's sway; –
> but if we should meet in battle, –
> if it tries to crush my work, –
> then, by Heaven, I'll fight not shirk! –   [iii, 115*]

The shared intensity of inner life creates at once a kinship and an opposition. Brand has encountered something other than the commonplace to react to, gentleness against his rigour.

Another kinship, more startling, seems suggested in Act III, where, after a typically long exposure to the normal – domestic concerns, visits from Mayor, Doctor, Man – which cumulatively threatens to sap away Brand's resolve, Gerd erupts into the iambic scene with her trochaic excitement:

> Have you heard? He's gone, the preacher! –
> From the hill and burial mound
> trolls and goblins swarm around,
> black and ugly, big and small, –
> ooh, and can't they hurt and all – !   [iii, 152*]

Outlandish, but she speaks straight to the core of Brand's inner struggle, projecting with nightmare exaggeration images of the moral chaos of his surrender; speaks so directly that Brand believes she has been sent by God. Her nightmare confirms him in his resolve, which he presses on Agnes until their son is sacrificed; but the effort costs him an agony of uncertainty and tears, and from now on his intensity of will seems coloured by association with Gerd's wildness.

By the beginning of Act IV Brand's vision has taken over the realm of ordinary life. The consequences lie heavy, in the gloom of a home, in the misery of a wife, in the sad discourse that goes on for page after page of tight, clipped trochaic exchanges that have become the staple of speech in the house since the child's death.

The Mayor's long iambic intervention comes with the force of a counter-attack and seems to shake Brand, to the extent that it is in that metre that he expresses doubt as never before.

> Have I here ever talked with God?
> And has He heard me? And bestowed
> a glance on grief in grief's abode?   [iii, 179*]

But only briefly; Brand's will reasserts itself and the last scene returns to the tone and metre of the first, with Agnes maimed and heart-broken. But again

Brand's exigency is coloured by the Gypsy who, like Gerd, serves as agent of Brand's inner mind, implementing his kind of ruthlessness with his kind of hard directness of metre. And the implacability of her detailed demands tinctures the whole protracted ordeal, makes it seem right that by a sudden reversal Brand should be the one now to come under direct pressure from his own imperatives: if Agnes obeys, she dies. Brand insists that he has no choice, but he wills her loss, and the Act ends with him, vulnerable to doubt, desperately mouthing slogans for his own reassurance:

> Soul be steadfast to the choosing!
> Triumph's triumph lies in losing.
> Loss of *all* brought forth your gaining; –
> Loss alone the gift remaining. [*iii*, 194*]

When, heralded by a shriek from the organ of his new church, Brand bursts into the iambic inanities of Act V, his trochees express an inwardness that is not of vision but of torment; with his wife's death he has lost all sense of direction. Page upon page of exposure to the voice and views of Mayor and Provost seem to wear him down, deprive him of his own voice; until his meeting with his own travesty in Einar stirs a great revulsion of spirit and he becomes again, at least sounds like, the Brand he was. He fires the mob with his old rhetoric, leads them towards the heights. But this Brand is different; he loses control, his voice is drowned by the 'Vox populi vox Dei. Kom!/The people's voice is God's. Come on!' of the Provost; he is rejected and enters the high wilderness, heroically alone but prey to doubts greater than any before:

> Have I dreamt? Am I now waking?
> All is grey, the mist-veil's making.
> Were they sickly dreams, no more,
> that I looked upon before? [*iii*, 241*]

There is no further change in metre for the rest of the piece. The ending comes to focus exclusively on Brand as he faces his own ordeal, his own testing by the trolls that he could so neatly tabulate at the end of Act I. They assail him in his own voice because they express impulses that he has always suppressed, the alternatives to the life he has chosen, rejected but not forgotten. Brand's doomsday. He survives the troll-temptations of weakness and of frivolousness in the apparition of Agnes but not the onslaught of the troll wildness, the emblematic figure in the piece endowed with incomparably more vitality and energy than all the other trolls together: the figure of Gerd, the obsessed nonconformist, the wildly passionate foe to compromise. She takes us to the heart of the Brand enigma by means of sharp, clear images: his dread of compromise in the hawk; the chill inhumanity of his mission in

a deathly church of ice in the wilderness; the spiritual arrogance of his ima-
gining himself a Christ performing the will of God in the terms of her naked
adulation:

GERD   Let me see your hands now, show me.
BRAND   Why my hands?
GERD   There's nails been ripping!
              From your hair there's blood-drops dripping,
              bitten by the thorn's fang surely,
              gashed about the brow so cruelly . . .
              yes, for you're the Saviour purely!
BRAND   Get thee from me!   [*iii*, 247–8*]

And at every challenge, Brand capitulates, recoils in revulsion from what
Gerd shows him until, in the most majestic image of all, his weeping seems
to release him into a new life based on warmth and love.

The piece does not, however, stop there. Brand's past errors cannot be
washed away in tears. There is one more vast error to be accounted for: the
subordination of love to will, crucial in all his terrible decisions. God's love
does not descend as he imagined, like a white dove bearing peace; the white
dove is the avalanche which wipes out a Brand still enough his old self to die
questioning his God. The imagery of the event identifies the greatest of
Brand's failures, but the mingling of peace and love with the implied chas-
tisement seems to suggest something other than simple condemnation.

Perhaps ambivalence itself, not simplicity, is what the piece aims at in its
presentation of Brand. For by a combination of poetic and dramatic means
the ending both is and is more than a 'proof' of Brand's mistaken mission,
more than an explanation in terms of boyhood deprivation. The imagery of
the ending makes Brand the focus of universal concern: his melting is a
cataclysm in nature, his annihilation a catastrophe, and his destruction is
attended by a more-than-human voice that evokes memory of another dove
that descended on Jesus at the start, not the end, of his mission proclaiming,
'This is my beloved son in whom I am well pleased.' God's love was not
incompatible with Christ's suffering.

Brand, a mere human, is not privy to the will of God; hence the error of
his life. Perhaps Ibsen sees him, within that inevitable limitation, as another
of the modern heroes that appear in his poems – another, as in 'Without
Name'; 'masterpiece frustrate' [N, 95] – necessarily flawed but worthy of
the deepest respect for his battle against the littleness of the modern world.
Whatever the conclusion, it can be reasonably claimed that the 'dramatic
poem' has achieved a scope and depth beyond any of the poems, and a
perception, beyond that of any of his plays to date, of the magnitude and
universality of the issues underlying that modern dwarfishness.

*

Ibsen's statement that *Peer Gynt* was 'the antithesis of *Brand*' (letter to Edmund Gosse, 30 April 1872) is manifestly true, in a sense: *Brand* is a work that implodes, narrowing from a world-wide mission to focus with wellnigh insupportable intensity upon the destiny of one prodigious individual fate and its universal significance; *Peer Gynt* explodes, from small farm to wide world, from fact to fantasy, in a prodigal variety. But Ibsen ascribed other qualities to it that carry more negative connotations: wildness and formlessness, a recklessness ascribable to his remoteness from Norway (to Peter Hansen, 28 October 1870). It was 'caprice', he wrote to Bjørnson on 9 December 1867, that led him to include the Strange Passenger, not the portentous symbolic intent alleged by a critic. In 1898 he confided to William Archer (reported in *The Monthly Review* 1906) that *Brand* and *Peer Gynt* were much easier to write than the severely logical *John Gabriel Borkman*, because 'you can introduce a bit of everything'. All seems to confirm Ibsen's other comment (in the above-mentioned letter to Hansen) that after *Brand*, *Peer Gynt* followed of its own accord.

Another pointer in much the same direction is Ibsen's copious borrowing from other writers and sources – Goethe, Byron, Oehlenschläger, H. C. Andersen, Wergeland, J. L. Heiberg, Kierkegaard and, time and again, the Bible; the sheer profusion and range of quotation, greater than in any other of his works, suggests magpie acquisitiveness rather than purpose. Ibsen's negotiations with Edvard Grieg for music to accompany the first stage production suggest a similarly cavalier indifference to the structure of his own work; the whole of Act IV, he proposed, should become a tone poem with tableaux, and several other scenes and characters should be excised [*iii*, 502–4]. Furthermore Ibsen draws on the world of folk-lore, stuff impervious to rational ordering.

There are some facts to be set against these intimations of spontaneous creation, formlessness and excessive eclecticism. *Peer Gynt* did not come of its own accord; for the whole of 1866, after *Brand* had been sent to the publisher, Ibsen was busy looking at other, and historical rather than modern, subjects. Draft material [*iii*, 454–82] suggests that the piece went through three stages of composition in the course of which verse forms were adjusted and details altered to conform more accurately with the facts of Ibsen's own boyhood. A whole range of characters that constitute a strong semi-mythical presence in the final work were added by after-thought: the Strange Passenger, the Bailiff, the Button Moulder, the Thin Man. The excisions proposed to Grieg turn out to have one common tendency, namely to preserve and strengthen the presence in the play of Solveig. As for quotations and references, Ibsen, like Beckett, makes them serve to define the character who borrows; and nowhere is the general opinion – that Ibsen, more borrower than innovator, always makes whatever he borrowed his own – more completely apposite than when applied to his use of folk material.

Ibsen claimed (letter to Frederik Hegel, 8 August 1867) that he had got little information about Peer from Asbjørnson's *Book of Norwegian Folk Tales* but on the other hand had had so much more freedom to invent. The translations in the *Oxford Ibsen* [*iii*, 482–6] bear him out. Events confronting the original Gudbrand Glesne and Peer Gynt may be extravagantly supernatural, but they plod through them with a degree of phlegmatic ordinariness that is unshakable. It is evident that Ibsen effects a superb transmutation of this stuff into poetry; equally evident that he integrates it into the very structure of the work's meaning.

There is one further respect, and a crucial one, in which *Peer Gynt* is not the antithesis of *Brand* but the twin: the ambivalence of its impact. The controversies have survived beyond the contemporary strife about whether Truth and Beauty and a positive Ideal were essential to genuine poetry. *Peer Gynt* raises as sharply as did *Brand* issues concerning religion or morality concentrated into an enigmatic ending, and disagreement has reigned. A story of salvation through Christian grace? A desperate dream of salvation in a man's disordered mind? A romantic happy ending or anti-romantic satire? Peer a poet redeemed by his poetic force? Peer a poetaster who speaks in verse because he exists in a verse play and for no other reason? Solveig an impressive figure of Christian constancy and forgiveness or a sentimental, insubstantial romantic cut-out? The answer, if single answer there is, must lie within the work itself, and in approaching that there is one more comment by Ibsen to be remembered: 'My book is poetry. And if it is not, then it shall be . . . !' (letter to Bjørnson, 9 December 1867). The poetry is the book, and the book is another 'dramatic poem', another convergence of poetry and dramatic form, with the poetry contributing to the dramatic structure, and the dramatic structure to the poetic imagery, and it asks to be approached as such.

A commentary on the poetry, in this sense, of the piece would be as long as the piece itself, so extraordinary is Ibsen's fecundity and versatility. Furthermore there is no current English translation that reproduces with any close accuracy the verse forms that contribute so much to the significance, hence no standard text to which reference can be made. I use here my own translations and, to abbreviate analysis, concentrate in the first instance on points of transition in the action.

The first scene is written in a metre of remarkable adaptability; it is the four-foot trochaic line that was used in *Brand* but loosened and lightened to meet many different needs; Peer can sweep confidently through his yarn on its back, so to speak:

> What a colt to ride – amazing!
> As we started on our run
> it was just like suns were blazing.
> Eagles, brown-backed every one,
> hung in space between us there
> and the way-down stretch of water, –
> specks of dust upon the air.   [*iii*, 256*]

Aase can grumble in the same metre. But above all the verse establishes a common language through which this pair share a life, present and past, that makes them decisively not specimens of romantic peasantry. They are not even peasants, not competent to run a small-holding; they are misfit survivors of a feckless and bankrupt marriage, with dreams and fantasies their only relief. On home ground, and with only his mother for company, Peer can revel confidently and cockily with words, but all changes when he leaves the farm for the wedding party at Hægstad. As he draws close to the place his physical hesitancy is reinforced by the way his verse changes:

> There it is, Hægstad. A step or two yonder …
> Will Ingrid be sitting there lonely, I wonder? …
> No. Wedding guests swarming like gnats down the track – …
> There's always the laughing behind your back …   [*iii*, 268*]

He withdraws from an encounter with hostile locals into a private world of fantasy whose defensiveness sounds in the new and tightly formal artifice of regular couplets:

> Peer Gynt's riding first and a crowd of folk follow…
>   Nobody sits quite so sturdily upright,
> Nobody glitters like him to the sunlight…
>   The women curtsey and each soul admires
> Emperor Peer Gynt and his thousands of squires …   [*iii*, 269*]

– only to make the intrusion of the world of real peasants that much the more abrupt and painful for the doggerel dislocation:

PEER	…The King, why he raises his crown and he says –
ASLAK	Look who's here! Peer Gynt, the drunken swine – !
PEER	Your Highness –
ASLAK [*grins*]	Wake up lad, rise and shine! [*iii*, 269*]

Peer tries to overcome the hostility of the other guests, adapts both voice and behaviour for them, but it does not work; and the pain is real and evident in the tautness of his initial reaction; until, that is, there is another immediate transition, back into liveliness at the first sight of Solveig and the first introduction into his life of the different values she seems to embody; a sense of wonder in the verse before disappointment sends him back to his old role of scapegoat wild-boy:

> She's lovely. And who's seen the like before?
> Eyes on her shoes and her pinny's brightness – !
> and she clutched at the skirts her mother wore,
> and carried a prayer-book wrapped in pure whiteness – !
>
> [*iii*, 273*]

It is a vision that is never to leave him, entirely. After his orgy with the sæter-girls in Act II it comes back as a longing to be free as the eagles, to be clean again and pure – but the aspiration collapses in the course of the passage, and the next transition is from Peer's unregeneracy to an appropriately debased troll world whose significance in the work is again effected by the poetry's movement and tone. The Dovre-king's first speech in Act I establishes immediately his function:

> Cool down now. Cool it! ... Less huffing and puffing.
> Now over the years our stock's taken a dive.
> It's touch and go if it's bust or survive.
> Refusing support from the public seems thoughtless.
> Besides that, this lad here's pretty near faultless,
> and well set up with it too, I'm sure.
> It's true he's got only one head for his ration,
> but even my daughter can't manage more.
> Three-headed trolls have gone right out of fashion ...   [*iii*, 294*]

The speech makes him the epitome, not of the semi-mystical or supernatural, but of the crashingly commonplace; folk-lore degraded as a reproach to Norway's degradation into narrowminded complacency. The lessons Peer learns in the Dovre palace are addressed to the nation at large; the brilliant scene with the Boyg, no mere troll grotesque but a symbol of a deep and insurmountable psychological impediment to action, registers the moment when Peer has them etched into his own inner consciousness and adopts them for his own, not to correct but to confirm his congenital evasiveness; by accepting the national slogans of 'to thyself be enough' and 'go round about', Peer becomes both an individual and a personification of national and, later, international inauthenticity.

Act IV provides a dazzling range of versatility for Peer in both functions; it defines both what he has made of himself and what sort of world it is that abets his unscrupulous pursuit of self interest. The brittle sophistication of the self-made man is caught in the complacent slickness of the verse as well as in the sentiments:

> I said just now, I am in fact
> a simple, plain autodidact.
> My study's not methodical;
> but still I've gained a sort of knowledge,
> and thought and read about it all ...   [*iii*, 328*]

and the outrageousness of his business amorality is highlighted by the tension between suave propriety of form and impropriety of content.

Transitions abound in this Act, all registered in the voice as well as in setting and costume, as Peer makes his crazy but not formless progress. Ibsen may not have known when he started that Peer would find himself in Africa, but he clearly conceived the notion with a structural purpose, absurd though the adventures are.

First after the international magnate comes Peer in the role of love-besotted prophet:

> Silence! Did she note, my sweeting?
> Has she heard my little song?
> Is she through the curtain peeking
> with her veils and so forth gone?   [*iii*, 350*]

It is in a tone not heard from him before, a new pitch of absurdity; but it reads as mere role-playing because he never allows himself to be convinced by his own protestations. The doting lover can still observe:

> Child, where love's concerned I'd claim
> tom-cats and prophets at the game
> work out at pretty much the same.   [*iii*, 351*]

And so he progresses along the coast of North Africa, his every role, costume, voice contributing to a madly exaggerated yet deliberately judged demonstration of the consequences of self-obsessed living, not just in Peer but in the world at large – in Sweden's obsession with its past, Norway's with its language, in German philosophical solipsism, the impractical Utopianism of Ole Bull's settlement in America. The final scene in the Cairo madhouse represents a universal bankruptcy, though its bitter ironies are focused on Peer. The would-be Emperor riding the clouds ends on his knees in the mud, mount for a madman, crowned in straw; and under the shock his old glibness appropriately collapses into the inarticulateness of terror.

Act V concentrates on Peer the person; there is no extravagant variety and diversity, no abrupt leap in roles; Peer no longer visits but receives visitants that force him to confront one or other aspect of his past and thereby acknowledge more and more openly the truth about what he has done with his life and to his soul. The start of the transition to this sober pilgrimage to the ultimate reality is beautifully managed through the lifelike movement of the verse against the growing threat of the storm that provides the welcome for an old, now, and lonely Peer:

> SKIPPER   Two hands to the helm – and see to the light.
> PEER   It's blowing up.
> SKIPPER   There'll be storms tonight ...
>   ... Here comes the weather.
> PEER   Now don't forget, –
>   if your people need helping, all or any,
>   I'll not be too strict about every penny.
> SKIPPER   That's right handsome. It isn't a lot they get;
>   they all have a missus at home and youngsters.
>   And just on their wages – well, ends don't meet ...
>
> [*iii*, 375–7*]

It is the realism that sets off the special character of Peer's first visitant, the Strange Passenger, who speaks with a suave urbanity of tone that makes him seem comically disengaged, until the incongruousness becomes serious, and he turns into an inquisitor from a wholly different realm of being, challenging Peer's capacity to rise to the spiritual challenge he presents. Peer fails the test of course; and his resolute obtuseness to his real condition is beautifully conveyed through the next transition, at the end of the Priest's graveside address. A fine speech, sparse of rhetoric but measured, deeply considered and humane, it ends:

> PRIEST   To try the heart and reins as arbitrators –
>   that is no task for clay, but its Creator's; –
>   I end on this clear, sure and hopeful chord:
>   it is no cripple stands before his Lord! ...
> PEER   Now that's what I call christianity, look!
>   There's nothing to seize the mind terrifyingly. –
>   The theme, one should be oneself undyingly, –
>   the line the preacher's sermon there took, –
>   works in a way, too, quite edifyingly.   [*iii*, 390*]

the slovenliness of Peer's understanding beautifully caught in the slovenliness of the verse.

But something begins to stir in him; the auction at Hægstad moves him to a new desperation reflected in the verse in which he throws himself away, so to speak, as so much rubbish. There is a new self-understanding in the onion-peeling scene, and a new genuineness in his response to the vision of Solveig waiting in the hut he once built for her:

> PEER [*stands up, quiet and deathly pale*]
> One who remembered – and one who forgot.
> One who has squandered – and one who has not. –
> O truth! – and that's not a game to be played!
> O horror! – Here's where my Emperordom stayed!
>
> [*iii*, 397*]

Still, he runs; but runs through images of desolation, encountering other emissaries from a realm where judgement is absolute and final. But Peer cannot simply capitulate, because, as the Button Moulder reveals, the threat is to the very essence of Peer's identity, his Gyntian Self. This ultimate threat seems to postpone further development to his understanding, revives his impulse to evade, to keep on running. His verse reverts to the flippant and trivial in his manoeuvrings with the Thin Man, but then the final and sudden transition occurs when Peer happens to look into the sky to see not Emperor Peer Gynt but an emblem of extinction, a brief shooting-star; and from that encounter comes a form of poetry that is, in one important respect, quite unlike any other that Peer has created. It is not just a matter of movement and tone, though the changes there are great and significant:

> [*A glimpse of a shooting-star; he nods to it.*]
> Cheers! from Peer Gynt, my brother the star!
> shine, fade and die in the void where you are – !
> [*Hugs himself in terror; . . . a moment of quiet, then bursts out.*]
> Is there no-one, none in this sixes and sevens – ,
> none in hell's bottomless pit, in the heavens – !   [*iii*, 418*]

It is the crisis in Peer's soul. He goes on to hold unswerving doomsday over himself in a poetry that is of a new kind in him:

> As unspeakably poor, then, a soul one day
> can turn back into nothing, in the overcast grey.
> You beautiful earth, don't be cross
> that I trampled your grass for nought worth telling.
> You beautiful sun, it was so much loss
> was your radiant touch on a folkless dwelling.
> There was no-one at home to be warmed and provided; –
> the owner, they say, had never resided . . .   [*iii*, 418*]

– down to the final epitaph on himself: 'Here lies NO-ONE below'. For this is the only poem, of all those created by Peer, that does not collapse at its ending into mundanity. Peer has become capable, after all, of directness, of honesty, of awareness; and it shows in a poem that is at last sustained and genuine. It is a negative vision at this stage, this acceptance of his own unworthiness, but it does not exclude, indeed it depends upon, a sense of all that was worth striving for though he never strove – he will climb to the topmost peaks again before he dies, to 'stare myself tired at the promised land' – just as the ending turns into an emblem of that promised land in tangible form as Peer comes upon his hut and sees Solveig.

Whatever one is inclined to think of the ending in itself, there is no denying the dramatic weight that Ibsen attaches to it; it is firmly crafted into the sequence of visitations; it is not presented as a sudden and unmotivated event. *Peer Gynt* is full of quotations from itself. Scenes echo one another in their chaos – the wedding party, the Dovre hall, the apes in Africa, the lunatic asylum; the connectedness is stressed by the use of catch phrases: the old one was bad but the young are worse; you can tell the nobs by their riding outfit; forward and back is as long a gait. Most originate in Peer's traumatic encounters with the trolls. It is a strand that binds together disreputable adventures into a composite definition of his philosophy at work.

The final scene is bound into place by a similar but opposing strand whose weaving began in the first Act, with Peer's first sight of Solveig. She is given an emblematic simplicity of both demeanour – with the modesty of her glance, the purity of her dress, and the prayerbook she carries – and, from Act II on, of speech, but she becomes immensely real in Peer's mind as more than just a pretty girl; she serves as a constant reminder of a world of values quite distinct from his own; a world that Ibsen gives dramatic substance to by bringing it back to haunt and reproach him again and again; sometimes as Solveig herself, sometimes as Aase, sometimes as a choir of women, but always womanhood associated with religion in some manifestation – church bells, hymn singing, procession.

Emblematic and idealistic as these images may be made to appear, they nonetheless become fused with reality in this final scene. After the wildness in the mountains, after the flat sterilities of the desert, after his flight through scenes of greater and greater spiritual desolation in Act V, Peer comes home. The final scene restores him to a community, for there is a church to be assumed and a congregation singing a hymn and the hut and the woman he could have made his wife. It suggests that it is here, against the example of selfless love and loyalty displayed in small things, that the pretensions of the Gyntian Self are finally to be measured.

Peer's final transition is characterized by verse of a new and desperate sincerity as he questions Solveig, no longer asserting self but questioning where he lost his own:

> Where was *I*, as myself, as the whole man, the real?
> Where was *I*, with my forehead stamped with God's seal?
>
> [*iii*, 421*]

And his final acceptance of the offered grace is not a matter of a few, unsupported words: to prepare for the moment Ibsen assembles images of the spirit: the Pentecostal procession and hymn; Solveig's appearance and her song; the gleam of Peer's transformation magnified, as in *Brand*, by the participation of nature through the rising of the sun; the swelling of Solveig's song confirmed 'in the splendour of the day' that ends the work. Solveig may be elderly and blind, and Peer old and battered by life; but like *The Winter's Tale*, *Peer Gynt* insists on our remembering the human sorrow, the irredeemable wastage, without thereby denying the ultimate affirmation.

Peer Gynt may be more than a single man's pilgrimage of self-discovery. There is the question of why his plight in particular should engage us. We are told that his destiny was to be a shining button on the waistcoat of the world; to have been a poet, perhaps. We may be invited to think back to the very beginning, to the vivid imagination, the gift with words, all wasted in mere fantasy until suffering begins to tell against his complacency – the genuine poet emerging with the genuine self. But the disembodied voices – of withered leaves and thread-balls – accuse him of failing to express the ideas, create the songs, formulate the watchwords, perform the deeds of which he was capable. The accusations relate to nothing in the work; they resemble Ibsen's allegations, in a poem of that name, against the Bards of Norway. The nation is the target – as it is again in the scene with the Old Man of Dovre which brings national satire back into the last Act, with Peer cast not as person but as personification. Peer may be intended both as the fully realized character that Ibsen claimed, and also as the conduit of a challenge to a people at large to rediscover its own gift for poetry – to find its roots again, its soul again, its sense of purpose, its smothered gifts of imagination: a poetry to be proclaimed against the engulfing prose of the world at large.

Peer Gynt engages the moral issues of Ibsen's world as did *Brand*, but at more points: the scope of social reference is broader, characters more varied and more sharply characterized in speech – there are no lay figures. The work is another in the line of moral epic, but with the epic more thoroughly humanized, and presented through a dazzlingly inventive dramatic imagination that provides both the wealth of fantasy and the means to shape it, until it presents the world, no less, with a compelling image of its own living likeness in the figure of one little man. The poetry is overt here and in *Brand*, but between them, by bringing the strength of commitment to the modern world that Ibsen had developed in his poems into harness with the dramatic instinct developed in the earlier plays, they stand as milestones on the way to the later works.

The volume published in 1871 under the title *Poems of Henrik Ibsen* was his fourth, though first successful, attempt to appear before the public in the role of poet – a fact that indicates the importance of the project to him. As, too, does the amount of time and energy that Ibsen, by then living abroad and relishing the fame that *Brand* and *Peer Gynt* had brought, was prepared to invest in its compilation. These positive indications have to be set against the self-deprecatory tone of his own comments on the volume – he said it contained much that he would now place little weight on, and much that was dated – and coupled with his manifest concern for its success and with his justification that the volume did, after all, possess a sort of unity and indicate a kind of development in his writing career.

There is not a great deal available to help the reader without Norwegian to come at the unity, development or indeed any sort of independent estimate of the fifty-odd pieces that make up the volume itself (omitting songs from plays) or of the considerably larger body of some 200 pieces that Ibsen had been writing from at least as early as 1847, while he was still a teenage assistant to an apothecary in Grimstad.

Norwegian scholars and critics, despite a frequent tendency to adopt a certain apologetic tone towards much of the poetry, especially pieces not included in *Poems*, have nonetheless laid the essential foundations for its study, but most of their work remains ountranslated: Didrik Arup Seip's introduction to the whole corpus of poems in volume XIV of the Hundreårs-utgave; Herleif Dahl's *Bergmannen og byggmesteren: Henrik Ibsen som lyriker*; Leif Mæhle's *Ibsens rimteknikk*; Pavel Frænkl's *Ibsens vei til drama*, and many others. It is by way of exception that Daniel Haakonsen's essay on 'Henrik Ibsens lyrikk' (originally published in *Edda* vol. 50, 1950) has appeared in English in *Contemporary Approaches to Ibsen* vol. VII (1991); and that Vigdis Ystad's selection in *Henrik Ibsen, Dikt* (1991) should bring together under a few broad, thematic headings pieces from the 1871 volume and pieces selected from elsewhere.

In English some of the same ground has been touched on by, for instance: Brian Downs's *Ibsen, the Intellectual Background*; James McFarlane's 'Ibsen's Poem-cycle "I Billedgalleriet"', in *Scandinavica*, May 1978 (a detailed study of revision undergone by the group 'In the Picture Gallery' as *Poems* was being shaped – see Northam, *Ibsen's Poems*, pp. 140–52); Halvdan Koht's *Life of Ibsen* and Michael Meyer's *Ibsen, A Biography*. Needless to say, many studies of the prose plays have drawn on individual poems for their thematic relationship to the later works: 'Blueprint' and *The*

Master Builder, 'The Miner' and *John Gabriel Borkman*, 'With a Waterlily' and *Little Eyolf* for instance; or on specific textual revisions of a poem for indications of shifts of emphasis in Ibsen's thinking and poetic sensibility. In general terms, however, the English-speaking public's access, direct or indirect, to this considerable body of Ibsen's creative output has been considerably hampered by the demise of the early enthusiasm for the poetry in its own right that inspired, for example, Philip Wicksteed (*Four Lectures on Ibsen*, 1892), R. A. Streatfield (*Lyric Poems by Henrik Ibsen*, 1902), F. E. Garrett (*Lyrics and Poems from Ibsen*, 1912) and most notably Muriel Bradbrook (*Ibsen the Norwegian*, 1959). There is at the moment of writing no current translation into English of the whole corpus, and only one of *Poems* (my own *Ibsen's Poems*, 1986).

Poems does not present us with a section cut evenly through the strata of Ibsen's previous work. Of the fifty or so pieces in the volume, a mere ten or eleven came from the close on a hundred written between 1847 and 1857, and many of those were heavily or significantly revised, some more than once, before they were included. Of the fifty-five or so written during Ibsen's second stay in the capital (1857–64), some twenty were chosen; and of the poems written abroad between 1864 and 1871, all were included. Thus by both selection and revision the 1871 volume became more a reflection of his sensibility in the late sixties than a mere chronicle of past work and past attitudes. The defining of that sensibility can best be achieved by comparing, like with like, pieces that had undergone Ibsen's editorial attentions with those that, for whatever reason, had not – where like refers to the loose and deliberately unexclusive categories into which all of his poetry can be thought to fall.

Ibsen began as a love poet in a wholly conventional fashion: 'Pallid star! bestow a sign / From those heights eternal!' ('To the Star', 1849); 'Dearest of blooms with your sweet-scented petal / Brief as a dream was your flowering's bright round, – ' ('To My Primrose', 1853); even a later poem to his wife-to-be ('To my Rose', 1857) is in similar vein, ending:

> And if you are gently dozing,
> Please remember in your doze,
> Please remember him whose only
> Dream is of his lovely rose.

Pretty compliments that nonetheless depersonalize and etherealize the real young women (Clara Ebell in Grimstad, Rikke Holst in Bergen, besides Suzannah) to whom they were written, turning them into abstract objects of veneration, emblems of love. They confirm the common estimate of Ibsen's early poems. But what is not accounted for in this estimate is the exercise, from the very beginning, of a critical self-scrutiny that leads Ibsen to write, alongside these romantic conventionalities, decidedly unromantic critiques of them. 'Memories of a Ball' (1849) begins with a resoundingly conventional prologue, a conflation of Wergeland's muse and Welhaven's autumnal asters:

> To Stella!
> Here I set before thy feet
> A bouquet of blooming flowers
> Burgeon of late summer's powers
> From the bed of Memory sweet;
> [...]
> – Stella! Those the blooms I gave
> Are but pale-as-alabaster
> Sheaves of sad, autumnal aster
> Burgeoned forth from out a grave!

But in the body of the poem it is a sardonic eye that reviews the manners and behaviour of real people at a real ball, noting

> ... a charming flirt-formation
> Rocket-launching invitation ...

and the devices of dress and make-up in the service of illusion:

> Even a thirty-year-old fair
> Becomes a sylphide out at dances! –
> [...]
> Arms shown whitely,
> Bosom sightly
> With its alabaster sheen
> There set off with lace resplendent;
> Here a pinkish ditto's been
> Kept from sight behind a pendant ...

The fixed smiles, hidden torment – even the envious uninvited, lounging in the street outside – are all included. And the verse part of the piece makes its unromantic point all the more sharply for being followed, under the shared sub-title, by the same ball-going experience mediated through the prose entries in the diary of an unmitigated idealist who commits suicide in an ecstasy of renunciation.

The challenging of the dreams of romantic love by the facts of life goes on in 'Autumn Evening' (1849), in 'A Leg-pull' (1851) (a hard knock at the Wergeland whom elsewhere Ibsen revered), and most successfully in 'Room to Let' (1850) where love is negotiated, or not, as the case may be, amid the frustrations and limitations of bachelor rooms and wary females. The room to let is Ibsen's heart:

> True there's many a miss or maid
> Dropped in, peeping through the entry,
> But a casual visit paid
> Only leaves the room more empty;
> When she's curtseyed her goodbyes,
> Thanked me kindly, formal-wise,
> She's forgotten but – the visit's
> Left me bored and with the fidgets.

And yet these accomplished and telling attacks on conventional Romanticism are no more represented in *Poems* than, understandably, the pretty clichés themselves, a fact that may go some way towards identifying the character of the volume overall.

For closer examination shows that the attacks are not pressed home. The poet of the Ball resolves, after all, to plunge unregenerately into the next to find either his heart's desire or oblivion, romantic lover to a T; the young Miss wooed in such seemingly pragmatic terms is as much the idealized, impossible She as the Pallid Star, destined to the old style of worship; 'A Leg-pull' merely exchanges one kind of romantic sentimentality for another. These pieces simply transpose the commonplaces of romanticized love into modern dress and circumstance.

The love poems selected for *Poems* are radically different. It is indicative that of four pieces written in the same year (1853) for the same Bergen girlfriend, Rikke Holst, Ibsen passed over two entirely conventional pieces: 'To My Primrose', and 'To R.H!' (Ah,I know a lovely land / Star-remote out yonder . . .); but included 'A Birdsong' and 'The Wild-flower and the Pot-plants'. They both offer, in place of idealistic abstraction, an immediacy and particularity that suggest truth to real, and felt, experience. From 'A Birdsong':

> I painted poem-pictures,
> with lively play of hue;
> two eyes of brown were shining
> and laughed and listened too.   [N, 22*]

Two real youngsters to the life, Ibsen showing off his special gifts, she playing up to him. And real life, too, in the handling of what followed, namely Ibsen's running for dear life at her father's approach. All the poem says is: 'But we, we took a fine farewell / and never met again. – '; but that wry laconism suggests a capacity to handle the absurdities and indignities of love in the real world without recourse to romantic extremities of despair.

'The Wild-flower . . .' – Rikke again – is specifically criticized by the voice of good sense as the negation of the conventional beloved: 'She's never a beauty, she's just a kind / of next-best-thing to a hussy – ' [N, 46*] to which Ibsen replies with one simple image that affirms a live, not conventional, admiration for a distinct and special individuality:

> she is a child of the open air
> and sixteen summers her age is! [N, 21*]

With their concern for truth to experience, circumstance and overt personality, these pieces, early though they are, go well with the later and infinitely more complex pieces in the volume where the concern simply probes more deeply in the same direction – to express not just the outer and verifiable truth but the hidden truth, the obscure and remarkable essence of relationship and character. And with that change in level of concern goes a change in poetic economy. If 'Birdsong' and 'The Wild-flower and the Pot-plants' exchange the exalted rhetoric of Romanticism for the simpler language of everyday, in these later poems the poetry seems to inhere in the very act of perception; form and language become so restrained and reduced that they serve now almost as a transparent envelope that contains rather than enhances. Two of the most moving poems in the volume are of this kind. 'Gone!' was written in 1864, soon after Ibsen settled in Genzano; it ends:

> A party, merely,
> till darkness came on;
> a guest here, merely, –
> and now she is gone. [N, 46*]

There is no mistaking the charge of desolation carried by the utter simplicity of the last line, or the emotive force of the sparsely but powerfully established setting. They hint persuasively of the hidden poignancies that can lurk behind the seemingly commonplace event – sudden discovery of one person's worth to another, recognized only through the process of loss. The simplicity works because of the total absence of rhetorical competition.

'A Swan' was written about 1865; it too registers, through the simplest of means, the amazed discovery of an unsuspected splendour, a swanhood, in a character revealed only at and through the ultimate severance, loss becoming thereby a mingling of affirmation and negation. It ends:

> With song's first breath
> your journey was gone.
> You sang in death; –
> you *were* then a swan! [N, 35–6*]

'With a Waterlily' (1863) [N, 26], too, is a world away from the decorative conventionalities of those other flower compliments, 'To My Primrose' and 'To My Rose'. It seems to penetrate a prim and preachy surface into levels of sexual relationship by their nature not openly acknowledgeable in a piece written originally to a sister-in-law – not, perhaps, openly understood by the poet himself. Its intimations of obscure tension between surface purity and lurking danger, between modesty and sexual threat, make the little poem appear to prefigure *Little Eyolf* and its hints of forbidden relationships and, with its fellows, to foreshadow the tragic procedures and ambivalences of Ibsen's later prose plays generally.

Much the same development, from convention to surface reality to essential truth, is to be seen in Ibsen's 'political' poetry – the term needs some elaboration. Understandably for a writer whose nation was still seeking a sense of its own identity and a code for its own moral and political conduct after centuries of dependency, Ibsen started out as a subscriber to the National-Romantic vision, compounded of myth, legend and history, of Norway's destiny: the heroic past, be it of Valhallan gods, Viking heroes or medieval kings; the long subservience and obscurity that followed its collapse; and then the promised birth of a new creation. It was a vision that ensured that, in Ibsen's view, political events and characters of his own times were to be judged not by the criteria of political science – 'A Balloon-Letter to a Swedish Lady' [N, 99] shows his detestation of that – but by the heroic values and standards of the past and the promise implied by a brave new world; an inheritance for all the folk to share and augment.

Perhaps his most dignified and moving exposition of the vision comes in the Prologue delivered in the Norwegian Theatre in Bergen on 15 October 1851, with its evocation of the long winter of Norway's inanition:

> Then all was hushed, like some deserted strand,
> Where shattered flotsam bobs upon the waters
> That ripple soundless on the whitened sand.
> No bird-call twittered through the forest quarters...

but the imagery distances and cloaks rather than confronts the experience of past ignominies.

Well before Sweden–Norway, in Ibsen's view, betrayed Denmark to German aggression in 1863, his expansive sense of a heroic folk with a common, conventionally heroic past changed to a recognition that in the modern world leadership and guidance must be looked for in the rare individual of visionary power. 'To the Survivors' (1860) [N, 44] and 'To Professor Schweigaard' (1860) [N, 44] celebrate such men: J. L. Heiberg, the Danish philosopher, writer, man of the theatre; Schweigaard, a liberal academic-cum-politician. '4th July' [N, 37] and 'A People's Grief' [N, 40], pieces written on the sickness and death of King Oscar in 1859, praise him precisely for having broken with the conventional role of kingship; he has been a great exemplar to his people by virtue of his peaceful and civilized pursuit of national arts. The true business of politics has become culture and quality of mind instead of power.

There is, however, a price to be paid. The individual distinction of the new hero can easily become isolation, and isolation can lead to persecution. Heiberg was, according to the poem, a martyr; Schweigaard a lonely pioneer; 'Without Name', however, is the poem (to King Charles XV) that elaborates the theme fully. It celebrates a ruler nameless because fameless, to be honoured for his possession of a distinct and personal inward vision that would, had it been realized, have set his nation in the van of progress. That his reward has been a martyrdom at the hands of the spiritual dwarfs of politics merely emphasizes his stature:

> Hence this monument's unveiling
> to a masterpiece frustrate;
> and while cunning's botch is failing,
> I his very *fault* am hailing
> my proud knight's true worth regaling:
> *In him was the bard too great!* [N, 97*]

The ambivalent linking of martyrdom and greatness, defeat and affirmation, similar in kind to the mingling of loss and affirmation in the best of the poems of love and intimacy, becomes one of the dominant characteristics of the 1871 volume.

Without the personal moral vision to inspire it, politics is, in Ibsen's view as expressed there, a corrupt game of an establishment that, if it cannot reform, should be destroyed; some of the bitterest political poems in the volume express that mood: 'Abraham Lincoln's Murder' (1865) ends with:

> Just let the whole system be wrenched away;
> the sooner comes vengeance and Judgement Day
> on us for the lies we have been! [N, 92]

'To My Friend the Revolutionary Orator' (1869) with:

> You fix up a flood to earth's farthest mark.
> I'll gladly, myself, torpedo the Ark. [N, 94]

But the bitterness is not nihilistic; it is inspired by Ibsen's passion for a politics of enlightenment, of enlargement of the human spirit, through the vision of thinkers and artists.

It is not, therefore, surprising that *Poems* should contain more pieces about art than about any other theme – indeed Ibsen signals the prominence by framing the contents between two pieces that record the human cost to the poet of his art: 'Fiddlers' to begin, 'Burnt Ships' to end – nor that pieces in this category should follow the kind of development by now familiar.

Some of the most immediately attractive amongst the unrepresented pieces indicate entirely conventional sources of poetic inspiration:

> The full moon is shining; – across the unending
> Slumber of sea-level tenderly spills
> In magical harmony glistening and blending
> Moonlight's broad torrent, while everything stills . . .
>
> 'Moonlight Voyage on the Sea', 1849

or:

> It is too bright, it is too bright
> Where Moon here sheds her glow, –
> My heart is by this calm of night
> Transfixed and trembles so . . .
>
> 'Evening Stroll in the Woods', 1849

or:

> Here where the carpet so rich in its bloom
> Decked the sweet meadow's light green with its treasure,
> Summer's farewell sounds a tremulous measure,
> Straws for its strings now, a poem of gloom! . . .
>
> 'Autumn', 1849

It is Nature at its most emblematic: generalized and unspecific, a largesse extended to all; as, too, were the other sources that Ibsen celebrates: the national treasury of history, myth and legend; the haunted countryside where spirits in streams and falls bewitch with their music; the nostalgia for home and homeland. These are represented as sources of inspiration common to all Norwegians, making them, if not themselves artists, responsive to art. Ibsen can refer to poets as bards, as a class with a clear social function, and can define poetry itself and art generally in confident and general terms:

> For art is like a harp's strong sounding-board,
> Lends power to the soul-strings of the nation . . .
>
> Prologue, 15 October 1851

> What more makes the people strong
> Than its life in mountain straitness,
> Than its forebears' deeds of greatness
> Drawn in imagery and song?

> Than its own reflection's gleam
> Glimpsed deep down in art's clear stream?
>
> Prologue, 21 August 1859

Ibsen would not be Ibsen if these emblematic generalities were not challenged by his own cheerful mockery of knee-jerk inspiration – in 'A Leg-pull' (1851, a skit on Wergeland's sentimental 'Romance of the Snowdrop'), or 'Voice of Nature' (1851), or 'The Lad in the Blueberry Patch' (1851), for instance; but, as with the love poems, the challenge is slight, the mere replacing of one form of sentimentality by another only superficially more substantial. And none of these pieces, nor many like them, appears in *Poems*, where art is treated not as a social function but as the product of deeply personal and individual experience.

It is notable that in the poems that Ibsen revised for his volume Nature now serves to symbolize not a universal plenitude but the impediments, doubts and fears that beset the actual as distinct from theoretical business of creation: 'The Eider' (1850) [N, 25], 'Bird and Birdcatcher' (1850) [N, 26], 'Fear of Light' (1853) [N, 27], 'The Gulley' (1864) [N, 31], 'The Power of Memory' (1864) [N, 48], are all instances. 'The Miner' (1850) [N, 27], common enough a romantic persona, goes far beyond an emblematic function by virtue of a rhythm that in its dogged violence convinces the reader of a pain and anguish that were Ibsen's own:

> No, deep delve I must, not cease;
> there lives an eternal peace.
> Break my way, you hammer, batter
> to the secret heart of matter! –
>
> Hammerblow on hammerblow
> to the day when life must go.
> Not a beam of brightness dawning;
> not a sun of hope's new morning.

The source of inspiration has changed from a generous external Nature to an obscure, tension-ridden, private inwardness. One of the most striking pieces in *Poems* registers the shift through its setting and simple, almost prosaic, imagery: the setting is Ibsen's room, he the sole occupant; everything else is the product of his own mind which romps with the offspring of his playful fantasy:

> But just as the playing was at its best
> I caught in the glass a reflection,
> And there there stood so sedate a guest,

with blue-grey eyes, and with buttoned vest,
and in slippers, saving correction . . .

'From my Daily Round', 1864 [N, 75]

The poem is Ibsen's most completely developed account of the creative imagination within his own experience: a matter now not of social function or of easily adopted and opposed stances, but of painful and difficult process, intensely intimate and self-sustained, where the poet's self-consciousness, not Nature, has become the inspiration, the subject matter and the impediment of his art.

This is the vision that inspires one of the two long pieces about art and the vocation of art that appear in *Poems*, namely 'On the Heights' (1859/60) [N, 79]; but not, significantly, the other, 'Rhyme-Letter to Mrs Heiberg' [N, 111], written for inclusion at the last moment before publication. 'On the Heights' subjects Ibsen's obsessive concern with this internal warfare between vocation and living to its most searching examination, using the expansiveness of quasi-epic form and the particularity of quasi-dramatic presentation not simply to state the predicament but to trace it through fluctuations between faith and scepticism, certainty and doubt. When Ibsen writes of another artist, Mrs Heiberg, however, he can, from his non-involvement, approach art through the splendour of the artifact, making it a matter for unalloyed celebration.

This involves no relapse into generalized romanticism about art on Ibsen's part. His tribute is highly specific. It is paid to a specific artist in a specific art form for the way her versatility has informed each specific role that she has played. It is in that sense characteristic of the general tendency of the volume for which it was written, aiming to define the essence of her genius not its superficialities, proceeding not by argument but, more nearly dramatic than 'On the Heights', by sharply etched images – of sailing ships in motion, of movement, atmosphere and setting. And there is just a hint, not enough, certainly, to imply that this treasure is discovered through the pain of loss, but of an awareness that it is all the more precious because it is now a matter for memory – a hint of another swan song, but without the spare simplicity; on this occasion Ibsen can let himself go in vicarious praise of an art which is, after all, inseparably connected with his own. But all such considerations apart, it is a poem that by itself makes the case for wider study of this body of work, and as such provides the perfect conclusion to this brief survey:

One contender,
dream-fraught maiden slim and slender,

now floats past me under sail.
She is like some legend hiding
wrapt behind a trembling veil;
she is like a vision gliding,
    never biding,
on some mystic, secret trail.
    Sea-elves sporting
    twist cavorting,
veiled in bowspray at their game;
    elf-pack chases
    keel-wave traces;
but within the flag's embraces
    hides *Agnete*'s name.

    . . .

Your art is the child of fragrance,
    inspiration,
    fervent senses,
character and fantasy, –
not a wood- and stone-erection,
    brain-confection
stuck down fast in black on white,
but, on vines of fair Perfection,
swings, forever free, its sprite

NOTES

1 The references in this chapter to *The Oxford Ibsen* are there primarily to enable
the reader to locate the various quotations and thus to place the passages in
context; the translations throughout this section are, however, my own: references to the *Poems* (in the form [N, page number]) are to John Northam, *Ibsen's
Poems* (Oslo, 1986); passages from *Peer Gynt* are from a new translation (Oslo,
1993).

Other sources relevant to this chapter include

'BRAND'

Bellquist, John E., '*Brand* and *Når vi døde vågner*', in *Scandinavian Studies*, 55
(1983).

Ewbank, Inga-Stina, 'Henrik Ibsen: National Language and International Drama',
Contemporary Approaches to Ibsen, vol. VI (Oslo, 1988).

Haakonsen, Daniel, *Henrik Ibsen: Mennesket og kunstneren* (Oslo, 1981).

Hemmer, Bjørn, '*Brand*', '*Kongsemnerne*', '*Peer Gynt*' (Oslo, 1972): in Norwegian.
Henrick Ibsen: *Samlede Verker* (16th edn Oslo, 1978) vol. II – postscript.

Lervik, Åse H., *Ibsens verskunst i Brand* (Oslo, 1969).

Thorn, Finn, *Lov og evangelium* (Oslo, 1981).
Ystad, Vigdis, '*Brand* og det umulige', *Nytt Norsk Tidsskrift*, 2 (1991).

'PEER GYNT'

Aarseth, Asbjørn, *Dyret i mennesket* (Oslo, 1975).
    Text and Performance: 'Peer Gynt' and 'Ghosts' (London, 1989).
Anstensen, A., *The Proverb in Ibsen* (Columbia University Press, 1935).
Blackwell, Marilyn, 'Spatial Images in *Peer Gynt*. Ibsen's Inversion of the Feminine
    Redemptive', in *Modern Language Review*, 85 (1990).
Fjelde, Rolf, 'Translating *Peer Gynt*' (with Sverre Arestad), *Modern Drama*, 10
    (1967).
    '*Peer Gynt*, Naturalism and the Dividing Self', *Drama Review*, 13 (1968).
Haakonsen, Daniel, *Henrik Ibsens 'Peer Gynt'* (Oslo, 1967).
Hageberg, Otto (ed.), *Omkring 'Peer Gynt'* [essays by various hands] (Oslo, 1967).
Shapiro, Bruce, *Divine Madness and the Absurd Paradox* (New York, 1990).

POEMS

Dahl, Herleif, *Bergmannen og byggmesteren* (Oslo, 1958).
Frænkel, Pavel, *Ibsens vei til drama* (Oslo, 1955).
Haakonsen, Daniel, 'Henrik Ibsens lyrikk', in *Edda,* 50 (1950).
McFarlane, James, 'Ibsen's Poem-cycle "I Billedgalleriet"', in *Scandinavica* (May
    1978).
Mæhle, Leif, *Ibsens rimteknikk* (Oslo, 1955).
Northam, John, *Ibsen's Poems* (Oslo, 1986).
Ystad, Vigdis, *Henrik Ibsen: Dikt* (Oslo, 1991).

4

ROBIN YOUNG

Ibsen and comedy

The title of this chapter might seem paradoxical, even a contradiction in terms. The forbidding seriousness of Ibsen's later works has become a legend, especially to those who know them mainly by repute. Yet the earliest of his plays to deal with contemporary social realities were all classed as comedies; to understand how he developed as an artist – and as a social critic – it is essential to know something about the ways in which he approached and adapted the conventional comedy of his day.

It is as well to remember at the outset that the term 'comedy', even leaving aside its more specialized modern uses and more general older meanings, is an equivocal one. It has been used to denote a tone of voice or mode of perception (something 'light' or 'amusing'); it can indicate a special kind of dramatic plot, a 'happy end' with the blend of assurance and strain which that can imply; and it can suggest a specific subject-matter – in Jonson's words 'an image of the times' which deals 'with human follies not with crimes'. In much classic comedy – in Shakespeare or Molière or Holberg – all three of these senses may apply. But there is no logical reason why, in all circumstances, they should. The appalling may also be funny, without suggesting redemption or a happy end; human follies can also be crimes. One could read Ibsen's entire *œuvre* as a deconstruction of the various, always potentially divergent, elements of what is classed as comedy.

It is significant, and very much germane to the theme of this chapter, that only three of Ibsen's plays were described as comedies – and that in each case the designation was somewhat different: *St John's Night* (1852–3: Eventyrcomedie or 'fairy tale comedy'); *Love's Comedy* (1862: Komedie) and *The League of Youth* (1869: Lystspil). If the appellation is in every case problematic, this is in no way beside the point. These plays were his earliest attempts to depict contemporary life in a realistic way. Each play takes as its starting point a particular strand of the theatrical tradition which Ibsen inherited – romantic comedy, intellectual comedy, social comedy. His struggle to adapt, develop or escape from these inherited models is a dramatic history in itself; and the tensions between the forms of classical comedy and specific problems of contemporary reality were fundamental to the development of realism in the theatre.

There used to be a common assumption – the more pervasive because seldom actually articulated – that Ibsen was a provincial who came (in effect) from nowhere, and that any debt he might owe to his predecessors was exactly that: a burden to be shuffled off.[1] Examination of these three (very different) plays suggests that this is not obviously the case. Even the first of them, *St John's Night*, though Ibsen refused to allow its publication in his lifetime, provides a fascinating glimpse not just of the sort of dramatic material he was working with in the early 1850s, but also of the ways in which his creative intelligence was beginning to make use of the apparently unlikely material of traditional romantic comedy and transform it into something more personal and substantial.

St John's Night is a play which, more than most, has to be read with a sort of double vision. On the one hand, seen from the perspective of its own time (and no doubt that of its first dissatisfied Bergen audience in January, 1853) it is an uneasy mish-mash of literary and dramatic influences, in which the matter of Shakespeare's Midsummer-festive comedy (quarrelling pairs of lovers set to rights by the benign influence of nature and super-nature) is subjected to clumsy dramatic treatment in the manner (but without the style) of Heiberg's Vaudevilles. *St John's Night* is not a good play. Its atmosphere is charming but derivative,[2] its plot unmemorable and uninteresting, its characterization feeble. One can understand why Ibsen felt unwilling to acknowledge it as part of the canon.[3]

Yet with hindsight one can see in the play's discontinuities, its discordant elements and styles, the shape of things to come. In the figure of Johannes Paulsen, Ibsen created the first of those weak, riven, driven poseurs who stalk the pages of his later works.[4] And in the contrasting pairs of lovers who discover their true selves in the course of the play, he initiated a pattern which was to recur in his dramas right to the end of his career. The ideas Paulsen is torn between – 'aestheticism' and national feeling – are localized in time and specific in reference; they bear little obvious relationship to the tensions of the later works. Even in terms of this play's dramatic action, they lead nowhere; in *St John's Night* the significance of the lovers' change of partners is lost in the trivial complications of (mostly retrospective) plot.

But it is entirely characteristic of Ibsen's development that ideas and motives which lead nowhere in one work can become central and enormously progenitive in another. The genre of the Midsummer comedy of love finds echoes surprisingly later in his work. *The Lady from the Sea* is in part a reworking of the same mode (in an earlier draft, that play too was to be set at Midsummer). And, especially in the first known draft ('Resurrection Day'), *When We Dead Awaken*, with its unhappy couples finding their true other selves in the 'summer night on the fells', reverts to the dramatic patterning of his earliest plays. That these patterns are now invested with a wholly different significance is evidence of how far his art had come (and with it European theatre) in the intervening half-century. But it also suggests the extraordinary consistency, resilience, self-reliance of the dramatist, that motives and structures from an almost unrecognizably different theatrical era could still be used for expressive and deeply personal ends, as the cutting-edge of the new.

In subject-matter, too, the ending of *St John's Night* points forward to much that would be crucial in the later plays. Certainly Paulsen's faintly sheepish admission at the end of the play:

> When in love, one takes a theoretical view of love. Betrothal and marriage . . .
> are practical matters, and theories – as one knows – can't always be made to
> work in practice. [*i*,261]

forms a direct and obvious link with the themes of *Love's Comedy*.

Love's Comedy is in one sense an intensely verbal play. Such dramatic tension as there is inheres almost exclusively in what people say rather than in what they do. The plot is vestigial. Much of the comedy consists of what Isherwood calls 'tea-tabling' – literally so, indeed, since (as E. M. Christensen has emphasized in a stimulating study)[5] the metaphor of the tea-plant itself has an important place in the play's structure of meaning. The central 'events' of the play, such as they are, happen inside and between the two main characters, Falk and Svanhild; and it is the counterpointing of their brief uncertain love against the beliefs and demands of the other couples in the group which gives the play its dynamism and richness.

Love or marriage – that appears to be the choice which the play leaves us with; and to anyone only familiar with Ibsen's later work this apparent dilemma might seem a startling one. After all, the whole burden of such plays as *The Lady from the Sea*, *Little Eyolf* and *John Gabriel Borkman* would seem to be that a marriage entered into without passion (just such a marriage as Guldstad seems to be recommending in *Love's Comedy*) will lead to unhappiness, even ruin, for all concerned. Is not *Love's Comedy*, through its conclusion, specifically rejecting Falk's passion, his all or nothing, in favour of Straamand's embattled domesticity and Guldstad's insidiously worldly good sense?

Yet nothing in an Ibsen play is quite as it seems; and a closer examination of *Love's Comedy* reveals a debate much more evenly conducted, more ambivalently handled than it might appear. Falk's comic assault on the tepidities of modern marriage foreshadows Brand's deeply un-comic attack on modern latitudinarian Christianity. In each case an ideal is posited; assessment of the validity of that ideal must have something to do with our view of the moral status of its proponent. Something, but not everything. Falk, in his hour-long engagement to Svanhild, is either inconsistent or an extreme (and extremely temporary) case of the triumph of hope over experience. But this does not necessarily invalidate what he says in the play – any more than Ibsen's own belief in 'the claims of the ideal' is negated by the destructive immaturity of a Gregers Werle. And what Falk says – his impassioned and witty assaults on the estate of bourgeois marriage – has more to commend it than Falk's own behaviour might suggest.

The debate is a close one, involved and involving. The other couples in the play – Styver and Frøken Skære, who have been living and partly living in an engagement for which passion (and the capacity for poetry) have long since been transmuted into the prose of single-minded duty and weary desperation; and Lind and Anna, for whom the whole process is just starting, but who show unmistakable signs of going the same way as the others – may seem to serve the playwright (and Falk) in making the points about what engagement and marriage mean if love and passion are too early, or too easily, or under too much external pressure, exchanged for the small coin of domestic contentment. Yet they are not objects of fun, nor mere mouthpieces for set, limited, wholly predictable points of view. Straamand – who seems for much of the play gentle, ludicrous, hopeless – surprises Falk with the passion and eloquence of his defence of uxoriousness. Styver has, in the end, less dignity; but he also, pathetic though he is, can deploy an eloquence in defence of his engagement to Frøken Skære which commands a sort of respect.

This is all a long way from the insipid generalities, the argument-by-default of *St John's Night*. But it is important to note that a greater depth of involvement of argument is not the only gain of *Love's Comedy*. The social and geographical setting of the later play is also much richer, more sharply defined, more integrated into the dramatic structure. *St John's Night* is ostensibly set in contemporary Norway ('Fru Berg's estate in Telemark'); and certain of the play's features clearly have some contemporary relevance. But it is a sketched-in topicality rather than something essential to the self-consciously timeless moralizing of the play as a whole; *Love's Comedy*, by contrast, is very consciously and precisely set. The time is very much the present and the action takes place in Fru Halm's *løkke* by the Drammensvej in Christiania. In the earlier prose version, 'Svanhild' (1860), the word used was *Landsted* – 'country estate'. By using the much more precise term in the later version – 'løkke' is (or was) used in Christiania to denote an idyllic, ostensibly rural villa at the edge of town – Ibsen was emphasizing the extent to which what happens in the play is self-consciously a holiday from social reality. But not entirely. What the guests bring to Fru Halm's Belmont is a pretty fair picture of life in the city just down the road – a society in which the exhausted consensus and benign autocracy of Schweigaard's party-less *Embedsmandsstat* was just beginning to give way to the tensions which were to destroy it, or at least transform it beyond recognition, only twenty years later. It is significant that all the major characters but one are members of the official class, their relatives, would-be relatives or dependants; and equally significant that it is the one exception – the businessman Guldstad – who supplies the necessary dose of moral and social realism at the end of the play, and wins the hand of Svanhild into the bargain.

Yet, despite the urgency and sharpness of its social comment, it is also central to the play's nature and dramatic effect that it is written in verse. Indeed, even more than *Brand* or *Peer Gynt*, *Love's Comedy* is quintessentially a verse-drama, unique amongst Ibsen's works in that it began life in prose, as the fragment which has come down to us as 'Svanhild', and that the content of the play seems more or less to have demanded it be recast in verse. On one level (and certainly judged from the viewpoint of his later dramatic practice) one might have expected that implicit tensions between the play's specifically contemporary setting and its highly stylized form might weaken or muffle its dramatic impact. Strikingly, it does not – or not, at any rate, in the original Norwegian.[6]

Indeed, more than any previous Ibsen play, *Love's Comedy* displays – even, at some points, parades – sovereign control over its expressive means. Full of energy and poise, the hard-edged rhyming decasyllabics of this play – so different from the octosyllabics of *Brand* with their obsessional, menacing jog-trot, and from the unstable, constantly shifting pyrometrics of *Peer Gynt* – are a formidable technical and artistic achievement. In its discovery of reality through artifice, *Love's Comedy* is one of Ibsen's most unexpected and beguiling achievements, and one vital to an understanding of his creative personality.

If *Love's Comedy* is Ibsen's first serious (one uses the word advisedly) exploration of the themes of bourgeois love and marriage, *The League of Youth* performs the same service for business and politics. The two plays form a fascinating contrast. Whereas *Love's Comedy* is set apart from the social milieu whose conflicts it nevertheless enacts, *The League of Youth* confronts directly the issues of money, class and power. The one play is a triumph of poetic style and artifice, the other set the pattern for all those realistic prose dramas which were to follow. This contrast is evident in the literary ancestry of each play: whereas *Love's Comedy* looks back to Heiberg and Overskou, *The League of Youth* is an attempt – fascinating if (indeed, partly because) not entirely successful – to adapt to contemporary conditions the satirical style of Holberg's comedies.

No less than *Love's Comedy*, *The League of Youth* can seem surprising to those acquainted mainly with Ibsen's later work. It is not at first sight a socially radical play – quite the contrary. Yet it represents, through the ostensibly reassuring glass of the comic vision, determinant social forces at their rawest and most blatant. Whereas *Love's Comedy* showed the governing, educated elite in the mid-afternoon of its prestige, power and influence, *The League of Youth* depicts a very different kind of reality. It is set in a small coastal town – one of those commerce-dominated societies, almost city-states in miniature, with their powerful merchant (not bureaucratic) elites which were to provide much of the intellectual and political leadership of the new Norway. Yet the social power-structure of this play is very different from that of Ibsen's later, more conventionally realistic exercises in the genre – *Pillars of Society*, *An Enemy of the People*, *The Wild Duck* – in which the commercial bourgeoisie is unmistakably in control, and the drama revolves around its abuse of near-absolute power.

On the contrary, in *The League of Youth* ultimate power rests with a figure, Chamberlain Brattsberg, who contrives to keep a foot in both worlds. He is simultaneously a representative, through his Chamberlainship, of the official order, politically the greatest power in this essentially pre-democratic society, and is also the most prosperous local businessman. On one level this reflects a precisely known reality – many elements of his position and character must be based on Severin Løvenskiold, former Norwegian Stattholder and also owner of Fossum Ironworks (and thus the Ibsens' immensely powerful and influential neighbour during their years at Venstøp).[7] But Ibsen turns this social reality into the focus of the play's personal and moral dilemmas. What is at issue in the play is not just an attack on the established social order by outsiders like Stensgaard and Monsen, but the tensions and weaknesses within that order.

Ostensibly the pattern of the play consists, in true comic style, of an attempt to subvert the harmonious order represented by Brattsberg's household, followed by the defeat of these discordant elements and the reassertion of the 'natural' order. And in this celebration of authority against its enemies, Ibsen might seem to be harking back to an earlier tradition of comedy, essentially conservative and non-subversive, which would accord very well with his own known beliefs at this period and with the whole ethos of his circle of friends in Christiania during the early 1860s. *The League of Youth* appears to run directly counter to the ethos of his later work. Certainly, that was how both radicals and conservatives interpreted the play on its appearance in 1869.

In Ibsen's work, however, surprise is often double-edged; and *The League of Youth* can itself be read as a much more subversive work than is immediately apparent. Stensgaard's political and amatory adventures and Monsen's unscrupulous wheeling and dealing are the most obvious focuses of the drama. But these are predictable bugbears, easily overcome. What gives the play its darker tone and much of its interest are the problems which Ibsen raises but fails to resolve – in particular the tensions in the Chamberlain's own family. His son Erik has been trained as a lawyer but lacks the opportunity, and perhaps the ability, to practise. Instead he has speculated in conjunction with Monsen, and has forged Brattsberg's guarantee on a cheque (thereby anticipating Nora's 'crime' in *A Doll's House*). Erik's wife Selma, furious at being excluded from the 'serious' life of his self-imposed woes, puts forward (with none of Nora's ambiguity, double-think or self-deception) a demand to be taken seriously as wife, woman, human being which exactly prefigures the terms of *A Doll's House*:

> How I've longed for even a little share in your worries! . . . You dressed me up like a doll. You played with me as you might play with a child . . . Now I don't want any of your troubles. I'm leaving you! I'd rather sing in the streets than . . . Leave me alone! [*iv*, 93]

Yet having raised these issues, so central to so much of his later work, this play explores them no further. How could it, since this is a conventional comedy and these are matters which threaten to subvert the affirmation of conventional values and power-structures on which such comedy traditionally depends? Instead, by a series of predictable comic manipulations the forged cheque is redeemed and normality, of a sort, is restored to the business life of the community – an existence hastily promoted by Brattsberg from being 'no great honour . . . quite the reverse, I very nearly said' [*iv*, 91] to 'an honourable and a valuable undertaking' [*iv*, 143]. As for Selma's problems, they are forgotten altogether in the entirely conventional jubilation of the play's final pages.

But not forever. Rather, as in the case of *St John's Night* nearly twenty years previously, ideas which lead nowhere in one play – which can lead nowhere, given the aesthetic framework within which Ibsen is working – become the starting point for revolutionary departures later. Erik's misdemeanours, Selma's frustrations, the unhappy, blighted childhood of Stensgaard:

> His father was a wizened little ne'er do well, a lout, a nobody . . . The mother was coarse, the most unwomanly woman I've known . . . Squalor at home . . .

high ideals at school ... mind, character, will, talents, all pulling in different
directions. What else could it lead to but a split personality?   [*iv*, 128*]
and of Monsen, 'whose father worked himself nearly to death, and in the
end got carried over the waterfall with the logs' [*iv*, 86] – all this is the raw
material of Ibsen's later drama. To see it here, in a context in which it can
be allowed to develop no further – and, indeed, puts a strain on the play's
comic design which only determined dramatic craftsmanship can contain –
is to realize how great was the distance Ibsen had to travel before he could
create the great cycle of prose *Nutidsdramaer* to which *The League of
Youth* affords such a fascinating and uneasy prelude.

Yet to see the comic form and spirit of these three plays as merely something which Ibsen had to outgrow would be to misunderstand the nature of
his achievement and to under-value the early comedies both in themselves
and as harbingers of important elements in the later plays. Whilst none of
the later works could be described as generic comedy, not even *Pillars of
Society*, *An Enemy of the People* and *The Lady from the Sea* (the three plays
which end in catastrophe of one sort or another), no Ibsen play however
grim is without its moments of humour. Sometimes, as in *An Enemy of the
People*, that comic vision constitutes the drama's central mode of seeing,
and it is only the subject-matter which is essentially un-comic. Indeed, much
of the energy of this play derives from the confrontation between Dr
Stockmann – really a larger-than-life comic character – and a social situation which is and remains to the end of the play unregenerately serious and
potentially tragic in its implications. It is as though the tensions between
form and subject-matter, so disruptive in *The League of Youth*, are here
re-channelled into a conflict of character and world-outlook – Stockmann's
radical yea-saying against the cramped, self-interested, dyspeptic negativism
of his brother – which makes of the play an experience both exciting and
uncharacteristically straightforward.

In the more complex plays that followed, these two views of life are fused
or held in balance.[8] Despite some recent attempts to represent it in this light,
The Wild Duck (for example) cannot in any acceptable sense be described
as a comedy – no play which ends with the death of a child could. Yet it
contains characters and situations which are unmistakably comic; and the
play's hybrid form challenges all conventional assumptions about the nature
of both tragedy and comedy. Hjalmar (obviously) and Gregers (perhaps less
so) are both ridiculous: the one a weak, vain self-deceiver, the other a neuro-
tic hero-worshipper and prophet of self-knowledge whose awareness of
other people and of his own inner motives is fatally skewed. Each character
in his own sphere – Gregers up at the ironworks brooding on family wrongs
and presenting the Claims of the Ideal to the startled peasantry; Hjalmar

lording it over his womenfolk, nourishing the self-delusions which sustain him and stunt Gina and Hedvig – is relatively harmless. But their individual weaknesses, combined, have the power to exert enormous pressure on those around them. The nonsense Gregers spouts has a terrible plausibility to the vulnerable Hedvig; and the special disturbing power of the play derives from the complexities of the audience's response to a process which is, at different levels, both tragic and absurd.

Gregers' self-deception is funny; its consequences are not. It is the particular task of the Ibsen-interpreter, in the study as in the theatre, to hold these two modes of seeing in balance. Even the temptation to play Hjalmar for laughs must be avoided scrupulously, as Ibsen himself emphasized: 'This part must definitely not be rendered with any touch of parody ... His sentimentality is genuine, his melancholy charming in its way ...'[9] Genuine, charming, dangerous – at least in conjunction with Gregers, for it is Hjalmar's innocence that makes him so apt and malleable an instrument for his friend's destructive neuroses. 'The ringing laughter grows harsh and hollow, and notes of ineffable sadness escape from the poet's Stoic self-restraint'[10] – C. H. Herford's comments on *Love's Comedy* have unmistakable relevance for the significance of the comic in Ibsen's drama as a whole. In each of the later plays the relationship between tragic and absurd is subtly different. But it is always present, a vital determinant of the play's mood, a touchstone of the playwright's sceptical, questioning view of the world. Any production or interpretation which does not keep this in mind must fail to take the measure of his dramatic method.

This interpenetration of comedy and tragedy in his works, the ironic distance which he keeps from even the most plausible of his heroines and heroes – all this surely reflects an irony and balance in Ibsen's own temperament perceptibly at odds with much in the cultural life of late nineteenth-century Europe. No major writer of the age was less disposed to indulge and pamper the demons of the absolute. On the contrary (and was there ever a writer with a more appropriate last word on his whole career?) much of the effectiveness of his radical social dramas derives from his refusal to allow idealism to cloud the realities of human nature. Indeed, what is most astonishing about *Love's Comedy* and *The League of Youth* is not how distant they are in political terms from the dramas which were to follow, but how much of their sceptical, ironic cast of mind is carried over into the later works.

This is not to say that *Pillars of Society*, *A Doll's House* and *Ghosts* are not revolutionary plays. Unmistakably, they are. What is at issue is rather the nature and antecedents of the revolution they effected. And one could argue that what happened in Ibsen's work in the late 1870s was not a repudiation of the worldly scepticism of his friends in the group known as *Lærde Holland* but the turning of that scepticism on even those social truths which they in their unquestioning conservatism had assumed to be self-evident. One might also suspect that it is exactly because Ibsen's vision was more complex, more ironic, less blinkered and more realistic than that of such radical contemporaries as Bjørnson and Kielland that his plays have retained, in quite other social contexts than their own, the power to move and to shock. As we watch in his early comedies these weapons being sharpened and turned, it is fascinating to see how profoundly, how creatively, the revolutionary playwright was indebted to the literature of the past.

NOTES

1 On Ibsen's indebtedness to Norwegian and Danish predecessors, see Brian W. Downs, *Ibsen: The Intellectual Background* (Cambridge, 1946); and H. Noreng 'Henrik Ibsen som komediedikter – med konsentrasjon om 1860-årene' in *En ny Ibsen?* ed. Noreng (Oslo, 1979), pp. 9–51.

2 On its derivativeness, and specifically on the issue of the play's multiple authorship, see Halvdan Koht, *Life of Ibsen* (translation of the second Norwegian edition, New York, 1971), pp. 79–81.

3 He specifically refused to allow its inclusion in the first collected edition of his works (1898–1902).

4 As was pointed out at the time of the play's posthumous publication; see the introduction to the edition of the *Efterladte Skrifter* (1909) vol. I, p. lxiv.

5 See E. M. Christensen, *Henrik Ibsens realisme: illusion katastrofe anarki* (Berlin and Copenhagen, 1985), pp. 288–300.

6 Even the translations which most faithfully reproduce the metres and rhymeschemes of the original – those of C. H. Herford into English (1900) and of Chr. Morgenstern into German (1898) – do not quite catch the elegance and power of the original. Nevertheless, they are essential reading for a Norwegian-less reader striving to assess the tone of the original.

7 For a summary and interpretation of evidence about the play's social background, see R. Young, 'Ibsen's "lykkelige adelsmennesker": Commerce and Nobility in *De unges Forbund* ', *Scandinavica*, 29: 2, 181–92.

8 For a remarkable early discussion of the interpretation of tragedy and comedy in Ibsen's later plays, see G. Groddeck, *Tragödie oder Komödie: Eine Frage an die Ibsenleser* (Leipzig, 1910).

9 Henrik Ibsen to Hans Schrøder, 14 November 1884.

10 C. H. Herford, Preface to his translation of *Love's Comedy*, part of which is reprinted in James McFarlane (ed.), *Henrik Ibsen*, Penguin Critical Anthologies (Harmondsworth, 1970), pp. 179–80.

5

BJØRN HEMMER

Ibsen and the realistic problem drama

FREEDOM, TRUTH AND SOCIETY – RHETORIC AND REALITY

During the night of 9 January 1871, a young Dane lay awake in his hospital bed in Rome writing. He was committing to paper a poem to which he had given the title 'To Henrik Ibsen'. He had recently received a letter from Ibsen – a letter carrying a powerful appeal to him to put himself at the head of the 'revolution of the human spirit' which the age cried out for. In the poem which formed his enthusiastic response, the young Dane – the critic Georg Brandes (1842–1927) – described how all those mendacious and authoritarian forces of the contemporary age would be brought low when 'the intellectuals' made their revolt. And he raised the banner of freedom and progress with the words: 'Truth and Freedom are one and the same.'[1]

Time after time in the years that followed, Ibsen was himself to raise this same revolutionary banner – with truth and freedom as the central watchwords. In later years these concepts could sound both abstract and ambiguous; nevertheless, within their historical context, they served as a battle cry in the struggle against the prevailing situation. 'Truth' alone – that truth of the new age such as a Brandes and an Ibsen saw it – could achieve liberation. Without truth there could be no change, no genuine 'freedom'. This was the ideological basis for that quartet of realistic social plays which Ibsen published in the years between 1877 and 1882: *Pillars of Society, A Doll's House, Ghosts* and *An Enemy of the People*. In both the first and the last of these plays the double-barrelled phrase 'truth and freedom' is used as a rallying cry and as a definition of what in the final instance the problematic reality of the day – 'society' – lacked. This was the battleground on which Ibsen and Brandes found each other and where they could make common cause. However unlike they may have been, one thing they were agreed on: that *they* were conducting the case for progress and the future. They did not stand alone, but they must be counted as the indisputable leaders in the campaign for a modern, radical and realistic literature in the cultural life of Scandinavia of this age. It was these two who most powerfully challenged the values of the existing middle-class society and who formulated the basic rights and liberties of the individual.

In the November of the same year in which he wrote his poem to Ibsen, Brandes began a series of public lectures in Copenhagen on the literature of nineteenth-century Europe. These lectures provoked great attention and controversy, precisely because in them Brandes called upon writers to revolt. He did it in the light of an ideology of liberation which he himself linked directly to the ideas of freedom which underlay the French Revolution of 1789. But Brandes's middle-class public of 1871 were not greatly receptive towards revolutionary ideas. The recent events of the Paris Commune had frightened the citizens of Europe even further away from their own ideological past.

His main concern, Brandes declared,[2] was not *political* opposition, for political liberty had very largely been assured. What was at stake was 'liberty of the spirit', 'liberty of thought and of the human condition'. The entire range of 'social values' would have to be changed radically by the younger generation before a new and vigorous literature could begin any new growth. But in Brandes's view it was surely the writers themselves who ought to take the lead in this work on behalf of progress.

What Brandes directs his criticism against is a conservative, stagnant society which 'under the mask of liberty has all the features of tyranny'. His target is Victorian society with its facade of false morality and its manipulation of public opinion. It is this same kind of society that Ibsen turns the searchlight on in his first realistic dramas. The people who live in such a society know the weight of 'public opinion' and of all those agencies which keep watch over society's 'law and order': the norms, the conventions and the traditions which in essence belong to the past but which continue into the present and there thwart individual liberty in a variety of ways. Not all see this as a problem. Consul Bernick, the bank manager Torvald Helmer and Pastor Manders have all accepted the premises for this kind of bourgeois living and have adapted to society's demands – without any awareness of the cost in human terms. In their own estimation, their task is to confirm the existing social structure – as 'pillars of society'. This position they are not prepared to give up at any price. But in these three Ibsen dramas – *Pillars of Society, A Doll's House* and *Ghosts* – it is precisely the defenders of this society who are presented as the least free.

The point that Ibsen and Brandes were making was that this kind of society could not satisfy the natural need of the individual for freedom. It all had to do with power, with status and with the role of the sexes. The repressive attitude of bourgeois society towards everything that threatened its own position of power demonstrated only too clearly how far it had moved from the standpoint of the revolutionary citizens of 1789. The question of political and spiritual liberty had been thrust into the background by what had constantly been the motivating force in the life of the individual: economic freedom. Capital gave a position of power in society; and once those positions had been won, the bourgeois individual had acquired something which had to be defended. In this way, the bourgeois individual became a defender of the status quo and a traitor to his own officially expressed values. Official rhetoric was one thing; the realities on the other hand were something else.

It is this which forms the background to Ibsen's and Brandes's criticism of contemporary society. They found in their age a clear dichotomy between ideology and practice, a contradiction between the official and the private life of the bourgeois individual. Behind the splendour of the Victorian family facade there was to be found a much murkier reality. It was precisely these contradictions, this problematical element, in the bourgeois world that Ibsen made his special field as a realistic commentator on contemporary life. Both Ibsen and Brandes wanted to make the individual the sustaining element in society and thereby dethrone the bourgeois family as the central institution of society. From the perspective of the bourgeois individual the family is a micro-society which mirrors the nature of the macro-society and which is to bear witness to its health. In *Pillars of Society* the scoundrelly Consul Bernick is praised by the young teacher Rørlund for his 'exemplary family life'; and the consul's fellow-conspirator, the businessman Rummel, delivers himself of the following pronouncement: 'A man's home ought to be like a showcase' [v, 104]. But he himself recommends an *arranged* family tableau behind the glass walls.

In the spirit of liberalism, Ibsen lets the individual's status in the family stand as an illustration of his position in the wider society. The power structure within the walls of the domestic home reflects the hierarchical power structures which prevail in the wider world. But those who participate in public life also encounter other repressive forces. Consul Bernick eventually admits that he feels like an isolated tool of an uncomprehending and crippled society, controlled in all his actions [v, 110].

The main social perspective in Ibsen's first realistic plays coincides with the perspective of Brandes's lecture series on 'Main Currents in Nineteenth Century Literature'. Here Brandes had presented a well-formulated programme for a new 'modern' literature. His challenge to his fellow authors was primarily that they should enter into their own times and make contemporary concrete reality the subject of their writing: 'What shows a literature in our own day to be a living thing is the fact of its subjecting problems to debate ... For a literature to submit nothing to debate is tantamount to its being in the process of losing all significance.'[3]

What sort of 'problems' he had in mind is illustrated by the examples he immediately adduces: marriage, religion, property rights, the relationships between the sexes, and social conditions. The objectives of his programme seem to have been both social and aesthetic. Brandes's idea was not that literature should become an instrument of abstract debate about prevailing social problems; his intention was to point out that if literature was to have any useful function at all, it had to come to grips with those conditions which invade and determine the concrete existence of the individual. Literature – as he put it – was to deal with 'our life', not with 'our dreams'.

If Ibsen's dramas in the period 1877 to 1882 have come to be designated as realistic *problem* plays, this has to be seen against the background of Brandes's formula-like statement. Some Ibsen scholars prefer the rubric 'critical realism'; others again have chosen to apply the term 'modern contemporary drama' to the whole series of works after 1877.[4] Each of these different designations nevertheless has a bearing on one or other of the central elements in the kind of literary realism which Ibsen practised: on social problems, on critical perspective and contemporaneity. Indeed this last is often accepted as one of the defining characteristics of realism: '*Il faut être de son temps.*'[5]

Within the framework of these dramas, Ibsen concentrates on some phase in the contemporary situation where a latent crisis suddenly becomes visible. In this way he was able to embody contemporary social problems through the medium of an individual's destiny. This is another of realism's main tenets in the matter of individual characterization: the particular is to throw light on the general, and from one's response to a particular individual one should be able to glimpse the socially representative type. This, according to René Wellek, is an almost universal demand in theories of realism. It marks not only a polemical break with romantic characterization, but is also linked to realism's demand for objective reality and to its implicit didactic tendency.[6] 'Truth' and 'sincerity' are concepts central to Linda Nochlin's account of the realists' own definition of where they stand.[7] It may sound paradoxical to say that the realists combined on the one hand a wish for the objective presentation of reality with a didactic purpose on the other; but the paradox is illusory. A work of realism aspires to convey a moral message of general validity, and this is why the realist has need of the socially representative type. In Ibsen this sometimes leads to a difficult balancing act between over-explicitness and caricatured characterization on the one hand, and on the other an objective evocation of plausible human types, where the author's presence is less evident. Viewed from a later standpoint in time, there are some things – particularly his treatment of selected male characters – that might prompt one to set a question mark against his 'realism'.

That Ibsen himself nevertheless considered himself a 'realist', and that he shared realism's mimetic view of literature, emerges clearly from his own estimate of *Ghosts*. In a letter from Rome to an acquaintance on 6 January 1882, he defended himself against those critics who had attacked him on account of his 'beliefs'; he specifically emphasizes his own 'absence' from the work and his striving for objective reality:

> They try to make me responsible for the opinions that certain of the char-acters in the play express. And yet in the whole book there is not a single opinion, not a single remark to be found that is there on the dramatist's account. I took good care about that. The method, the technique underlying the form of the book was in itself quite enough to prevent the author making himself apparent in the dialogue. My intention was to try and give the reader the impression of experiencing a piece of reality. But nothing would more effectively run counter to this intention than inserting the author's opinions into the dialogue. Do the people up there at home think I haven't enough dramatic sense to realize that? Of course I realized it, and I acted accordingly. In none of my plays is the author so extrinsic, so completely absent, as in this last one.[8]   [v, 476]

Ibsen refers to reality, to an impression of a world of experiences which both reader and author have in common. Now it is a truism that every discussion of reality in art will in time run up against the ambiguity that resides in the very concept of 'reality'. Moreover, reality (which reality?) does not permit of literary expression, and objectivity is an impossibility. 'The truth' will necessarily be a controversial and ambiguous phenomenon.

As was said above, a realist's use of terms must be seen in the light of his own personal interpretation of them. This is very much the case with Ibsen's and Brandes's use of the slogan 'Freedom and truth' in their criticism of contemporary society. When they use these words, and similarly terms like 'reality' and 'society', they invest them with a different content from that which these same terms have in the bourgeois rhetoric of the time. This is very clear in *Pillars of Society*, where the term 'society' shows itself as poss-essing a whole range of different meanings, depending on who is using it. In his poetic practice, Ibsen demonstrates time after time that he conceives of truth as something individual and subjective. It is always the minority which is right [*vi*, 96]. This is why he lets Nora go out into the world alone both to find out who she really is and to be able to re-assess values and concepts. Ibsen has her sweep aside any doubts about what the problem is: 'I must try to discover who is right, society or me' [*v*, 283]. She admits her husband is right when he says she no longer understands the society they live in. As a dramatist, Ibsen must make it evident to his audience that Nora, as the drama moves towards its close, is truer and freer than before – and that her path is one of general validity. Helmer has mobilized the rhetoric of established society to keep Nora within the framework of the community and of the family. The reaction of the public was – and possibly still is – dependent on whether Nora's (and Ibsen's) use of an alternative rhetoric carries greater weight and conviction.

Nora's situation illustrates the pattern central to Ibsen's realistic problem dramas: the individual in opposition to a hostile society. The structure of the conflict is simple – and nobody can be in any doubt as to where the author's sympathies lie. Collective aberration about which ideals or values are true and which are false means that Ibsen sets in motion a process whereby concepts which are central to the bourgeois world are subject to re-definition. It is a striking feature of, for example, *Ghosts* that the reactionary Manders and the radical Helene Alving both make use of the concept of 'the ideal', despite their having totally contradictory views of the meaning of 'truth' and of individual 'freedom' in life. Ibsen clearly saw that the concepts of established bourgeois society needed a new content – something which he himself drew attention to in a letter to Brandes. In this same letter he writes of the need for 'a revolution of the human spirit', and claimed that the 1789 rallying-cry of 'Liberty, equality, fraternity' needed filling with new meaning.[9]

Perhaps the battle-lines between the conservative bourgeoisie and the radical intelligentsia in Scandinavia in this age of Ibsen and Brandes were not as clearly drawn as all this might suggest. The literary history of Northern Europe has very largely been based on the premises of radicalism. The perspective may not entirely falsify history, but it does somewhat over-simplify it. There are distinctly conservative elements to be found in Ibsen's works of social criticism; and he gave clear acknowledgement of the part he played within the society he was attacking: 'One never stands totally without some share of responsibility or guilt in the society to which one belongs' [xvii, 402]. This is why he defines, in one and the same breath, the writing of poetry as the passing of judgement upon one's own self. Some of the phenomena he criticized were things he well knew from his own inner life. Honest introspection – what he was inclined to call 'self-anatomy' – had made it clear to him that he too bore the stamp of the Victorian society of the day. Life and learning were not always the same, as he admitted in a speech to Norwegian students in Christiania in 1874. The irony directed at those who histrionically held high the banner of the ideal at no great cost to themselves lost none of its point when applied to himself and to fellow writers.

Nevertheless he stood distanced, an outsider, from the society he was criticizing. Like Brandes, he was marginalized in respect of the collective life of his own people – not least by the concrete fact of his own twenty-seven years in exile. It was a stance which gave Ibsen both a personal freedom as an artist and also the clarifying perspective of distance – something he always claimed as a necessity for himself as a writer.

It is something of a paradox that, in this socially critical phase of his authorship, he was able to create a large and broadly based market among the wider European public for his art. What he had to offer to this bourgeois public was a successive chronicling of their own vices and lies. Granted the setting of his works was Norwegian, but the perspective on Victorian morality was international enough when he allowed it to reveal its defects.

It is not to be wondered at that Ibsen's dramas provoked scandal and outrage. Yet at the same time he won a large following, including many of those whom he had attacked. Even a proportion of 'the pillars of society' found it worthwhile to listen to what this author had to say. This could well imply that bourgeois society had not entirely lost its sense of its past and of its own lost ideals. Even bourgeois society was ready to acknowledge that contemporary reality might have its problems – with socially destabilizing phenomena like industrialization, positivism, liberalism, secularization, political polarization and the like. Society in the 1870s was becoming increasingly fluid. Only the most conservative forces wished to defend its 'law and order' by neutralizing such 'enemies of the people' as Ibsen and Brandes. But strong resistance could be found – and this gave Ibsen an adversary and the stuff of conflict for his dramas. The opposition consisted of all those who wished to withdraw within the circle of their own little community, their small township or their family – there to defend their world against the threat from the new or larger world 'out there'. Ibsen himself in these years was a resident of this wider and freer European cultural scene. And he wrote about Norwegian provincial life. When for his first realistic problem drama he chose as its setting 'a small, Norwegian coastal town', this was clearly connected to its being a milieu he was greatly familiar with from his childhood and early years. As an observant outsider he had lived in a small community of this kind – in Grimstad in the 1840s –

and it was here he had first begun his career as a writer. Patterns and tensions – social, economic and psychological – present themselves much more clearly in a small and easily surveyable community of this kind than in a larger and more pluralist society. For a dramatist, a society of this sort could nicely function as a social laboratory.

THREE DRAMAS – THREE STAGES OF DEVELOPMENT

In his comments about *Ghosts*, noted above, Ibsen played down his role as a critical interpreter of reality. His strategy had been rather to get 'reality' itself to speak – by way of artistic illusion.

Ghosts brings to life a threatening and deeply tragic world – a world totally devoid of hope. In his Notes to *A Doll's House*, which he regarded as a developmental stage on the road to *Ghosts*, Ibsen referred to it as 'nutidstragedien', 'the tragedy of the contemporary age' [*v*, 436]. But at the same time *A Doll's House* is a tragedy in which Nora ultimately leaves by a door to a world of new possibilities. Even though the main dramatic conflict between the partners to the marriage remains unresolved, the end of the play sees the tragic element muted. *Pillars of Society*, for its part, stands far removed from tragedy.

Viewed retrospectively, one can see more clearly that Ibsen's path to realistic drama led him via earlier stages in his development as a dramatist. There are elements in the intrigue of *Pillars of Society* which remind one how in his day he had learned from Eugène Scribe (1791–1861) the art of giving logical motivation to a complex succession of scenes within the dramatic action. It is also clear that Ibsen's road to realism led through *comedy*. In form and structure, *Pillars of Society* is closely related to *The League of Youth* of 1869, something which Ibsen himself indicated in a letter to his publisher on 23 October 1875 [*v*, 430]. He regarded both these plays as structurally innovative, and he was clearly proud of his mastery of a modern, realistic form, in which through the medium of natural stage dialogue he had succeeded in creating an impression of reality, of 'contemporary life'. Moreover he saw a clear relationship between comedy and realism. In 1870 he wrote to a correspondent that in *The League of Youth* he had used characters which to some degree were typical of the society of the day; and he continued: 'Comedy today must, in my opinion, bear a strongly realistic stamp' [*iv*, 554].

Nor is it so very remarkable that Ibsen's way to realism should have gone via comedy: comedy has traditionally stood very close to its age and to social 'reality'. The public's laughter draws sustenance from this close relationship.

In *Pillars of Society* there are glimpses here and there of elements of human tragedy. But this side of the play is overshadowed in the final phase by a comprehensive move to resolve the conflicts which have been brought to light and to lay the foundations of a new start for practically all the parties involved. This urge to normalize the social situation and to re-integrate the guilty Bernick into the community bears witness to the affinity between *Pillars of Society* and comedy. This is reinforced also by its broad purpose as a social drama, virtually a *comédie des mœurs*, with a range of caricature types: windbags, hypocrites, speculators, domestic tyrants, gossips, self-deceiving fools – together with a newly returned Norwegian–American feminist. The sleepy little coastal town lies bathed in the light of ridicule, smugly proclaiming its own virtues and its contempt for everything new and alarmist from the world outside, the so-called 'big communities' [*v*, 25].

But the laughter dies when one is permitted to see behind the facade of this bourgeois splendour: one then finds brutality, oppression and self-seeking in those who occupy positions of authority in the community. It is at this point – and particularly where money and morals impinge on each other – that *Pillars of Society* most obviously tends towards serious social drama, with its references to actual contemporary factors such as the Plim-soll line and its associated 'coffin ships'. Ibsen made no attempt to conceal the fact that he had had a serious intent with this drama. True, in his letter to King Oscar II of 20 September 1877, he sensed that it would be tactful to play down any idea that he had criticized the established social institutions. What he had intended, he claimed, was

> ... to lead the vision and the thoughts of the public in a different direction and to show that untruth does not reside in institutions but in the individuals themselves within the community; that it is the inner life of the people, the life of the mind, which has to be purified and liberated; that it is not the external liberties which are to be desired but on the contrary a personal and cultural liberation, and that this can only be acquired and taken possession of by the individual himself, in that his conduct has truth as its basis and point of departure.[10]

Of course, Ibsen is quite right when, later in this same letter, he claims that this set of beliefs lies at the heart of his writings. The focus is on the indi-vidual – the liberation and the 'renaissance' of the individual. But he demon-strates in his writings that this also has consequences for the institutional-ized aspects of community life: marriage, the family, religious and economic life. This perspective was to become very much more evident in *A Doll's House* and in *Ghosts*. Here Ibsen allows the individual to engage in a much more radical encounter with society's institutionalized authorities. In

Pillars of Society the prime objective is to strike a reformist balance between the individual and society. Those who represent the main challenge to the small-town milieu – Dina and Johan – do indeed leave for the newer and freer world of America to follow their fortunes. But the drama also opens up a vista of 'a new age' for those who remain behind, an age wherein people are to live a truer and a freer life than before [*v*, 122]. It is the guilty one himself, Consul Bernick, who allows the notion of 'a new age' to play a central part in his address to those fellow-citizens who have come to pay him homage. But he takes over the phrase directly from the spokesman of the congratulatory party, Mr Rørlund, who has just delivered himself of a parodistic piece of bourgeois rhetorical speech-making, and in so doing pointed up the gap between rhetoric and reality. But is Bernick's response any closer to reality?

It is possible that at this stage Ibsen had an optimistic and naive faith in the liberating effect which 'truth' would have on the life of the individual, and that he was still simply *en route* towards a more dystopian view of society. Furthermore, it is probable that the prevailing dramatic convention in respect of comedy contributed to the harmonization of the finale. It could also be that Ibsen's most immediate model – Bjørnson's drama of 1875 entitled *A Bankruptcy* – prompted him to give his fellow author and rival a run for his money. All these factors might help to explain why the conclusion of *Pillars of Society* is less than wholly persuasive. Ibsen's own belief in the reformatory function of literature was neither optimistic nor naive at the time he wrote this play. In a letter of 30 September 1877 to a woman reader he said of his own book: 'It rakes about in all sorts and manner of conditions of things, which it is presumably not within the power of literature to reform but upon which literature may nevertheless try to shed a true and proper light' [*v*, 430].

The problem which has engaged the attention of a number of Ibsen scholars is the matter of what light Consul Bernick stands in at the close of the drama. The first to ask bluntly whether or not the final situation was savagely *ironic* was James McFarlane in 1965. His argument was that the hitherto traditional interpretation of the drama might have overlooked its 'ironic potential':

> I felt that there were other possibilities that at least merited scrutiny: that, for instance, the play might conceivably be construed as a deceptively mordant ironic piece in which simple honest virtue, far from triumphing at the end to a chorus of sentimental moralizing, is on the contrary seen to be once more duped and deceived, manipulated, hoodwinked, led by the nose by a very smart operator indeed who knows all the tricks. There is no doubt that in the end Bernick leaves himself sitting very pretty – prettier, probably, than he has

ever sat before – and taking full advantage of the domestic and public sympathy that an apparently repentant sinner who knows how to play on heartstrings can count on.[11]

McFarlane is surely right in stating that Bernick treats 'the truth' in a highly arbitrary and cavalier fashion. Bernick declares that people must know the whole truth about him, but he conceals his worst crime: that he had been willing to sacrifice the lives of others in order to preserve his own position in society. His public confession is thus selective and retouched. He alone – and we – know the whole truth; the women who champion the truth, Lona and Martha, know nothing of these murky corners of Bernick's secret life. The question remains, therefore, whether Lona is only partially successful in her plan to save her one-time hero.

Central to the drama's ethical perspective is Lona's project: she means to help Bernick to find himself again, to rediscover the person he once was when he was living in a freer and larger community in London and Paris. It was a time when he dared to be in love with Lona. When he returned home, he betrayed that love in order to ensure his own financial and social standing. Disloyalty and deceit have since served as the dubious ground on which he has based his role as public benefactor and establishment figure in society. He himself believes that in order to prosper in this society, the individual must be prepared to betray: 'Isn't it society itself that forces us into these devious ways?' he asks [v, 89].

The second major project in the drama is the desire of Johan and Dina to rescue their freedom and their dawning love. Society cannot tolerate their happiness; their only allies are the two self-sacrificing women, Martha and Lona, who represent an unselfish love for a man who himself little understands their innermost motives.

The combination of these two projects creates a situation the impact of which on Bernick is such that he appears to lose control. He makes public confession of the wrong he did to Johan fifteen years before. He also discloses his own part in the secret conspiracy relating to the railway. For a few moments he risks the condemnation of the people, but then seizes control of the reins once more. He knows the weaknesses of the people and he plays on them. Earlier he had said to Lona: 'Look into any man's heart you will, and in every single case you will find *some* black spot which he has to keep covered up' [v, 85]. Now he himself 'covers up' his own blackest spot; and after publicly presenting himself as 'a sinner' subject to the judgement of the people, he suddenly adopts an almost Christ-like role: He who is without sin, let him cast the first stone. Bernick enjoins each one of his fellow citizens to scrutinize himself; and later he re-affirms this injunction: 'I ask each one of you to go to his home ... to compose himself ... to look into his heart. And when we have all calmed down, it will be seen whether I have lost or gained by speaking out' [v, 123].[12] There is no denying the business-man: the concepts of profit and loss are still central to his thinking. At the same time he offers himself to fill the continuing role of leading financier of the community.

What the ultimate judgement of the people will be remains an open ques-tion. But there is every reason to believe, as McFarlane indicates, that Bernick sits more securely than ever before at the centre of the community. He gains the full support of the women about him, whom only now does he realize he has misjudged. Lona and Martha can step back; they have both been 'foster mothers' to men they have wished to make happy. In Lona's eyes, Bernick has finally gained *himself*. The projects, linked to the two men central to the drama, have apparently succeeded.

But the harmonization covers up many a smouldering question. There is not merely the ambivalence of Bernick's moral balance-sheet and the ironic overtones of the final settlement. There is a more general unclarity about the author's own attitude. What is one to think of the form of rhetoric Bernick has recourse to in his final words: 'Just as long as my two loyal and true-hearted women stand by me. *That's* something else I've learned this last few days: it's you women who are the pillars of society'? At which point he is immediately corrected by Lona: 'That's a pretty feeble piece of wisdom you've learnt ... No, my friend, the spirit of truth and the spirit of freedom – *these* are the pillars of society' [v,126]. Has Bernick really understood which values are in question, and has he altered his view of what was the woman's task? His final words are ominously reminiscent of something he said before ever he discovered he had things to learn in this regard: 'People should never think primarily of themselves, least of all women. We all have some sort of community, large or small, to support and work for' [v, 66]. Such a placement for women itself refers back to the dubious book from which the local pedagogue, Mr Rørlund, reads out passages to the fashion-able ladies of the town: *Women in the Service of Society*.

It is possibly not Bernick alone who seems to be caught up in a traditional view of the role of women. The author's own attitude also has ambiguous overtones. The character of Lona Hessel admittedly carries a number of features which bear witness to the then emergent ideas of women's liber-ation. Martha too, to say nothing of Dina, protests against the oppression of women by the male-dominated society. But Lona and Martha are presented throughout in a situation of servitude to the man – a man they love and wholly sacrifice themselves for. This self-sacrifice seems to be the one thing which has given meaning to their lives. When Bernick, who understands little of this, asks Lona why she has acted towards him as she has, he is given the answer: 'Old friendship does not rust' [v, 124]. But the phrase betrays something of what her inmost thoughts are, for she hides her actual meaning behind the variation she plays on the old Norwegian folk-saying that 'Old *love* does not rust.' Nor does Bernick understand the deeper meaning in Lona's words even here. She has acted out of love, and it is here that she tells him the real reason why she has returned home: 'When Johan told me all that about the lie, I swore to myself: my girlhood hero shall win through to truth and freedom' [v, 124]. It has thus been of fundamental importance to her that the *man* who brought love into her life must legitimize that love and confirm the values she believes in and which give meaning to life: truth and freedom. These are to set the basic values of the new age. But the resistance of the older society to 'a new age' is strong. Nor is it apparent to her the extent to which Bernick continues to hold fast to the status quo, and how yet again he adopts 'devious ways' to ensure his position. On this point perhaps also the *woman* Lona is a target for the ironic potential of the text. Whether it is conscious irony on Ibsen's part is open to doubt. The ambiguous element in his conception of woman's role relates rather to that conflict between the two ideals of woman which we constantly encounter in his works.

On the one side there is the woman who is determined to stand up as a proud and independent individual, a Dina who will not allow herself to be 'a thing there for the taking' [v, 107]. On the other side Ibsen seems to give heroic stature to the woman who devotes her whole life to the service of others, like a Lona or a Martha. The first of these types is the man's equal, the second serves him as his good spirit. In *A Doll's House* and *Ghosts*, it is above all the Dina-type character which Ibsen gives full range to. But in the shadow of Nora one can find the self-effacing Kristine Linde, who sees life's meaning exclusively in terms of service to others. This two-sided ideal of woman is to be found in all phases of Ibsen's authorship, and it re-emerges in later dramas like *Hedda Gabler* and *When We Dead Awaken*. Both types of woman are freer than men when it comes to the social situation; and in consequence they are truer and more complete – in the sense that they more frequently dare to be themselves. But in a society that oppresses 'truth and freedom', it is not the woman who sets the standard for individual living. The family tableau which rounds off *Pillars of Society* – Bernick surrounded by his loyal women – may well appeal to posterity as a sublime example of tragi-comic irony; and also, indeed, as a kind of 'triumph of realism'. Independently of the author's conscious intentions, the tableau goes to confirm that if the women are not necessarily the servants of society, they nevertheless continue to be the servants of the male pillars of society.

Whether the public of Ibsen's day regarded the final scene as ironic is open to doubt. But to a later generation, with its greater socio-historical insight and a cooler approach to the rhetoric of the age, the scene is flooded with what Northrop Frye calls 'sophisticated irony': 'Irony is naturally a sophisticated mode, and the chief difference between sophisticated and naive irony is that the naive ironist calls attention to the fact that he is being ironic, whereas sophisticated irony merely states, and lets the reader add the ironic tone himself.'[13]

Pillars of Society is above all an ambiguous drama – with its rhetoric, its uncertain view of who is morally right and capable of leading's society's development, its double-sided view of the role of women, and not least with its combination of serious problem drama and satirical comedy. Something of the same ambiguity hangs over that other drama most closely related to *Pillars of Society: An Enemy of the People* (1882). Ibsen himself was not unfamiliar with the problem. Two days after completing *An Enemy of the People* he wrote to a correspondent: 'I am still a bit uncertain how far I should call the thing comedy [*lystspil*] or a straight drama [*skuespil*]; it has something of both elements, or else lies in between . . .' [*vi*, 425].

Between these two works of broadly social perspective lie the 'marriage drama' *A Doll's House* and the 'family drama' *Ghosts*: two works where the treatment is no longer ambiguous, but where the woman – and the man – are presented as tragically unfree within an oppressive bourgeois society, and where *the family* is perceived – to use Bernick's words – as 'the nucleus of society'. But it is only on the surface that this nucleus seems to be healthy.

The situations in which Nora Helmer and Helene Alving have for many years found themselves show clear points of similarity. Both women have elected to play a game of deceit, 'that long ghastly farce', as Mrs Alving calls it [*v*, 378]. They felt compelled into it in the interests of those they loved: in the one case the husband Torvald, and in the other the son Osvald. But they were also under social pressure, and this was the reason they had to have recourse to 'devious ways'. They lived the whole time in fear that the masquerade would be exposed. In her fear Nora constructed a dream in which the man would spring forth as her strong protector, as the knight protecting his loved one. Mrs Alving's defence is more down to earth: first, a period of hard and exemplary work carried out in the man's name, followed by the endowment of a building in the public interest which would forever ensure an unspotted reputation for the Alving family.

Ibsen takes the 'retrospective technique' of *Pillars of Society* and develops it in these plays a stage further. He lets the action begin just before the projects of the two women seem to be successfully accomplished. The family's facade is preserved and success seems assured. But then events over which they have no control reach into their lives. The past beats upon the door and creates chaos in their previously well-ordered ménage. The two women are forced to see their lives in a new and merciless light – both of them incited by men they have loved but can now neither love nor respect any longer (Torvald and Manders), whilst Mrs Alving is also urged towards her new insights by what Osvald tells her.

This revaluation of their own inner lives also becomes for them a show-down with the society which has created the pre-conditions of their lives. Thus it is that Ibsen here chooses the *woman* to lead the battle for 'the revolution of the human spirit' under the rallying-cry of 'truth and freedom'.

From the preliminary notes to the 'contemporary tragedy' about Nora, and in part also to those for *Ghosts*, it clearly emerges that Ibsen at this time sees the position of women as a dominant social problem. He uses strong phrases: women (he declares) can in no way be themselves in this society [*v*, 436]; and he further asserts that women are mistreated and deprived of their economic inheritance [*v*, 468]. Ibsen's ideas bear the clear stamp of the liberal thinking of the age and are strongly reminiscent of the ideas in John Stuart Mill's *The Subjection of Women*. (The Danish translation by Georg Brandes had appeared as early as 1869.) Both Mill and Ibsen make the point that it is not only women who suffer under the prevailing regime. Men too, as well as public morals and society as a whole, would benefit from greater equality between the sexes. The women problem is society's problem, and Ibsen sheds light on this through individual destinies and confrontations.

A Doll's House may be said to be the story of a quite immature woman who suddenly wakes up and sees her marital situation, sees the 'life-lie' on which she has based her life. She is married to and has had children by 'a stranger', somebody who has always treated her like a child and a possession. She had believed she was happy, but discovers that this kind of happiness was based on a much more comprehensive masquerade than the one she herself had invented. For this reason she quits her earlier world and the inauthentic existence of her 'doll's house'. She feels she must go out into the real world to discover the truth about herself and her values. At which she takes her first step out into a different, harsher and lonelier world – but a world which also carries the hope of something better. Ibsen, in a letter of 3 January 1880, comments on her situation: 'The moment she leaves her home is the moment her life is to begin ... In this play there is a big, grown-up child, Nora, who has to go out into life to discover herself'.[14]

A different way of formulating Nora's development might be as follows:

She is forced to give up her dream and her favourite rhetorical phrase '*det vidunderlige*' ('the miraculous') because it no longer has any relevance to the world of reality. What is striking is that at the very final moment she reaches out for a new but apparently closely related rhetorical phrase '*det vidunderligste*' (literally 'the most miraculous', frequently translated as 'the miracle of miracles') [*v*, 286]. A certain sense of hope is associated with this phrase – which could be taken as tempering the tragedy played out when the break is a fact, and a mother has to leave her three small children.

Right up to the final showdown Nora has clung to the notion of 'the miraculous', to the dream that Helmer will take upon himself the complete and full responsibility for her actions and thereby courageously defy the threat of society's condemnation of her. Her illusory picture of the husband is valid only for some romantic-patriarchal dream world. The real Helmer is in his mental make-up much less liberated than Nora herself; he reveals himself as being a pitiable and egotistic slave of the male society of which he is so conspicuous a defender. It is not the human being in him which speaks to Nora at their final confrontation; it is society, its institutions and authorities, which speak through him. Ibsen's exposure of him is total; and Helmer's *oratio morata* when the danger is past – 'I am saved! Nora, I am saved!' [*v*, 277] – is on the verge of caricature.

It is only when she discovers the emptiness behind her notion of 'the miraculous' that her mind is fully liberated. At this point she clearly stands as one of Ibsen's most 'liberated' characters – in the sense that she then acknowledges no constraints on her individual freedom. Equally she is determined to cut any of the ties that bind her husband to her: 'There must be full freedom on both sides' [*v*, 285]. She grants him the freedom which she implies might allow him to become a different person. It is to this 'changed' Helmer that she holds out this straw of hope – 'the miracle of miracles' – at the last moment: the almost utopian hint that they might at some future time meet again as two independent and free individuals on an equal footing.

Something which in many critical analyses of *A Doll's House* is lost sight of is that Nora's winning of her individual freedom is not in itself the objective: it is a means, a preliminary to her own self-development whereby she is to become a person in her own right and also in the sight of others. 'As I am now, I am no wife for you,' she says to Helmer; and shortly afterwards she adds that the same applies to her relationship to the children [*v*, 285]. She has made the painful discovery that she is a nullity, and that this must be changed. It is this she will use her freedom for – something which, in the author's view, she has every right to do: 'With the view of her marriage which Nora has formed this night it would be immoral of her to continue living together with Helmer; this she cannot do and therefore she leaves.'[15]

But *A Doll's House* is not just about one marriage. The last Act where the break occurs is introduced by a conversation between two people who have endured crisis and who now find a new basis for companionship and happiness. The somewhat melodramatic relationship between Mrs Linde and Krogstad counterpoints Nora's individualistic need for freedom and her demand for separation. For an understanding of the thematic structure of the drama, Kristine Linde's declaration that she needs somebody *to live for* is an essential part of the whole. Her voice is admittedly a muted one in the drama; and it is easily drowned by Nora's shriller demand for freedom. But Kristine is the one who understands that the Helmers can no longer keep truth out of their shared life. She is also a person who addresses herself to life's realities and who has faith in reason. As with Krogstad, life has taught her not to believe in 'pretty speeches' [*v*, 264]. Action is to replace rhetoric – therein there is hope and happiness.

Nora, too, rejects all Helmer's rhetoric about what is required of a wife and mother in contemporary society. *He* appeals to her conscience; but conscience no longer functions for her as a guide in matters of morality. On the contrary conscience in such cases becomes – as in *Ghosts* – an organ of authoritarian and repressive social forces, an internalized control mechanism which conflicts with the newly won insights of the individual. It is thus that conflicts can arise within the individual between a socially determined 'conscience' – which gives its allegiance to the past – and a newer ('free and true') conception of what is right and wrong, positive and negative. Ibsen himself defined this conflict in a letter he wrote on the subject of *Rosmersholm* (1886), but the comment is equally applicable to *Ghosts*: 'The acquisitive instinct rushes on from one conquest to the next. Moral consciousness, however, "the conscience", is by comparison very conservative. It has its roots deep in tradition and in the past generally. From this comes the conflict within the individual' [*vi*, 447].

It is this kind of 'conscience' – a persistent and recurrent element in Ibsen's work – with which Helene Alving has struggled for many years of her life and from which she is still unable to liberate herself. It is 'her bad conscience' – her own words – which has driven her to build this false icon to Alving: the Children's Home [*v*, 377]. But, seen rationally, this conflicts with the values she has herself come to believe in.

The building of the Children's Home *In memoriam Captain Alving* has its clear parallel in the false idealization of the father figure which Mrs Alving undertook in the letters to her son Osvald. She herself feels that it was wrong of her to suppress the truth, but Pastor Manders – this defender of Victorian values – has no scruples in sanctioning her actions:

MANDERS   Don't you feel your mother's heart prompting you not
               to shatter your son's ideals?
MRS ALVING   But what about the truth?
MANDERS   What about his ideals?   [v, 382]

She sees only her own cowardice here, the fact that she has felt under pressure to behave as she did in acting out a lie. But the Pastor tries to pacify her: 'You have built up a beautiful illusion in your son's mind, Mrs Alving ... and really, that's something you shouldn't underestimate' [v, 383]. What the Pastor does not realize – nor Mrs Alving as yet – is that lies and illusion form a dubious foundation for living. But there is nevertheless something in this society which favours the generation of such false ideals within both the public and the private sector and the concealment of the more chaotic conditions of private life. 'Law and order' is the objective; and a rigid code of duty and the power of public opinion are the effective instruments of control.

But rebellion against this oppressive social system comes when the individual no longer feels at ease with this illusion of a satisfying life. When she was young and newly married, Mrs Alving had known the conflict between her own demands for happiness and the demands which society imposed on her. In despair she rebelled and ran away from her husband. But she did not manage what Nora appears to achieve: to resist those forces which would send a married woman back to the path of duty. Manders compelled her to return with his doctrine: 'All this demanding to be happy in life, it's all part of this same wanton idea. What right have people to happiness? No, we have our duty to do, Mrs Alving' [v, 371].

These painful experiences made Mrs Alving begin to doubt the values on which this society based itself. Her reading of those authors representative of the new thinking confirms her in her misgivings. But she has also made an interesting discovery: that there is in effect nothing new in the writings of these thinkers. All they do is give expression to what most people discover to be right and true as soon as they dare to be themselves and to be free in their thinking. It is the *natural* understanding of life – something most people are confused about or else dare not acknowledge. Not even Mrs Alving herself. It is Osvald whom she allows to speak in her stead; and it is he who first succeeds in getting her to see what a destructive society she continues to belong to. She had believed she could control the truth about her late husband, such as she had presented it in the scene with Pastor Manders. But Osvald is able to make her see that the image of the depraved

Alving is only a part of the truth. Osvald himself replicates the image of his father as a young man when he stood for an alternative way of life to that bleak and grey existence prevailing in his birthplace. He has known life in the wider and freer world, in Paris and in Rome, where values are entirely different. His experience is thus the same as that of the young Bernick when *he* was abroad, and when his ideas had not yet been corrupted by small-town society. As a painter Osvald had ceaselessly endeavoured to capture that good life: 'Mother, have you noticed how everything I've ever painted has turned on this joy of life? Always and without exception, this joy of life. Light and sunshine and a holiday spirit ... and radiantly happy faces' [*v*, 403].

Osvald is here telling his mother about the life *she* has never known, and which he now conjures up in positive opposition to the world she has known and adopted. And when he declares that he would never have been able to live at home because everything of value in him would have become perverted, she suddenly sees the young Lieutenant Alving in a new light. In the light of this same recognition she must also re-assess her own conduct towards her husband. The young lieutenant had been a lively and happy man with something of the direct simplicity of a child, and full of the joy of living [*v*, 412]. But in that oppressive pietistic milieu he was paralysed and broken. And what of her? She admits unreservedly that she also contributed towards making her husband's life insupportable: 'They'd taught me various things about duty and suchlike, and I'd simply gone on believing them' [*v*, 413].

In her eyes her husband can now take a rightful place as a person of genuine qualities, as a representative of that life-style which Osvald glorified in his art, 'that glorious free life out there' [*v*, 370]. After this she can at least tell Osvald the truth about Alving's career without his losing his status as an ideal, either for herself or for her son. She has freed herself from the pressures of the past and of society, and this freedom brings truth. In parallel to this development, the false image of the Alving ideal literally burns down to make room for the new image of him.

But Mrs Alving's recognition comes too late, altogether too late. The past holds her captive at Rosenvold, at the same time as Osvald is now singled out as the innocent sacrifice – not merely 'for the sins of the fathers', as the doctor put it, but also for the misdeeds which society and his mother have committed against his father.

The tragic irony of *Ghosts* is that when Mrs Alving finally sees the truth about the past it is then too late. The drama's tragic analysis of the past reveals that she who believed herself innocent is by no means without guilt. And that she who has experienced the need to work her way out into freedom – and who indeed achieves this intellectually – is caught. Thus she too becomes a sacrifice of that society and of the past to which for so many years she has been opposed but to which she has also felt an obligation. She has long had the instincts of the rebel, but the forces of reaction proved too strong for her. She has belonged to the 'lysredde' (those who are afraid of the light), those who banished the sun from their own lives and from the lives of others. This is what she admits.

In *Ghosts* Ibsen directs a blistering criticism at society and its annihilating forces. But it is a criticism which also targets the most agreeable representative of that milieu and who is its one rebellious element. It is precisely the presentation of Mrs Alving's battle against the reactionary forces within herself that demonstrates Ibsen's insight into the psyche of the bourgeois rebel. The rebel too bears a share of responsibility in respect of the society which denies the new 'truth and freedom', and which thereby resists change. Mrs Alving is a rebel who fears rebellion.

When the sun finally rises, Mrs Alving has come to a full realization of the individual's right to light and happiness in a natural life. She still has hope that she and her son will be able to share that sun-filled existence, even though she knows that he is seriously ill. But he sweeps away her 'pretty speeches' and asks her to face up to the reality which is now hers and his: that of a child who sees his life running out.

Against this brutal background, the stricken Osvald gives voice to the drama's most devastating rhetorical expression: 'Mother, give me the sun' [v, 421]. But this is no 'pretty speech'; it is a declaration that all hope is lost and that the whole thing is now impossible. Here the rhetorical stands in direct relationship to the drama's reality – and to the tragedy of real life. Ibsen's scepticism about mankind's sense of the rhetorical appears quite clearly in the three dramas *Pillars of Society*, *A Doll's House* and *Ghosts*. Time after time we see him showing how rhetoric can serve to keep reality at a distance. But by degrees this scepticism also seems to bear on his own rhetoric. In *Ghosts* – this rigorously structured '*bürgerliches Trauerspiel*' (tragedy of middle-class life) – there is no slogan-dominated conclusion, no proclamation of 'truth and freedom', no 'miracle of miracles'. There is only the *sun* to indicate those dimensions of life which are denied, and to symbolize an ideal, natural way of living.

So it seems that it is precisely the natural life and the natural individual that Ibsen is concerned to defend in these works, where he otherwise submits society to debate. Society it is which prevents natural humanity from emerging and developing. Dina dreams of a society where people are wholly and completely 'natural'; Nora dreams of escaping from an artificial doll-like existence in order to become 'a human being'; and Osvald's ideal is of a community where people find happiness merely by virtue of 'existing'. These are ideas carrying associations with Rousseau and Romanticism, and are clearly based on a positive view of people as individuals. But not as social beings, for in organized bourgeois society the individual is coerced into giving up any right to be himself in any natural or positive way.

But 'truth and freedom' also seems to have had another function for Ibsen. It did not simply represent an ethical demand on the individual as a member of society; it also had relevance to Ibsen himself in his role as dramatist and realist. In the course of these three dramas he made increasingly severe demands on himself as an artist in respect of truth. By degrees he found the courage to take a freer attitude towards the bourgeois society which he was challenging in these dramas of contemporary life. 'Truth and freedom' can therefore stand as something characteristic of himself as author – he who felt that he *had* to write *Ghosts*, and who declared: 'For me freedom is the highest and the first condition for living' [XVII, 449].

NOTES

1 The term which Brandes used here for those who were to make their revolt was 'Aanderne', a term which in this context has no simple approximation in English. Literally it translates as 'the spirits'; a modern idiom might try 'cultural activists'. For a translation of the text of Ibsen's letter and of Brandes's poem, see James McFarlane, *Ibsen and Meaning* (Norwich, 1989), pp. 348–9.

2 Georg Brandes, *Emigrantlitteraturen* (originally published 1872, reprinted Copenhagen, 1971), p. 23; an English translation of this work is to be found in Georg Brandes, *Main Currents in Nineteenth Century Literature*, 6 vols. (London, 1923), vol. I.

3 Ibid., pp. 15–16.

4 See Hermann J. Weigand, *The Modern Ibsen: A Reconsideration* (New York, 1925), p. vi.

5 Linda Nochlin, *Realism* (Harmondsworth, 1987), pp. 25–8.

6 René Wellek, *Concepts of Criticism* (New Haven, 1963), pp. 222–55.

7 Nochlin, *Realism*, pp. 35–6.

8 On the matter of the author's absence, his 'detachment', *impassibilité*, see René Wellek, *A History of Modern Criticism 1750–1950*, vol. IV, *The Later Nineteenth Century* (New Haven, 1966), p. 6.

9 See note 1 above.

10 *Henrik Ibsen. Brev*. Newly collected by Øyvind Anker (Oslo, 1979), p. 218.

11 James McFarlane, 'Meaning and Evidence in Ibsen's Drama', in *Contemporary Approaches to Ibsen*, vol. I (Oslo, 1966), p. 38.

12 The Bible allusion is very clear in the fifth draft of the play: 'Let him who is without sin cast the first stone' – see *v*, 193.

13 Northrop Frye, *Anatomy of Criticism* (New York, 1967), p. 41.

14 *Henrik Ibsen. Brev*, pp. 247–8.

15 Ibid., p. 248.

6

GAIL FINNEY

Ibsen and feminism

The question of Ibsen's relationship to feminism, whether one is referring specifically to the turn-of-the-century women's movement or more generally to feminism as an ideology, has been a vexed one. The view supporting Ibsen as feminist can be seen to lie along a spectrum of attitudes with Ibsen as quasi-socialist at one end and Ibsen as humanist at the other. Proponents of the first stance might point to an amateur performance of *A Doll's House* (1879; dates following plays refer to publication) in 1886 in a Bloomsbury drawing room in which all the participants were not only associated with the feminist cause but had achieved or would achieve prominence in the British socialist movement: Eleanor Marx, the daughter of Karl, in the role of Nora; her common-law husband Edward Aveling, who played Helmer; William Morris's daughter May, portraying Mrs Linde; and, as Krogstad, none other than Bernard Shaw.[1] Together with Aveling, Eleanor Marx (who learned Norwegian to enable her to translate Ibsen) also produced *The Lady from the Sea* (1888) in London in 1891. Looking at Ibsen's advocates in terms of political groups, one may safely claim that his strongest supporters were found in socialist circles.

Ibsen himself often linked the women's cause to other areas in need of reform, arguing for example that 'all the unprivileged' (including women) should form a strong progressive party to fight for the improvement of women's position and of education.[2] Similarly, in a frequently quoted speech made to the working men of Trondheim in 1885, Ibsen stated: 'The transformation of social conditions which is now being undertaken in the rest of Europe is very largely concerned with the future status of the workers and of women. That is what I am hoping and waiting for, that is what I shall work for, all I can' [*vi*, 445–7]. The question of Ibsen's relationship to socialism is illuminated by the fact that, in the nineteenth century, socialism and feminism were familiar bedfellows. The most prominent socialist thinkers of the day, male and female, saw that true sexual equality necessitates fundamental changes in the structure of society; it is no accident that progressive attitudes toward women in Scandinavia have been bound up with overall liberal trends.

At the other end of the spectrum, those arguing that Ibsen's concerns were not narrowly feminist or political but broadly human invariably cite the speech he made at a banquet given in his honour by the Norwegian Women's Rights League on 26 May 1898:

> I am not a member of the Women's Rights League. Whatever I have written has been without any conscious thought of making propaganda. I have been more poet and less social philosopher than people generally seem inclined to believe. I thank you for the toast, but must disclaim the honour of having consciously worked for the women's rights movement. I am not even quite clear as to just what this women's rights movement really is. To me it has seemed a problem of humanity in general.[3]

This statement is perhaps best understood, however, against the background of Ibsen's frequently voiced disinclination to belong to parties or societies of any kind. In general, it seems unproductive to regard these three 'causes' – the socialist cause, the women's cause, and the human cause – as mutually exclusive for Ibsen. His concern with the state of the human soul cuts across class and gender lines. Yet this is not to say that he did not at times concentrate his attention on the condition of women as women, and it is this attention to which this essay will be devoted. Consideration of the plays themselves, in particular the twelve major prose dramas, will follow some introductory remarks on Ibsen and feminism.

His speech to the Norwegian Women's Rights League notwithstanding, the younger Ibsen made a number of claims which would indeed qualify him for the position of 'social philosopher'. In notes made for *A Doll's House* in 1878, he writes that, 'A woman cannot be herself in contemporary society, it is an exclusively male society with laws drafted by men, and with counsel and judges who judge feminine conduct from the male point of view' [*v*, 436]. Bearing out this sentiment, in a speech delivered the following year to the Scandinavian Society in Rome Ibsen urged that the post of librarian be filled by a woman and that the female members of the Society be granted the right to vote in meetings. Even more politically charged was his support in 1884 of a petition in favour of separate property rights for married women; in explaining why women and not men should be consulted about the married women's property bill, Ibsen commented that 'to consult men in such a matter is like asking wolves if they desire better protection for the sheep'.[4]

A crucial element of Ibsen's relationship to feminism is the role played by actual feminists in his life and work. Their influence began within his own family, with his wife Suzannah Thoresen Ibsen and her stepmother and former governess Magdalene Thoresen. Magdalene Thoresen, Danish writer of novels and dramas, translator of the French plays the young Ibsen staged at the Norwegian National Theatre in Bergen, and 'probably the first "New Woman" he had ever met',[5] was a key role model for Suzannah, an independent-minded woman whose favourite author was George Sand. Suzannah left her mark on Ibsen's conception of such strong-willed heroines as Hjørdis of *The Vikings at Helgeland* (1858), Svanhild of *Love's Comedy* (1862), and Nora of *A Doll's House*.

But perhaps even more important in affecting Ibsen's attitudes toward women was Camilla Collett, who is usually regarded as Norway's first and most significant feminist. Her realist novel *The District Governor's Daughters* (1854–5), which attacks the institution of marriage because of its neglect of women's feelings and its concomitant destruction of love, finds echoes in *Love's Comedy*. During the 1870s Ibsen had extended and impassioned conversations with Collett about issues such as marriage and women's role in society. His great esteem for her is evident in a letter written in anticipation of her seventieth birthday in 1883, in which he predicts that the Norway of the future will bear traces of her 'intellectual pioneer-work', and later he writes her of her long-standing influence on his writings.[6]

No introduction to the topic of Ibsen and feminism would be complete without mention of his reception. Whether or not one chooses to regard his work itself as feminist, there is no denying that much of it – above all *A Doll's House* – was enthusiastically welcomed by feminist thinkers in Norway and throughout Europe. In closing the door on her husband and children, Nora opened the way to the turn-of-the-century women's movement. To mention only a few examples of the play's impact, Gina Krog, a leading Norwegian feminist in the 1880s and first editor of the feminist journal *Nylænde*, called the drama and its likely reformative effects a miracle. Amalie Skram, Norway's foremost naturalist writer and the first Norwegian author to treat female sexuality, praised the play dramatically and psychologically and saw it as a warning of what would happen when women in general woke up to the injustices that had been committed against them. Such sentiments were not confined to women, as the admonishment of pastor M. J. Færden to his congregation in 1884 attests:

> Just as Nora appears in the final scene, free and unfettered by any bond, divine or human, without commitment or obligation to the man whom she has given her promise or to the children she has brought into this world – likewise we will find the wife in the modern marriage, from beginning to end . . . The emancipated woman has taken her place at the door, always ready to depart, with her suitcase in her hand. The suitcase – and not, as before, the ring of fidelity – will be the symbol of her role in marriage.[7]

Entirely different in tone but essentially similar in its evaluation is Strindberg's lambasting of Ibsen, inspired by the publication of *A Doll's House*, as 'the famous Norwegian bluestocking, the promoter of the equality mania'.[8] *A Doll's House* did indeed have a significant impact on the improvement of women's condition in Scandinavia, as is documented for instance by Anna Agerholt in *The History of the Norwegian Woman's Movement* (1937).

I will approach the topic of feminism in the major prose plays themselves by considering four sub-topics: briefly, the double standard and marriage and, more extensively, the emancipated woman and motherhood. It is telling that beliefs in differences between masculine and feminine character and behaviour are repeatedly put into the mouths of narrow, stodgy, hypocritical, or otherwise unsympathetic characters. To mention only a few examples, in *Pillars of Society* (1877) the priggish, platitudinous schoolmaster Rørlund reads from *Women in the Service of Society* to a group of town ladies dubbed the 'Society for Moral Delinquents' in an attempt to uphold their dedication to the purity of the family and the community – a wholly farcical value in the light of the lies, pretence, and selfishness on which this society is based. Likewise Karsten Bernick, the primary generator of this deception, observes that 'here the women are content to assume a seemly, if modest status' and that 'People should never think primarily of themselves, least of all women' [*v*, 66]. Similarly, Torvald Helmer of *A Doll's House*, whose most avid concern is for keeping up appearances regardless of the psychological cost, is given to statements about feminine helplessness and childishness versus manly strength and resourcefulness.

A particularly blatant example of the double standard is found in *Ghosts* (1881), where Pastor Manders expresses moral censure for the Alving's former servant Johanna as a fallen woman but scoffs at Mrs Alving's characterization of her deceased husband as a fallen man [*v*, 381]. Similarly, he is horrified at the mention of cohabitation outside of marriage, or free love [*v*, 369]. Since these views are voiced by a man who is shocked by any hint of free-thinking and whose unswerving adherence to principle had once sent Mrs Alving back to her dissolute husband and hence ruined her life, it is not difficult to infer Ibsen's attitude toward them. In the light of characters like these, it is not surprising that the twelve major prose plays contain only one extensive portrayal of a relatively healthy marriage, that between the Stockmanns in *An Enemy of the People* (1882), and even this depiction shows the pragmatic Mrs Stockmann to be sceptical toward the idealism of her husband.

Given Ibsen's sensitivity to feminist issues, it comes as no surprise that he has often been praised for his creation of female characters. James Joyce's evaluation of 1900 is representative: 'Ibsen's knowledge of humanity is nowhere more obvious than in his portrayal of women. He amazes one by his painful introspection; he seems to know them better than they know themselves. Indeed, if one may say so of an eminently virile man, there is a curious admixture of the woman in his nature.'[9] Although the majority of Ibsen's protagonists are male, some of his most memorable and well-known characters are female, such as Nora Helmer, Helene Alving, Rebecca West, and Hedda Gabler; Elizabeth Robins speaks for all turn-of-the-century actresses in claiming that 'no dramatist has ever meant so much to the women of the stage as Henrik Ibsen'.[10] The power of his female roles has continued to attract top-calibre performers down to our own day, as is evident in the homage paid him by Julie Harris, Jane Fonda, Liv Ullmann, Glenda Jackson, Susannah York and others.[11]

Of the four sub-topics of feminism listed above, female characters are of course featured most prominently in depictions of the last two, the emancipated woman and motherhood. These two issues are of central concern in illuminating Ibsen's relationship to feminism. Regarding the first, Ibsen was widely credited with virtually inventing the emancipated woman in the last Act of *A Doll's House*. Because Nora's self-realization occurs so late in the play, however, I will focus here on four other figures who may to varying degrees be seen as emancipated women: Lona Hessel of *Pillars of Society*, Petra Stockmann of *An Enemy of the People*, Rebecca West of *Rosmersholm* (1886), and Hilde Wangel of *The Master Builder* (1892).

These characters are distinguished by their rejection of a strict division between conventional masculine and feminine behaviour, by their disdain for public opinion, and by their freedom from the hypocrisy that often accompanies maintenance of the status quo. Their emancipated status is reflected in their appearance, language and behaviour. In the first Act of *Pillars of Society* we learn from the townswomen's gossip that Lona Hessel, stepsister of Bernick's wife Betty, had scandalized the town before her departure to America to join Betty's younger brother Johan by cutting her hair short and wearing men's boots; returning now from America, she is initially taken for a member of the circus because she carries a bag over her shoulder by the handle of her umbrella and waves at the gawking townspeople. Similarly, Hilde Wangel appears in Halvard Solness's office dressed in walking clothes with her skirt hitched up, complete with rucksack, plaid, and alpenstock and 'slightly tanned by the sun' [*vii*, 375], flaunting her disregard for traditional standards of feminine attire and beauty. The unconventionality of both characters is further evident in their speech, which is dotted with colloquialisms, topics traditionally regarded as unmentionable for young middle-class women, and swear words. Lona exhorts the Bernicks' young son to 'Give us your paw, lad!', describes Johan during the crossing to Europe as 'filthy as a pig', and greets a former acquaintance with the words, 'Well, I'll be damned if that isn't Mrs Rummel' [all quotations *v*, 47]; in like manner Hilde speaks in a natural, uninhibited fashion, mentioning her filthy underwear to Solness and using expressions like 'hell' and 'Good Lord'.

The aggressive and forthright behaviour of these female characters is shaped by their lack of concern for what people think. In *Pillars of Society* the townswomen disclose that, prior to her trip to America, Lona had slapped Bernick in the face when he announced his engagement to Betty; her scandalous behaviour continued abroad, they report, where she sang in saloons for pay, gave public lectures, and published 'a quite outrageous book' [*v*, 35]. Upon returning home she shocks observers by washing her face at the pump in the middle of the marketplace. Rebecca West defies public opinion by continuing to live as a single woman beneath one roof with Rosmer following his wife Beata's death; as Rebecca says to Rosmer, 'Oh, why must we worry about what others think? We know, you and I, that we have no reason to feel guilty' [*vi*, 338]. Concomitantly, in contrast to the traditional female of the day, she seems wholly lacking in maternal inclinations, observing to the housekeeper that Rosmer is better off childless, since he is not the kind of man who can 'put up with a lot of crying children' [*vi*, 347]. Similarly, the younger Hilde Wangel of *The Lady from the Sea* balks when her father describes her as marriageable, and already here she is portrayed as a saucy, naughty girl with the desire to be a 'horrid child' for spite [*vii*, 55]. When Mrs Solness warns the older Hilde of *The Master Builder* that people might stare at her if she ventures into town in her unconventional garb, she responds that that would be fun [*vii*, 397].

A further trait indicative of the emancipated character of these women figures is their high level of education. Lona's authorship of a book speaks for itself; Petra Stockmann, a full-time teacher who first appears on stage with a pile of exercise books under her arm, expresses unalloyed liking for her work. Rebecca, largely educated at home by her (foster) father Dr West, reads radical newspapers in an effort to keep abreast of new developments and shares books and ideas with Rosmer. Significantly, it is she who takes the initiative in attempting to support the impoverished revolutionary writer Ulrik Brendel by asking the radical journalist Peter Mortensgaard to come to his aid. Reportedly inspired by Ibsen's stepmother-in-law Magdalene Thoresen, the character of Rebecca West was hailed by feminists. Gina Krog heard the 'gospel of the future' proclaimed in *Rosmersholm*: 'Ibsen's belief in women, in the women of his country, has never been expressed so proudly as here.'[12]

In keeping with their liberated tendencies, these figures typically serve to unmask the lies which shadow the lives of other characters. Petra, a free-thinking young woman who refuses to translate a story because it defends conventional Christian beliefs, is repelled by the hypocrisy of a school system which requires her to teach things she does not believe in and declares that she would prefer to start a school herself if she had the means. She wholly supports her father's plan to expose the pollution infecting the municipal baths, like him subordinating the individual well-being of their family to a commitment to truth, principle and the general welfare. In a similar vein, Lona Hessel favourably compares the air of the American prairies to the shroud-like smell of moral linen she encounters back home and, when Rørlund questions her as to her intention regarding their society, expressly announces her mission: 'I want to let in some fresh air, my dear pastor' [v, 48]. The primary target of her campaign is Bernick, whom she finally exhorts to confess the multiple deceptions on which his business, his marriage and his reputation are founded.

Like that of Rebecca West, the conception of Lona Hessel was inspired by an actual feminist contemporary of Ibsen's, Aasta Hansteen. A portrait painter by profession and an outspoken suffragette who often wore men's boots and carried a whip when she spoke in public, Hansteen achieved her greatest notoriety in 1874 by supporting the cause of a Swedish baroness who claimed to have been seduced and abandoned by a Norwegian medical student. In presenting the baroness's cause as an issue concerning all women and in arguing for the expulsion of the student in articles, speeches and demonstrations, Hansteen succeeded in ostracizing herself. Ibsen was sympathetic to Hansteen and disturbed by her fate at the hands of the press and public. Her influence on *Pillars of Society* is perhaps most obvious in Lona's remarks to Bernick about the treatment of women, both his own and that of society at large. When Bernick complains that his wife Betty has never been any of the things he needed, Lona counters: 'Because you never shared your interests with her. Because you've never been open or frank with her in any of your dealings. Because you let her go on suffering under the shame you unburdened on her family' [v, 111]. Lona generalizes this observation in her famous comment to Bernick near the play's end: 'This society of yours is like a lot of old bachelors: you never see the women' [v, 126].

These four female characters share many properties with the New Woman, a literary type which flourished above all in Victorian fiction of the 1890s. The New Woman typically values self-fulfilment and independence rather than the stereotypically feminine ideal of self-sacrifice; believes in legal and sexual equality; often remains single because of the difficulty of combining such equality with marriage; is more open about her sexuality than the 'Old Woman'; is well-educated and reads a great deal; has a job; is athletic or otherwise physically vigorous and, accordingly, prefers comfortable clothes (sometimes male attire) to traditional female garb.[13] Yet while Ibsen's emancipated women characters were influential for the conception of the New Woman, they cannot be wholly identified with this type. A recognition of the qualifications to their emancipation is important for an understanding of Ibsen's position *vis-à-vis* feminism.

Taking a close look at the figures discussed above, we see that all four are ultimately defined in terms of male characters. Lona Hessel's 'character and strength of mind and independence' [*v*, 71] notwithstanding, she tells Bernick that she has returned from her new life in America because of her feelings for him, in order to help him re-establish himself on honest ground. Furthermore, referring to her role as 'foster-mother' [*v*, 108] to her younger stepbrother Johan in America, she observes: 'Heaven knows, it's about the only thing I have achieved in this world. But it gives me a sort of right to exist' [*v*, 59]. Throughout *An Enemy of the People* Petra Stockmann's views are shaped by those of her father, an influence underlined by the drama's final word: the curtain falls as Petra grasps Thomas Stockmann's hands and exclaims, 'Father!' [*vi*, 126].

Even Rebecca West, so enthusiastically championed by contemporary feminists, reveals herself to be decidedly oriented around men. When Rosmer's brother-in-law Kroll observes (referring to her remaining with Rosmer): 'You know . . . there's something rather splendid about that – a woman giving up the best years of her young life, sacrificing them for the sake of others,' Rebecca responds: 'Oh, what else would I have had to live for?' [*vi*, 97]. Her visions of ennobling humanity are focused on Rosmer, the object of her love, rather than on herself; when Rosmer asks her towards the end of the play how she thinks things will be for her now, she replies that it is not important [*vi*, 363]. Kroll's comment that what she calls her emancipation is only an abstraction, that it never 'got into [her] blood' [*vi*, 357], may be an accurate one; it is in any event supported by her confession that when she reached twenty-five she began subtracting a year from her admitted age, since she felt she was 'getting a bit too old' to be unmarried [*vi*, 356].

Rebecca West is also stereotypically feminine in her seductiveness, her tendency to use her wiles and great attractiveness to manipulate others. Kroll, saying 'Who is there you couldn't bewitch . . . if you tried?' [*vi*, 353], accuses her of having used his former infatuation with her to gain entrée to Rosmersholm; Brendel calls her 'my enchanting little mermaid' [*vi*, 375] in warning Rosmer not to build on her in carrying out his goals. As Kroll points out, Rebecca had succeeded in captivating the unstable Beata as well, and her removal of Beata through psychic murder – prompting Beata's suicide by leading her to believe that Rebecca was pregnant by Rosmer and that a childless wife was in the way – hardly resembles feminist solidarity.

Directly or indirectly responsible for the deaths of Beata, Rosmer and of course herself, Rebecca has as much in common with another literary type that flourished at the turn of the century as she does with the New Woman, the *femme fatale*. Her high degree of sensuality, characterized by as early an observer as Lou Salomé as a 'wildness that resembles a beast of prey at rest and which hungers for spoil',[14] further associates her with this type. Like the conventional *femme fatale*, she is incapable of moderating her passion, but rather either allows it to lead her to irrational acts such as the psychic murder of Beata or represses it completely.

Consideration of Rebecca West as *femme fatale* links her to Hilde Wangel, whose vision of the younger Solness atop the church tower and whose entreaties that he do the impossible goad him into climbing the tower of his new house, from which he falls to his death. As in the case of Rebecca *vis-à-vis* Rosmer, Hilde's emancipated ways clash with her virtual idolization of Solness, her desire to see him achieve greatness; in the words of Nada Zeineddine, 'Hilde's dreams are mirrored in Solness and through him'.[15] Claiming that he has made her what she is [*vii*, 441], Hilde seems to have spent the past ten years anticipating the moment when she would be reunited with him and become his 'princess', he her 'king'. It is difficult to imagine a more blatant counter-narrative to that of the New Woman.

Examination of the complex, hybrid characters of Lona Hessel, Petra Stockmann, Rebecca West and Hilde Wangel sheds new light on Ibsen's observation, quoted earlier, that 'a woman cannot be herself in contemporary society, it is an exclusively male society'. Through these powerful dramatic creations Ibsen suggests that even for potentially or partially emancipated women, the male-dominated nature of his society, affecting their thinking from birth, stands in the way of total autonomy. This belief is reinforced by the multiple portrayals of motherhood – whether actual, prospective, foster or metaphorical – in his major prose plays.

Insofar as the female ability to bear children is the most crucial ramification of the physiological difference between women and men, the issue of motherhood has been central to every feminist movement or programme. As Julia Kristeva writes, it is not woman as such who is oppressed in patriarchal society, but the mother.[16] A focused look at Ibsen's mother figures discloses a similar message: maternity is viewed most positively by those who are not biological mothers, whereas his actual or prospective mothers either deny their pregnancy, abandon their children, give them away to be cared for elsewhere, raise them in an atmosphere of deception, or neglect them. The victimization these unmotherly mothers inflict results from their own victimization by a powerful social norm equating anatomy with destiny; in Ibsen's notes to *A Doll's House* he conjectures that a mother in modern society is like 'certain insects who go away and die when she has done her duty in the propagation of the race' [*v*, 437]. Hence Ibsen bears witness to a larger nineteenth-century historical strategy which Michel Foucault has termed 'hysterization', or the process of defining women in terms of female sexuality, the result of which was to bind them to their reproductive function.[17]

It is no accident that Ibsen's most famous emancipated woman character achieves self-realization by turning her back on her husband and children. For whereas parenthood in literature is traditionally a sign of attaining adulthood, as the drama's title announces and as Nora Helmer herself confirms, marriage and motherhood have been for her a kind of protracted doll's house existence in which she has played with her children just as Helmer, and her father before him, played with her [*v*, 280–1]; in order to reach genuine maturity she must leave this life behind. Yet her progression from doll–child to adult is not as smooth and sudden as the many critics who characterize it as over-abrupt would have it. Careful examination of the first two Acts of the play reveals that the role of Helmer's little skylark and squirrel is one in which he casts her and which she self-consciously plays. The childlike pose she assumes with him – 'I would never dream of doing anything you didn't want me to'; 'I never get anywhere without your help' [*v*, 205, 232] – appears in a highly ironic light in view of her revelations that she forged her father's signature in order to secure a loan to save Helmer's life and that she has done, for example, secret copying work in an attempt to pay off the note.

Further chinks in the image of Nora as cheerful doll–child are evident in behaviour which can most accurately be labelled hysterical. There is already something desperate and insistent about her often repeated exclamations in the first Act about how happy she is [*v*, 209, 210, 215, 216, 220]. After Krogstad threatens to reveal her crime, her nervousness increases to the point that she feels she might go mad [*v*, 255]. Her hysteria culminates in her rehearsal of the tarantella which she is to dance at a party the following day; she dances with abandon, wildly, her hair coming undone and falling around her shoulders, in a manner perceived by Helmer as 'sheer madness' [*v*, 259]. This scene is illuminated by Catherine Clément's discussion of the tarantella's origins in southern Italy, where it serves as a form of hysterical catharsis, permitting women to escape temporarily from marriage and motherhood into a free, lawless world of music and uninhibited movement.[18] In analogous fashion, Nora returns from her frenzied state to her role as wife and mother, but only as a springboard from which to emancipate herself.

Concomitantly, *Ghosts*, the play centring more than any other on the mother–child bond, ultimately casts maternity in a tragic light. The quintessential mother, Helene Alving tells her son Osvald that he is 'The one thing I have in all the world. The one thing I care anything at all about . . . I have nothing to live for but you' [*v*, 397, 417]. Yet her maternal devotion, based on deception rather than on power, backfires at every juncture: sending Osvald away as a child to shield him from the influence of his dissolute father could not prevent him from inheriting the syphilis which is now killing him; the orphanage she founds as a memorial to the supposedly honourable Captain Alving burns to the ground; and the son to whom she has sacrificed so much begs her in his suffering to be the instrument of his death.

In *The Wild Duck* (1884) the powerlessness associated with motherhood also results in a web of lies and deceit. The pattern according to which Gina Ekdal conceals her seduction as a servant by the wealthy Werle by marrying Hjalmar Ekdal and leading him to think her child is his echoes the sub-plot of *Ghosts*, in which Mrs Alving finds a husband for the maid her husband has impregnated. Gina's power is confined to the domestic sphere, which she epitomizes, typically depicted as sewing or adding up accounts and described by Hjalmar's friend Dr Relling as 'pottering about in her slippers all nice and cuddlesome, and making the place all cosy' [*vi*, 193]. As if in an attempt to counteract the kinds of unpredictable forces that led to the conception of her daughter, this model housekeeper has become compulsively obsessed with order, subordinating humaneness to neatness. But as in *Ghosts*, all endeavours to maintain tranquillity prove futile once the long-standing deception is unmasked, leading to the sacrificial suicide of the child it has sought to protect.

Few portrayals of victimization by motherhood, or more accurately imminent motherhood, are as memorable and yet as subtle as that in *Hedda Gabler* (1890). While it is nowhere expressly stated that Hedda is pregnant, the play abounds in intimations of her condition; as Janet Suzman claims, Hedda's pregnancy draws together every strand of the play.[19] Yet Hedda is nearly the only main character who does not refer to her expectations; in response to the allusions to the possibility of pregnancy made by her husband Tesman, his aunt Juliane Tesman, and Judge Brack, she changes the subject or reacts with irritation or even anger. She supplies the reason herself; when Brack mentions the prospect of 'a sacred and . . . exacting responsibility', she angrily retorts, 'I've no aptitude for any such thing' [*vii*, 213].

For the maternal calling of the conventional nineteenth-century woman is thwarted in Hedda by tendencies that were at the time viewed as masculine. The influence of her motherless, father-dominated upbringing is everywhere evident: in her taste for horses and pistols; in her eager anticipation of a contest between Tesman and Løvborg for the available university professorship; even in General Gabler's portrait, which is described in the opening stage directions, before we meet any of the actual characters, as occupying a prominent place in the Tesmans' drawing room. Explaining the play's title, Ibsen wrote: 'I intended to indicate thereby that as a personality she is to be regarded rather as her father's daughter than as her husband's wife'.[20] As Elizabeth Hardwick points out, Hedda's husband is 'much more of a girl than she is',[21] since while she was brought up by a general, he was raised by two maiden aunts.

Hedda's society provides few outlets for her masculine ambitions, however. Her comment to Brack – 'I just stand here and shoot into the blue' [vii, 203] – is loaded in multiple respects. In the face of her own aimlessness, she seeks masculine experience vicariously, pressing Løvborg to confess his debaucheries to her as her only insight into a world 'that she isn't supposed to know anything about', conjecturing that she could make it her life's goal to encourage Tesman to go into politics [vii, 223, 212].

As in A Doll's House, the clash between Hedda's unfeminine inclinations and the step she takes down the feminine path of marriage and, inevitably, pregnancy results in hysteria. Her gestures are as telling as her words: drawing the curtains, seeking fresh air, walking nervously around the room, raising her arms, clenching her fists, drumming her fingers, physically abusing Thea Elvsted. And as in the case of Nora, her hysteria finds release in music, in the 'wild dance tune' she plays on the piano [vii, 267]. Yet unlike Nora, Hedda is still too much the victim of traditional thinking to move from hysteria to feminism. Trapped by Brack between two conventional attitudes – her fear of scandal and her abhorrence of adultery – she fulfils the prediction she had made upon Tesman's joyous response to the news of her pregnancy: 'Oh, it'll kill me . . . it'll kill me, all this!' [vii, 255].

Significantly, the character who is most positive about Hedda's expectations is one who has never experienced biological motherhood. Certain that Hedda must have become pregnant during the couple's six-month honeymoon, Miss Tesman presses for a revelation, hinting to Tesman that a use might be found for the empty rooms in the house and to Hedda that there will soon be sewing to do. As an unmarried, childless woman, she has taken on one foster-child after another; having raised Tesman, who gratefully acknowledges to his 'Auntie Julle' that 'You've always been both father and mother to me' [vii, 175], she has recently filled her life by nursing her ailing sister Rina, and after Rina's death she plans to replace her with another invalid. The contrast to Hedda, who regards such care as a 'burden' [*vii*, 253], is evident.

The antithesis between Hedda Gabler, a (prospective) mother in spite of herself, and Juliane Tesman, who idealizes motherhood from the vantage point of one who has known it not as a biological necessity but as a chosen, foster calling, is paradigmatic in Ibsen's *œuvre*, recurring with somewhat different contours in *Little Eyolf* (1894) and *John Gabriel Borkman* (1896). In what is probably the most explicit treatment of female sexuality in all of his works, Ibsen investigates in Rita Allmers the psychology of a woman whose enormous sensuality renders her unsuited for motherhood. Showing great self-awareness, she sums up her situation to her husband:

> I can't go on just being Eyolf's mother. And only that ... I want to be every-thing to you! To you, Alfred! ... Motherhood for me was in *having* the child. But I'm not made to go on *being* mother to it ... I want you! All of you! You alone! The way I had you in those first glorious, throbbing days.   [*viii*, 60]

Bearing witness to Adrienne Rich's contention that women who refuse motherhood are perceived as dangerous,[22] Rita's neglect proves fatal to her small son, insofar as he drowns because his lameness prevents him from swimming and this handicap is the result of a fall he suffered as an infant when she had left him unattended in order to make love with Alfred.

As in *Hedda Gabler*, maternal indifference is counterbalanced here by the love and devotion of an (assumed) female relative whose feelings are all the more heartfelt because they are chosen rather than biologically imposed. The first action we see Alfred's (supposed) half-sister Asta take is to look in on Eyolf, to whom she refers as 'the poor little lad!' [*viii*, 41]; her empathy with him is symbolically reinforced by the revelation that she would have been named Eyolf if she had been a boy and that Alfred had often called her by that name when they were children. Having frequently taken care of Eyolf, she is blamed by Rita for usurping his affections, when in fact her love was at least as much directed toward Alfred Allmers, to whom she has learned she is not related after all.

A strikingly similar constellation is found in *John Gabriel Borkman*: the struggle between a natural and a foster mother for their son (figure) vicari-ously mimics their former rivalry for his father. If Rita Allmers is 'too hot' to be a proper mother, it might be said that Gunhild Borkman is too cold; described as sitting 'erect and motionless' and as feeling 'always cold' [*viii*, 155, 156], she views her son Erhart merely as a tool to avenge the scandal of his father's embezzlement and imprisonment by making something of himself and restoring the family name. By contrast, her sister Ella Rentheim, who took over the care of the boy Erhart during the five years his father was in prison, has returned eight years later to regain the young man's affections. Although her motives are also selfish in part, insofar as she wants Erhart to change his name to Rentheim and thus carry on her line, she is concerned for his happiness as well and clearly loves him more than his own mother ever has.

Erhart's gratitude recalls that of Tesman to his Aunt Juliane: 'Aunt Ella ... you have been unbelievably good to me. With you, my childhood was as happy and carefree as ever any child could hope for' [viii, 212]. Unlike the unfortunate Eyolf, Erhart manages to save himself from this struggle between two women by escaping with a third, Mrs Wilton. In the light of her felicitous role, it seems Ibsen would have us put credence in her views, such as her subordination of often happenstance biological maternity to chosen foster-motherhood: 'A good foster-mother often deserves more thanks than one's real mother' [viii, 173].

Ibsen's awareness of the difficulties of motherhood on the one hand and of the overwhelming power of the myth of maternity as the proper calling for women on the other hand is expressed by several memorable instances in the major prose plays in which women who have either lost their children or never had any remain trapped in maternal thinking toward metaphorical offspring. Although the tragic secret at the heart of *The Master Builder* is the Solnesses' loss of their infant twins as the indirect result of a fire that had destroyed their home years before, Aline Solness reveals that she in fact grieves not for the babies but for her nine dolls lost in the blaze, which she had carried under her heart 'like little unborn children' [vii, 425]. In the cases of Thea Elvsted in *Hedda Gabler* and Irene de Satow in *When We Dead Awaken* (1899), childless women develop a rhetoric of maternity to describe their roles in the production of works of art. Just as Thea refers to the book she helped Løvborg write as their child, Irene says of Rubek's masterpiece sculpture for which she sat as model, 'Our child lives on after me. In honour and glory' [viii, 254]. Yet the true nature of the two women's contributions is revealed by Thea's despairing question on learning that Løvborg has no further use for her – 'What am I to do with my life, then?' [vii, 246] – and Irene's admission to Rubek that once he no longer needed her as his model, she died inside. Their role is more accurately that of midwife or muse than metaphorical mother; if they were genuine artists, it goes without saying that they could go on to create further works alone. The rhetoric of artistic maternity shows Thea and Irene to fall between the two stools, as it were, of the nineteenth-century division of labour which assigned artistic creativity to men and childbearing to women. Although Thea and Irene have failed to participate in either area, the myth of maternity as women's destiny is so powerful that they appropriate its language in compensatory fashion to describe their artistic midwifery.

This consideration sheds new light on Ibsen's claim late in life that 'it is the women who are to solve the social problem. As mothers they are to do it. And only as such can they do it.'[23] Whereas this statement is often interpreted to mean that Ibsen viewed motherhood as the proper calling for women, he may in fact be suggesting that it is the only vocation truly open to them. The many female figures in his plays demonstrate the enormous and often detrimental influence of the notion that maternity is woman's duty: women who have motherhood imposed on them against their will, mothers unsuited to motherhood, childless women for whom the maternal model is so strong that they take on foster or metaphorical children.

Ibsen's implication that the best mother is the one who assumes this calling not because of biological determinism, as was so often the case in his day, but out of free choice, finds its most wholehearted endorsement in *The Lady from the Sea*. In a kind of counterpoint to *A Doll's House*, where Nora must create her own freedom by leaving behind the domestic environment which has confined her, Dr Wangel grants his wife Ellida the freedom to choose between joining the mysterious seafaring stranger to whom she has been so powerfully attracted and remaining with Wangel and his children. Where Nora exchanges motherhood for autonomy, Ellida is able to truly embrace (step)motherhood only because Wangel has rendered her autonomous.

The Lady from the Sea may stand as the last word on the question of Ibsen and feminism. For insofar as it reverses the pattern of *A Doll's House*, it does not present women with the choice between motherhood and solitary New Womanhood but rather powerfully advocates women's right to choose their destiny and combine roles as they desire. Supporting the belief that a woman's mind and body are hers to control as she wishes, Ibsen's *œuvre* allies him with feminist thinkers not only of his era but of our own day as well.

NOTES

1 Ian Britain, 'A Transplanted Doll's House: Ibsenism, Feminism and Socialism in Late-Victorian and Edwardian England', in *Transformations in Modern European Drama*, ed. Ian Donaldson (London, 1983), pp. 16–17.
2 Henrik Ibsen, *Letters and Speeches*, ed. Evert Sprinchorn (New York, 1964), p. 229.
3 Ibsen, *Speeches and New Letters*, trans. Arne Kildal (1909; New York, 1972), p. 65.
4 Ibsen, *Letters and Speeches*, ed. Sprinchorn, p. 228.

5 Joan Templeton, 'The *Doll House* Backlash: Criticism, Feminism, and Ibsen', *PMLA*, 104 (1989), 36. I am indebted to Templeton for information on Magdalene and Suzannah Thoresen.

6 *The Correspondence of Henrik Ibsen*, ed. Mary Morison (New York, 1970), pp. 365, 423–4.

7 Translated and quoted by Katherine Hanson, 'Ibsen's Women Characters and Their Feminist Contemporaries', *Theatre History Studies*, 2 (1982), 86–7. Hanson is the source of much of my information on the reception of *A Doll's House* in Norway.

8 Quoted by Roslyn Belkin, 'Prisoners of Convention: Ibsen's "Other" Women', *Journal of Women's Studies in Literature*, 1 (1979), 145.

9 Quoted in *Ibsen: The Critical Heritage*, ed. Michael Egan (London, 1972), p. 388.

10 Elizabeth Robins, *Ibsen and the Actress* (1928; New York, 1973), p. 55.

11 See Robert A. Schanke, *Ibsen in America: A Century of Change* (Metuchen, N.J., 1988), pp. 171–280.

12 Translated and quoted by Hanson, 'Ibsen's Women Characters', 88.

13 On the New Woman in literature see especially Gail Cunningham, *The New Woman and the Victorian Novel* (New York, 1978), and Leone Scanlon, 'The New Woman in the Literature of 1883–1909', *University of Michigan Papers in Women's Studies*, 2:2 (1976), 133–59.

14 Lou Salomé, *Ibsen's Heroines*, trans. Siegfried Mandel (original 1892; Redding Ridge, Conn., 1985), p. 86.

15 Nada Zeineddine, *Because It Is My Name: Problems of Identity Experienced by Women, Artists, and Breadwinners in the Plays of Henrik Ibsen, Tennessee Williams, and Arthur Miller* (Braunton, Devon, 1991), p. 74.

16 Julia Kristeva, *La Révolution du langage poétique* (Paris, 1974) p. 453.

17 Michel Foucault, *The History of Sexuality*, vol. I, *An Introduction*, trans. Robert Hurley (New York, 1978), pp. 104–5.

18 Hélène Cixous and Catherine Clément, *The Newly Born Woman*, trans. Betsy Wing (Minneapolis, 1986), pp. 19–22.

19 Janet Suzman, '*Hedda Gabler*: The Play in Performance', in *Ibsen and the Theatre: The Dramatist in Production*, ed. Errol Durbach (New York, 1980), p. 89.

20 Letter of 4 December 1890 to Count Moritz Prozor [*vii*, 500].

21 Elizabeth Hardwick, *Seduction and Betrayal: Women and Literature* (New York, 1974), p. 57.

22 Adrienne Rich, *Of Woman Born: Motherhood as Experience and Institution* (New York, 1976).

23 Ibsen, *Speeches and New Letters*, trans. Kildal, p. 66.

Other sources relevant to this chapter include

Bhalla, Brij M., 'The Feminine Self in Ibsen', *Journal of the School of Languages* 3:2 (1975–6), 22–31.

Ewbank, Inga-Stina, 'Ibsen and the Language of Women', in *Women Writing and Writing about Women*, ed. Mary Jacobus (London, 1979), pp. 114–32.

Finney, Gail, *Women in Modern Drama: Freud, Feminism, and European Theater at the Turn of the Century* (Ithaca, 1989).

Lester, Elenore, 'Ibsen's Unliberated Heroines', *Scandinavian Review*, 66:4 (1978), 58–66.

Popovich, Helen, 'Shelf of Dolls: A Modern View of Ibsen's Emancipated Women', *CEA Critic*, 39:3 (1977), 4–8.

Rogers, Katharine M., 'A Woman Appreciates Ibsen', *The Centennial Review*, 18 (1974), 91–108.

Sprinchorn, Evert, 'Ibsen, Strindberg, and the New Woman', in *The Play and Its Critic: Essays for Eric Bentley*, ed. Michael Bertin (Lanham, Md., 1986), 45–66.

7

JANET GARTON

The middle plays

Rebecca, Ellida, Hedda: the three heroines of Ibsen's plays from this period, *Rosmersholm* (1886), *The Lady from the Sea* (1888) and *Hedda Gabler* (1890), have names which have a similar ring to them; all sound slightly unfamiliar to a Norwegian ear, have an air of 'otherness' which marks them off from convention. The centrality of the heroines in these plays is underlined by the fact that two of them give the plays their titles, the only Ibsen plays where this occurs apart from the early *Lady Inger* (1857) – whereas as many as ten plays refer to the names or functions of male characters in their titles (*Catiline, Olaf Liljekrans, The Pretenders, Brand, Peer Gynt, Emperor and Galilean, An Enemy of the People, The Master Builder, Little Eyolf, John Gabriel Borkman*).

The otherness of these heroines is apparent from the beginning of the action; all are outsiders in their society, at odds with the mores of the community in which they find themselves, unhappy with an environment which forces them to live inauthentically. They have all to a greater or lesser extent tried to conform, but at the cost of the repression of their 'wild side'. They are pagans living in a Christian society. All are passionate women who, it could be argued, have got themselves involved with the wrong man. Neither Rosmer, Wangel nor Tesman are as their partners would have them be; they lack the passion to respond to their women's needs. As a result all three women have focused their sensuality on a substitute figure. Rebecca has invented for herself an idealized 'Rosmer' who bears little resemblance to the actual man, Ellida recalls her dream lover from the past and Hedda turns her energies to rekindling her highly charged relationship with Løvborg. The clash between aspiration and reality drives them all to breaking point.

Yet an investigation of the similarities between the central characters of these plays takes us only so far; there are major differences too. Ibsen is well known for returning to a similar theme in adjacent plays but casting an entirely different light on it; like the two faces of egoism in *Brand* and *Peer*

Gynt, or the positive and negative aspects of idealism in *An Enemy of the People* and *The Wild Duck.* The most striking difference between these three plays emerges in their endings; the middle play, *The Lady from the Sea,* culminates in a reconciliation, and is often cited as the only one of Ibsen's later plays in which the institution of marriage is shown in a positive light. In the other two plays, on the other hand, the curtain falls on the suicide of the heroine, in *Rosmersholm* on a double suicide. In Ibsen's plays, as in the society of his day, women's chances of self-realization are largely dependent on the attitude of the men nearest to them, and it is the reaction of the men which is the key factor here in deciding the outcome. Wangel has wisdom enough to realize what his wife needs, and courage to give her it; whereas Rosmer practically demands that Rebecca sacrifice herself, and the men in Hedda's circle between them corner her like a trapped animal.

The blame cannot be laid entirely at the door of the male characters, however; such a black-and-white division of responsibility would make the plays too programmatic and fail to explain their continuing fascination. Rebecca, Ellida and Hedda are tormented at least as much by their own internalized repression and guilt as they are by external restrictions. They are divided within themselves, and turn in upon themselves in a conflict more destructive than mere lack of opportunity could make it. After all, there are women who break free, even in Ibsen's world.

Are these, then, three plays about three frustrated women? The answer must be yes. They contain three of the most demanding roles in an *œuvre* which has been notoriously fruitful for actresses: 'No dramatist has ever meant so much to the women of the stage as Henrik Ibsen.'[1] A list of those who have played the parts reads like a roll-call of modern acting talent. Ibsen's studies of female psychology have lost none of their subtlety over the last hundred years, and his assessment of their clash with society's norms is still as fresh. Whatever he might have said in other contexts about not knowing what the women's rights movement was all about,[2] his plays know what it is about, and that in a sense which extends beyond the political aims of the late nineteenth century and does not look out of place alongside modern critiques of the patriarchal society.

But the plays are about many other things as well. Ibsen was an eager follower of contemporary debate, and alert to all the burning issues of the day, including this one. He was resident in Munich throughout the period when these three plays were written, although he was travelling too, most importantly to Denmark and Norway; and from his vantage point in central Europe he was well placed to follow both European and Scandinavian developments. His plays can be plotted along various axes: politically, as a commentary on the struggles of the growing movement towards parliamentary government and national independence in Norway; intellectually, as a barometer of the influence of contemporary European thinkers such as Darwin, Mill and Brandes. He drew on past literary and oral tradition, particularly, in the case of these middle plays, on folklore and the folk ballads of the Germanic area. And he anticipated later developments, such as the Neo-Romanticism and Symbolism of the 1890s, the decadence of *fin-de-siècle* writing, the emphasis on the 'unconscious life of the soul' of the young Knut Hamsun, and especially, of course, Freudian psychoanalysis. It is no wonder that initial public and critical reaction to these plays was most often puzzlement or dismissal.

Rosmersholm (1886) stands at a crossroads in Ibsen's works. It exhibits a political awareness and a critical attitude towards socio-political thinking in Norway reminiscent of his earlier social dramas; and at the same time it is the first of a series of studies in modern psychology, in which all of the later plays show a marked interest.

Ibsen's involvement in Norwegian politics was rekindled by a visit to Norway in 1885, his first for eleven years. 1884 was an important year for the government of Norway; the election of the first Liberal administration under Johan Sverdrup signalled the advent of full parliamentarianism, and was a decisive step in weakening the power of the Swedish king and furthering Norway's struggle for independence in the union with Sweden. Ibsen's reactions to the new administration are recorded in a speech he made to a workers' procession in Trondheim on 14 June 1885, and they were not altogether positive:

> I have found that even the most necessary rights of the individual are still not as secure under the new regime as I felt I might hope and expect them to be. The majority of those in control do not permit the individual either freedom of faith or freedom of expression beyond a certain arbitrarily fixed limit. Much remains to be done here before we can be said to have achieved real freedom. But our democracy, as it now is, is hardly in a position to deal with these problems. An element of nobility must find its way into our public life, into our government, among our representatives and into our press. Of course I am not thinking of nobility of birth, nor of money, nor a nobility of learning, nor even of ability or talent. What I am thinking of is a nobility of character, of mind and of will. [*vi*, 445–7]

Thus far, Ibsen's words, composed at a time when the ideas for *Rosmersholm* were germinating in his mind – he began work on the play in December of that same year – could serve as a programme declaration for Rosmer himself. Favouring neither the old nor the new regime, represented by Kroll and Mortensgaard respectively, Rosmer has a vision of a third way:

the creation of an aristocracy of mind. A generation of 'happy, noble men' is what he will inspire [vi, 340]. But the next words from Ibsen's speech should give us pause; for the new nobility, he says, will come from two new directions, from 'two groups which so far have not suffered any irreparable damage under party pressure. It will come to us from our women and from our workers' [vi, 447].

Rosmer is not from a new unaffected group; quite the opposite. In fact, his words come to sound more and more hollow as the play progresses, and it becomes clear that he has indeed suffered irreparable damage. For Rosmer is a man weighed down with baggage from the past, in both a political and a personal sense. This prophet of the new age is the last scion of a dying stock, formerly employed as a priest, for the whole of his life a pillar of the conservative society, and, moreover, a personal coward. In the first words of the play we learn that he does not 'dare' to cross the footbridge on his way home [vi, 293–4]; and when he enters the scene, he postpones for as long as possible explaining his change of heart to his reactionary brother-in-law Kroll.

Rosmer is not strong enough to challenge the establishment on his own, and he is aware of that. He needs to enlist the support of one of Ibsen's 'undamaged' groups; and this indicates the importance of Rebecca to him. She will support him in his task and help him to communicate his ideas. Yet even with her help, it never begins to look like a practical proposition. Not only do Rosmer's ideas fail to carry any great conviction, they are also so vague as to be practically incoherent. They are based on notions of 'purity' which seem to include sexual abstinence (expressed in the Norwegian text as 'vor fælles tro på et rent samliv mellem mand og kvinde' [x, 396] – literally 'our joint belief in pure cohabitation between man and woman'). Here again, the personal becomes entangled with the political. The pan-Scandinavian 'sexual morality debate' was raging during this period, and advocates of chastity versus free love were reviling each other in the press and from the lectern.[3] Ibsen's great contemporary Bjørnson was a doughty champion of chastity for both men and women before marriage, as in his recent play A Gauntlet (1883). But advocates of chastity after marriage were few and not normally to be found among the male participants in the debate; Rosmer's insistence on this point, and Rebecca's acquiescence in it, are personally rather than politically motivated. Repression is synonymous with Rosmersholm, and we come gradually to realize that both characters are locked in mutual guilt.

Past crimes return to haunt their perpetrators with unerring appropriateness in Ibsen's plays, and never more so than here. The death of Rosmer's first wife Beata by suicide in the mill-race has left both feeling implicated; Rosmer at first somewhat obscurely, as he fears he may not have done enough to help his wife in her neurosis, and Rebecca more directly. For as she later confesses, she deliberately made Beata feel inadequate as a wife for not giving Rosmer children, made her suspicious that Rosmer cared more for her than for Beata, and finally hinted that she, Rebecca, would have to leave Rosmersholm because she was pregnant. When this emerges, Rosmer realizes the extent of his complicity, in that he made his preference for Rebecca obvious.

This much responsibility is acknowledged by both during the course of the play; yet there is in both cases another and deeper level of guilt which is never publicly and to some extent not even privately acknowledged. Although he admits to some complicity in Beata's death, Rosmer is not willing to explore his possible involvement in the causes of her illness. She was an unbalanced, unreasonable woman, neurotically obsessed with giving him a child and horrifying in her demands on him; she appalled him, he confides to Kroll, by 'her wild fits of sensual passion' [vi, 324]. But if he was obsessed with purity to the extent of not consummating his marriage or having ceased to sleep with her, then her childlessness may be his fault rather than hers and her 'wild passion' not a symptom of neurosis but a natural reaction from a strongly sexed woman; being made to feel that her sexuality is monstrous is more likely to have caused neurosis.

It is Rosmer's fate, it seems, to arouse a passion he cannot satisfy. For Rebecca admits to a similar feeling; when she first came to Rosmersholm, she was overwhelmed by 'a wild and uncontrollable passion' for Johannes Rosmer [vi, 369]. (In Norwegian, a different word is used in the two instances; Rosmer calls Beata's feeling *'lidenskabelighed'* (passion), whereas Rebecca, being more direct, uses the more direct word *'begær'* (sexual desire) [x, 377; 426].) Desire was the mainspring of her actions, of her resolve to supplant Beata and take over as mistress of Rosmersholm.

Yet when it seems, finally, that Rebecca has achieved her aims, when Rosmer asks her in Act II to become his wife, she refuses. Why should this be? The reasons, I think, are complex; it is the nub of the play.

Rebecca too conceals a deeper level of guilt than the acknowledged crime against Beata; and her guilt, like Rosmer's, is connected with sex, though in her case it is a sin of commission rather than omission. She has, as she delicately puts it, a past. She knows from the beginning of the action that she has been the mistress of her foster-father Dr West; through Kroll's agency she discovers later on that her foster-father was in fact her real father, and thus is guilty not just of immoral conduct – which, with her liberated views, might not have weighed too heavily on her – but of incest. In his essay on the play, Freud suggests that she is obscurely aware of this fact before Kroll spells it out to her, and that it has in fact helped to dictate her actions.[4] She has transferred her original Oedipus complex (supplanting her mother with her father/husband) to her new situation, supplanting Beata with a new father/husband figure. When the new father seems about to become a husband, old incest fears are reactivated, and block her initial impulse of delight, effectively paralysing her realization of what she most desires.

This is a convincing explanation, and given further plausibility by the context of the proposal scene; it follows immediately upon a scene where the two of them have been reminiscing about the quiet happiness of the old days, planning the creation of a society of noble men. Rosmer has confessed to Rebecca that he has now lost the one thing that makes life wonderful; and when she asks expectantly what that is – hoping presumably that he will say love – his reply is: 'Quiet, happy innocence' [vi, 340]. This is the one thing she cannot give him, and it makes her realize how far apart their aspirations are; at the same time it reminds her of the guilt she brings with her as well as what she has incurred in that house. It is not the best foundation for a coming together in mutual understanding.

There are yet more reverberations set up by this scene, however, which add a further dimension. Let us consider how the proposal is worded in the Oxford Ibsen version:

ROSMER   Then do you know what I think? Don't you? Don't you see how I can best rid myself of all those nagging memories ... from all the misery of the past?

REBECCA   Well?

ROSMER   By confronting it all with a new and living reality.

REBECCA   [feels for the back of the chair]. A living ...? What do you mean?

ROSMER   [comes closer]. Rebecca ... if I were to ask you ... will you be my wife?

REBECCA   [for a moment speechless, then gives a cry of joy]. Your wife! Your ... ! Me!

ROSMER   Good. Let us try. We two will be one. The space left here by the dead must remain empty no longer.

REBECCA   Me ... in Beata's place!

ROSMER   Then that puts her out of the picture. Right out. For good.

REBECCA   [in a soft, trembling voice]. Do you think so, Johannes?

ROSMER   It must do! It *must*. I will not go through life with a corpse on my back. Help me to throw it off, Rebecca. And let us stifle all memory in freedom, in joy, in passion. You shall be to me the only wife I ever had.

REBECCA   [masters herself]. Let us have no more talk of this. I will never be your wife.   [vi, 342]

In one detail only is this translation not entirely faithful to the original – but it is a significant detail. The actual wording of Rosmer's proposal is not the entirely conventional 'Will you be my wife?' but 'Vil du være min anden hustru?' [x, 396] – 'Will you be my *second* wife?' What kind of proposal is that? It is tactless to say the least; surely not even a man who has had several wives would choose that moment to remind his intended of her place in the list. With a playwright so conscious of every word, this insertion must be a pointer; and when one considers the rest of the conversation closely, it becomes apparent that a great deal more is said about the first wife than about the second. Rosmer's declaration is born not of love but of fear. He wants Rebecca not because he returns her desire but because she must pull the corpse off his back – though his appeal makes it clear that he is not entirely convinced that she can. He does finally offer her freedom, joy and passion ('*lidenskab*') – but these are desperate words from a desperate man, who cannot deliver on his promises. It must be dawning on Rebecca here that she would be 'in Beata's place' in more ways than one, that marriage to Rosmer could never fulfil her impossible dream. Thus her refusal contains not only an awareness of her own burden of guilt, which would prevent her from restoring to Rosmer his child-like innocence; it also contains a realization of his inadequacy – that what he is able to offer her is not marriage but an unremitting struggle with a ghost which will always 'cling to Rosmersholm' [vi, 294].

Why, one feels driven to ask, should a man like this, reliant on help from others and incapable of sexual passion, inspire precisely such passion in two sensuous women? To dismiss him as simply weak is to miss an aspect of his character which does indeed lie dormant for much of the play, but surfaces strongly towards the end. Ibsen's notes on the play from around the time he was composing the first draft can give a clue to this:

> She is an intriguer and she loves him. She wants to become his wife and she pursues that aim unswervingly. Then he becomes aware of this, and she openly admits it. Now there is no more joy in life for him. The demonic in him is roused by pain and bitterness. He determines to die, and she is to die with him. This she does. [vi, 445]

'The demonic' in Rosmer indicates a link with a tradition much older and much less civilized than the traditions of Rosmersholm, that of Nordic folklore and legend. During the nineteenth century, Norwegian researchers and authors rediscovered the oral folk tradition which had largely been forgotten during the centuries of Danish rule, and many of the old stories were recorded in written form for the first time. Ibsen's interest in them is documented in an essay from as early as 1857, entitled 'On the Heroic Ballad and its Significance for Literature' [*i*, 672–84]. Here he expresses his view that a poet needs to derive his material from the art of the people, to give literary life to what has fermented in the popular consciousness. The Danish poet Adam Oehlenschläger has shown what can be done with saga material, but the dramatist will find his best source in the heroic ballads, which originated in the Germanic tribes before they became separate nations.

It is well known that Ibsen drew on folk legend and popular mythology for material for his early plays, most famously in *Peer Gynt*.[5] What has been much less investigated until quite recently is his use of ballad material in the later plays.[6] In fact *Rosmersholm* marks a turning point in his writing in this respect too; with this play Ibsen returns to incorporating references to folk legend, and particularly to the ballads, in a way which provides important clues to characterization in all of his last seven plays.

The name Rosmer is significant. It was not the first name Ibsen chose for his protagonist; as often in his composition, he tried out other alternatives first: Boldt-Rømer and then Rosenhjelm. Both names have an unmistakably aristocratic ring, which Rosmer does not – but what it does contain is a direct reference to the ballad of 'Rosmer havmand', a troll/merman who lures a young maiden away from home and family, away from this world to his other-world kingdom. Although his conscious mind would not admit it, Rosmer has lured Rebecca – and lures her most dramatically at the end, away from a world in which their love cannot be realized. His old tutor Brendel plays a role in making this clear. Brendel is a caricatured *alter ego* of Rosmer; he goes out into the world attired in Rosmer's cast-off clothes to bring a message of redemption to the people, a message which turns out to be as hollow as Rosmer's notions of nobility are impractical. And it is Brendel who makes it clear to both Rebecca and Rosmer what he is really demanding of her: to cut off her finger and her ear, i.e. to sacrifice herself to preserve his belief. It is only after this that Rosmer allows his demonic nature to surface to the conscious level; in the last Act, the power balance swings over, as Rebecca loses the dominance she has had throughout.

Rebecca does not give up without a fight; she too has a demonic streak, which is clear from early on. She comes from the North, in Scandinavian folklore the home of magic, of trolls, of Lapp shamanism and ancient lore; '*nordlandsmystikken*', the mystery of the North, is a common feature in nineteenth-century Norwegian literature. She has a fascinating power which she has used not only to capture Rosmer but also to ensnare Beata, who became totally dependent on her. Brendel calls her 'my enchanting little mermaid' [*vi*, 375], and even the unsusceptible Kroll is moved to exclaim: 'Hvem kunde ikke De forhekse, – når De la' an på det?' [x, 409] – which translates as 'Who is there you couldn't bewitch ... if you tried?' [*vi*, 353] –

except that the Norwegian '*forhekse*' carries a stronger charge of witchcraft than the rather more everyday English 'bewitch'. It is a word used more than once about Rebecca, and which she uses about herself. There is even a suggestion, slight but as always with this author, not to be overlooked, that she is a shape-changer. When she is preparing to leave Rosmersholm, she asks for her 'brown sealskin trunk' [*vi*, 364], suggesting that she is a creature from another world, a seal maiden who has left her native element for a life on land with a mortal husband, and who cannot return to the sea without her seal skin.[7]

Ancient folklore and modern psychology come together in this play; indeed they are different ways of describing the same thing. Whether it is called demonic possession or sexual guilt and repression, a life together in this world has been rendered impossible for Rosmer and Rebecca. She has lost her powers, been 'ennobled' as she puts it, but her description makes it sound anything but positive: 'It is the Rosmer philosophy of life . . . that has *infected* my will . . . and made it *sick*. Made it a *slave* to laws that had meant nothing to me before . . .' [*vi*, 371; emphases mine]. She is a sea-creature dying on the land; she is a woman of passion for whom sex can no longer be disentangled from guilt and fear. Neither she nor Rosmer have fully acknowledged their past repressions, and as a result neither can resolve them and move on; the repressions therefore express themselves destructively, as each lures the other to the other world, into the water.

Water surrounds this play. It begins with Rosmer attempting, and failing, to cross the path over the mill-stream, and ends with the fall into those same waters, whose pull has been felt behind the whole of the action. Rosmer and Rebecca are both sea-creatures; she speaks near the end of her fear of being a 'sea-troll slumped over the ship that is to carry you forward' [*vi*, 379]. Many of the most dangerous spirits of Norwegian mythology are connected with the power of river, waterfall and sea; and nowhere in Ibsen's writings is this power more strongly felt than in his next play.

The writing of *The Lady from the Sea* (1888), like that of *Rosmersholm*, was preceded by a journey, this time to Denmark in the summer of 1887. The Ibsens stayed at Sæby on the coast of Jutland, where Henrik spent much time staring out to sea. Several contemporary comments indicate the extent to which the sea was occupying his thoughts; the Norwegians, he was to claim in 1888, 'are spiritually under the domination of the sea'.[8] His unusually extensive notes for the play were to a large extent a meditation on the sea, some of which has survived into the play itself. He was familiar with the writings of Darwin, whose *On the Origin of Species* (1859) and *The Descent of Man* (1871) had been translated into Danish by J. P. Jacobsen in

1871–3 and 1874 respectively, and pondered what would have happened if evolution had continued in the sea, rather than moving to the land. His original title for his next play was 'Havfruen', 'The Mermaid'; and indeed the final title, *Fruen fra havet*, is linguistically much closer to the mermaid idea than the English language, using different derivations for the two concepts, can achieve without contortion.

Ellida is presented from the start of this play as a creature from another world. The first words of the painter Ballested, painting a picture of a mermaid, link the motif explicitly to her: 'She has strayed in from the sea and can't find her way out again. So here she lies dying in the brackish water' [*vii*, 30]. When she comes in, her appearance confirms the comparison; she comes straight from bathing, her wet hair hanging loose about her, complaining about the 'sick' water of the fjords. In a quite literal way she comes from the sea; she grew up as the daughter of a lighthouse keeper right out by the open sea, and she even bears a 'heathen' ship's name rather than a 'decent Christian' one [*vii*, 41]. The sea represents all she has lost; it has become an obsession which dominates her consciousness. This is the only one of Ibsen's late plays, with the exception of the final *When We Dead Awaken*, which takes place entirely outside – a contrast to the enclosed living-rooms of *Rosmersholm* and *Hedda Gabler*. Yet even this is of no help to Ellida, for whom the very outdoors in this place represents confinement.

This fey creature, at the beginning of the play, is in the most prosaic of situations; she is at the centre of a domestic scene, imported into a ready-made family. She has become a 'second wife' in a family still full of memories of the first. Although not a direct threat like Beata was, the dead wife is still a barrier, particularly between her and the two daughters, Bolette and Hilde. Their reluctance to give her a mother's place combines with her unwillingness to be integrated into the family to underscore her outsider position. And her husband, Dr Wangel, has accepted the situation; he moves between the two halves of his family – literally, as the girls always sit on the verandah and Ellida in the summer house – and makes no determined effort to bring them together. This is in part because he does not really want to; he is fascinated by the otherness of Ellida, and content for it to remain, until he realizes that the situation is critical.

The situation has in fact become critical when the play opens. Ever since Ellida lost her baby a couple of years earlier, she has shut herself off from Wangel, refusing to make love and yearning to be away by the sea, at the same time as showing a nervous dependence on him: she hurries over to seize his hands when she first enters, and is agitated by his absences throughout the play. Wangel, one of the least egotistic of Ibsen's husbands, has tried inviting her old friend Arnholm for a visit, believing him to be a former suitor who might revive her spirits, and even suggests moving out to the sea with her, which would mean abandoning his profession. Her refusal of this offer is the clearest indication that her yearning for the sea is a symptom of her distress rather than the real cause: 'I won't have you making yourself unhappy on my account. Especially as it wouldn't do us any good' [vii, 60].

The crisis comes to a head with the arrival of the Stranger, an enigmatic figure whose presence is heralded by several conversations about him. The sculptor Lyngstrand first mentions him as a man he had met at sea, and who swore to avenge himself on his faithless fiancée who had married another man. He subsequently, according to Lyngstrand, perished in a shipwreck. Ellida then tells Wangel about him. He was the mysterious lover who had married them both to the sea, and who has ever since been her spiritual husband; her marriage to Wangel has felt like a betrayal from the start, as spiritually she is possessed by the Stranger. She even fears that he was physically the father of her child, as the baby had his eyes. That was why it could not live, and that is why she dare not conceive again.

When the Stranger actually appears, his appearance comes at first as something of an anticlimax. This is no ghost, returned dripping from a watery grave, but a most substantial man, dressed in travelling clothes, with bushy red hair and a beard [vii, 76]. He is visible to Wangel as well as to Ellida; and the latter even fails to recognize him at first despite having thought about him day and night. The same is true of him as of the sea; it is not the man himself but what he stands for in Ellida's mind that matters. He is the focus of her longing for what life cannot offer her.

Ellida has married Wangel without loving him; he was an older man who was attracted by this young girl, and she had no prospects in life. As she sees it now, he bought her: 'The plain truth is . . . that you came out there . . . and bought me. . . . And I, for my part . . . there I stood, helpless, bewildered, and quite alone. It wasn't really surprising that I accepted . . . when you came along and offered to . . . provide for me for the rest of my life' [vii, 98]. In a way reminiscent of Nora in A Doll's House, she has been an acquisition 'looked after in your house' [vii, 99]. She has grown genuinely fond of Wangel, but at the same time increasingly aware of what he cannot offer her: the reckless passion which laughs at society's laws and conventions, the white heat of sexual desire which melts her willpower and has nothing to do with the settled domesticity of life in the village. This is what the Stranger had offered her and she had taken, and what she thought she had rejected when he left; but it resurfaces when the attempt to deny that part of herself breaks down. She is not like the tame carp in the fishpond, content because they have no knowledge of life in the great open sea; once aroused, her senses crave the excitement she briefly tasted.

In this play too, Ibsen has drawn on folk belief and legend, which carry much intuitive knowledge of intoxication and possession. It was established at the beginning of the play that Ellida belongs to a different world; and it is a world she shares with the Stranger. The whole play this time takes place in Northern Norway, with its brief hectic summers and isolated winters. Ellida belongs to the wilder shores of this land, and the Stranger comes from even further north. At the start his origins are mysterious; Lyngstrand calls him 'the American', associating him with 'the free world' in the era of emigration, and his name seems to be Johnston. Later we learn from Ellida that his original name was, significantly, Freeman, and that he came from the northernmost part of Norway, Finnmark, and had actually been born in Finland. This makes him a '*kvæn*', a Finnish immigrant; the name carries untranslatable connotations both of mysterious foreignness and of suspicious unreliability. He possesses the demonic powers associated with the far North, and can cast spells on things and people. His declaration about Ellida when he discovers her faithlessness has the incantatory ring of a Lappish curse: 'Men min er hun og min skal hun bli'. Og mig skal hun følge, om jeg så skal komme hjem og hente hende som en druknet mand fra svarte sjøen'[XI, 74] (literally translated: 'But mine she is, and mine she shall be. And me she shall follow, if I have to come home and collect her as a drowned man from the black sea').

As a rural community heavily dependent on the sea, it is not surprising that Norway has many legends of drowned sailors returning to haunt the living.[9] Lyngstrand's image of a drowned man standing over his sleeping wife who has been unfaithful is based on one such legend, and the belief that a revenant can actually father a child is another. In another sense, the Stranger is a merman, is even the sea itself. His eyes, like the baby's, change with the sea. Ellida has been enticed by this sea creature as is the maiden in the eighteenth-century ballad of 'Agnete og Havmanden' (Agnete and the Merman), and in the play based on that ballad by Hans Christian Andersen, *Agnete og Havmanden* (1833), to which Ibsen's play bears many resemblances.[10] Another story of Andersen's with which comparison is clearly invited is his *Den lille Havfrue* (The Little Mermaid, 1837), in which the mermaid chooses life on land at great sacrifice to herself and without ever finding a home in her new environment.

To associate Ellida's longing for the sea not just with demonic possession or with a mythical 'first home' but directly with her sexuality – which Ibsen clearly does, if not so explicitly as outlined above – is of course to invite a Freudian interpretation of the play, to which psychologically minded critics have eagerly responded.[11] This interpretation sees the play as a study of neurosis. Ellida is ill – is, indeed, in a state bordering on hysteria – because she is repressing a part of herself. Her dreams of the Stranger are a fantastical embodiment of what is excluded from her life with the family. Wangel has never asked for her love, only for her consent. Faced with the Stranger, he at first thinks to assert his authority and continue making the decisions for her, ignoring the fact that what makes the greatest impression on Ellida is the Stranger's assertion that she should come with him 'frivillig' – 'of her own free will' – a phrase which she repeats like a mantra four times in the next two minutes [*vii*, 80–1].

Wangel is, for obvious reasons, not a man who has had any training in psychoanalysis, but he is a caring doctor, used to examining his patients carefully and studying their symptoms. He is also a wise man who loves his wife, and sees that his attempts to protect her are pushing her further into madness; if he keeps her apart from the Stranger it will be at the cost of her sanity. The only thing he can do is to give her the freedom to leave, as he truly believes she will. But freedom, as we have seen, is the key; now that Ellida for the first time has a really free choice, she can also choose not to go. And that is what she does choose; the Stranger loses his hypnotic power over her mind, and her marriage to Wangel becomes a mutual bond rather than a one-sided guardianship.

Seen in this way, the play becomes a study of a crisis happily resolved, of a neurosis cured. Yet such a neat summing-up leaves too many questions unanswered. For it is undeniable that not only Ellida but also Wangel has lost something in the process. He admits to Arnholm in Act IV that he knows he should have helped her earlier to analyse her own feelings, but deliberately refrained, because 'I wanted her as she was' [*vii*, 92]; and in the last Act, she tells him that there is nothing to hold her in his house, because she has not put down any roots, and 'you were the one . . . and you alone . . . who wanted it that way' [*vii*, 108]. It was her feyness, her dreaminess, her elusiveness, that attracted him, and that will now be lost. For her too, the choice means a loss. She will now have a home in his house, ties to his children and a more equal partnership; but he will never be a passionate lover, and she will never feel the wildness in her blood again – the Stranger has departed forever. There must be some part of most women that would like her to have gone with the Stranger.

The other characters surrounding these three main combatants have their own comments to make on the action, and, as often in Ibsen's plays, provide by their actions a comically larger-than-life reflection or a grim underlining of the consequences of following a certain course. They are never there just as confidants or extras. Ballested provides an amusing running commentary on the importance of acclimatizing oneself to new surroundings, and at the same time displays a rather pathetic lack of commitment to anything. Lyngstrand's male chauvinist comments on the importance of a wife modelling herself on her husband – no doubt funnier now than they were in 1888 – throw into relief the extraordinary progressiveness of Wangel in releasing his wife from her vows. There is a whole intrigue around the relationships between Lyngstrand and Arnholm on the one hand and Hilde and Bolette on the other, ranging from calculated flirtatiousness to genuine solicitude, in which both gentlemen completely misinterpret the signals. Again, Wangel seems much less obtuse by comparison.

The sub-plot which most nearly mirrors the main intrigue, however, is the one involving Arnholm and Bolette. Arnholm has come to find a wife, in the mistaken belief that Bolette has formed a romantic attachment to him; and even when he discovers his mistake, he still persists. Her eventual agreement to marry him has ominous overtones of the 'trade agreement' between Ellida and Wangel years before. She, like Ellida, has no prospects if she stays at home, and he is effectively buying her with a promise to take her abroad to see the world. The deal is put in crass terms: her instinctive reaction to his proposal is to recoil 'in horror' [*vii*, 112], after which he loses no time in telling her that her fate will otherwise be to let life pass her by, be left alone and helpless when her father dies and then perhaps be forced to marry anyway, just to stay alive. (In a recent Oslo production of the play this message was driven home by having Arnholm actually strip her at the end of the scene, to look at what he had just bought – which is surely to sacrifice credibility to explicitness, but the implication is nevertheless there.) Apart from the fact that this relationship threatens to lead to a crisis in the future not dissimilar to the one at the centre of the play, the most depressing thing about it in terms of the present action is that Wangel seems prepared to let it happen. What he has learnt about his wife's needs does not make him any more sensitive to those of his daughters, for both of whom catching the right man seems the only way out.

Thus to see *The Lady from the Sea* as the one late play by Ibsen with a happy ending is to paper over rather a lot of cracks. It does not end in death, as most of the others do, and compared with the endings of *Rosmersholm* and *Hedda Gabler*, it presents us with at least a workable compromise. But a compromise it is, a renunciation of passion in favour of affection. Taken as a whole, it does not go very far towards providing a corrective to the bleak portraits of marriage of Ibsen's other mature plays.

In the opening scenes of *Hedda Gabler* (1890), we are presented with a bleak marriage but recently begun, between two of the most incompatible characters in Ibsen's entire *œuvre*. It takes only a few minutes for the extent of that incompatibility to be made clear.

As we wait for the appearance of Rosmer in *Rosmersholm* and Ellida in *The Lady from the Sea*, so we wait for that of Hedda in this play. And here as in the earlier two plays, much of the conversation circles around the imminent arrival. It is a technique of which Ibsen is by now past master, to give us necessary information and build up expectation whilst at the same time indicating latent tensions. Rosmer's avoidance of the footbridge and Ellida's nervousness are obvious causes for concern. In *Hedda Gabler*, however, the tensions lie more deeply buried, and the conversations between Berthe and Miss Tesman and between the latter and Jørgen Tesman indicate first and foremost satisfaction: Jørgen has every prospect of becoming a professor, has triumphed over his previous rival Eilert Løvborg, has bought the house of his dreams, and best of all, has just returned from his honeymoon with 'the lovely Hedda Gabler' [*vii*, 175]. The indications of stress are but slight, in Berthe's worry that she won't suit her 'particular' new mistress, in some unease about money and in a lack of consideration on Hedda's part in preferring to bring her cases home rather than give Miss Tesman a lift. So slight are the indications indeed that it is not unusual in modern performances for a glimpse to be shown of Hedda *before* Ibsen's text starts, to give the conversations more resonance, for example in Ingmar Bergman's London production in 1970, or in the 1991 Dublin production: 'We first see this Hedda, in fact, in a pre-textual scene prowling round the drawing-room in darkness, possibly after sex with Tesman, in a state of sighing desperation.'[12]

When Hedda enters in the play proper, however, it does not take long for the tensions to surface. She makes it clear that she is not at all pleased to see Miss Tesman so early in the morning, she has not slept well, and she has any number of complaints about her surroundings: too much sun, too many flowers, wrong furniture. She is soon gratuitously rude to the aunt, and her tone to Tesman suggests that she can but barely tolerate him. No-one and nothing in the domestic arrangements suits her, whereas they all suit each other very well, as Ibsen underlines in a letter about the casting: 'Jørgen Tesman, his old aunts, and the elderly serving-maid Berthe together form a whole and a unity. They have a common way of thinking; common memories, and a common attitude to life. For Hedda they appear as an inimical and alien power directed against her fundamental nature' [*vii*, 505].

How, then, has this unlikely match come about? From Tesman's side it is not difficult to grasp; Hedda was a fêted beauty, with an elegance and refinement which made her seem like a being from a higher sphere; he can hardly believe his luck in carrying her off. He is not observant enough to have seen the dangerous undercurrents. She could see advantages in the marriage too; she had been left after her father's death with little to live on and an awareness that she was rapidly passing through 'marriageable age'. Tesman had prospects, could offer her a status and possessions that she could no longer maintain on her own; a footman and riding horse were part of the agreement. For Hedda, however, disillusion has set in quickly. She has sold herself too cheap, and discovered a life of such sheer banality and stifling domesticity with Jørgen and his embroidered slippers that not even the prospects can make it bearable. In any case, they look increasingly fragile as it becomes evident that promotion is by no means assured.

It may seem strange to describe Hedda in the introduction to this essay as a passionate woman. When she enters in Act I and for most of the play, her appearance and her manner exude coldness. In the stage directions her eyes are described as 'steel grey, and cold, clear, and dispassionate' [*vii*, 179], and in later directions indicating her tone of voice, words like 'cold' and 'collected' ('*behersket*' – really closer to 'controlled') frequently recur. She cannot bear to be touched, and hates any suggestion of intimacy, verbal or physical. Symptomatic of this need to keep everyone at a distance is the fact that she cannot bring herself to use the familiar term of address, '*du*', to Miss Tesman, refuses to continue talking to Løvborg if he uses it, and addresses her husband by his surname, except when she needs to appeal to his affection in order to manipulate him. There are even suggestions of sexual frigidity; she is physically revolted by her unborn child and by its father, and refuses the offer of sex from men whom she otherwise obviously finds attractive, Brack and Løvborg.

Yet there are many indications that Hedda's behaviour is dictated by a control imposed by a relentless effort of will. For most of the time the lid is kept on tight, but just below the surface is boiling rage and frustration, and occasionally the pressure erupts in a snarling insult or a sardonic laugh. It can be seen more directly the first time she is left on stage on her own, when she 'walks about the room, raises her arms and clenches her fists as though in a frenzy' [*vii*, 183]. And although she may not take a lover, she clearly carries a potent sexual charge; all the men who come near her lust after her. Although it is less fully developed in this play than in the previous two, there is a suggestion here too that she is a creature from another world, with the power to entice and bewitch. In a letter about the play, Ibsen draws attention to 'the demonic aspect of the character' [*vii*, 502]. She has been associated with a 'pagan priestess' officiating at a Dionysiac rite; her reiterated vision of a triumphant Løvborg with 'vineleaves in his hair' is one of several references in the play to Bacchanalian revels.[13] Closer to home, she has been compared to a free Viking spirit, related to the indomitable Hjørdis of

The Vikings at Helgeland (1858), and also to a '*hulder*', a beautiful and seductive maiden from Scandinavian folklore who lures men into the forest – but when she turns round, reveals a cow's tail hanging down behind.[14]

The cause of Hedda's frustration – put in more modern psychological terms – is not the facts of sexuality but the fact of being a woman, with all that implied at that time both physically and socially in terms of submission and dependence. She wants to be on top; or as Ibsen put it: 'She really wants to live the whole life of a *man*' [*vii*, 488]. She is a girl who has been brought up by her father, and brought up, it seems, in a manner more befitting a boy than a girl; there is no mention of her mother. The portrait of her father watches over her throughout the play, and she is still known as Hedda Gabler rather than Hedda Tesman. She has an insatiable curiosity for aspects of life that a young girl 'isn't supposed to know anything about' [*vii*, 223], and absolutely no vocation for those aspects that she is supposed to know something about. She glories in flirting with both Brack and Løvborg – so long as she has the upper hand. The moment either of them threatens to make love to her, to remind her physically that she is a woman, she panics – and reaches for her pistols.

The fact that Hedda Gabler's pistols are a Freudian phallic symbol seems so obvious in 1990 that Ibsen's genius in inventing them in 1890 can all too easily be forgotten. That they are in her possession is perfectly well motivated on a realistic level; they are the one thing the general left to her. They console her for everything she lacks in her present existence. Symbolically, they supply her with her defence against male invasion; with them, she has a strength – and a power to shock – not available to most women. They keep Løvborg at a distance, and deter Brack – though significantly, not for long. The latter takes her pistol from her after she fires at him as he will ultimately take from her the last vestiges of her self-determination.

Yet despite all her wishes to deny her womanhood, Hedda cannot actually be a man. Not only her body but also her mind betrays her; she has internalized the repressions of her society, and her exaggerated fear of scandal renders her incapable of defying public opinion. All she can do is to achieve her aims vicariously. Tesman has shown himself to be too lightweight to carry the burden of her ambitions, so she turns to Løvborg. This is why the competition with Thea becomes so fierce; Løvborg is to realize Hedda's dreams, and she cannot bear the thought that silly little Thea has inspired him. She is jealous of the new book, and when Løvborg suggests that the book is the child of his union with Thea, her hatred of it is intensified by and intensifies her hatred of the unwanted child she is carrying. As she burns the book at the end of Act III, she is no longer sure whether it is the book or the child she is destroying: 'Nu brænder jeg dit barn, Thea! –

Du med krushåret! ... Dit og Ejlert Løvborgs barn. ... Nu brænder, – nu brænder jeg barnet' [XI, 375]. ('Now I'm burning your child, Thea! You with the curly hair! Your and Eilert Løvborg's child. Now I'm burning ... I'm burning the child.' My translation; the Oxford Ibsen renders the last sentence as 'I'm burning *your* child' [*vii*, 250], which obscures the fact that Hedda is not just talking about Thea's child but widening the reference to include her own.) Ironically, she not only fails to inspire Løvborg either to live or to die in accordance with her ideals, but even loses the despised Tesman at the end to the influence of a woman she thought she could twist round her little finger.

By the end of the play, all her outlets are sealed off. Løvborg is gone, the baby is coming, and Tesman is gravitating towards Thea, who will fit effortlessly into the cosy group with Miss Tesman and Berthe. Only Brack is still drawn to her, but the playful badinage of their earlier relationship has been transformed into a sexual blackmail which he makes brutally clear he will exploit to the hilt. Mother and mistress are the roles left to her, roles with no power in the world that interests her. Geographically she is squeezed off the stage, and all that is left to her is one pistol. The one act of defiance she can perform is an act of self-destruction, a pitiful parody of the glorious self-assertion of which she had dreamed.

At the same time as Ibsen was writing *Hedda Gabler*, Jonas Lie, another of the 'four greats' of Norwegian literature's Golden Age, was composing a book of tales entitled *Trolls* (1891). In the introduction, he explained what he understood by that word: 'That there are trolls in people is understood by anyone who has an eye for such things ... Troll magic lives ... within people in the form of temperament, natural will, explosiveness ... And how far this troll stage follows mankind further into civilized society, would be a useful and instructive study, possibly also a somewhat surprising one.'[15] Like Ibsen, Lie was aware that trolls and the like were not just decorative national symbols but an expression of an intuitive understanding of the forces that determine people's actions and cannot be explained in terms of logic and rationality, the forces that are hidden away from the daylight. What Ibsen is doing in the plays I have looked at could be defined as an investigation of the way in which 'the troll stage' has followed mankind into civilized society. His central characters are driven to the brink of self-destruction, and sometimes beyond, by conflicts between conscious and sub-conscious drives. In a post-Freudian age a different vocabulary is available to explain the process, but it does no more than provide a rational theory to demonstrate what is already embodied in the folklore.

As contemporary reception indicates, however, Ibsen's mixture of folkloric theme and psychological insight was not readily appreciated – although *The Lady from the Sea* did have a more positive reception in Norway, where 'it was felt to make a special appeal to the Norwegian temperament' [*vii*, 471] than in Denmark, where Georg Brandes, who had hoped for more plays from Ibsen taking issue with contemporary social problems, disliked it. *Rosmersholm* had very few performances in Norway, and was reviled by the British press when it was produced at the Vaudeville Theatre in 1891 [*vi*, 449–50]. *Hedda Gabler* was obscure and difficult, and early performances provoked laughter in all the wrong places [*vii*, 505–7].

In retrospect, it seems extraordinary that even those critics whom one might expect to be sensitive to the psychological nuances of the plays were slow to appreciate them. Knut Hamsun is a case in point. His declared aim in his Christiania lectures in 1891, which Ibsen attended, was to herald a new way of writing, a modern psychological literature in which types were to give way to characters governed by contradictory impulse and divided motivation. Yet he could not see the merit of Ibsen's latest plays, castigating him as a bad psychologist. Rosmer was a type, who represented nobility and nothing else, and *The Lady from the Sea* was 'a book for Germans'(!), so obscure that he could make no sense of it at all.[16]

A recent study of the Norwegian reception of *Hedda Gabler*, however, argues that it was the male critics, who dominated in the press, who dismissed Ibsen's plays of this period, whereas several female critics showed a more ready appreciation: 'Ibsen was ahead of his time in terms of dramatic technique and psychological understanding. In my opinion, the same can be said of the female critics when it comes to analytical understanding of the link between the female psyche and the repressive mechanisms of their society.'[17] In a society which had given rise to Camilla Collett's and Amalie Skram's novels, investigating the sufferings of girls for whom marriage, often not of their choice, was the only available vocation, the dilemmas confronted by Ibsen's female characters were immediately recognizable.

NOTES

1 Elizabeth Robins, *Ibsen and the Actress* (1928; New York, 1973), p. 55.
2 E.g. Ibsen's speech to the Women's Rights League, 26 May 1898 [*v*, 456].
3 For a summary of this debate, see Elias Bredsdorff, 'Moralists versus Immoralists: The Great Battle in Scandinavian Literature in the 1880s.' *Scandinavica*, 8 (1969), 91–111.
4 Sigmund Freud, 'Some Character-Types Met with in Psycho-Analytic Work' (1916). Reprinted in James McFarlane (ed.), *Henrik Ibsen*, Penguin Critical Anthologies (Harmondsworth, 1970), pp. 392–9.
5 See e.g. Henning K. Sehmsdorf, 'The Romantic Heritage: Ibsen and the Uses of

Folklore', in Oscar Bandle et al. (eds.), *Nordische Romantik*, Beiträge zur nord-ischen Philologie vol. XIX (Basel and Frankfurt, 1991), pp. 160–5.

6 See Per Schelde Jacobsen and Barbara Fass Leavy, *Ibsen's Forsaken Merman. Folklore in the Late Plays* (New York and London, 1988).

7 See Jacobsen and Leavy, *Ibsen's Forsaken Merman*, Part I.

8 See Michael Meyer, *Henrik Ibsen* (Harmondsworth, 1971), pp. 598–605.

9 See e.g. Reimund Kvideland and Henning Sehmsdorf (eds.), *Scandinavian Folk Belief and Legend* (Oslo, 1988).

10 Jacobsen and Leavy, *Ibsen's Forsaken Merman*, p. 135.

11 See e.g. Lou Andreas-Salomé, *Henrik Ibsens Frauen-Gestalten* (Jena, 1892); M. Esther Harding, *Women's Mysteries* (New York, 1935); P. Lionel Goitein: 'The Lady from the Sea', *Psychoanalytic Review*, 14 (1927), 375–419. See also Barbara Fass Leavy, 'Ellida as Seal Maiden', in Jacobsen and Leavy, *Ibsen's Forsaken Merman*, pp.196–210.

12 Michael Billington's review in *The Guardian*, 5 September 1991. See also the chapter 'Messenger from a Closed Country: *Hedda Gabler*', in Frederick J. Marker and Lise-Lone Marker, *Ibsen's Lively Art. A Performance Study of the Major Plays* (Cambridge, 1989).

13 See James McFarlane's essay on the play [*vii*, 14].

14 Jacobsen and Leavy, *Ibsen's Forsaken Merman*, pp. 136–41, and especially chapter 7: 'Hedda Gabler and the Huldre.'

15 Jonas Lie, *Trold. Samlede verker* vol. IV (Oslo 1975), p. 3.

16 Knut Hamsun, *Paa Turné* (Oslo, 1971), pp. 33–7.

17 Kari Fjørtoft, *'Hedda Gabler' i samtid og ettertid* (Oslo, 1986), p. 120.

Other sources relevant to this chapter include

Bredsdorff, Elias, *Den store nordiske krig om seksualmoralen* (Copenhagen, 1974).

Engelstad, Fredrik, '*Rosmersholm* – et forvekslingsdrama om skyldfølelse', in Irene Engelstad (ed.), *Skriften mellom linjene* (Oslo, 1985).

Finney, Gail, *Women in Modern Drama. Freud, Feminism, and European Theater at the Turn of the Century* (Ithaca and London, 1989).

Hageberg, Otto, *Frå Camilla Collett til Dag Solstad* (Oslo, 1980).

Harding, M. Esther, *Women's Mysteries: Ancient and Modern: A Psychological Interpretation of the Feminine Principle as Portrayed in Myth, Story, and Dreams* (New York, 1935).

Høst, Else, *'Hedda Gabler.' En monografi* (Oslo, 1958).

Kvideland, Reimund and Henning K. Sehmsdorf (eds.), *Scandinavian Folk Belief and Legend* (Minnesota, 1988).

Lyons, Charles R., *'Hedda Gabler.' Gender, Role and World* (Boston, 1991).

Nissen, Ingjald, *'Vildanden'* – *'Rosmersholm'* – *'Hedda Gabler'* (Oslo, 1973).

Østerud, Erik, *Det borgerlige subjekt. Ibsen i teorihistorisk belysning* (Oslo 1981).

8

INGA-STINA EWBANK

The last plays

Never had I more
Excited, passionate, fantastical
Imagination, nor an ear and eye
That more expected the impossible
(W. B. Yeats, 'The Tower')

'I have to keep working – creating one work after another – until the day I die.'[1] When Ibsen gave these words to Arnold Rubek, to define what it means being an artist, he did not know, nor intend, that *When We Dead Awaken* was to be his last play – the Epilogue to the whole long row of 'one work after another' created over fifty years.[2] To us the irony is twofold: Rubek is to die that very night, in his attempt to awaken, as a man and as an artist, from the 'dead'; Ibsen was to become too ill or frail to keep working until the day he died. For all that, Rubek's words may serve as a paradigm of the extraordinary drive which was an essential part of Ibsen's creativity, which had resulted in a regular output of 'contemporary' plays from *Pillars of Society* (1877) onwards, and which did not slacken when he returned to live in Norway in 1891, there to produce that series of plays which he somewhat grudgingly admitted to having had in mind when he used the term 'A Dramatic Epilogue': *The Master Builder* (1892), *Little Eyolf* (1894), *John Gabriel Borkman* (1896) and *When We Dead Awaken* (1899).

This chapter is written in the conviction that, as with Yeats in the poem quoted above, 'decrepit age' – or, as Henry James put it when reviewing *John Gabriel Borkman* in 1897, 'his extreme maturity'[3] – did not mean a falling-off of Ibsen's imagination. In creating figures like the protagonists of these late plays (all of whom expect 'the impossible'), let alone in creating the kinds of plays that could hold them, that imagination had never been more 'excited, passionate, fantastical'. Nor – as evidenced by the contemporary reception of the plays and the continuing critical debate about them – had he more expected the almost impossible of his readers and audiences. Are we to see these works as realistic, or symbolical, or mythical – or even, as Archer saw *When We Dead Awaken*, as 'self-caricature'?[4] Are we to understand them as pre-Freudian studies of psychopathological cases or as post-Hegelian, post-Nietzschean dramatizations of the consciousness of man?

The aim of this chapter is not to give categorical answers to such questions but rather to show why they come to be asked in the first place. Seen 'one after another', each of the late plays has its own concerns and uses its own particular means to exercise the 'spell' which Henry James, for one, found himself under when watching any Ibsen play: 'the surrender of the imagination to his microcosm, his confined but completely constituted world'.[5] But the four plays also clearly have thematic concerns and formal and stylistic features in common. In their preoccupations – with the alienated artist, with the a-morality of the creative impulse, with strange and mysterious areas of human consciousness – and in their challenge to the conventions of realistic, bourgeois theatre, they are very much of their time, products of a decade in European literary and dramatic history which saw the flourishing of Symbolist theatre and the beginnings of Modernism. But the very same qualities also make them characteristically the product of their self-conscious, ever-developing author, who in any case at this stage of his career was influencing, as much as being influenced by, developments in European literature and theatre. Hence, I propose to discuss them mainly in relation to his own work as a whole rather than to external models, and to begin from the context of the more macrocosmic – or group – features of the plays, to end with a brief study of the dramatic art of each microcosm.

A purely formal approach to these plays would hardly be fruitful. Each by itself and all together the plays point to Ibsen sitting in judgment over himself, questioning the nature, the value and the cost of his commitment to his art. In the immediately preceding plays a row of female protagonists – Rebecca West, Ellida Wangel and Hedda Gabler – had, each in her way, been searching for freedom and self-fulfilment. There are powerfully realized women in the late plays, too; but, with the exception of Hilde Wangel, they are in various ways presented as the victims of the egocentric drive of male protagonists: a builder, a (would-be) moral philosopher, a financier and a sculptor. Each of these – Solness, Allmers, Borkman and Rubek – is driven by a 'calling' which is at odds with 'life', in the sense of viable human relationships and domestic happiness. Two recurring verbs – *skape* ('create') and *bruke*, with the cognate noun *bruk* (English verb and noun, 'use') – point the tension between the man whose self-perceived 'calling' is to create and the woman whose love he uses as enablement, because of her influence, or her money or her perfect body – and uses at the expense of her own creativity.

In many ways this is well-known Ibsen territory: a return to central themes of vocation and the sacrifices it demands and to the problems of the aesthetic versus the ethical life. Without minimizing the complexity of the later protagonists, the 'I' of the early poem 'On the Heights' is a forerunner of a Solness, an Allmers, a Rubek, even a Borkman. So is Brand, who pursues his calling uncompromisingly, at the cost of the lives of his child and his wife, through to his death high up the mountain, in an avalanche. Brand is a priest, though Ibsen said that he could just as well have been a sculptor, or a politician.[6] 'Life's the real work of art', Brand tells Einar, the painter. In *When We Dead Awaken* Rubek, who is a sculptor, dies in the same manner as Brand, but in the pursuit of the 'life' he has betrayed for 'art'; the 'child' he sacrificed is a piece of sculpture which he has deconstructed; and the 'death' of Irene, the 'mother' of that child, is of the soul.

There are, of course, compelling reasons to see such internalizing of the symbolism in autobiographical terms. Rubek, who returns to his own country but finds himself in a spiritual no man's land, is as *déraciné* as Ibsen must have felt when, speaking with the voice of many a nineteenth-century cultural exile, he lamented to Georg Brandes in 1897 that he had only a 'native', not a 'home', country.[7] Rubek is internationally famous (though aware of the hollowness of fame), as Ibsen had become by the 1890s: published, translated, performed – and written about – all over Europe as no Norwegian had ever been. And Rubek is the object of the most devastating criticism of 'the poet' (*'dikter'*) delivered in any Ibsen play, as Irene turns on him:

IRENE   [*hard and cold*]   Poet!
RUBEK   Why poet?
IRENE   Because you are soft and spineless and full of excuses for everything
          you've ever done or thought. You killed my soul – and then you go
          and model yourself as a figure of regret and remorse and penitence
          . . .   [*viii, 279*]

Rubek's response is a defiant, or obtuse, refusal to recognize the point of Irene's accusation: 'I am an artist, Irene . . . I was born to be an artist. And I'll never be anything other than an artist.' Ibsen could hardly have undercut his own position more deeply. In the words of James McFarlane, *When We Dead Awaken* 'pronounces upon the author a meta-judgment of extreme severity'.[8]

Is Ibsen then to be identified with Rubek any more than with Brand? Can we understand Solness's paranoic fear of 'youth' only as an echo of Knut Hamsun's attack on Ibsen as a representative of the older generation of writers? And, to take just a few more examples from traditional biographical readings of the last plays, are Ibsen's more or less intense friendships with young women in the late 1880s and the 1890s the 'key' to Hilde Wangel and her impact on the Master Builder; and are the churches, homes and castles in the air which make up Solness's past, present and prospective building programme, to be seen as allegorical references to Ibsen's early, middle and late plays?

The answer to such questions is surely that Ibsen is a writer of dramatic fictions in which autobiography fits where it touches. Sometimes it touches very deeply, but rarely (as I hope the rest of this chapter will demonstrate) at the expense of what James called 'the completely constituted world' of the fiction. Ibsen liked to stress that everything he had written was 'lived through' ('*gjennemlevet*'), but he was also as insistent as T. S. Eliot on the separation between 'the man who suffers and the mind which creates'.[9] The ruthlessness which is one aspect of such a separation is of course one of many things that the last plays, and in particular *When We Dead Awaken*, are about. And in the man who, like Rubek, 'was born to be an artist', the very knowledge that an experience will be used, turned into art, is bound to affect the experience itself. Thus, when Ibsen writes to Emilie Bardach that he is 're-living again and again – and yet again' his experiences with her, and that he finds it impossible as yet ('*vorläufig*') to translate these into art ('*Dichtung*'),[10] then we need not be professed deconstructionists to point out that the verb he uses for the translation process is '*umzudichten*': the '*um*' carrying the suggestion that the experience itself was a kind of '*Dichtung*' – the meta-judgment in this case probably unintentional.

When the plays written after 1891 examine the artist in his relationships with other human beings, this is in keeping with the increasingly self-reflexive temper of European literature in the 1890s. 1891 was also the year of, for example, the publication in book form of *The Picture of Dorian Gray*. In the literature around 1900, writers like Hauptmann, Hofmannsthal and Thomas Mann were exploring the conflict between life and work. But very likely it is also *partly* because a homecoming after twenty-seven years of voluntary exile meant an acute confrontation between earlier and present selves. Equally likely, if the examination is particularly rigorously conducted in *When We Dead Awaken*, this is partly because, in preparing a collected edition of his works in 1898, Ibsen had to re-read them all, presumably 'one after another'. One result was the revival of a long-abandoned idea of writing an autobiography: 'a book that will link my life and my authorship together into an illuminating whole'.[11] Another was the well-known preface 'To my readers' ('*Til læserne*': Ibsen's Norwegian leaves out the familiarizing pronoun) in the Norwegian edition of his collected works, in which he asks that each play be read in the order in which it was written, for 'only by apprehending and absorbing my entire production as a coherent, continuous whole will you be receptive to the specific impression the individual parts are intended to convey'.[12] By the summer of 1898 the autobiography project had been superseded by the composition of *When We Dead Awaken*. He could read himself, and expect to be read, through the 'continuous whole' of his texts; and this, it turned out, was also the only way he could write himself. Unembarrassed by theories of the death of the author, let alone of the intentional fallacy, he could present himself as the figure in the carpet of his works rightly read 'one after another'. This collapses intentionality into textuality: it gives us Ibsen's own authority to concentrate our critical attention not on biographical data, but on his texts and their intertextuality. And by 'text' we must understand not merely the words, spoken or on the page, but the entire system of signs – verbal, visual, situational, structural – which constitutes each play. Printed to be read, the texts were conceived for performance.

If we accept Ibsen's view of his work as a dynamic process (never was a *corpus* less like a corpse), of the figure being revealed only as his carpet unrolls, we are bound to ask how the last group of plays complete the figure. Among many possible ways of answering this, the notion of self-reflexiveness offers itself as one which embraces questions both of themes and of technique, and which also suggests parallels in the history of the theatre. At the end of great periods of dramatic activity – in fifth-century Athens or Jacobean and Caroline London – dramatists can be seen to found their art on self-conscious manipulation, involving transgression as much as use, of the conventions of the genres and traditions within which they are working.[13] By the 1890s Ibsen's 'tradition' was largely his own *corpus* and, without wishing to make him into a complete solipsist, we may understand his late dramatic art in terms of how he marks and manipulates the conventions he has himself established. His audiences and readers had come to expect plays that created an illusion of reality and that contained individuals in quest for selfhood, driven to realize their idea of themselves, against obstacles raised by their society. The last four works, in a number of ways, play with these expectations, both fulfilling and subverting them.

Making significant action out of two or three hours of realistically rendered life depends on coincidences – an orphanage burning; the right person arriving at the right moment – and on language which, within the limits of verisimilitude (if straining at them), points that significance (Osvald's 'And I am burning, too'; Lona Hessel's assurance that she has come 'to bring in fresh air'). In the late plays Ibsen thrusts such coincidences and pointers at us, as if to challenge the very principle of verisimilitude. Solness voices his fear that 'one of these days youth is going to come here knocking on the door', and immediately Hilde Wangel knocks and enters –

as pat on her cue as the Rat-wife in *Little Eyolf* on hers.[14] Borkman agrees to Ella's plea that Erhart change his surname to hers, and her grateful 'When I am gone, Erhart Rentheim will live after me' produces the violent entry, through 'the concealed door', of Mrs Borkman: 'Never. Erhart shall never bear that name.' *When We Dead Awaken* is structured as one large, escalating coincidence, forcing confrontations of attitudes and of time past and present, the significance of which is relentlessly pointed by the dialogue. Unlike Strindberg in most of his post-Inferno plays, Ibsen has not abandoned the conventions of bourgeois realism but, even as he uses those conventions, he challenges them with explicit symbolism, melodrama, even allegory. Each play offers a variety of levels of reality. As audiences we are kept on our toes, watching actions which range from the mundane to the impossible, listening to language which moves between the obvious and the inexpressible, between colloquial directness and poetic intensity. We are denied the security of a single mode or tone. When Borkman, at the end of the family battle for Erhart in Act III, proclaims that he is going 'out into the storm alone' and then amends the phrase to 'out into the storm of life', as if Ibsen wanted to mark the clichéd nature of the metaphor, then the effect would seem to be as much comic as tragic, and certainly not heroic. And yet, within a few moments Borkman is quite literally in the storm (of death rather than life, as it turns out), having walked, as it were, through the looking glass and into his own heroic vision. And yet again, Ella Rentheim is there to refute that vision – but still her language is coloured by it, as she speaks of the 'icy wind' that comes from his 'kingdom'. By the time Borkman dies on the cold mountain-side, his heart gripped by 'a hand of ice', genre expectations and questions of what is realistic and what symbolical have been both generated and transcended.

The ending of *John Gabriel Borkman* is also an example of how the late plays break away from the bourgeois parlour to use outdoor settings, interwoven with their thematic textures. The mental landscape of Ibsen's protagonists had always been a vertical one; their thrust is upwards, as they strive, or at least yearn, for 'something higher than this life'; and downwards, as they try to '*grunne til bunns*' (literally: 'think through to the bottom of it') who they are and why. In *Brand* the physical setting embodies the spiritual quest. In the contemporary plays it is the language that maintains the mental geography of peaks and abysses, its metaphors fed at times by literal, if off-stage, presences: the distant mountain tops at the end of *Ghosts*, or the mill-race in *Rosmersholm*. Inner and outer landscapes merge in the multiplicity of meanings in, for example, 'the depths of the sea' ('*havsens bunn*') in *The Wild Duck*. The late plays make the up/down grid literal, as Solness, Borkman and Rubek all realize their deepest sense of themselves in a climb which leads to their death, the last two before our eyes and in a mountainous landscape. Alfred Allmers has just come down from the mountains when his son drowns and lies, we are told, 'on the bottom' of the fjord; and the last two Acts of *Little Eyolf* are set by the shore of that fjord. It is as if Ibsen had decided to put on stage the verbal metaphors of his earlier texts, confronting us with the paradox that the literal setting makes the action more symbolical.

This does not mean that Ibsen had become a symbolist, in the sense of seeing and representing the world as merely a storehouse of signs and symbols.[15] There were those, notably among the French Symbolists, who thought he had. Maeterlinck greeted *The Master Builder* as a 'somnambulistic drama' in which everything that is said 'at once hides and reveals the sources of an unknown life'.[16] For all that Maeterlinck wrote illuminatingly on what he called 'the inner and the outer dialogue' in *The Master Builder*, what was life to him was death to Ibsen, who thanked Edvard Brandes for emphasizing, in his review of that play, the realistic qualities of the characters,[17] and who generally insisted that he did not 'seek symbols', he 'portrayed people'.[18] If his 'people' are as doomed as those in Maeterlinck's *L'Intruse* (The Intruder), published the same year as *The Master Builder*, it is because they actively aspire, create and destroy, not because we all 'give birth astride of a grave'.[19] Yet, his people tend to turn into symbolist poets in their attempts at self-analysis and in their reaching out to each other, even as what they do, and the settings in which they do it, evoke meanings beyond the literal. His texts, in other words, show that the two aims need not be as mutually exclusive as his *dictum* suggests. But the earlier drafts of texts also show that very often the images one thinks of as crucial to the symbolic structure of a play entered the text at a late stage. The 'harps in the air' which Hilde says she heard as the Master Builder stood on top of his tower, and the floating crutch and wide open eyes of the drowned child which haunt the parents in *Little Eyolf*, are examples. They seem to have been the ultimate articulation of mind complexes and of structural connections, rather than part of the original impulse for the play. This is not to deny that the last four plays are 'more metaphoric, mythopoeic, visionary and mysterious'[20] than the earlier ones, but to stress – again – the variety of levels of reality offered. Borkman's aims, compared to those of his forerunner, Bernick in *Pillars of Society*, are indeed 'mythopoeic'. He has visions of a Dionysian vigour and Wagnerian grandeur, of 'the spirits that serve me ... earth-bound millions', of 'veins of iron ore stretching out their arms to me ... branching, beckoning, enticing' [*viii*, 231]. Solness, whose very name evokes myth (Norwegian '*sol*' meaning 'sun', and '*ness*' an 'isthmus' – placing him half-way between gods and men?),[21] challenged the Almighty

from the church tower at Lysanger ('*lys*' meaning 'light') and aims to do so
again from the top of his own tower. Ibsen evokes resonances of a Lucifer, a
Faust, a Prometheus, even an Apollo – but without locking Solness into an
identification with any one of these myths. Allmers walks in the mountains
with Death as 'a good travelling companion', and the Rat Wife lures his son
into the waters of the fjord as irresistibly as she draws those other little
unwanted, 'nagging' creatures; but *Little Eyolf* is also a naturalistic study of
sexual and familial relationships, of frustration, bereavement and guilt.
Rubek, like a latter-day Tempter, has twice promised to take a young
woman to the top of a high mountain and show her 'all the glory of the
world' [*viii*, 244, 283]; but it is as a man and artist that he has failed to keep
his promise.

Ibsen is not a myth-maker but a fiction-maker who uses myth – Norse,
Classical, Christian – where it serves to open our minds to the potentials of
the action – to what the Yeats poem terms 'the impossible'. Myth, according to Frank Kermode, is 'a sequence of radically unchangeable gestures';
fictions are 'for finding things out'.[22] Not only is this what Ibsen's dramatic
fictions are for, but they also make us, readers and audiences, take part in
the finding out, by destabilizing our sense of reality – of what the world and
people are 'really' like. They do not allegorize their protagonists to make
them and their fate conform to pre-existing myths, but invite us to apply to
them a number of varied viewpoints, some of which are located in myth.
We see Solness as a kind of god to Hilde, a man with vertigo to his wife, and
Borkman as both a Nietzschean *Übermensch* and an embezzler.

Such dialectical strategies are of course characteristic of all Ibsen's plays.
We are kept alert, adjusting and modifying our understanding of motives
and meanings until the end of a play, and beyond. We have to 'read' characters through '*tegn imot tegn*' – one kind of evidence challenging another.[23]
From *The Master Builder* onwards Ibsen makes these signs both more compelling and more contradictory. In particular, while he maintains his characteristic preoccupation with individual identity, characters' self-images are
both magnified and questioned as never before.

The four male protagonists are all committed to the idea of fulfilling their
own unique potential – 'the irresistible calling inside me', as Borkman puts
it [*viii*, 207]. As *Little Eyolf* opens, Allmers is obsessed with what he perceives as a re-born self. He recounts an epiphany in the 'infinite solitude of
the mountains' which taught him to 'become master of [himself]' and so to
re-define his calling. The other three protagonists are obsessed with a sense
of self as absolute and unchanging. Solness is 'half desperate' (stage direction) to explain why he is unable to give a younger man a chance to build: 'I
am what I am! And you can't expect me to change myself!' [*vii*, 363].[24]

Borkman insists that he had to speculate with the bank's funds, 'because I was me – because I was John Gabriel Borkman – and not somebody else' [*viii*, 207]. And Rubek, as we have seen, is similarly categorical: 'I am an artist . . .' [*viii*, 280]. The rhetoric of assertion which they share is both compelling and compulsively tautologous.

Against this affirmation of identity, no doubt related to Nietzsche's insistence that 'all truly noble morality grows out of triumphant self-affirmation',[25] each of the plays presents the protagonist as profoundly affected by relationships with others. Earlier Ibsen plays had been structured to focus on the individual's road to self-realization. In *Brand* we part, Act by Act, with one relationship after the other: mother, child, wife, parishioners. To find herself, Nora frees herself of the patriarchally instituted ties of wife and motherhood; and by the end of *Ghosts* Mrs Alving is left appallingly lonely, her attempt to re-interpret those ties having failed catastrophically. But from the mid-1880s onwards – whether we date it from *The Wild Duck* and the web of parental, filial and marital relationships into which Gregers Werle crashes, or from *Rosmersholm* with its exploration of the power one mind can wield over another – Ibsen's protagonists are far more deeply involved in patterns of interaction. Such patterns are foregrounded in the last four plays. Solness climbs heroically alone at the end, like Brand, but it is to affirm Hilde's image of him. Both Borkman and Rubek share their climb with a woman they have loved and betrayed, and Alfred Allmers presumably clasps the hand his wife holds out to him at the end. Each play places the protagonist's quest for self within a different version of the two-women pattern familiar from earliest Ibsen drama. Both *John Gabriel Borkman* and *When We Dead Awaken* give more space to the women's viewpoint than to the man's, to seeing him in terms of how he has *used* the woman whom he did not marry and the one whom, more's the pity, he did. *When We Dead Awaken* almost flaunts its diagrammatic positionings in this respect. The structure of *John Gabriel Borkman*, where the 'hero' is kept off stage for the entire first Act and lies dead for the last few minutes of the last Act, sets Borkman's own vision of his power to create against the two women's vision of their wasted lives – his murder, as Ella puts it, of '*kjær-lighetslivet*' ('the ability to love and be loved').

That the two women in *John Gabriel Borkman* are not only sisters but twins – a significant afterthought of Ibsen's between draft and final version – suggests that he was pushing his characteristic pattern to an extreme. Having shared life before birth, they are left at the end of the play to share a kind of death-in-life. In between they have 'fought to the death', first over a lover and then over his son. The play's last two lines of dialogue, spoken as Ella and Gunhild join hands over the dead body, were added at a late draft stage, as if only then did Ibsen feel that the dramatic pattern demanded an ending focusing on the interwovenness of three lives rather than on the death of Borkman:

MRS BORKMAN   We two – twin sisters – over the man we both loved.
ELLA RENTHEIM   We two shadows – over the dead man.   [*viii*, 233]

But nearly every line in this text demands of readers – let alone of directors and actresses – an awareness of the pressure put on apparently ordinary words by speakers who are 'a little more than kin, and less than kind'.[26]

In *Little Eyolf*, too, Ibsen drew the network of kinships and coincidences more tightly between draft and published text, to produce a formidable combination of familial and sexual bonds. Allmers married Rita for the means to 'follow [his] calling' and to provide for Asta, who he assumes is his half-sister. But his commitment to the calling – the book on 'Human Responsibility' – has made him an inadequate husband and father, with a sexually and emotionally frustrated wife, who is also jealous of Asta and, to make Allmers jealous, claims to be prepared to throw herself at Borgheim, who wants to marry Asta. Obviously there is not much room in this tangle for the title character, little Eyolf; before and after his death in Act I he serves mainly as a nexus for the relationships of the adults. In Act II Asta reveals to Allmers that she is not his half-sister, which throws doubt on the a-sexuality of their feelings for each other, past and present. Their closeness in the past is coloured by both narcissism and homoeroticism, as we learn that Allmers used to make Asta dress as a boy and to call her Eyolf. Furthermore we learn (in the printed text but not in the draft) that he told Rita of this transvestite 'Eyolf' at the very moment that the real little Eyolf, left neglected on a table while his parents were making love, fell and was crippled for life. A strange topic of conversation for the occasion, one might think, but a coincidence pregnant with implications for our understanding of Allmers and his overlapping relationships with the two women and the two Eyolfs.

Emphatically, then, Ibsen is subverting the expectation that his plays will focus on an individual's quest for selfhood. In all the late plays such a quest is dominated by what James McFarlane has aptly defined as 'a sense of the world as an arena of relationships and meta-relationships'.[27] Relatedly, he is subverting judgments such as the one delivered by Knut Hamsun in his notorious lecture on 7 October 1891 when, with Ibsen sitting in the front row, he declared that 'whenever Ibsen treats individual problems that are supposed to be psychological, it is only in so far as they are related to social problems'.[28] How far a conscious desire to contradict this helped to shape *The Master Builder* and the plays that followed, we cannot know. Nor, of course, do we need Ibsen's famous disclaimer of 1898 – 'I have been more of a poet and less of a social philosopher than people generally seem inclined to believe'[29] – to question Hamsun's verdict in the first place. The point is that in the last four plays society – whether in the shape of particular 'problems' or as the weight of 'old dead ideas and beliefs' – is no longer a major antagonist.

The worlds of these plays are intimate, internalized spheres with their own private demons. When society impinges on them, it is not through figures – such as Torvald Helmer, or Pastor Manders or Judge Brack – whose social attitudes operate as constraints on the protagonists, but in a strangely collective, anonymous fashion. When Aline Solness receives a visit from 'several ladies', they are unnamed, unlike the firmly localized ladies who make up the moral sewing circle in *Pillars of Society*, and unspeaking (except for one choric scream and a call for the doctor), unlike the dinner guests who so robustly establish the social ethos in the first Act of *The Wild Duck*. Their function, apart from peopling the stage for Solness's climb and fall, is to oblige Mrs Solness to exercise her 'duty' as a hostess (and so to leave Hilde Wangel to have a last and decisive duologue with Solness); just as, when she goes out to buy a respectable outfit for Hilde, it is her obsession with 'duty' (the word *'plikt'* which Hilde finds so 'cold and sharp and prickly') that is being foregrounded, and not Hilde's defiance of social etiquette. The children, some of them in 'folk costume', who sing and dance in Act II of *When We Dead Awaken* may be picturesque icons of a normal, harmonious society but their importance lies in how Rubek, Maja and Irene, each in his or her way, react to them. Society in these plays exists, almost expressionistically, as something on which the few central characters project their emotions of fear and hostility. That Rubek's public – the consumers of his art of sculptured portraiture – do not recognize the animal features he manages to conceal under superficially 'striking likenesses' tells us more about Rubek than about the society whose materialist criteria of success he has, after all, himself adopted. Solness gave up building churches to build 'warm, cheerful, comfortable homes, where fathers and mothers could live together, secure and happy, and feeling that it's good to be alive' [*vii*, 405]. But as we see him, he builds only for himself, although Ibsen's stage directions pointedly place his new home with a tower next to 'a street with mean dilapidated buildings'. The crowd of walk-ons who gather at the end 'to see him too scared to climb his own building' is as anonymous as are the unseen urchins down by the jetty who make no attempt to save little Eyolf from drowning.

Ibsen creates a powerful sense of confinement. There is no world elsewhere for someone like Rita who, we are told, 'can never thrive anywhere else but here' and has no longer a God to turn to. When little Eyolf dies there are no sympathetic condolences from outside, just black crape to be sewn on sleeves and hats, and three – or four, counting the wondrous necessary Borgheim – bereaved people to torment themselves and each other, in a kind of fjordside *Huis Clos*. *When We Dead Awaken* starts in the social ambience of a spa but moves out into the wild which becomes the setting for a society of four – Ulfheim, the bear-hunter, who first appeared as a radical outsider, pairing off with Maja as in a game of elective affinities. The isolation of the Borkman household may be motivated by the disgrace of John Gabriel's trial and imprisonment, but as we meet the inhabitants it has become a state of the soul. Self-imprisoned on separate floors of the house that is not theirs, husband and wife endlessly rehearse their individual grievances and their separate and mutually contradictory visions of 'redemption'. When Borkman lists the contributions he would have made to society, their only reality is as extensions of his ego: 'Mines, in infinite numbers! Waterfalls! Quarries! Trade routes and steamships all over the world. I would have created all this, alone' [*viii*, 186]. As so often in the late plays, there is a sense that characters move in a medium entirely made up of their own obsessive visions of reality.

This sense is achieved through a mode of selective naturalism. Whatever Hamsun said, later critics have recognized Ibsen's ability to take us into the inner lives of characters via external circumstances as trivial as a bag of macaroons. In the last plays the probing is at a depth, and the inner lives are of an intensity, which – unlike the case of, say, Hjalmar Ekdal – does not easily translate into bread and butter. We learn of Irene's diet of milk, water and 'soft, squashy bread' only because it – and she – is polarized against Ulfheim's 'fresh meat-bones . . . Raw with lots of warm blood' [*viii*, 253]. It is impossible to envisage Solness or Rubek eating herring salad – or the Borkman family eating at all. When Mrs Wilton tells Erhart Borkman to 'stay at home like a good boy and have tea with Mother and Auntie' [*viii*, 173], audiences in the theatre laugh at the discrepancy between the cosy domestic scene conjured up by the words and the household, tense to breaking-point with spoken and unspoken conflicts, which they see before them. Allmers was offered champagne when he returned from the mountains but, despite the 'rose-coloured shades' which Rita had put over the lamps, he 'touched it not' – an in-action which only too clearly, whether we recognize the Welhaven quotation or not,[30] signals his lack of response to, indeed his fear of, his wife's sexuality. Not all the documentation is as high-flown – there is comic bathos in Allmers countering Rita's undressing with questions about Little Eyolf's 'tummy' – nor as relentlessly symbolical: nothing could be more realistic than Allmers confessing to having found himself, in the midst of his acute grief, wondering what was for dinner. But the phenomenological pressure is away from externals. So, for example, in dramatizing Allmers's and Rita's reaction to the death of Little Eyolf, Ibsen left out of his final version of Act II those lines in the complete draft where they both voice their 'sense of loss ... even in the smallest things ... the empty chair at table ... his coat not hanging where it should in the hall'. Instead he added lines in which Allmers sado-masochistically insists on the 'wall'[31] now forever between the two of them because 'the large, wide-open eyes of a child will be looking at us, night and day' [viii, 83].

This focusing on the obsessions of a small nucleus of characters also means that, where there are middle-ground figures with some sense of a life of their own, figures like the Broviks in *The Master Builder* or the Foldals in *John Gabriel Borkman*, they still function mainly as sounding chambers for the protagonist's condition. The Broviks, father and son, endorse Solness's complex of feelings about his own past (when he displaced the father), present (when both embarrass him) and future (when he fears the son will displace him). The infatuation of Kaja Fosli, Ragnar's fiancée, is a means of bringing out the sexuality which is inseparable from Solness's will to power. She has the makings of a frustrated Chekhovian anti-heroine – but simply fades out when not needed. Vilhelm Foldal, author of an unperformed tragedy and representative of the little people who lost everything through Borkman's high-handed use of funds, has been Borkman's only audience, listening to his Napoleonic dreams of restored greatness; and young Frida Foldal is the only one to play for him – the *Danse macabre* to which he responds, from inside his obsession, as to the 'singing' of the iron ore down the mines of his childhood. Thanks to Erhart Borkman's bid for freedom and Mrs Wilton's foresight in providing 'somebody to fall back on', Foldal is to lose even Frida, the one member of his family who does not 'despise' him, and to supply a grimly farcical interlude as he rejoices at having been run over by the splendid covered sleigh that bore her off. But not before he has functioned to provoke what is possibly the most devastating scene in any Ibsen play. In Act II Ibsen makes us watch Foldal and Borkman feed each other's illusions, his of being a poet and Borkman's of 'coming into power again', until an incautious word from the impatient Borkman, '*dik-tersnakk*' ('poetic nonsense'), cracks the thin surface under which doubts and fears have hovered. Reversing the direction of the dialogue, the two of them set about stripping pretences not only off each other but off the very bond that appeared to link them:

FOLDAL   It wasn't a lie as long as you believed in my vocation. As long as you believed in me, I believed in you.

BORKMAN   Then we've been deceiving each other. And perhaps deceiving
           ourselves, too, each of us.
FOLDAL   Isn't that what friendship really is, John Gabriel?   [*viii*, 191]

And they part because, as Borkman tells Foldal, 'I've no longer any use for
you.'

This may be the nadir of human relations in the late plays, but it is not
untypical. What bonds people is use. To Hilde, being 'used' is having her
'kingdom'; but when people no longer have any use for each other (as
Rubek dismissed Irene when she had served her use as a model), or when
characters refuse to be used (as does Erhart Borkman, or Maja, used by
Rubek as 'a kind of emergency currency'), then bonds of family, love or
friendship become meaningless or irksome, or both, to them. Then, too,
truthfulness or sincerity comes to equal that unremitting awfulness of
people to each other which injects both tragedy and comedy into the plays.
Characters do and say things which, as Judge Brack would say, people
don't. Alfred Allmers tells Rita that he married her for money: 'gold and
green forests'. Solness tells old Brovik that he must lump it and 'die as best
[he] can'. Rubek agrees with Maja that he is 'tired' of her, and then expands
the admission into one of being 'made unbearably sick and tired and listless
by living with [her]'. This particular piece of plain-speaking is part of an
extended duologue of mutual dismantling which is also made to comment,
self-reflexively, on the way it operates:

RUBEK   ... [*Bursts out vehemently.*] But do you know what it is that drives
        me absolutely to despair? Have you any idea?
MAJA   [*quietly defiant.*] Yes. I suppose the fact that you went and took me
        – for life.
RUBEK   I wouldn't put it into such heartless words.
MAJA   But the meaning is just as heartless, all the same.   [*viii*, 270]

Such 'heartless' words and meanings, challenging any neat division between
dark comedy and tragedy, are concentrated in the wisecracks with which
Borkman dismisses others' sorrows, but they dominate the entire dialogue
in *John Gabriel Borkman*, through to the closing exchange in which 'the
cold heart' ['*hjertekulden*'] is both subject and object.

Being driven, in Rubek's words, 'absolutely to despair' is a structural as
well as emotional determinant. *The Master Builder* opens on an exclama-
tion: (literally) 'No, now I can't stand this much longer!'; and while the line
is old Brovik's and 'this' refers to Solness's oppressive power over him and
his son, we soon discover that Solness himself has reached a similar crisis
point. So, within her private angst, has Aline. Brovik's line sounds awkward
in a literal translation: colloquial Norwegian sprinkles the adverb '*nu*' more

liberally than idiomatic English uses 'now'. But Brovik's '*nu*' is not just a throat-clearing or mild modifier, it signals an unbearable *now* – a condition from which each of the last four plays starts. In the earlier 'contemporary' Ibsen plays the action leads up to a crisis, a situation which is perceived as unendurable by the central character, or characters. At that point they resolve it by a counter-action which either contains a new beginning or is a choice of death. Only Mrs Alving is left, in 'speechless anguish', suspended in a crisis which, she has cried out, 'cannot be endured'. With the obvious exception of Hilde Wangel, all the main characters in the last plays reach for Mrs Alving's phrase, and long before their play ends. Because it articulates the sub-text of the entire Act, Mrs Borkman's curtain line to Act I – 'I can bear this life no longer!' – transforms a melodramatic cliché into a dramatic equivalent of Edvard Munch's famous painting, 'The Scream' (1893). The plays begin at a breaking-point and follow a structural pattern where an arrival – Hilde Wangel, the Rat Wife (and Asta), Ella (and Mrs Wilton), Irene – forces a crisis condition into an active crisis. The charismatic power of the protagonists is then manifested in that, out of this, they draw the strength to assert a vision which would turn despair into hope or, in the language of *When We Dead Awaken*, 'death' into 'life'. They do not choose death, as do Hedda Gabler and Rosmer and Rebecca, but death is the natural consequence of the thrust of their will and the magnitude of their self-assertion. There is a kind of triumph, as well as defeat, in the suspended closure of these endings.

Little Eyolf does not at first sight fit this pattern very well. The play opens with Alfred Allmers's return from the mountains and his determination to begin a new life devoted to his son, and ends with Rita and Allmers determined to begin a different new life, devoted to underprivileged children. Yet, looked at more closely, the contrary indications turn into dark ironies, subverted expectations. By the end of Act I Allmers's intentions for Eyolf, which in any case have only deepened Rita's crisis, are thwarted by the drowning of the child; and retrospectively they are proved, under Rita's ruthless questioning, to have been guilt-driven, self-deceptive and ultimately self-serving. In Acts II and III the two of them struggle to bear the unbearable implications of Eyolf's death, but instead they unravel one terrible truth after another about their life together, even as Allmers learns through Asta's revelation that he has lost both little Eyolfs. In the end Asta goes off with Borgheim, the road-builder, and Allmers and Rita are left to proclaim a resolution, a happy ending which the context profoundly questions (a point which I shall return to shortly), making this play the most subversive of all, in terms of genres and categories.

Like the other late plays, then, *Little Eyolf* is dark, but with the kind of darkness which enables us to say of Ibsen what Peter Brook, with rather less justification, has said of Beckett: that his 'no' is forged 'out of a longing for "yes" and so his despair is the negative from which the contour of its opposite can be drawn'.[32] If the plays leave us with a sense of irreconcilable conflicts – between self and others, art and life – and with unanswered questions, it is also with the questions sharpened, and with a sharpened awareness of the dramatic art which, in Archer's words, makes 'people think and see for themselves'.[33] We must turn to the art which makes of each play a 'completely constituted world'.

In *The Master Builder* Ibsen creates a world where time and space have a remarkable interdependence which also controls our responses to the play. As Solness stands on top of his tower, Hilde thrusts the past into the present: 'At last! At last! Now I see him great and free again!' A visual pattern supports her affirmation: the three Acts have moved through settings progressively more appropriate to the protagonist's name, to an end against 'an evening sky with sunlit clouds'. Forming, like Shakespeare's *Richard III*, an arch from an opening to a closing 'now',[34] the structure may seem to celebrate Solness's achievement of greatness and freedom. But the end of the arch splinters, as Hilde's 'nows' proliferate, gain in intensity, and drift into bewilderment: 'Now he swings his hat! ... For now, now it is finished! ... Now I can't see him up there.' As the Master Builder falls, 'right into the quarry', the downward forces in the play are also affirmed: 'So in fact he couldn't do it.'

In the two or so hours' traffic of the stage a world is created, largely by what we *hear*, which gives a unique geography and time scale to the twenty-four hours of fictive life which we *see*. The operative heights and depths in this play are man-made structures; the characters are preoccupied with buildings – burned down and erected, finished and unfinished, buildings existing only as drawings or 'castles in the air'. In the theatre, directors have been fond of putting a model of Solness's new villa on stage; and in Adrian Noble's 1989 production for the Royal Shakespeare Company, Solness's fall was marked by a huge canopy, cantilevered over the stage throughout the performance, suddenly turning to display a model village of houses and church. With or without such visual aids, the text shows Solness defining his own identity by what he has built, is building and intends to build, and Aline's by what he has prevented her from building. She too 'had a talent for building ... for building children's souls', and her talents are now 'like the heaps of rubble after a fire' [*vii*, 406–7].

Two moments in time past keep being re-activated in the process of reminiscences and reconstructions which makes up the text: the burning-down, some 'twelve–thirteen years ago', of Aline's family home, and Solness's climb, ten years since to the day, to the top of the tower he built for the church at Lysanger. In each case, what matters is not what 'really' happened, but how, and how differently, different characters perceive the significance of what happened. In each case, too, what is revealed at any given time depends on the nature of the interaction between speakers. When, on the subject of the fire, Solness and Aline in Act II drain each other with half-understood accusations, with self-explanations that are not wanted and with intended consolations that misfire, then words serve merely to alienate. Prompted by Hilde, on the other hand, each of them is able to reach down to the deepest sources of guilt and grief. With her, in Act III, Aline is drawn beyond the 'unbearable' sense of dereliction of duty to husband and newborn children which she tried to tell Solness about in Act II, to speak of the loss of the 'little things' that were her past and future: the family heirlooms and the nine dolls whom she 'carried under [her] heart. Like little unborn children.' And with Hilde, in Act II, Solness passionately lays bare his sense of responsibility for having *wished* the fire and the irrational guilt and fear of retribution which for ever undercut his achievement: 'That is the price my position as an artist has cost me – and others.'

Guilt clings to every version of the fire and drags people downwards. After hearing Aline's story, Hilde feels that she has been down a 'tomb', and earlier Solness speaks of his 'abysmal [literally, 'bottomless'], immeasurable debt' to Aline [*vii*, 372]. Downward and upward forces clash in Solness's consciousness that, as he repeatedly says, the fire was what enabled him to rise ('*brakte meg i været*'). Hilde authenticates this sense of his calling as an upward trajectory, for which he has been singled out: 'Nobody but *you* should be allowed to build. You should do it all alone' [*vii*, 400]. To see him 'standing free and high' on his own tower will affirm her faith in his power to do 'the impossible'.

The Lysanger episode comes alive in the play, not so much by gradual reconstruction as by Hilde imposing her construction of it on the Master Builder who, whether or not it is a fiction, is ever more willing to make it his own truth. If she is a '*dikter*', he begins as an ideal audience and ends up as a co-author, in a series of remarkable duologues where words and images are not only bridges but meeting points. By the end of Act I her account of events ten years ago has become 'something *experienced* [he] felt [he] had forgotten' (and it is a measure of the range of tones in their encounters that Hilde can teasingly praise him to Dr Herdal for his 'quite incredible memory'). In Act II her will-power is seen to empower him. Their dialogue begins like an illustration of Nietzsche's *Genealogy of Morals*,[35] shot through with Solness's intense combination of self-castigation and self-affirmation. Knowing himself one of the 'specially chosen', his will implemented by mysterious 'helpers and servers', he is yet also living 'as if my chest was a great expanse of raw flesh' which never heals though 'these helpers and servers go flaying off skin from other people's bodies to patch my wound' [*vii*, 412]. Hilde's unpitying response and accusation of 'a fragile conscience' mark a turning-point, with Solness, questioning the 'robustness' of Hilde's own conscience, beginning to take the lead in the dialogue. It is he who names as 'trolls' the motivating force about which she herself is inarticulate – 'this thing inside me that drove and forced me here' – and who feeds her images of other reckless creatures – Vikings and birds of prey. Jointly, completing each other's sentences, they build their identification with these images, across a sub-text of sexual and spiritual affinity, charging every word with significance and creating a mythical world of their own. This Act closes with Hilde alone on stage, an image of Nietzschean 'reckless self-assurance',[36] an a-moral will intent on a 'terribly exciting' repeat of Lysanger.

But by the time Hilde and Solness next meet, her scene with Aline at the beginning of Act III has moralized that will by empathy. Standing in her way is now 'somebody one knows'. For a moment the action threatens to turn into a concern for others. But the new strength of self in Solness means that 'duty', paying his debt by being 'chained alive to that dead woman', is not a real choice. He pulls Hilde up from the 'tomb' by a mesmeric use of their own metaphors; and the only real 'debt' now is the 'kingdom' promised at Lysanger and being cashed in as a 'castle in the air'. Their final duologue completes both the rejection of others – building houses for them has added up to 'nothing' – and the (re)construction of the significance of Lysanger, as Solness only now tells of the 'retribution' he invoked by doing the 'impossible' and challenging the Almighty's call on him to build churches. As he goes to climb his own tower and deliver an even bolder challenge, the magnitude of the act makes questions of right and wrong seem irrelevant. At the same time their shared language moves beyond symbol and image to the kind of transparency that simply exalts what is:

SOLNESS [*looks at her with bowed head*]. How did you become as you are, Hilde?

HILDE   How did you make me become as I am?   [*vii*, 441]

As she is, Hilde is allowed to appropriate the final image of the play: '*My, – my* master builder!' *Her* master builder 'got right to the top', and as at Lysanger she heard 'harps in the air'. The others' master builder 'couldn't do it' and had 'his head ... all smashed in'. Triumph and defeat, upward and downward pull, co-exist. Which is the true ending and genre, the heroic romance of the achieved impossible, or the *de casibus* tragedy of the inevitable, even retributive, fall? The antiphonal structure sets imaginative intensity against observable fact, in a suspended closure.

In one sense, *Little Eyolf* is an answer to *The Master Builder*. It is possible at the end of *The Master Builder* to feel the elation of Nietzsche's 'I know of no better purpose in life than to be destroyed by that which is great and impossible.'[37] No such upward thrust is sustained in *Little Eyolf*. I have already suggested that the play subverts its own surface pattern of hope. This, we may note here, involves a subversion of space and time structures. These might seem to open out and up, as the play moves out of doors after the first Act, and as the ending has the protagonists planning a future (unlike *The Master Builder*, where a post-play existence of the characters is unthinkable) in which they will look 'Upwards, – towards the mountain peaks'. But the movement outside is not felt as a release. Between the complete draft and the final version of the text Ibsen internalized the physical setting by changing the weather of Act II, down by the fjord, from 'a brilliantly sunny day' to 'a heavy damp day with driving mist'. And the changes to Act III, set on a 'rise' above the fjord, effect a closing-in on Rita and Allmers. The steamer, merely mentioned in the draft, comes to figure prominently in the dialogue, not as a symbol of the new life of Asta and Borgheim who are going away in it to build roads in the North – one thinks of Dina and Olaf sailing off on *The Palm Tree* at the end of *Pillars of Society* – but as a projection of the fearful obsessions of the couple left behind. Rita dare not look at the steamer because its lights are 'great staring eyes' and evoke the image of the 'great open eyes' of the child lying at the bottom of the fjord. She identifies the ship's bell with the 'death-knell' ringing forever in her ears, '"*Kryk-ken fly-ter.*" "*Kryk-ken fly-ter.*"'[38] And the fact that the steamer anchors on the very spot where little Eyolf died becomes a proof of their isolation from a world that is indifferent, or worse:

ALLMERS   Life is pitiless, Rita.
RITA   People are heartless. They don't care. Either about the living or the dead.
ALLMERS   You are right. Life goes on. Just as if nothing at all had happened.
RITA   [*stares vacantly ahead.*] But then nothing has happened. Not to the others. Only to the two of us.   [*viii*, 97]

For the first time in the play the two of them truly meet in a dialogue, but only to affirm the alienation of 'us' from 'the others' and from 'life'. Ibsen is making ironic use of the symbolic potential of the action space, to point the lack of space, the emotional and spiritual claustrophobia, of the Allmers world.

The wider geography of the play, constructed by the language, takes the irony further. *Apparently* the frame of reference is here, as it is not in *The Master Builder*, the usual Ibsen one, with its extremes in the depths of the sea, where little Eyolf has been swept out by the undercurrent, and the mountain heights from where Allmers returns to recount two epiphanies – both of which he constructs as points of conversion from the uncompleted book on 'Human Responsibility' to real-life paternal responsibility. The first, told to Rita and Asta in Act I, is a Wordsworthian 'spot of time',[39] a tale of deriving renovating virtue from communion with nature. The second, told to Rita alone in the final scene, is a Keatsian account of falling more than 'half in love with easeful Death'[40] while wandering lost in the mountains. The first is an expansion of a mere reference in the draft to 'the great solitude' as promoting reflection. The second is altogether absent in the draft where, at the corresponding point in the action, Allmers reads Rita a poem he has just written, 'They sat there, those two' – a poem about a couple raking the ashes of their burned-down house for an indestructible 'gem', their 'peace' and 'happiness' lost forever [*viii*, 147]. In the 1898 edition of his *Collected Works* Ibsen published this as 'the first preliminary work for *The Master Builder*'; and its appearance in the draft of *Little Eyolf*, where Allmers insists that it is about himself, Rita and both Eyolfs, 'the big and the little', suggests an association at a symbolical level between relationships in the two plays. This disappears from the text in favour of Allmers's self- and death-centred story, and the difference between the two kinds of fiction is important. Whatever 'really' happened to Allmers in the mountains, in the final version of the play he twice translates it into the common idiom of European Romanticism. He borrows a ready-made symbolic geography for which what we see of him – his 'character' – provides no underpinning. Solness's self-analytical images are part of an overall spiritual thrust. With Allmers it is a question of bad fit between language and inner landscape; the thrust is in the rhetoric alone.

It is difficult not to feel that the same is true for the ending, where Allmers's great thrust is virtually spoken in inverted commas, a citation of his earlier imagery: 'Upwards, – towards the mountain peaks. Towards the stars. And towards the great silence.' As a formula for the proclaimed transformation of his and Rita's attitude in the last few moments of the play – the recognition that they have been lacking in sympathy for others and the decision to devote their lives to the less fortunate – this visionary statement is in itself incongruous and is, furthermore, subverted by his recent account of the allure of death in the solitude and silence of the mountains. As a spiritual thrust 'upwards' it is also counteracted by Rita's downward admission that the compelling force behind this apparent wakening to a social conscience is the need to placate the wide-open eyes of little Eyolf. Her verb, '*smigre meg inn hos*' ('win over by flattery'), hardly suggests an authentic redemptive alternative to the unbearable. There is nothing to indicate that Allmers is able to love anything other than his idea of himself, or that Rita's passionate sexuality, hitherto so resentful of the two Eyolfs, will achieve successful sublimation because she lets the urchins live in little Eyolf's rooms and 'take turns at sitting in his chair at table'. The play closes on another fiction, another illusion. Rita is no Gina whose practical stoicism in the midst of grief is the one consolation we are given at the end of *The Wild Duck*. To see the parents of little Eyolf hand in hand and looking towards the stars is paradoxically less reassuring than the sight of Hjalmar and Gina helping each other to carry the dead Hedvig to 'her own little room'.

The triumphal aspect of the ending of *The Master Builder* is a fulfilment of potential from the past. In *Little Eyolf* the dialogue draws two areas of the past into the present. One is the precise moment when little Eyolf fell from the table even as Allmers 'fell' for Rita's sexuality – a source, to Allmers, of guilt, of which the crippled child is the living (and dead) embodiment, but complex and compound guilt because it involved a betrayal of himself and both Eyolfs. The other is the more extended period of Alfred and Asta Allmers's '*samliv*' ('life together'), remembered by him as a kind of Garden of Eden, a prelapsarian state of joyful innocence. By the end of Act II he is proposing a Paradise Regained: to come back 'home' to Asta in order to be 'cleansed and purified' of his '*samliv*' with Rita and her sexual demands. By this time, however, we also know that this life of half-brother and -sister, with her dressing up as a younger version of himself, was more narcissistic than pure. And, as Asta reveals that she is not in fact his half-sister, past and present have to be re-interpreted in sexual terms. Asta's self-consciously symbolical farewell gift of waterlilies – 'the kind that grow up to the surface, – from deep down below' ('*bunnen*') – leaves Allmers to close the Act on a declension of his loss: 'Asta. Eyolf, Little Eyolf – !' In terms of this relationship, the last Act conveys frustration, and not a gain out of loss. In the draft Allmers makes something of a heroic sacrifice, in that it is he who tells Asta to leave. In the final version he persists in imploring her to stay, and Asta's last words show that she perceives her departure with Borgheim as 'fleeing from you [Allmers] – and from myself' [*viii*, 96]. Altogether *Little Eyolf* is closer in its ending to *The Wild Duck* than to *The Master Builder*, and not just because a child has died by going to '*havsens bunn*' ('the depths of the sea'). At the end of *The Wild Duck* there is Relling to deconstruct Hjalmar Ekdal's language of grief which has persuaded

Gregers Werle that 'Hedvig has not died in vain', and to subvert any possible tragic or heroic effect of Gregers's exit line. At the end of *Little Eyolf* the whole structure of the play cries 'The devil it is' to Allmers's and Rita's assurance that the two Eyolfs have not been lost in vain and that their own way is together and 'upwards'.

Like *Little Eyolf*, *John Gabriel Borkman* ends with two survivors clasping hands; but in the later play – as if in a dialectical opposition to its immediate predecessor – that closing stance embodies no illusion, no imagined upward thrust. The twin sisters unite, at last, as 'two shadows – over the dead man', and the dialogue that brings them together, 'over the man we both loved', is one of acceptance, beyond either hope or despair. At the same time it completes a pattern which, from the vantage point of this ending, we see as having been immanent in the play as a whole: a tightening stranglehold by ineluctable winter, with all its concomitants of cold, whiteness, death. Winter has been at work inside and outside: in the snow driving beyond the window-panes as the curtain rises on Mrs Borkman alone with her crochet-work; in her phrase 'I'm always cold' [*viii*, 156] and in Ella's white hair; in the human relationships demonstrated, and in the snowy setting where they are finally played out. In various ways the characters have been fighting the cold: Mrs Borkman by clutching Erhart and his 'mission'; Ella by reaching out for the same Erhart to bring some warmth into the last few months of her life; Borkman by striding 'out into the storm' to recover his lost vision. Edvard Munch, who apparently felt an affinity with Borkman, is reputed to have called the play 'the best winter landscape in Norwegian art'.[41] What is perhaps most remarkable is the interpenetration of external and internal landscapes in this exploration of 'the cold heart'. Intensity and imaginative wholeness are achieved by extraordinary concentration and control of all the available means of communication in the theatre.

The four-Act structure of *John Gabriel Borkman* is so telescoped that each of the last three Acts begins just when, or in the case of Act II just before, the previous one ended. Only the theatre could provide such moments, of shocked surprise merging with fulfilled expectation, as when the curtain rises at the opening of Act II to show translated into the figure of Borkman the footsteps of the 'sick wolf' heard in Act I, while Frida Foldal is still playing the *Danse macabre* which downstairs drove Erhart to cry out 'I can't stand this any longer!' [*viii*, 177]. Locations take on a peculiar significance. Downstairs and upstairs become terms of irreparable alienation, and inside means imprisonment in the past, while outside means the illusion of escape to 'freedom', or 'life'. The play starts from a kind of deadlocked equilibrium, where characters are identified with their position on the downstairs/upstairs and inside/outside grid, and any movement from those positions has disproportionate and generally disastrous consequences. Ella Rentheim comes, in Gunhild's words, 'to the wrong house'; Mrs Wilton comes in and draws Erhart *out* and to the South; Mrs Borkman suddenly stands in the door *upstairs*; Borkman goes *downstairs* and then *out*. In a tragi-comic exchange near the beginning of Act IV, when Erhart is escaping with Mrs Wilton in a covered sleigh, Mrs Borkman's whole devastated life becomes suspended on the question of whether or not Erhart is sitting 'inside' the sleigh yet [*viii*, 221].

Time and space are not really perceived as separate dimensions in this play. On the compressed present rests the intolerable weight of the past: sixteen years of shame for Gunhild Borkman since 'the storm broke over – over this house'; eight years upstairs for Borkman, after five years in prison and three years, before that, in custody (presumably while the details of the fraud were sorted out). Remarkably, and unlike the case of the immediately preceding plays, no character attaches to the past a sense of guilt. 'Redemption' to Borkman means rehabilitation, the restoration to power in the bank which he expects every time there is a knock on his door. To Mrs Borkman it means obliteration of shame: the 'monument' she will raise over the grave of the husband she regards as already dead 'will be like a cluster of living plants – hedges, trees and bushes – planted closely, so closely round the spot that marks your life, the grave that is your life – hiding it for ever' [*viii*, 210]. With religious intensity she sees Erhart as her redeemer who 'must make his life a shining light – a light so strong and steady that no one – throughout this land – can see the shadow his father cast over me – and over my son' [*viii*, 161]. Husband and wife, then, live for fictive and mutually contradictory visions of a future, against which Erhart asserts his actual demands of the present ('happiness', realized as a somewhat dubious *ménage à trois*). Only Ella's future is certain and short (though 'the winter is long here', as the self-absorbed Borkman responds to her news of a mortal illness [*viii*, 202]). Ironically, it is Ella's arrival, to secure Erhart for her few remaining months, that brings back the past and eliminates the future. Space and time, then, in *John Gabriel Borkman*, are perceived as measured by the individual obsessions of characters who are also peculiarly alienated from each other. Those obsessions control their language, spoken and unspoken, down to minute details such as their extreme self-consciousness about the personal pronouns they use – or do not use. Mrs Borkman, throughout Act I, refers to her husband upstairs as 'he' or 'the Chairman of the Bank' and speaks his name only when recalling 'what it used to stand for', in the days when 'all over the country they called him by his Christian name, as if he was the King himself'. He, in Act II, refers to her as 'someone downstairs'. Seeing him downstairs at the beginning of Act III, she at first speaks not *to* him but to Ella *about* him, still as 'he'. Everyone's discourse is I-centred. Wedded to her grudge, Gunhild cannot really say 'we' to Ella until they join hands over the corpse of Borkman. Earlier in the play, a 'we' is almost meaningless. Erhart, when told that Aunt Ella is coming to live 'with us', has to ask 'With us? With all of us?' [*viii*, 176]. And Mrs Wilton can shock and hurt Mrs Borkman with her casual 'we' in Act I, let alone her triumphant 'We are leaving, Mrs Borkman' in Act III, which resolves the three-cornered battle over Erhart, who can only cry out 'I want to live.' In this verbal climate, apparently unremarkable lines may become strangely poignant. When Ella insists on coming with Borkman on his walk to freedom [*viii*, 229], his unexpected emphasis on 'we' – 'Well, we two belong to each other, don't we, Ella' ('*Ja vi to, vi hører jo også sammen, vi, Ella*') – gives a momentary glimpse of what could have been, if he had not sold Ella's love and his own soul for the chairmanship of a bank.[42]

Until Borkman actually walks out into the snow, the world outside serves only as a language for inner worlds. Mrs Borkman draws everything into her angst which, she admits to Ella, 'comes drifting over me – like a storm – and engulfs me' [*viii*, 161]. Ella is most articulate about the landscape of lovelessness:

> Compassion! [*laughs*]. I have never been able to feel compassion – Not since you betrayed me ... You have made everything as empty and barren as a desert. Inside me – and all round me as well. [*viii*, 200]

Borkman 'proudly' admits, in his confrontation with both women in Act III, that his only real love was 'power ... The power to create human happiness, in ever-widening circles around me' [*viii*, 209]. What he wanted to create is realized in the visionary fervour of his own speeches; what he has created is the wasteland of the women's speeches. In the last scene those two opposed worlds merge into the external landscape. Any division between external and internal disappears, as Borkman projects his vision onto the snowy hill and the fjord below, creating in his language the non-existent steamships and factories, much as Edgar creates the drop from Dover Cliff in *King Lear*. Only here, a contrary vision is antiphonally pitched against Borkman's, as in a mighty incantation he offers his love to 'the spirits that serve me ... deep in the darkness' while Ella speaks for the 'warm and human heart which beat for you' and he 'shivers', acknowledging that he sold her heart 'for the kingdom – the power – and the glory' [*viii*, 231]. If this line marks a moment of recognition, it is as close as any of the protagonists of the late plays gets to *anagnorisis*. But it is also the beginning of dying. As the twin sisters clasp hands, we are left with no sense of simple right versus wrong. *John Gabriel Borkman* is an electrifying exploration of the human capacity to create and destroy.

When, in *When We Dead Awaken*, that capacity is lodged in an artist, the world of the play is rarefied into a stark representation of the heart of the matter. As Joyce wrote about the play, it 'expresses its own ideas as briefly and as concisely as they can be expressed in the dramatic form'.[43] The three Acts, all out of doors, are set on a rising gradient, beginning at sea level and ending in the high mountains; the geography is very tangible but also as utterly internalized as in any of Strindberg's 'wander plays', for the rise is also of the mind and spirit. The play begins in the sterility and stagnation of the opening dialogue between Rubek and Maja, gathered into the image of their journey 'home' on a train which stopped for no reason at endless little wayside halts where no-one got on or off, and where it stood silent 'for what seemed like an eternity', while railwaymen walked the platform, talking 'softly, tonelessly, meaninglessly ... about nothing' [*viii*, 241–2]. It ends in elation, with Rubek and Irene climbing to 'celebrate [their] wedding feast', Irene 'rapturously' envisaging their route: 'Up into the glory and splendour of the light. Up to the promised peak! ... right to the very top of the tower, lit by the rising sun'; and with Maja's Ariel-like song, as she is carried by Ulfheim down the mountainside: 'I am free! I am free! I am free!' The 'dead' of Act I – where the life of Rubek and Maja is shown to be void of creativity and joy, as mute and meaningless as the train journey; and where Irene is first seen as a silent walking corpse, her dress shroud-like, her face pale, her features 'stiff and immobile', a ghostly Nun in attendance – have awakened. The sound of the naturalistic storm which is to produce the avalanche is to Rubek 'the prelude to the day of resurrection'. But, more than ever in these plays, there is the orchestration of dissonant voices at the end: the roar of the killer avalanche answers Rubek and Irene's call to triumph, and the Nun's '*Pax vobiscum*' is followed by the faint sound of Maja's song. Resurrection, or 'sound and fury,/ Signifying nothing'?[44]

How we answer this depends on how we read what Joyce described as 'the whole scroll of [Rubek's] life unrolled before us'.[45] The upward movement of the play's present has to be reconciled with the simultaneous movement into time past performed in language. More keenly and explicitly than in any other Ibsen play we are asked to *interpret* what we hear. This is because the play is constructed almost entirely as a series of confrontational duologues – Rubek–Maja, Maja–Ulfheim, Rubek–Irene – and because in these confrontations speakers interact through metaphors which feed into the play's central theme of creativity in art and life. Every character is, more or less self-consciously, a '*dikter*', making sense of life through fictions. In one rare cross-grouping, Maja and Irene have an interchange about opening 'a casket of [Rubek's] that's somehow got locked' [*viii*, 273]; and in another Ulfheim and Rubek agree on the similarity between the raw material of their respective arts, and between their struggles to subdue that material [*viii*, 251]. Maja is initially drawn to the bear-killer (as is Desdemona to Othello) by his stories, and drawn to go with him up the mountains to find out if they are true. The ultimate rapprochement of Maja and Ulfheim, in an extra-ordinary scene which begins like a date rape, takes place through their fictionalizing into fairy-tale their respective pasts – and, in a stichomythic exchange, their shared future. Maja's life with Rubek was a descent and an imprisonment. He 'gave her the idea that she was going up with him to the top of the highest mountain where the sun shone ever so bright', but instead 'he tricked her into a cold, damp cage, without sun or fresh air ... only gilded walls, and round them a lot of great spooky figures in stone' [*viii*, 291]. The fact that both Rubek and Irene refer to his art of sculpture as '*dikte*' is a semantic (if virtually untranslatable) pointer to the tight *nexus* of ideas at the heart of a play where everyone turns life into figures, whether of marble or of words, and where the *Laokoön* problem is solved in that not only is the statue rendered through words but the very point of describing it is to show it as changing and developing in time.[46]

The central confrontations, of course, are between Rubek and Irene, and the 'scroll' that they unroll is the history of the creation of the statue which he calls 'The Day of Resurrection' and she calls their 'child'. It began, with Irene as model and inspiration, as a single figure: 'a pure young woman, untainted by the world, waking to light and glory' [*viii*, 278]. When, thanking her for the 'episode', he dismissed her, he 'killed' her and – it turns out – his inspiration. Her afterlife seems to contain only madness and destruction; his is identified with the deconstruction of the statue. Re-interpreting 'The Day of Resurrection' has meant de-centring the young-woman figure and subduing her radiance, foregrounding a figure of his own guilt-laden self who knows that 'never in all eternity will he win free to achieve the life of the resurrection', and surrounding both with images of mankind as animals [*viii*, 278–9]. This work has brought him fame and wealth, but his own art has degenerated into the veiled satire of the busts that unsuspecting citizens commission from him.

Irene is the key-figure in the art of the play, as in the history of the statue. She belongs in a half-world between psychology and allegory – a precarious mode which threatens to collapse if we start asking how mad or sane she is, and what she has *really* been doing since she left Rubek, or whether he and she are *really* intending to have sexual intercourse on a snow-covered moun-tain. She forms a link between the play that is and the statue that it is about.

In Act II, approaching across the plateau, she looks to Maja 'like a marble statue' and to Rubek 'like the Resurrection incarnate'. But she is not, unlike Hermione in *The Winter's Tale*, a 'statue' come alive to bring forgiveness and a new life; she is there to confront Rubek with, she insists, the dead self left by 'the artist who calmly and casually took a warm living body, a young human life, and ripped the soul out of it – because you needed it to make a work of art' [*viii*, 276]. She served the artist, naked body and soul, and jointly they created the 'child', but for the sake of his art he never dared desire her as a woman: 'The work of art first – the human being second.' In this sense she represents his guilty conscience, his betrayal of life for art, as well as the darkest fear of the play: that when we dead awaken, it is only to see 'that we have never lived' [*viii*, 286]. But she also represents a kind of Catch 22, for had he touched her, she would have killed him with the sharp needle she kept hidden in her hair. The play is not offering easy solutions, either in a regretful could-have-been – saying that Rubek should have made love to Irene and begot flesh-and-blood children – or in an uncontested epiphanic closure, a marriage of life and art in the sunrise among the peaks. The ending is bound to produce a sense of elation – a feeling, as in *The Master Builder*, that it is better to have climbed and fallen than never to have climbed at all – but also a fearful sense that there can be no artistic creation without human destruction, including ultimately that of the creator.

Rubek's life has to be read in the unrolling history of 'The Day of Resurrection', much as Ibsen wanted his read through his production of plays, 'one after another'. *When We Dead Awaken* completes the figure in Ibsen's carpet by confirming his self-critical and yet ardent stance – and by not delivering a message. Henry James's story 'The Figure in the Carpet' (1896) continues to be the subject of debate on how to read it: in terms of structuralist ambiguity – seeing a co-existence of mutually exclusive readings – or of deconstructionist 'unreadability', which implies a text that both generates and frustrates the desire for interpretation.[47] Whatever terms we apply to the figure completed by *When We Dead Awaken*, it seems, it retains the contours of a question mark.

NOTES

1 Here, as occasionally elsewhere, I have used my own translation; but citations from Ibsen in this chapter are mainly from *The Oxford Ibsen*, with the exception of the text of *John Gabriel Borkman* which is cited from the translation by I-S.

Ewbank and Peter Hall (London, 1975). For consistency, where quotations are located, this is without exception to volume and page number of *The Oxford Ibsen*.

2 For an account of Ibsen's different identifications of the series of plays to which he intended *When We Dead Awaken* to form an 'Epilogue', see [*viii*, 1–2].

3 *Harper's Weekly*, 6 February 1897. Reprinted in Allan Wade (ed.), *Henry James: The Scenic Art* (London, 1949), p. 292.

4 See Thomas Postlewait (ed.), *William Archer on Ibsen: The Major Essays, 1889–1919* (Westport, Conn., 1984), p. 287.

5 *Harper's Weekly*, 23 January 1897. In Wade, *The Scenic Art*, p. 289.

6 Letter to Georg Brandes, 26 June 1869 [translated *iii*, 441].

7 Letter to Georg Brandes, 3 June 1897 [see xviii, 397].

8 See *viii*, 34.

9 'Tradition and the Individual Talent' (1919). Cited from *Selected Essays* (New York, 1952), p. 8.

10 Letter to Emilie Bardach, in German, 15 October 1889 [translated *vii*, 548].

11 Speech at a banquet in Christiania, 23 March 1898 [translated *viii*, 360].

12 See [I, 7–8, translated *viii*, 359].

13 See chapter 10, 'Genre and Transgression' in Simon Goldhill, *Reading Greek Tragedy* (Cambridge, 1986).

14 The Rat Wife enters and asks if there is anything 'gnawing' ('*gnager*' – but shortly she expands this to '*nager og gnager*') in the house, moments after Allmers has exclaimed that Eyolf's debility 'gnaws' ('*nager*') at his heart.

15 On Symbolist poetry and drama, see Maurice Valency, *The End of the World: An Introduction to Contemporary Drama* (New York, 1980), chapters 1–3.

16 'Le Tragique quotidien', in *Le Trésor des humbles* (1896). Translation in Toby Cole (ed.), *Playwrights on Playwriting* (New York, 1965), pp. 35–6.

17 Letter to Edvard Brandes, 27 December 1892 [see xviii, 329].

18 See Edvard Beyer, *Ibsen: The Man and his Work* (London, 1978), p. 170.

19 Samuel Beckett, *Waiting for Godot* (London, 1959), p. 89.

20 Brian Johnston, *The Ibsen Cycle: The Design of the Plays from 'Pillars of Society' to 'When We Dead Awaken'* (Boston, Mass., 1975), p. 254.

21 See Johnston on Solness, in *The Ibsen Cycle*, pp. 253–311.

22 Frank Kermode, *The Sense of an Ending: Studies in the Theory of Fiction* (London, 1966), p. 39.

23 The phrase occurs in *Emperor and Galilean*, Part I, Act III, and *The Lady from the Sea*, Act IV. See also James McFarlane, 'Meaning and Evidence in Ibsen's Drama', *Contemporary Approaches to Ibsen*, vol. 1 (1965/66), pp. 35–50.

24 The echo of the divine 'I AM THAT I AM' (Exodus 3:14)) is in the translation only (Original: 'Jeg er nu engang slik som jeg *er*'). However, 'change myself' corresponds to an untranslatable phrase – 'skape meg *om*': 're-create myself' – of implicitly Lucifer-like (if negated) ambition.

25 See '*The Birth of Tragedy*' and '*The Genealogy of Morals*', translated by Francis Golffing (Garden City, N.Y., 1956), p. 170.

26 *Hamlet*, I.ii.65.

27 'The Structured World of Ibsen's Late Dramas', in Errol Durbach (ed.), *Ibsen and the Theatre* (London, 1980), p. 131.

28 Lecture printed in Knut Hamsun, *Paa Turné* (Oslo, 1960). Translation in James McFarlane (ed.), *Henrik Ibsen*, Penguin Critical Anthologies (Harmondsworth, 1970), p. 142.
29 Speech at a banquet of the Norwegian Women's Rights Association, 26 May 1898 [translated *viii*, 363].
30 See J. S. Welhaven, *Samlede digtverker*, 4 vols. (3rd edn Oslo, 1928), vol. II, p. 105. (Last line of the poem 'Republikanerne', from the sequence *Reisedigte* (1836): 'De havde Champagne, men rørte den ei'.)
31 For emphasis Ibsen uses the two words for 'wall': 'vegg og mur'.
32 Peter Brook, *The Empty Space* (Harmondsworth, 1972), p. 65.
33 William Archer, 'Ibsen and English Criticism', *Fortnightly Review*, 46 (1 July 1889). Reprinted in Michael Egan (ed.), *Ibsen: The Critical Heritage* (London, 1972), p. 119.
34 That is, from Richard's 'Now is the winter of our discontent' (I.i.1) to Richmond's 'Now civil wounds are stopped, peace lives again' (V.viii.40).
35 See the section on 'Guilt' and 'Bad Conscience' in *The Genealogy of Morals*, especially the discussion of the material source of '*Schuld*', of man's need for self-torture, and the connection between guilt and physical pain. On Nietzsche and *The Master Builder*, see also Egil Törnqvist, 'Individualism in *The Master Builder*', *Contemporary Approaches to Ibsen*, vol. III (1977), pp. 134–45.
36 Nietzsche, *The Genealogy of Morals* (see note 25, above), p. 229.
37 Nietzsche, *Thoughts Out of Season* (*Unzeitgemässe Betrachtungen*) (New York, 1974), II, paragraph 9.
38 'The crutch-is-float-ing'. Cf. p. 132. above, on the image of the crutch.
39 William Wordsworth, *The Prelude* (1850), XII, 208.
40 John Keats, 'Ode to a Nightingale', line 52.
41 See Ragna Stang, *Edvard Munch: The Man and the Artist* (London, 1979), pp. 159 and 260.
42 Ralph Richardson, who took the part of Borkman in the National Theatre (London) production of the play, 1975–6, declared this to be his favourite line.
43 'Ibsen's New Drama', *Fortnightly Review*, 1 April 1900. Reprinted in Egan (ed.), *Ibsen: The Critical Heritage*, p. 386.
44 *Macbeth*, V.v.26–7.
45 Egan (ed.), *Ibsen: The Critical Heritage*, p. 387.
46 See Lessing's *Laokoön* (1766), on the differences between verbal and plastic arts. See also Daniel Haakonsen, *Henrik Ibsen: mennesket og kunstneren* (Oslo, 1981), pp. 258–9, on Rodin as a model for Rubek and in particular 'The Gate of Hell' as a source for 'The Day of Resurrection'.
47 See the debate between J. Hillis Miller and Shlomith Rimmon-Kenan in *Poetics Today*, 1:3 (1980), 107–18; 2:1b (1980/81), 185–8 and 189–91.

9

JAMES McFARLANE

Ibsen's working methods

From the very start of his career, Henrik Ibsen learned the compulsions of working to a rigorous deadline. When in the autumn of 1851 he was offered a post at the newly established theatre in Bergen, his contract stipulated that he was to 'assist the theatre as dramatic author'. The unwritten assumption was that he would be expected to come forward with an original dramatic work, all ready and rehearsed for performance, every 2 January – the anniversary of the founding of the theatre. This, as he soon discovered, was to be achieved alongside a punishing regime of daily practical work in the theatre as 'Instructeur'.

His first 'anniversary' occasion, on 2 January 1852, clearly allowed him insufficient time to compose a new full-scale dramatic work; but he did go some way towards meeting his obligations by writing a 'Prologue', partly in rhymed and partly in unrhymed verse, the sentiments of which placed the young author very firmly behind the nationalistic endeavours of the new theatre [i, 619–20].

The succeeding five anniversary occasions – and the nature and quality of the works performed – clearly testify that during these years Ibsen found himself having to work at the composition of his dramas under severe time pressure. On the first of these, in 1853, *St John's Night* flopped, running for only two performances; although at the time he was quite ready to acknowledge the play as having come from his pen, in later life he tried to disown it [see i, 686]. For the second occasion, in 1854, he offered a hastily revised version of an earlier play, *The Burial Mound*, which had already been performed in its original form [i, 127–51] in Christiania in 1850; this too was a resounding failure with the public and was taken off after only one performance. For the 1855 occasion, when he presented *Lady Inger*, he was initially deeply uncertain about the quality of the work, pretending that it had been submitted to him for performance by a friend; it was only much later, actually during rehearsals, that he admitted to the authorship of it. It too made a disastrous showing on its first night, and was taken off after its second performance two days later.

Following these three theatrical failures, his next 'anniversary' work for 1856, *The Feast at Solhoug*, was a distinct and welcome though still limited success with the public. It ran to five performances in Bergen in the course of the year, was played in Trondheim as part of a guest visit by the company that same spring and achieved six performances later that year in Christiania.

The fifth and final play of these years in Bergen was *Olaf Liljekrans*. The starting point for this was a short dramatic fragment from 1850, originally planned as a work in four Acts with the title of 'The Grouse in Justedal', and written at the time he was still sheltering behind the pseudonym of Brynjolf Bjarme [*i*, 427–58]. The links between this fragment and the finished drama were only tenuous, however, and most of the latter was written in the summer of 1856. For this occasion Ibsen served not only as the play's author and as its director in the theatre but also as costume designer: eight water-colour sketches from his brush of designs for the costumes have survived.[1] They show the characters in peasant national costume, all executed with considerable technical facility and close attention to detail. Once again, however, the public's response was disappointing, and the play was withdrawn after only two performances; the text also remained unpublished until 1902.

In the late summer of 1857 Ibsen severed his connections with the Bergen Theatre, and on 11 August of that year signed a new contract with the Norwegian Theatre in Christiania. Thus ended his first and formative period as a dramatist: six years or so of anguished endeavour, of many-faceted dramatic apprenticeship, of hard and demanding practical work on the production side, and of unremitting strain to meet the obligations of his contract as a dramatic author. In contrast to the circumstances of his later career, he could afford neither the time nor the energy to devote himself wholly to dramatic composition, and the disciplined regularity of routine which characterizes his maturer years was lacking. Moreover, the public acknowledgement he craved for his work remained disappointingly meagre and contributed little towards his self-confidence.

Little in the way of *working* draft material has survived from these years that might throw light on Ibsen's methods of composition, though what little there is bears significantly on what we know of Ibsen's later practices. Admittedly, there are the 1850 and the 1854 versions of *The Burial Mound*, a comparison of which yields some insight into the general direction Ibsen's mind was taking at this time. And the 1850 manuscript of 'The Grouse in Justedal' by its very format – thirty quarto leaves, in two gatherings of sixteen and fourteen leaves, and embodying minor emendations in Ibsen's hand – sheds some light on his working methods, even though the relationship between this manuscript and the finished drama of some seven years later is not really that of working draft. The one exception in these years is *Catiline*, for which two working notebooks have survived; they contain an almost complete draft of the play, together with two fragmentary scenarios. The physical make-up of these notebooks anticipates in large measure what Ibsen in later life came to adopt as his basic working method: each of them originally consisted of sixteen leaves, to which extra leaves were added – some loose, some stuck or sewn in – whilst others were torn out; this eventually resulted in two separate items of eighteen and twenty-nine leaves, respectively, making forty-seven leaves in all for the full draft; of this, the two brief scenarios were written on the last two pages of the first of these notebooks [see *i*, 576–80]. The manuscript is dated 1849.

During the next phase of his career – between taking up his new job in Christiania in 1857 and his departure for Italy in 1864 – the obstacles to the free development of his dramatic powers changed in kind, but were in no way diminished; rather the reverse. In place of the earlier contractual constraints, he was faced with new domestic responsibilities – as husband and father – and with increasingly fraught economic circumstances. The theatre he had joined went into decline; he was himself repeatedly beset by feelings of inadequacy; he began to neglect his duties and find solace in the bottle. Finally the theatre itself went bankrupt, and Ibsen was left with no regular income, and eked out a living on free-lance fees, the odd grant or stipendium, an occasional loan and even a whip-round among friends.

Between the completion of *The Vikings at Helgeland* in 1857 and the publication of *Love's Comedy* in the winter of 1862–3 there occurred the longest gap between major dramatic works in the whole of his career – those years between the ages of twenty-nine and thirty-four which might well in ordinary circumstances have been some of the most productive.

Of *Love's Comedy* itself, two earlier drafts have survived: a short prose fragment entitled 'Svanhild' [*ii*, 203–16], and an earlier version of the full play in verse [*ii*, 352–8]. Together they shed some light on the genesis of the play itself without adding greatly to our understanding of Ibsen's working methods. Even less helpful on this score is *The Pretenders*; circumstantial evidence seems to suggest that it was written at high speed, mostly in the summer months of 1863, but no preliminary notes or draft dialogue of this play have survived.

Perhaps the most striking thing about this period of his authorship is the close juxtaposition of two works so very different from each other in terms of form and style: the one a light comedy, contemporary in theme and setting and shot through with satire, the other portentously historical, heavy with fateful significance; the one very much a personal declaration, the other an assertion of national destiny; and, most evidently of course, the one in rhyming verse, the other in what is for the most part rather solemn prose. *Love's Comedy* met with much public hostility and was deemed 'immoral' for what it seemed to be saying about the sanctity of marriage; it had to wait eleven years for its first performance. But the reversion to a historical theme and the adoption of prose as the medium of *The Pretenders* still did not seem to come from any genuine inner conviction: 'I am at present writing an historical drama in five Acts,' he confessed in a letter in the summer of 1863, 'but in prose, I *cannot* write it in verse.' This evident anguish over the right choice of medium between verse and prose persisted for many years until, in the mid-1870s, he was at last to declare himself unequivocally for prose.

The years between 1864 and 1877, between the start of his self-imposed exile from Norway and his eventual emergence as a dramatist of international status, were crucial to the development of his dramatic technique. Over these years, two things worked in dialectical relationship to mould his patterns of life and work. The first was that once he had freed himself from the obligations and constraints of National Romanticism, once he had put behind him the compulsions of serving as an instrument of the chauvinism of the age, his creative imagination was released to explore areas of dramatic potential previously embargoed. The second was that very shortly he was to enjoy not merely artistic success but also a measure of material well-being which opened the way to a wholly new kind of life-style and encouraged him to explore new and more audacious themes and materials for his work.

He began planning on a grandiose scale, asking himself why he should not address himself to writing a drama in ten Acts since he simply could not find room for what he had to say in five – a plan, incidentally, which he was to realize before the first ten years of his exile were up. He then seems to have switched to writing a long – very long – narrative poem in rhyming verse, of which a 'fragment' of some 212 eight-line stanzas has (miraculously) survived. This work, which by virtue of its theme and content has come to be known as the 'Epic Brand', occupied him for about a year; he then abruptly, in consequence of one overwhelming moment of insight and inspiration, abandoned it in favour of a large-scale *dramatic* poem on the same general themes and with the same characters as the narrative poem. It was then as though a floodgate had been opened; and Ibsen did not conceal the exhilaration he felt at this newly won fluency of composition:

Then one day I went into St Peter's – I was in Rome on an errand – and there, suddenly, the form for what I had to say came to me, forcefully and clearly. Now I have thrown overboard the thing that has been tormenting me for a whole year without my having got anywhere with it; and in the middle of July I began on something new, which progressed as nothing has ever progressed for me before. It is new in the sense that the writing of it began then; but the content and the drift of it have been hanging over me like a nightmare since those many unhappy events back home made me look within myself and look at our way of life there ... I work morning and evening, something I have never been able to do before. It is blessedly peaceful out here [in Ariccia], no visitors; I read nothing but the Bible – it is powerful and strong.

[*iii*, 424–5]

The five long Acts of this major new work were completed in a matter of four months, between July and November 1865, in what can only be thought of as a kind of *raptus*.

The uninhibited exuberance which characterized the writing of *Brand* continued into his next play. 'After *Brand*,' Ibsen later confessed, '*Peer Gynt* followed as it were of its own accord.' Once again it was in verse, and long. He completed it at high speed in some nine to ten months, mainly between the January and the October of 1867 whilst resident in Southern Italy, in Ischia and in Sorrento. It grew prodigiously under his hands: a vast, free-ranging invention, audacious in its imagery, headlong in its movement.

Full draft versions of both *Brand* and *Peer Gynt* have survived, together with a number of other preliminary jottings, scraps of trial dialogue, revisions and additions on separate sheets of paper. In both cases, the draft versions represent a relatively late stage of composition, with the constituent parts carefully collated and numbered, from which Ibsen was able to prepare the final fair copy [see *iii*, 433–9, 454–82]. Moreover, in the case of the *Peer Gynt* draft, Ibsen carefully dated his work at certain key points, such as the beginnings and ends of the Acts; this was to be a continuing feature of his working method in later life. In their physical make-up, these drafts tended to take the form of two folded sheets, quarto, one inserted within the other, giving an eight-sided 'gathering', which he was then careful to number sequentially. Revisions could then take the form of (a) minor corrections and emendations to the emergent text; (b) the insertion of extra single or folded sheets, sometimes unnumbered, sometimes identified and ordered by letters; and (c) the occasional excision of certain pages and the substitution of new ones. It was a pattern of work which, with various modifications, was to serve Ibsen for most of the remainder of his authorship.

Prompted partly by the ambiguous and (to him) disappointing reception given by the critics of the day to *Peer Gynt*, Ibsen began to read warning signals in the situation. He became aware that this undisciplined mode of composition had its dangers. Soon he was to refer to this period of his life as an 'intoxication'; five years after its publication – in a letter to Edmund Gosse – he was calling *Peer Gynt* 'wild and formless, recklessly written' [*iii*, 491]. Much later in life he confessed that he had written both *Brand* and *Peer Gynt* at high pressure, ceaselessly writing verses even when asleep or half-awake, thinking them splendid at the time but having to admit later that they were 'veriest nonsense'. Such plays, he asserted, were easy to write compared to the strict consistency of a *John Gabriel Borkman* [*iii*, 493–4].

Ibsen's reaction against this spirit of 'recklessness' was in its own idio-syncratic way almost equally intemperate. Pausing only to fire off *The League of Youth* as a furious riposte to the critics back home, he then took up again the plan he had had in his sights for a number of years and for which he had already collected a fair amount of material: that of writing what he had described as 'a fairly considerable dramatic work, the material of which is drawn from Roman history' [*iv*, 557]. The result was a work which occupies a unique position in Ibsen's *œuvre*: *Emperor and Galilean*, a 'double drama' in ten Acts. No other play of his was so carefully researched [see *iv*, 597–603]; no other is so fully documented with preliminary notes and other draft material [see *iv*, 562–97]. His repudiation of the earlier insouciant mode of composition was total. He himself acknowledged that the play gave evidence of a new Germanic thoroughness – ascribed by him in part to his having left Italy behind and moved to Dresden to live. It deliberately set out to give dramatic expression to his own personal 'Welt-anschauung' – the word is Ibsen's – and he was eager that the play should be designated as 'a world-historic play'. The high seriousness of his purpose is evident.

Although he never again embarked on a dramatic project remotely matching *Emperor and Galilean* in motivation and temper, there is one ancillary aspect of the work which does mark a genuine policy decision and left its mark on all his subsequent endeavour. The work is in prose; not tentatively so, as some of the earlier prose dramas might be considered, but very deliberately and indeed – as he was quick to assert – irrevocably so. He politely but firmly corrected Edmund Gosse when the latter hinted that the work would have been improved by being in verse [*iv*, 606]; and from this moment on he rejected verse as an appropriate medium for drama in this modern age.

His career of authorship was almost half over before Ibsen found and adhered to a creative rhythm with which he felt entirely at ease. In these years, which made up almost exactly the last quarter of the nineteenth century, there were published those twelve 'Ibsenist' plays which transformed Ibsen from a dramatist of modest Scandinavian dimensions into one of towering international status. Typically, the compositional cycle for each individual play occupied two years. *Pillars of Society* came in 1877; *A Doll's House* and *Ghosts* in 1879 and 1881 respectively. *An Enemy of the People*, fuelled by his anger at the reaction of the critics back home, took him exceptionally only one year. There then followed, every second autumn for the next fourteen years, that astounding succession of plays which took Europe and the world by storm: *The Wild Duck*, *Rosmersholm*, *The Lady from the Sea*, *Hedda Gabler*, *The Master Builder*, *Little Eyolf* and *John Gabriel Borkman*. Finally came a further untypical period of three years which he took over his 'dramatic epilogue' *When We Dead Awaken*, published in the last December days of 1899.

Henrik Jæger, Ibsen's first biographer, recorded in 1887 some anecdotal details about his working methods:

> When he has chosen his material, he ponders it carefully for a long time before he sets pen to paper. Much of this thinking takes place on his long walks; moreover, the long time he takes over dressing is also given over to this preparatory thought. When he has thought the thing through in broad outline, he writes an outline sketch.

Jæger suggested to him that since he worked out his scenarios so carefully he might just as easily write the last Act first and the first one last. This Ibsen did not accept, indicating that many of the key details did not emerge until he was actually engaged on the writing of the play itself. Jæger continued:

> On the basis of this outline, he then sets about giving the thing shape, and this goes relatively swiftly. . . . In this way the first manuscript grows from day to day until it is finished. But this version is then for Ibsen nothing more than a preliminary. Only when this is complete does he feel he is familiar with his characters, that he knows their natures and how they express themselves. Then comes the revision in the second manuscript, and finally the fair copy in the third. He does not allow the work to leave his possession until there is one complete fair copy in existence.[2]

Although there would inevitably be minor deviations from this tidy norm as he moved from play to play, the publication in 1909 of the three volumes of Ibsen's literary remains, his *Efterladte Skrifter*, gave surprisingly precise confirmation to Jæger's account. For the first time public access to his working drafts and 'foul papers' was available on a broad scale. With only a few gaps of any significance, mainly relating to one or two of the early plays, these papers cover the whole span of his authorship from *Catiline* to *When*

We Dead Awaken; they comprise preliminary notes and jottings, scenarios, drafts, fragments of trial dialogue, marginal annotations, occasional pen and ink illustrative drawings, all for the most part sequentially numbered and/or lettered and physically sorted to preserve their essential sequentiality. Moreover the care which Ibsen habitually gave to dating his papers, often furnishing precise dates for the start and finish of individual Acts of a play, makes it possible in a great many instances not merely to sort and order with confidence the various and separate fragments into a coherent succession of events, but also to place them with rare precision in historical time: by year, month and day.

A brief chronology of the genesis of *The Lady from the Sea* not only provides a representative sample of the nature and range of these draft papers but also gives a quite startling example of the disparity between 'brooding' time and active writing time that was possible within the Ibsenist two-year cycle of composition. His previous play, *Rosmersholm*, had been published on 23 November 1886. Circumstantial evidence from Ibsen's correspondence and the testimony of friends suggests that he probably did not actually put pen to paper during the whole of 1887, and possibly not until the middle of 1888, though William Archer (who visited Ibsen on holiday in Denmark) did report Ibsen as having said that he was turning over several plans and that he hoped 'to have some tomfoolery ready next year'.

Among the surviving documents directly relating to the play [see *vii*, 448–58], none can be ascribed to a period earlier than the summer of 1888. The earliest notes were dated, by 5 June in his own hand. In terms of bulk they covered just over nine quarto sides of handwriting, and consisted of: (a) a relatively full outline, in generally narrative form, of the events of Act I as then envisaged; and (b) a later outline of Act I, in which the characters are identified impersonally as the Painter, the Tutor, the Sculptor, the Young Girls, the Lawyer, etc., together with notes for the set of Act II. A second item consisted of one folded sheet, quarto, which originally contained only a list of named characters; subsequently two of the remaining sides of this item were used for brief notes on the structure of the play by Acts as far as the opening of Act IV, and alterations were then later made both to the names and to the descriptions in the original list of characters.

The chief constituent item is a complete working draft of the play in fifty numbered folios, extra to which are two separate and differing title-pages with varying names for the characters. To this working draft were made many subsequent deletions, alterations and additions entered on the folios themselves; and, additionally to these, some extra dialogue, notes, etc. were written up on loose sheets and inserted in the draft as part of the revisionary process. Changes in the characters' names from one Act to another, and sometimes even within the course of a single Act, make up a fairly complex pattern; these changes are helpful to the reader, as they surely were also to the author, as an aid in ordering the drafts and other manuscript notes in sequence.

Furthermore, the individual Acts were then dated by Ibsen top and tail, thus:

Act I	10 Jun 88 – 16 Jun 88
Act I	21 Jun 88 – 28 Jun 88 / 18 Aug 88
Act III	2 Jul 88 – 7 Jul 88 / 20 Aug 88
Act IV	12 Jul 88 – 22 Jul 88 / 31 Aug 88
Act V	24 Jul 88 – 31 Jul 88

Seemingly, therefore, in round terms: a couple of months to complete a first version; another month to complete the revision; and (since it is known that the completed manuscript was despatched on 25 September) about another three weeks to make the fair copy – the whole preceded by some eighteen months of 'brooding'. The drama was published on 28 November 1888 – two years almost to the day after the publication of *Rosmersholm*.

Taken all together, these papers offer many a fascinating insight into Ibsen's creative processes. They illuminate with rare clarity the onward progress of a work's dramatic development, often from the first seed of an idea, through successive stages of revision and re-structuring and re-direction right through to the meticulously formed handwriting of the fair copy, despatched with scrupulous timing to achieve (it must be admitted) maximum market impact. Most obviously, these drafts show Ibsen to have been an extremely methodical writer at this important stage of his authorship and testify to the enormous care with which he adjusted and amended the elements in the work, refined its dialogue, re-aligned its constituent parts, and re-worked its emphases in the pursuit of effective dramatic communication. At the same time, however, what they also demonstrate beyond doubt is that, for Ibsen, dramatic composition emphatically did not mean the mere supervention of language on an inspiration which was already complete. They leave no doubt that the writing of an Ibsen play was a highly interactive procedure, a dynamic process full of shifts and retreats and advances and semantic flux as the creative invention of the author, the imperatives of the linguistic medium and the latent potential of the thematic material acted upon one another during the entire period of active composition.[3]

Throughout these maturer years of authorship, those vast sources of creative imagination which Ibsen so prodigally exploited in *Brand* and *Peer Gynt* continued to serve him; but the difference now lay in the control – the iron, unrelenting control – which he now exercised over them.

NOTES

The two works indispensable for a study of Ibsen's draft manuscripts (and thus of his working methods) *in Norwegian* are: Henrik Ibsen, *Samlede Verker*, Hundreårs-utgave (The Centenary Edition) ed. Francis Bull, Halvdan Koht and Didrik Arup Seip (Oslo, 1928–57), 22 vols.; and Henrik Ibsen, *Efterladte Skrifter*, ed. Halvdan Koht and Julius Elias, 3 vols. (Christiania, 1909).

Those without a knowledge of Norwegian might consult *The Oxford Ibsen*, ed. James McFarlane, 8 vols. (London, 1960–77), passim; and *The Collected Works of Henrik Ibsen*, ed. William Archer, 12 vols., (London, 1906 ff.) vol. XII (1912) *From Ibsen's Workshop*, trans. A. G. Chater. See also James McFarlane, 'Drama in the Making', in *Ibsen and Meaning* (Norwich, 1989), pp. 67–83 – the text of the second Popperwell Memorial Lecture in the University of Cambridge, April 1987.

1 See Otto Lous Mohr, *Henrik Ibsen som Maler* (Oslo, 1953), pp. 42–3.

2 Henrik Jæger, in a newspaper report of December 1887, reprinted in Henrik Ibsen, *Efterladte Skrifter* (Christiania, 1909), ed. Halvdan Koht and Julius Elias, vol. I, pp. xix ff.

3 This is something perhaps most clearly illustrated by the draft manuscripts to *Little Eyolf* – see James McFarlane, 'The Structured World of Ibsen's Late Dramas' in *Ibsen and the Theatre*, ed. Errol Durbach (London, 1980), pp. 131–40.

10

SIMON WILLIAMS

Ibsen and the theatre 1877–1900

There can have been few periods of theatrical malaise as extended and as acute as that of the 1870s and early 1880s. Theatre, it was generally agreed by most who wrote about it, did not reflect the intellectual and scientific advances of the nineteenth century, nor did it address the fundamental problems created by an age of industrialization and urbanization. Zola's famous call-to-arms, the essay 'Naturalism in the Theatre' (1880), was but the most inflammatory contribution to what was becoming, by the late 1870s, an escalating critical assault upon the theatre. Zola accused French and, by implication, European drama of being mechanical, superficial, lacking in authentic characters, and perpetuating the outworn clichés of Romanticism. These objections were shared by critics elsewhere. The brothers Hart, leading theorists of the German naturalist movement, bewailed the decadence of German theatre, claiming that no great drama had been written since Schiller and that acting had been in decline since the Napoleonic wars. Everything presented on stage was intended either to complement the 'trivial, shallow taste of the public'[1] or to underpin those values that created a complacent, materialistic society. In England things were little better; Harley Granville-Barker, looking back on the 1880s, suggests that theatre was all 'a rather childish affair'.[2]

Since then, the theatre has never fully grown up; in Britain and America, in particular, it still apparently feels that one of its major functions is the depressing duty of providing pure entertainment and buttressing the values of the status quo. However, since the 1880s, that has never been its sole duty. Indeed, in the last hundred years theatre often served as a forum for the discussion of the formative forces of modern life and the drama as a polemical medium through which these forces are represented. The plays of Henrik Ibsen were pivotal in the first phase of this transformation of the theatre. They had a vitalizing effect on a stagnant repertoire, they stimulated new modes of acting and staging and they influenced profoundly major playwrights of the twentieth century. This essay will be concerned with the first two of these issues.

In Europe, the most spectacular event in the introduction of Ibsen to national repertoires was usually the first performance of his most controversial play, *Ghosts*. As *Ghosts* had to be performed privately, usually under the auspices of independent theatre societies especially constituted to avoid the censor, myth has commonly associated Ibsen with these theatres. But his introduction was actually more various and his plays were seen by, and had an impact on, audiences wider than the select intelligentsia that patronized the independent theatres.

With the exception of Scandinavia, where his plays had had a tenuous hold in the repertoire since his early days as a theatre director in the 1850s,[3] Ibsen's works first found a stage in Germany. His introduction here came in two waves. The first of his plays to be produced were not the social dramas but those pieces that appealed to the historicist tastes of the time. *The Pretenders* was staged by the Meiningen Court Theatre, first at Meiningen, then as part of the company's tour to Berlin in 1876. In the same year, *The Vikings at Helgeland* was given with mild though not lasting success in Munich, Dresden and Leipzig. Then, two years later, Ibsen rose into prominence with spectacular suddenness when *Pillars of Society* was given simultaneous production in five private theatres in Berlin, followed by twenty-six productions elsewhere in Germany over the next year.[4] So popular was the play that his next work, *A Doll's House*, was taken up by court and municipal theatres throughout Germany immediately after its première in Copenhagen in December 1879. Although, to satisfy conservative opinion, it was occasionally given with an ending in which Nora did not leave for the sake of her children, *A Doll's House* succeeded in stimulating vigorous critical debate.

The spate of German premières came to a halt, mainly because the next play, *Ghosts*, was banned, Ibsen remaining in public attention primarily through critical essays. The second and more important wave of premières began in 1886, when *Ghosts* was given under private auspices, first in Augsburg, then by the Meiningen Court Theatre, finally in Berlin in January 1887. *Ghosts* was also chosen in September 1890 as the opening production of the Freie Bühne, an independent theatre society in Berlin devoted primarily to the production of new drama. By this time *An Enemy of the People*, *The Wild Duck*, and *Rosmersholm* had already been seen in Germany and Ibsen's plays were gradually acquiring a permanent place in the repertoire. Some were even given their first performances in Germany; *The Lady from the Sea* was first performed at the Weimar Court Theatre in February 1889,[5] *Hedda Gabler* had its première at the Munich Court

Theatre in January 1891, while both *The Master Builder* and *Little Eyolf* were first given full productions at theatres in Berlin. Toward the end of the century, even the reputedly unperformable works were staged, notably *Emperor and Galilean* at Leipzig in December 1896 and *Brand* in Berlin in March 1898.

The readiness with which the Germans staged Ibsen seems to lend support to his claim that he was better understood in Germany than elsewhere,[6] but opinions of theatre critics about him were far from unanimous. The earlier polemical prose plays were not especially controversial; indeed, they were mostly welcome as Germany had a tradition of theatrical protest through the work of Hebbel and Otto Ludwig. It may, in fact, have been the expectations created by this reputation and by Ibsen's affinity with the German naturalist movement that gave rise to the critical confusion, at times outright hostility, that greeted most of his plays from the first performance of *Rosmersholm* (Augsburg, 6 April 1887) on. Even Julius Hart, an ardent early advocate of Ibsen, confessed he was at a loss to understand *Hedda Gabler*,[7] a complaint that sounded more frequently until the end of the century when the personal, enigmatic nature of the late plays found acceptance. Nevertheless, while critics fretted in the theatre Ibsen flourished, especially after 1894 when the Deutsches Theater in Berlin, then the *de facto* national theatre, became a centre for Ibsen performance under the direction of Otto Brahm.

Ibsen's introduction to Britain was very different. It occurred over a shorter period of time, was centred around one city, London, and aroused one of the most violent critical controversies in the history of the theatre. After a few obscure or bowdlerized productions during the 1880s, Ibsen's arrival effectively took place on 7 June 1889 with a production of *A Doll's House* at the Royalty Theatre, with Janet Achurch as Nora. The production was planned to run for one week; it lasted for three. But while audiences were united in approval, critics were in an uproar. They considered the play to undermine that most sacred of Victorian institutions, marriage. The controversy quickly gathered steam under the leadership of Ibsen's insistent champion, the critic William Archer. In fact, Archer, aware of the vacuous triviality that passed for drama on the London stage, did not initially believe Ibsen should even be staged. Nevertheless, he was the moving force behind several productions in the *annus mirabilis* of 1891, when Ibsen first became a major presence in the London theatre. In addition to two separate revivals of *A Doll's House*, there were four first performances of Ibsen plays. *Rosmersholm* at the Vaudeville Theatre in February attracted little attention, because of inadequate acting, but the next première, in March, the opening production of the new Independent Theatre Society, was of *Ghosts*.

Although it received only one performance, the outpouring of critical venom it aroused has rarely been equalled in vituperation and volume, over 500 articles appearing on the subject of the play.[8] Tempers were running high when *Hedda Gabler* was produced at the Vaudeville in April, but surprisingly the play, which had been a critical failure in Germany, enjoyed a popular success, mainly due to the striking performance of the American actress Elizabeth Robins as Hedda. The five matinée performances planned for the production were extended to a month's run of evening performances. Ibsen's cause then suffered something of a set-back due to an undistinguished production of *The Lady from the Sea* in May. By now, though it would take years for conservative critics to accept Ibsen, their attempt to stifle him had failed,[9] and performances rather than the critical reaction they aroused began to attract public interest. In February 1893 Robins did for *The Master Builder* what she had done for *Hedda*, demonstrating the stage-worthiness of a difficult work after its lukewarm German première. Soon after, Herbert Beerbohm-Tree became the first of the actor–managers in the commercial theatre to take up Ibsen, specifically *An Enemy of the People*, which seemed to offer him a juicy leading role. Though he was ineffectively comic as Stockmann, his production brought Ibsen to a substantially wider audience than hitherto. In 1894, there was an unremarkable *Wild Duck* and in 1896, a star-studded *Little Eyolf*, with Janet Achurch as Rita, Elizabeth Robins as Asta, and Mrs Patrick Campbell as the Rat Wife, a production of uneven quality, but one that proved that even Ibsen's most apparently 'undramatic' plays could attract an audience. *John Gabriel Borkman* followed in May 1897 and, some weeks later, Ibsen was accorded the most complete acceptance when Queen Victoria and the Archbishop of Canterbury attended a revival of *Ghosts* by the Independent Theatre.

It was in France more than anywhere else that Ibsen's plays were most exclusively associated with the independent theatre movement. The Théâtre-Libre, founded by André Antoine in 1887 mainly for the production of original French plays with little commercial potential, introduced Ibsen with *Ghosts* in May 1890. The play was staged mainly on the promptings of Zola, for no other contemporary work so powerfully fulfilled his ideal of naturalistic drama. Even though Antoine's performance as Oswald had some impact, public response was mixed and the critics generally indifferent. Nevertheless, the next year Antoine followed *Ghosts* with *The Wild Duck*, a production that enjoyed a marginally better reception. *Hedda Gabler* made little impact when produced commercially at the end of 1891. In fact, it was not until the performance of *The Lady from the Sea* by the avant-garde group, Cercle des Escholiers, under the direction of Aurélien Lugné-Poë in December 1892 that Ibsen began to attract wide attention. The overtly poetic idiom of the play in which the dramatic focus seemed directed more toward extra-human realms of experience indicated the particular interest of the young director and the company that he subsequently founded, the Théâtre de l'Oeuvre, which was noted for the dream-like quality of its productions. In fact, l'Oeuvre gave no less than eight of Ibsen's plays their first French performance – *The Master Builder* and *Rosmersholm* in 1893, *Little Eyolf* and *Brand* in 1895, *Pillars of Society* and *Peer Gynt* in 1896, and *Love's Comedy* and *John Gabriel Borkman* in 1897. Only the Deutsches Theater in Berlin was as exclusively associated with Ibsen, and then in a naturalistic style that was radically different from the symbolism of l'Oeuvre. So strongly was Lugné-Poë identified with Ibsen in the French mind, that even the celebrated Réjane as Nora in a boulevard performance of *A Doll's House* in 1894 could not steal his thunder. Naturally, critical controversy surrounded his productions, which were widely pronounced to be too gloomy for French tastes.

In Russia, Ibsen arrived late and unremarkably. Solitary performances of *A Doll's House* were given in St Petersburg in 1884 and Moscow in 1891, followed by an insignificant *Vikings* in 1892, a dreadful production of *An Enemy of the People* in Moscow, also in 1892, and an undistinguished *Pillars of Society* in St Petersburg in 1897. Not until the foundation in 1898 of the Moscow Art Theatre in which a realistic mode of acting and production was systematically explored did Ibsen start to appear with any frequency on a Russian stage, but even then only *An Enemy of the People* and *Brand* were major successes, mainly because the Russians prized the visionary aspects of Ibsen's work over the naturalistic. It was not until the early twentieth century, with the performances of Vera Kommisarjevskaya and the rigorously non-realistic productions of Vsevolod Meyerhold, that Ibsen came into his own on the Russian stage.[10]

While critical controversies over Ibsen in different countries varied in emphasis, most objections were consistently repeated and hence can provide us with a means of identifying specifically the changes his plays introduced to the theatre. The most persistent complaint was that his plays did not elevate, but focused primarily on degrading aspects of human conduct; consequently they were dismissed as appealing solely to people with morbid interests. Certainly they confuted what was then conceived to be the fundamental purpose of art, namely to create only what is ideal and beautiful. In Germany especially, this was the ethos of Weimar Classicism that still dominated the theatre of the 1880s. As a minor, though representative critic put it: 'It has never been the business of art to bring that which is offensive to the fore. Harmony and quiet, elevated beauty are her characteristics. It is time we once again recall to memory the words of our deathless poet: "Life is serious; art is serene."'[11] A similar lack of ideality disturbed the doyen of English conservative critics, Clement Scott. He condemned Janet Achurch's Nora for not being 'the pattern woman we have admired in our mothers and sisters', and was deeply disturbed by Elizabeth Robins's persuasive performance as Hedda, who seemed to be an advocate of all he felt theatre should not express. 'She has made vice attractive by her art. She has almost ennobled crime . . . She has glorified an unwomanly woman. She has made a heroine out of a sublimated sinner. She has fascinated us with a savage.'[12] Ibsen subverted rather than affirmed the status quo. So strong was this sense of subversion that even a liberal critic like the Prussian Theodor Fontane, who had an acute appreciation of the technical qualities of the plays, could endorse neither Ibsen's deterministic vision nor what he considered to be 'the theses of the plays'.[13]

Many critics, generally the more obtuse ones, would not even grant Ibsen technical proficiency. For them, his sins against the canons of good playwriting were legion. They were especially irritated by his desire to mystify, a tendency that became more pronounced after *The Wild Duck*. Françisque Sarcey, the dean of French critics, claimed to be constantly baffled by the symbols, which he found entirely unnecessary, preferring instead the clarity of a well-made play by Scribe.[14] Critics were angered too by the difficulty of determining the attitude one should adopt toward his characters; *Hedda Gabler* and *The Master Builder*, with their equivocal central figures, even riled German critics otherwise in sympathy with the social plays where the 'message' seemed unambiguous and necessary. Then Ibsen was accused of being too gloomy, his characters belonged to hospitals, dissecting rooms, even morgues, and all of them were unpleasant people with whom it was impossible to sympathize. Some supposedly enlightened writers, like Edmond de Goncourt, hid their unease behind the excuse that his plays were too foreign.[15] Others, Sarcey and Scott especially, protested at the seeming lack of action, and at the extended passages of exposition. Consequently they dismissed Ibsen as unstageworthy. The last resort, of London critics in particular, was to accuse Ibsen of obscenity and coarse language, a complaint that flew in the face of their contention that he was also verbose and allusive.

A particularly interesting source of infuriation for critics in England, France and Germany arose from the presence in the audience of people who actually appreciated Ibsen. The critics' determination to isolate them as a body of eccentrics deserving of nothing but contempt can be traced back to the very first production of Ibsen in Germany – the Meiningen *Pretenders* in Berlin in 1876 – when Karl Frenzel, also a noted conservative, objected to the obtrusive presence of friends of the Norwegian poet in the audience.[16] In

London, where critics were incensed by Ibsen's challenge to conventional values, 'friends' of the poet were routinely dismissed as being on the margins of society, 'Ibsenites, Socialists and Agnostics',[17] 'members of a fanatical sect'. In France and Germany, critics displayed reverse intellectual snobbery, pouring their scorn on Ibsenites who, they claimed, only pretended to understand the obscure message of the master while the common sense of the audience remained healthily baffled. Behind this hostility, one senses a fundamental concern that, in contrast to the theatre of the previous generation, a common consensus could no longer be found among audiences. The polemics of Ibsen's drama divided the audience and revealed rather than covered broader rifts within society as a whole. Ibsen challenged the most basic assumption of the function of theatre – his work did not create a community, it divided it.

To dwell too long on the negative critical reaction can unbalance our view of Ibsen's importance to the theatre, first because the critical response was not all adverse, secondly because he was surprisingly popular with audiences. Even the most hostile critics commented in puzzled tone on the enthusiasm with which the plays were received. It has been convincingly demonstrated that, in London at least, Ibsen was more popular with audiences in the last decade of the nineteenth century than in the first decades of the twentieth.[18] The main reason for this was that while his ideas and vision were unfamiliar, he exploited all aspects of the popular idiom of nineteenth-century theatre to give them convincing expression. As Otto Brahm observed after the 1887 Berlin *Ghosts*, it was the content rather than the form that disturbed people.[19] In fact, Ibsen fitted with ease into the familiar aesthetic of contemporary theatre. Although *Pillars of Society* may have, as Alfred Kerr put it, 'laid a torpedo in the ark',[20] that torpedo came in the form of an immaculately constructed well-made play that manipulated tension as skilfully as Scribe ever did. Even though focus in the later plays centred more on character, symbol or discussion, Ibsen never failed to craft a well-structured plot. Furthermore, in the stage world he created, the illusion of a seamless whole was maintained. Consequently, his plays appealed to audiences raised on the aesthetic of the *Gesamtkunstwerk* which, despite Richard Wagner's revolutionary claims for his theories, had prevailed in the European theatre for several decades.

There were, of course, striking innovations in Ibsen's drama, but in retrospect they appear more as evolutionary developments than radical breaks with past practice. Although conservative critics deplored the vast amount of time devoted to exposition, the more discerning welcomed the greater structural cohesion this gave the action, finding exposition to invest the realistic drama with unwonted classical proportions and to intensify the tragic perspective on a mundane world. Attention to exposition and the self-exploration this required of major characters meant that an Ibsen play struck contemporaries as, in Henry James's words, 'the picture not of an action but of a condition ... of a state of nerves as well as of soul, a state of temper, of health, of chagrin, of despair'.[21] The consequence of this focus on character was an apparent de-theatricalization; in fact to the admirer of Ibsen, the word 'theatrical' had negative connotations, implying whatever was 'inauthentic'. Looked at historically, it is clear that through Ibsen the conventions of an earlier generation were beginning to lose their credibility. The plays and their performers were constantly praised for their denial of theatricality and their capacity to create a strikingly convincing illusion of everyday life. 'The effect of the play,' Ibsen wrote about *Ghosts*, 'depends a great deal on making the spectator feel as if he were actually sitting, listening, and looking at events happening in real life.'[22] However unsettling their impact was upon the audience, aesthetically his works remained within the range of conventional thinking about theatre.

Two further qualities of Ibsen's work made it historically important. First, as he was concerned not with ideal models of behaviour but with revealing motives that lie beneath the surface of behaviour, Ibsen's plays were not especially pleasant. While George Bernard Shaw's claim – that attending an Ibsen play was like the fascinating but painful experience of going to the dentist[23] – should be taken for the rhetoric it is, it indicates a new dimension to theatregoing. The play was no longer staged solely for entertainment, and the actors needed no longer to ingratiate themselves with the audience. A novel and potentially antagonistic relationship was thereby set up between stage and auditorium, an antagonism that was a prime stimulus for the initial critical outcry. Secondly, as characters became complex and revealed their personalities through the non-linear medium of memory and as much of this revelation centred around symbols that were difficult to grasp, Ibsen seemed to be asking for more imaginative effort from his audience than any playwright prior to him had done. He was not easy to follow, though as the French critic Jules Lemaître put it when discussing *Hedda Gabler*, sometimes it is necessary in the theatre 'to reflect, to make an effort, to work'.[24]

The accumulated new dimensions of Ibsen's drama had a radical effect upon production and performance practice in British and European theatre. Methods of staging were not instantly affected, as it was only in the twentieth century that systematic efforts were made to materialize psychic and symbolic landscapes on stage. In fact, the immediate effect of Ibsen was mainly to make the stage director, at that time an emerging figure, alert to the need for choice and exactitude in stage setting. As interaction between character and environment was a crucial dimension of Ibsen's drama, the environment should be carefully constructed. William Bloch at the Royal Theatre in Copenhagen was scrupulous down to the last detail in the setting and staging of *An Enemy of the People* and *The Wild Duck*,[25] a quality characterizing the work of other Scandinavian directors, especially the Swedish August Lindberg who, among other services to Ibsen, directed the European première of *Ghosts*. The settings devised by Antoine for his production of *Ghosts* and *The Wild Duck* at the Théâtre-Libre attracted as much interest as the acting. He was concerned with authentic national details as an expression of character and, in *The Wild Duck* especially, began to develop a sense of how each stage object expresses an aspect of the predicament of one or more characters.[26] Recent research has also indicated that the success of *Hedda Gabler* in London may have been due largely to the exiguous direction of William Archer who advised actors on all aspects of blocking, gesture and interpretation.[27]

The theatre artist who benefited most from Ibsen's plays was the actor. A common theme in all theatrical criticism of Ibsen, friendly or hostile, is the compelling quality of the acting the plays demand of the performer. 'More than anybody who ever wrote for the stage,' Elizabeth Robins stated, 'Ibsen could, and usually did, cooperate with his actors.' He regarded the actor as a 'fellow-creator'.[28] Henry James is more explicit.

> He will remain intensely dear to the actor and actress. He cuts them out work to which the artistic nature in them joyously responds – work difficult and interesting, full of stuff and opportunity. The opportunity that he gives them is almost always to do the deep and delicate thing – the sort of chance that, in proportion as they are intelligent, they are most on the lookout for. He asks them to paint with a fine brush; for the subject he gives them over is our plastic humanity.[29]

Prior to Ibsen, unless one played leading roles, acting was probably a rather uninteresting activity. Rarely did actors receive roles that represented peculiar and original personalities, rather ones written according to type. The little training they received was never intended to develop their powers of characterization, but to encourage them simply to be ' "graceful", "emphatic" or just "expressive" '.[30] In Germany, most actors imitated the elegance of the Weimar style, while in France the classicism of the Comédie Française was a widely adopted model.

Such approaches to acting were inadequate when applied to Ibsen. Rather than types, he created characters in 'minute and elaborate' detail,[31] paradoxically investing some of them with such immense passions that they would not be out of place in classical tragedy. The impossibility of tying Ibsen's characters down to type was compounded by the interrelationship between character and environment and by the manner in which characters' personalities were often shown as a product of their relationships with others and therefore as infinitely variable. Furthermore, Ibsen's characters are the essence of contradiction, marked by division rather than the wholeness that was the hallmark of the traditional nineteenth-century type. There was a technical innovation too that Ibsen's actors had to deal with, that character was not revealed chronologically as it was in conventional drama. Hence, in order to play the character fully, the actor had to anticipate action toward the end of the play while acting early passages. As Herbert Waring observed, on first reading A Doll's House struck him as entirely commonplace. Only on re-reading the play with full knowledge of the conclusion did 'every word of the terse sentences seem . . . to give a value of its own and to suggest some subtle nuance of feeling'.[32] The source of the Ibsen character's appeal was different from those in conventional drama, consequently the performer's technique had to alter. Beauty in appearance, voice and gesture were not essential attributes for the actor of Ibsen. Furthermore, traditional gender roles were often reversed, a heroic quality being required of the women, while actors playing Ibsen's men had to suffer 'the shameful extremity of a weak soul stripped naked before an audience looking for heroism'.[33] But perhaps the most formidable challenge faced by the Ibsen actor was the questionable moral quality of his characters, which could easily alienate them from the audience. The real challenge to the performer of Ibsen was therefore to make the character 'sympathetically unsympathetic' as Shaw put it.[34] All in all, Ibsen required the actor to be an interpretative artist, critical of the role and discriminating in choice. 'Line of action for the play and the character' are issues for the Ibsen actor to deal with rather than 'choice of passions and accompanying gestures'.[35] This laid a heavy responsibility upon the actor for, as A. B. Walkley observed, 'all [Ibsen's] drama is internal, the evolution of successive "soul-states"'.[36]

As Ibsen was the antithesis of the formulaic dramatist, the problems he set his actors could not be solved by formulas. Accordingly a variety of approaches to performing his plays was required, one which makes late nineteenth-century theatre one of the richest periods in the history of acting. The most obvious though not always easiest solution was the purely naturalistic one, whereby actors sunk themselves into the role, at times losing any sense of their own personality, an experience Antoine claims he went through when playing Osvald.[37] Stanislavski's most successful role was that of Stockmann in An Enemy of the People. While he never descended into the quasi-catatonic state Antoine claims he did, he identified totally with the character, with his situation, his values, his personality. However, in contrast to Antoine, Stanislavski avoided the unconscious realms of the character and discovered himself very carefully constructing Stockmann from various gestures and idiosyncrasies of people he had known.[38]

The greatest naturalistic renditions of Ibsen probably took place at the Deutsches Theater during the directorship of Otto Brahm between 1894 and 1904. As a drama critic in the 1880s, Brahm had campaigned against the ideality and artificiality of contemporary actors. If the actor 'wishes to embody modern forms', Brahm wrote in 1883, 'he should embody them in the style of our society. He should listen attentively and receptively to the thousand-voiced echo that comes back to him . . . however various its combination is of all the classes of the great city, high and low, rich or poor in intellectual life'.[39] As chairman of the Freie Bühne he encouraged actors to observe how the physiological both expresses the psychological and determines it. The physiological exactitude he encouraged in his actors was apparent in September 1890 at the inaugural production of the Freie Bühne, *Ghosts*, which was widely recognized as a more impressive performance than the 1887 production. Critics commented on the novel and effective use of 'artistic pauses' that allowed actors freedom to explore implied meaning and to observe an unusually accurate interdependence of word and gesture. Agnes Sorma as Regine won approval for she showed 'no sign of theatricalism';[40] neither did Arthur Kraussneck as a simple and mild Manders. The noted Burgtheater actor Emmerich Robert had been hired to play Osvald, and he gave 'a fine physiological study, rich in nuances', a graphic expression of degeneration, though he distanced himself sufficiently from the role to create a double response in Theodor Fontane, who felt 'not only miserable pity for the invalid, but heartfelt sympathy with the man'.[41] Marie Schanzer as Mrs Alving was considered too 'ideal' for the role and therefore unsuited to Ibsen.

When he took over the Deutsches Theater, Brahm displayed no interest in the classics as one or two failed productions taught him they could not be effectively performed in the style of acting he favoured. While part of the company continued to play the classics, Brahm centred his energies on developing an ensemble that would be a perfect medium for the performance of Ibsen and other naturalistic playwrights. For ten years he trained a notable ensemble at the centre of which were four actors who realized with completeness and accuracy the interpenetration of the physiological and the psychological. They were Emanuel Reicher, who portrayed in his roles a 'whole conglomerate of dominant, subordinate and subsidiary characteristics'[42]; Else Lehmann, most effective at moments of silence, who communicated a powerful sense of oneness with the physical world; Rudolf Rittner, whose peasant upbringing led him to express a profound melancholy and scepticism toward the modern city; and Oscar Sauer, the most interesting member of the company, an even more melancholy actor who radiated a sense of loss, as if the modern world were a decline from a previous, ideal state of existence, 'the dethroned king, the derided saint, the patriot without a home'.[43]

From all accounts, these actors had a palpable and disturbing influence upon their audiences, though in all four there was a common quality limiting their effectiveness, which is that they were bound by the matter of their roles. They could express the experience of oppression and the struggle against it, but none of them overcame it. Their final condition was therefore one of defeat. This, it might be argued, was distinctive of the naturalistic approach. Stanislavski's Stockmann, for example, was often criticized because it lacked the more striving aspects of Ibsen's character. In fact, in the cause of psychological truth the naturalists extracted so much theatre from the theatre that they were in danger of depriving the plays of much of their vitality. Certainly, Brahm's company looked very lacklustre when Max Reinhardt eventually took over the Deutsches Theater in 1905.

The naturalists had ignored the debt Ibsen owed to the more traditional modes of drama. While his characters are incomparably more complete and his settings generally more quotidian or 'suburban' than those of earlier dramatists, his plays still contain carefully structured plots, replete with *coups de théâtre* more powerful than any Scribe or Sardou could devise. Hence, in order to find an acting style to complement his theatricality, actors may have occasionally resorted to the gestural techniques of pre-Ibsen drama. It has recently been suggested that some of the most popular actors called upon the gestures and tricks of the melodramas and well-made plays in which they also acted so as to give theatrical form and effect to their psychologically realistic performances,[44] a technique that complements Ibsen's position as a playwright who bridges traditional concern with dramatic form with a modern interest in symbolism and depth psychology.

Not all actors focused on the minutiae of motivation as this on its own reduced the stature of the role. Some adopted overtly stylized means that occasionally bordered on the eccentric. For example Lugné-Poë, whose spare productions diminished attention to the physical environment and anticipated minimalism, indulged in hollow intonations and dreamlike gestures when acting Ibsen that infuriated several critics. As a Symbolist, he suggested ideas beyond the characters rather than represented behavioural traits within them; hence, in his production of *The Lady from the Sea*, 'each character seemed to be itself and its own ghost at the same time'.[45] The quality of Lugné-Poë's acting varied. When his company toured Scandinavia in 1894, he impressed critics with his forceful Solness, but was considered too robust for the languid Rosmer,[46] which was very different from the

French view of him. However, Ibsen himself was impressed by the one-sided passionate approach of Lugné-Poë and l'Oeuvre. 'The French', Lugné-Poë reports him as saying, 'are far more qualified than many others to play me. People do not wish to understand that I am an author of passion and ought to be played with passion and not otherwise.'[47]

To judge from contemporary criticism other celebrated interpreters of Ibsen did not in fact lack passion; indeed, the discovery by his female characters of basic needs and urges that demanded expression, gave rise to acting of great vigour that could invest such characters with a 'demonic' energy. Nora in *A Doll's House* was Ibsen's most famous rebel, creating almost singlehandedly his reputation as a polemical dramatist. The role, performed by actresses throughout Europe, was subject to such widely differing interpretations, that critical attention centred less on Ibsen's purported 'message' about the need to end incompatible marriages, than upon the more interesting dilemma as to how the actress combined the two disparate aspects of Nora's character, the 'song-bird' and 'squirrel' of the early parts of the play with the mature woman who leaves her husband at the end.[48] Betty Hennings, the Nora of the première in Copenhagen, was successful mainly in the first aspect, while Janet Achurch made a more powerful impact as she effected a gradual transformation from naiveté to 'melancholy dignity [and] subdued intensity of feeling',[49] though in later performances she darkened her interpretation. This may have been due to the influence of continental Noras she had seen. Eleanora Duse's rendering of the role was widely praised by those who deplored theatricality. Archer felt she achieved a perfect balance between the various facets of Nora's character, and while he felt her pedantically untheatrical at times, he approved of her dignified refusal to do the tarantella.[50] He and several other critics acclaimed her outburst of Latin temperament at the end, but when she performed in Vienna, she made a more powerful impression on Hofmannsthal who compared the contrast between her martyred feelings and her calm self-possession to that of a passion-play actor in the role of Jesus Christ.[51] Duse may have seemed idealist when compared with the German actress Agnes Sorma, who performed the role for Brahm at the Deutsches Theater. Early in the play, through impressionistic details she suggested disquiet beneath the bright surface, the tension between the two states giving her performance great power. At the end, she resolved the dilemma by representing Nora as deeply hurt by the betrayal of her love. Her final reckoning was so full of profound scorn for her husband, that the scene had a feral, Strindbergian quality so that when she left, there was no doubt that she was never to return. The decision was a natural result of the resolution of the two conflicting aspects of her character.[52]

Perhaps the most complete Ibsenian actress in the English theatre was Elizabeth Robins, who captured the 'demonic' quality of Ibsen's heroines without any of the one-sided quality that, one suspects, characterized the work of several l'Oeuvre actors. Certainly, her compelling acting, nurtured under the watchful direction of William Archer, saved both *Hedda Gabler* and *The Master Builder* after their undistinguished German premières. Clement Scott, despite his boorish attitude toward Ibsen, was nevertheless a competent judge of acting and, after seeing her Hilde, reported that she made her impact not by cultivating consistency of character, but by her capacity to carry the audience into a world of 'pure fantasy'. Despite his unease at the moral ambivalence of her performance, he could still write, 'Our stage history . . . furnishes no record of another such vivid combination of the realistic and imaginative side of the histrionic art.'[53] If he granted Ibsen nothing else, Scott acknowledged the tremendous impetus his plays gave to the development of acting.

Actresses rather more than actors have drawn attention in the history of early Ibsen performance as his plays so spectacularly redefined their artistic importance in the theatre and provided them with roles of unprecedented complexity and breadth. But the challenge of Ibsen to the male actor must not be underestimated. One of the most distinctive of these challenges was to create 'the treble strata of self, character, and *the role the character plays*',[54] except that 'roles' may be a more apposite word. For the actor, the challenge was often to create compellingly a character, weak at the centre, who nonetheless plays a series of roles projecting heroic images of his self. Indeed, through contrasting these multiple roles and the multiple personality they imply Ibsen achieves several of his most telling ironic effects. Few actors of the time had a technique that would allow them to embody credibly this important aspect of his characterization. Perhaps the only one to do so with complete success in the first generation of Ibsen actors was the German Friedrich Mitterwurzer. He had acted professionally since the 1860s, but had had great difficulty adapting to the theatre that required actors to represent a wholeness and unity of character. Heinrich Laube, the preeminent director of the middle decades of the century, had dismissed him as capable of playing only 'fissured characters'.[55] It was precisely 'fissured characters' that Ibsen created, hence they suited Mitterwurzer's talents perfectly, a compatibility Ibsen himself acknowledged.[56] He had performed several Ibsen roles on tour, his Osvald being particularly celebrated in America, but in Vienna he was known for Consul Bernick, Hjalmar Ekdal, and Alfred Allmers. As Bernick, there was no centre to his character: it was a series of masks that changed depending upon whom he was talking to and the situation in which he found himself.[57] So complete was each transformation and so equally was each mask an expression of Bernick that he did not appear to be a hypocrite, but someone who lacked any identifiable personality. The play therefore appeared to be less the satire that it was normally regarded to be, more a study of the damage that can be caused by one who lacks any coherent sense of his own self. As Hjalmar, whom he played as a failed artist, Mitterwurzer used his capacity to embody each role with complete conviction to draw audiences' sympathy toward the character.[58] At the same time, according to Hermann Bahr, he could always make the audience aware of his understanding as an actor of the irony between the different roles the character played,[59] which would have provided a wry commentary on the character and have fulfilled what Shaw described as the key challenge of the Ibsen actor, to make his characters 'sympathetically unsympathetic'. As Allmers, Mitterwurzer represented the point of crisis where a man's sense of his own identity collapses and the moral crisis which is composed of his search for a new centre. In this painful journey of self-discovery, Mitterwurzer's Allmers moved from heaviest depression to the faint possibility of redemption.

By the end of the century, Ibsen's plays had proved to be irresistible. They had established themselves in the repertoires of all regional theatres in Scandinavia and in central and eastern Europe, and were beginning to make some headway in the commercial theatre of London. In France, things took a little longer. For example, it was not until June 1921 that an Ibsen play, *An Enemy of the People*, was first staged at the Comédie Française. Nevertheless, by the turn of the century Ibsen was widely recognized as a playwright who had returned to the theatre a sense of truth and had first explored the potential of the medium as a means to diagnose the peculiar quality of modern life. As Alfred Kerr wrote

> The best and most momentous things that Ibsen has given us are the impulse to truth in an artistically untruthful time; the impulse to seriousness in an artistically superficial time; the pleasure of agitation in a time of stagnation; and the courage to grasp whatever contains something human, wherever it grows.[60]

Kerr quite rightly saw him as the 'grandfather' of the modern theatre.

NOTES

1 Heinrich and Julius Hart, *Kritische Waffengänge*, vol. IV (Leipzig, 1882), p. 3. (All translations are mine, unless otherwise noted.)
2 Harley Granville-Barker, 'The Coming of Ibsen', *The Eighteen-Eighties*, ed. Walter de la Mare (Cambridge, 1930), p. 162.

3 See Frederick J. Marker and Lise-Lone Marker, *The Scandinavian Theatre* (Totowa, N.J., 1975), pp. 138–51.

4 *Ibsen auf der deutschen Bühne*, ed. Wilhelm Friese (Tübingen, 1976), p. xi.

5 In fact this was a joint première, as the play was performed in Christiania on the same day.

6 Alfred Kerr, *Das neue Drama* (Berlin, 1905), p. 21.

7 *Berlin – Theater der Jahrhundertwende*, ed. Norbert Jaron, Renate Möhrmann and Hedwig Müller (Tübingen, 1986), p. 198.

8 See William Archer's famous digest of the critical opprobrium heaped on *Ghosts* in 'Ghosts and Gibberings', *William Archer on Ibsen*, ed. Thomas Postlewait (Westport, Conn., and London, 1984), pp. 23–7.

9 *Ibsen: The Critical Heritage*, ed. Michael Egan (London and Boston, 1972), p. 15.

10 Nils Åke Nilsson, *Ibsen in Russland* (Stockholm, 1958), pp. 29–162, provides a play-by-play survey of the early Russian reception of Ibsen.

11 H. von Pilgrim, quoted in William Henri Eller, *Ibsen in Germany* (Boston, 1918), p. 71.

12 Egan (ed.), *Ibsen: The Critical Heritage*, pp. 114 and 227.

13 See especially his review of the 1887 Berlin production of *Ghosts* and an 1888 production of *The Wild Duck* at the Lessingtheater in Theodor Fontane, *Sämtliche Werke*, 22/2 (Munich, 1964), pp. 690–8.

14 Françisque Sarcey, *Quarante ans de théâtre*, vol. VIII (Paris, 1902), p. 338.

15 *Paris and the Arts, 1851–1896: From the Goncourt Journal*, ed. and trans. George J. Becker and Edith Philips (Ithaca, N.Y., 1971), pp. 288–9.

16 Friese (ed.), *Ibsen auf der deutschen Bühne*, p. 10.

17 Egan (ed.), *Ibsen: The Critical Heritage*, p. 171.

18 Tracy C. Davis, 'Ibsen's Victorian Audience', *Essays in Theatre*, 4 (1985), 21–38.

19 Otto Brahm, *Kritiken und Essays*, ed. Fritz Martini (Zürich and Stuttgart, 1964), pp. 185–92.

20 Kerr, *Das neue Drama*, p. 24.

21 Henry James, 'On the Occasion of *Hedda Gabler*', *The Scenic Art*, ed. Allan Wade (New York, 1957), p. 250.

22 Henrik Ibsen, *Letters and Speeches*, ed. and trans. Evert Sprinchorn (New York, 1964) p. 222.

23 George Bernard Shaw, *Our Theatres in the Nineties*, vol. II (New York, 1931), pp. 249–50.

24 Jules Lemaître, *Impressions de Théâtre*, vol. VI (Paris, n.d.), p. 51.

25 See Frederick J. Marker and Lise-Lone Marker, *The Scandinavian Theatre*, pp. 167–72 and *Ibsen's Lively Art* (Cambridge, 1989), pp. 129–40.

26 Jean Chothia, *André Antoine* (Cambridge, 1991), pp. 49–57.

27 Thomas Postlewait, *Prophet of the New Drama: William Archer and the Ibsen Campaign* (Westport, Conn., and London, 1986), pp. 72–4.

28 Elizabeth Robins, *Ibsen and the Actress* (London, 1928), pp. 52–3.

29 James, *The Scenic Art*, pp. 253–4.

30 George Taylor, *Players and Performers in the Victorian Theatre* (Manchester and New York, 1989), p. 150.

31 Herbert Waring, 'An Actor's View of Ibsen', in Egan (ed.) *Ibsen: The Critical Heritage*, p. 328.

32 Ibid., p. 327.

33 Shaw, *Our Theatres in the Nineties,* vol. II, p. 252.
34 G. B.Shaw letter to Elizabeth Robins, quoted in Marker and Marker, *Ibsen's Lively Art,* p. 165.
35 Gay Gibson Cima, 'Discovering Signs: The Emergence of the Critical Actor in Ibsen', *Theatre Journal,* 35 (March, 1983), 14.
36 A. B.Walkley, *Playhouse Impressions* (London, 1892), p. 57.
37 André Antoine, *Memories of the Théâtre-Libre,* trans. Marvin Carlson (Coral Gables, Fla., 1964), p. 138.
38 Jean Benedetti, *Stanislavski* (London, 1988), pp. 103–5.
39 Brahm, *Kritiken und Essays,* p. 98.
40 Maximilian Harden, in *Berlin – Theater der Jahrhundertwende,* p. 83.
41 Fontane, *Sämtliche Werke,* 22/2, p. 706.
42 Emanuel Reicher, letter to Hermann Bahr, quoted in Heinrich Braulich, *Max Reinhardt* (Berlin, 1969), p. 22.
43 Julius Bab, quoted in *100 Jahre Deutsches Theater Berlin* (Berlin, 1983), p. 54.
44 Tracy C. Davis, 'Acting in Ibsen', *Theatre Notebook,* 40 (1985), 113–23.
45 Henri de Régnier, cited by Bettina L. Knapp, *The Reign of the Theatrical Director* (Troy, N.Y., 1988), p. 113.
46 Jacques Robichez, *Le Symbolisme au théâtre* (Paris, 1957) pp. 274–5.
47 Lugné-Poë, *Acrobaties* (Paris, 1931), p. 111.
48 Frederick J. Marker and Lise-Lone Marker, *Ibsen's Lively Art,* pp. 47–8. The Markers provide detailed reconstructions of several early Noras.
49 William Archer, *The Theatrical World for 1893* (London, 1894), p. 161.
50 Ibid., pp. 159–60.
51 Hugo von Hofmannsthal, *Prosa,* vol. I (Frankfurt, 1950), p. 76.
52 Based mainly on essays by Otto Brahm and Siegfried Jacobsohn in Agnes Sorma: *Ein Gedenkbuch,* ed. Julius Bab (Heidelberg, 1927), pp. 51–5, and Marker and Marker, *Ibsen's Lively Art,* pp. 58–9.
53 Quoted in Egan (ed.), *Ibsen: The Critical Heritage,* p. 272.
54 Cima, 'Discovering Signs', 19.
55 Jakob Minor, *Aus dem alten und neuen Burgtheater* (Zürich, 1920) p. 169.
56 Ibid., p. 188.
57 Eugen Guglia, *Friedrich Mitterwurzer* (Vienna, 1896), pp. 103–10.
58 See Simon Williams, *German Actors of the Eighteenth and Nineteenth Centuries* (Westport, Conn., and London, 1985), pp. 136–9, for a reconstruction of Hjalmar and other of Mitterwurzer's Ibsen roles in Vienna.
59 Hermann Bahr, *Wiener Theater* (Berlin, 1899), p. 140.
60 Kerr, *Das neue Drama,* p. 35.

Other sources relevant to this chapter include

Bernhardt, Rüdiger, *Henrik Ibsen und die Deutschen* (Berlin, 1989).
Franc, Miriam, *Ibsen in England* (Boston, 1919).
George, David E. R., 'A Question of Method', in Ian Donaldson (ed.), *Transformations in Modern European Drama* (London, 1983).
Henrik Ibsen in Deutschland (Göttingen, 1968).
Gregersen, H., *Ibsen and Spain* (Cambridge, Mass., 1936).
Henderson, John A., *The First Avant-Garde, 1887–1894: Sources of the Modern French Theatre* (London, 1971).

Jasper, Gertrude, *Adventure in the Theatre* (New Brunswick, 1947).

Knowles, Dorothy, *La Réaction idéaliste au Théâtre depuis 1890* (Paris, 1934).

Moe, Vera Ingunn, *Deutscher Naturalismus und ausländische Literatur* (Frankfurt, Bern and New York, 1983).

Osborne, John, *The Naturalistic Drama in Germany* (Manchester, 1971).

Pasche, Wolfgang, *Skandinavische Dramatik in Deutschland* (Basel and Stuttgart, 1979).

Schanke, Robert A., *Ibsen in America: A Century of Change* (Metuchen, N.J. and London, 1988).

Waxman, S. M., *Antoine and the Théâtre Libre* (Cambridge, Mass., 1926).

11

FREDERICK J. MARKER and LISE-LONE MARKER

Ibsen and the twentieth-century stage

At the outset of his career, as a stage director in Bergen and subsequently in Christiania (now Oslo), Ibsen developed a keen sense of the practicalities and performance conditions of the living theatre that never left him. That intimate knowledge of the stage and its conventions which the playwright derived from these early experiences fostered his extraordinary sensitivity to the poetry of environment in the theatre. In staging his own early saga dramas, he taught himself to write a carefully visualized, highly charged *mise-en-scène* into his plays, aimed at concretizing the psychological states and spiritual conditions of the characters, and designed to create a specific mood that would enhance and strengthen the inner action. Costumes, settings, objects, colours, sounds and lighting effects thus remained, from the beginning of his career to its close, the basic syntax of his dramatic poetry. In turn, the intense theatricality inherent in his work has been the source of its continued vitality in performance, long after the specific theatrical conditions for which a given play seems intended have changed irrevocably.

By 1906, the year of Ibsen's death, revolution was again sweeping through the theatre, and the great European Modernists of the day seemed particularly drawn to the challenge of forging an alternative to the minutely detailed, solidly realistic style of production to which Ibsen's 'modern' plays had hitherto seemed unalterably wedded. The immediate result was a series of pioneering productions by these innovators that proclaimed an entirely new approach to Ibsen on the stage, shaped by the New Stagecraft's triple goal of simplification, stylization and suggestion. Max Reinhardt's *Ghosts*, Edward Gordon Craig's *Rosmersholm* and Vsevolod Meyerhold's *Hedda Gabler*, all produced in 1906, were quite distinct but analogous manifestations of a shared anti-naturalistic determination to present a heightened conceptual image of the inner thematic rhythm and spirit of the work at hand, rather than a photographic reduplication of its surface reality. Craig might have been speaking for all three men when he wrote (in the programme for the *Rosmersholm* which he designed for Eleonora Duse):

1 One of Edvard Munch's designs for Max Reinhardt's Kammerspiele production of *Ghosts*, Berlin, 1906

'Realism has long ago proclaimed itself as a contemptible means of hinting at things of life and death, the two subjects of the masters. Realism is only Exposure, whereas art is Revelation: and therefore in the mounting of this play I have tried to avoid all Realism . . . Let us leave period and accuracy of detail to the museums and to curiosity shops.'[1]

A key aspect of the new Modernism, inspired by its distaste for the alleged 'drabness' of stage naturalism, was the renewed emphasis which it placed upon the role of the designer as an artist enjoying equal standing with the director. Out of this concern with the interpretative power of stage design and pictorial art in the theatre arose Reinhardt's historic invitation to Edvard Munch, Scandinavia's foremost painter during the Ibsen era, to create a series of designs for *Ghosts*, the production with which the director opened his intimate Kammerspiele in Berlin in November of this momentous year. Instead of confronting the spectator with an objectively rendered environment, made up of a complex filigree of naturalistic details in which no one element was given special emphasis, the Munch–Reinhardt collaboration stressed certain specific visual motifs, intended to heighten and deepen the dominant mood of oppressiveness and dread overhanging the Alving household. When we look at the room envisaged in Munch's sketches, we do indeed recognize numerous items one would call realistic: a table with chairs, a *chaise longue* on a carpet, a coffee table beside it, a fireplace, a grandfather clock, paintings on the wall, even a potted plant. The end result of Munch's technique is, however, a distillation – what could be called a regenerative decimation of strict, old-fashioned realism in the service of an inner world behind and beneath the word surface of Ibsen's play. Held in dark colours of reddish brown, black, grey and violet and dominated visually by a large, black armchair, Munch's prison–parlour virtually exuded a heavy atmosphere of joylessness and entrapment. In this way, the setting not only lent the Kammerspiele performance its distinctive visual tone and texture but also shaped the entire directorial concept of the play decisively. By transferring the drama from the realm of reality to an imaginative (but not abstract) plane, it was possible to make poetic and atmospheric values far more emphatic than any naturalistic production could have done. As the darkness which gradually enshrouds the action set in, the Kammerspiele stage grew shadowy and dim; as contours were erased, the darkly clad figures on the stage began to appear weirdly unreal, like their own ghosts. And as the end of the play ('the grandiose symphonic finale', as Reinhardt called it) came on, light and shadow acted out a drama of their own. As the past into which the characters are helplessly locked is at last fully revealed, the sinister shadows that hover in Munch's designs sprang to life. 'In the last, despairing moments of the play,' Julius Bab tells us, while cold, pitiless shafts of the dawn before sunrise pierced the darkness, 'as Mrs Alving rushed behind her son, towards the lamp, shadows as high as houses cast on the walls accompanied her like pursuing demons.'[2]

Only two days after the Kammerspiele *Gespenster*, Vsevolod Meyerhold staged his equally well-known production of *Hedda Gabler* in St Petersburg. Here, the aim of this far more radical and comprehensive deconstruction was to reveal Ibsen's play to the spectator in a new and deliberately unfamiliar manner, shorn of the intrusive weave of peripheral detail so dear to Stanislavski, his former teacher at the Moscow Art Theatre. As early as 1906, in his first significant manifesto, Meyerhold formulated his view of Ibsen as a playwright whose works confront the director with particularly serious pitfalls. The naturalistic director, he writes, inevitably tends to approach an Ibsen play intent upon 'enlivening' its 'boring' dialogue and bringing out its 'complicated' meaning by indiscriminately embroidering on the lifelikeness of every detail. As a result, prominence is given to the most insignificant nuances and the most 'secondary, parenthetic scenes', as Meyerhold calls them – with the consequence that the audience loses sight of the essentials and the leitmotif becomes obscured because, in his words, 'the director has placed it in a distracting frame'. For, he goes on to insist (in italics), '*the truth is that the sum of the meaning of the parenthetic scenes does not add up to the meaning of the entire play*'. Rather, a single decisive moment, emphatically presented, 'decides the fate of the act in the mind of the audience, even though everything else slips by as though in a fog'.[3] In other words, without a dynamic, virtually musical scoring of the dramatic text by the director–interpreter, the essence of Ibsen is lost, he would contend, in a plethora of distracting detail and stage business (such as the elaborate breakfast serving he recalls in the scene between Tesman and Aunt Julia in Stanislavski's production of *Hedda Gabler*).

In Meyerhold's own production of this play, created in collaboration with another noted painter of the time, Nikolai Sapunov, his *mise-en-scène* attempted (in the words of Pavel Yartsev, his assistant director) 'to give primitive, purified expression to what it senses behind Ibsen's play'. All considerations of actual period and place were boldly set aside. Instead, a purely symbolic scheme of chromatic values, shapes, and groupings was utilized to project a heightened sensual impression (rather than a naturalistic representation) of a cold, regal, autumnal Hedda, enthroned in a huge armchair covered in white fur and seen against a vast, blue, receding expanse that suggested her aesthetic longings.[4] A shallow, bas-relief stage, nearly four times as wide as it was deep, produced a flattened, two-dimensional effect that contradicted naturalist (in-depth) pictorialism and brought the actor into closer, more direct contact with the spectator. This exceptionally wide, shallow stage facilitated non-realistic, lateral patterns of movement – notably, widely spaced groupings – that undercut the very idea of 'life-likeness.' The whole purpose of such stylization was to subject the pictorial and choreographic elements of the theatre to the 'inner' voice of Ibsen's play – the 'subterranean forces and powers' he himself alludes to in his notes for *Hedda Gabler*. Accordingly, Meyerhold would argue, the director must enable the actor's movements, gestures, and mime to probe and reveal an area beyond the mere word text. To accomplish this, the factitious and divisive 'fourth wall' upon which the naturalistic aesthetic depends must be eliminated – regardless of its place in Ibsen's own personal assumptions about theatre. Only by doing so can the actor attain the closest possible rapport with the spectator, whose emotional participation in the inner action of the drama is essential.

Using entirely different methods, Gordon Craig arrived at much the same kind of conclusion. In Florence less than a month after Meyerhold's radical experiment, Craig staged *Rosmersholm* for Duse in a hazy, mysterious 'house of shadows' ('a vision of loveliness,' the actress called it) that consisted solely of vast greenish-blue space, soaring lines and an immense window in the distance to conjure up the 'powerful impression of unseen forces closing in upon the place' which he felt was the essence of the play. The avowed intent of Craig's design scheme was to create 'a place which

2   As *Rosmersholm* usually looked in the early years of this century: a production at Svenska
teatern, Stockholm, 1908

harmonizes with the thoughts of the poet', rather than yet another cluttered
facsimile of a Victorian parlour. As such, his work on *Rosmersholm* reflects
the same basic approach taken in his more visionary productions of two of
Ibsen's poetic dramas, *The Vikings of Helgeland* (in 1903) and *The Pretenders* (in 1926) – an approach characterized by his observation that 'drama is
the product of our inner life, and so we create on the stage a world for that
inner life'.[5] 'Ibsen can be acted and staged so as to be made insignificant and
mean,' he warned his Florentine audience at the Teatro della Pergola.
'Therefore we must ever remember our artistry and forget our propensity
towards photography. We must for this new poet re-form a new Theatre.'[6]

In St Petersburg less than two weeks later, Meyerhold again startled the
traditionalists with his new version of *A Doll's House*, the fourth in this
remarkable cycle of 1906 productions. Again, the focus of concentration
was the inner spirit of the work itself, not the fortuitous social or psychological circumstances of Nora's personal plight. The goal of Meyerhold's
Symbolical Theatre was, in each production, to present a charged, allusive
image of this inner spirit, rather than an allegedly exact and complete
replica of life. 'The urge to *show* everything, come what may, the fear of
mystery, of leaving anything unsaid turns the theatre into a mere illustration

of the author's words,' he writes. Hence, the realistic Norwegian environment conceived by Vera Kommisarjevskaya, his employer and leading lady,
was defiantly dismantled and replaced by a stylized set stripped to the barest
essentials. A decrepit piano in one corner, an equally dilapidated three-
legged stool, a pair of inconspicuous chairs, and an arbitrarily suspended
window framed by ballooning, cranberry-coloured drapes that reached the
full height of the stage completed the iconography of this uncosy doll's
house. Above all, Meyerhold insisted, 'a bridge must be built' between the
actor and the spectator, whose engaged imagination is able and willing to
supply that which is left unfinished or unsaid. For this reason, even Kommisarjevskaya's tarantella – the crucial moment in Meyerhold's interpretation,
toward and away from which Nora's life-dance moved – became, in the
director's own words, 'no more than a series of expressive poses, during
which the feet simply tapped out a nervous rhythm. If you watched only the
feet, it looked more like running than dancing.' How, he asks us rhetoric-
ally, would the spectator be affected if instead 'a naturalistic actress trained
by a dancing-master ceases to act and conscientiously shows every step of
The Tarantella?' Far less profoundly, he would contend, than by a situation
in which room is left 'for the play of allusion', for 'conscious under-
statement' and for 'the power of suggestion' to do its work.[7]

The underlying sense of irony inherent in Meyerhold's approach finds a
most unexpected parallel in the English-language premier of *Peer Gynt*
which Richard Mansfield staged in Chicago, at the height of a veritable
insurgency of Ibsen performances in America, on 29 October 1906. At the
core of this otherwise conventional, heavily pictorialized production was
Mansfield's own unyouthfully sardonic, at times even critically detached
interpretation of the central character. Over fifty and very near his death by
the time he attempted the part, the popular actor created a Peer that came
several steps closer to the perplexed and suffering non-heroic hero familiar
in many modern readings of the play. 'I propose playing *Peer Gynt* in a spirit
of travesty, and to present it as a phantasmagoria,' Mansfield had written to
his puzzled friend and biographer William Winter, an astute theatre critic
but perhaps the most pigheaded Ibsen opponent of his day. Yet even Winter
was obliged to admire the unusual power of 'the actor's revelation of
himself' that he achieved in the role – a revelation that proceeded from
Mansfield's layered, self-reflexive attitude toward the 'preposterous vaga-
bond' and complacent impersonator he enacted and (almost in Meyerhold's
terms) disclosed to the audience. A description of his desentimentalization
of Aase's death provided by Winter aptly illustrates Mansfield's ironic,
arrestingly 'modern' attack: 'His conduct in the death scene ... expertly
simulated wild passion and acute suffering, combined with self-pity and

theatrical delirium; the whole showy, extravagant outburst, however, being suffused with the attentive, observant, obvious self-consciousness which is inseparable from the endeavour, whether made in speaking or writing or anything else, to express something that is unreal or unfelt.'[8]

Hence it could be said that, in the autumn of the year of Ibsen's death, this brace of productions served to transport his plays from the nineteenth century into the twentieth, compelling the modern theatre to reconsider the playwright's work in a decisively new and sharply contemporary light. Needless to say, however, Craig's hopeful vision of a poet's theatre for Ibsen never materialized. By 1918, in fact, Pär Lagerkvist's brilliant commentary on the importance of Strindberg to the Modern movement seemed able to dismiss with confidence 'the typical Ibsen drama with its silent tramping on carpets through five long acts of words, words, words'.[9] ('Even now,' Lagerkvist adds with a twinkle, 'when the worst of the Ibsen affliction has passed, there is certainly no one who will deny that it was a great blessing that we were stricken by it, but also likewise a happy occasion that we have recovered.') Nor is it so very surprising that *A Doll's House*, presented in contemporary dress as a rotogravure image of 'reality', might strike a London reviewer of 1921 as 'a mere curiosity' so outdated that 'you can feel nothing but a detached interest in it as a great piece of drama that was once something like life' (*Daily Telegraph*, 11 July 1921). Five seasons later, even Madge Titheradge's otherwise highly regarded performance as Nora prompted the *Times* (10 January 1926) to dismiss the play itself as no more than 'a melodrama written by a man of genius in his spare time'. The theory and practice of the New Stagecraft had, it would seem, little immediate impact on the conventional period productions of 'mutton-chop whisker Ibsen,' given *au pied de la lettre* in those 'dingy parlours hung with penitential gloom' that James Agate always deplored in the English Ibsen tradition.

Unlike an early work such as *Peer Gynt*, which has continued to foster new and imaginative conceptual reinterpretations, Ibsen's major prose plays have, by their very nature, tended to inspire comparatively less formal experimentation on the part of directors and designers. Reinforced as it is by the detailed *mise-en-scène* which Ibsen has written into each of them, the style of theatrical representation initially evolved by André Antoine, Otto Brahm, William Bloch and their contemporaries in the naturalistic movement has continued to shape revivals of these plays throughout the present century. Even their best European productions – by such directors as Halvdan Christensen in Norway and Jürgen Fehling and Rudolf Noelte in Germany – have remained predictably rooted in an approach whose outward sign is the museum-like reproduction of a recognizable period interior. The enduring influence of this older tradition in Ibsen's own

3   Photograph of Halvdan Christensen's intricately detailed production of *The Wild Duck*
at Nationaltheatret, Oslo, 1949

country was perfectly exemplified by the 'intricately detailed, intimately
realistic' production of *The Wild Duck* that Halvdan Christensen staged at
Nationaltheatret in 1949. The Swedish critic and historian Agne Beijer best
describes Christensen's quietly intense approach in this revival, as one which
'inobtrusively and objectively placed the milieu for the action in the decade
to which it belongs, with dialogue that remains everyday speech, without
undue emphasis on profound pauses and vague symbolic images'.[10] As late
as 1955, one would have found this same production again in the repertory
at Nationaltheatret, resurrected by Gerda Ring on the basis of Christensen's *mise-en-scène*, with most of his original cast. In Stockholm in that very
same year, even the innovative Alf Sjöberg's highly successful rendering of
The Wild Duck at Dramaten still adhered faithfully to the same time-
honoured conventions of this representational pattern, with its period settings, costumes and accessories.

   Many would agree with Meyerhold and Craig, meanwhile, that a naturalistic production's preoccupation with material reality – indisputably rooted
though it may be in Ibsen's own stage directions – nevertheless constricts
and ultimately reduces a work whose vision extends far beyond the realistic

4 H. W. Lenneweit's spacious, open setting for the Ekdal studio in Rudolf Noelte's revival
of *The Wild Duck* at the Freie Volksbühne, Berlin, 1979

or the social plane. 'The disservice that the drawing-room, teacups,
wallpaper productions do to Ibsen is that the drama becomes invisible. It
gets lost in the teacups and the "pass the butter" and so on,' argues Michael
Zelenak,[11] whose American Ibsen Theatre began in 1983 with a bold stylization of *A Doll's House* that assertively rejected both the drawing-room
stage and the politely restrained 'underplaying' that traditionally goes with it
(particularly in English-language performances). At least two decades before
this ambitious Ibsen festival was launched in Pittsburgh, however, a
renewed search for an alternative style had again begun to gather force in
European theatre. With his first production of *Hedda Gabler* at the Royal
Dramatic Theatre in Stockholm in 1964, Ingmar Bergman literally altered
the perception of this particular play by showing how effectively the dusty
impedimenta of accumulated tradition could be swept aside. In the process,
he defined a new way of looking at all of Ibsen's so-called realistic plays in
the theatre – although Meyerhold, for one, would have recognized some of
his own aims and methods in it.

'With Ibsen, you always have the feeling of limits – because Ibsen places
them there himself. He was an architect, and he built,' Bergman has said in

an interview. 'He always built his plays, and he knew exactly: I want this and I want that. He points the audience in the direction he wants it to go, closing doors, leaving no other alternatives.'[12] Bergman's *Hedda* was thus a conscious attempt on his part to transcend these perceived limitations. His production translated the play into a new theatrical dimension, as it were, by freeing it of its naturalistic mosaic of details – the thick carpets, the 'necessary' porcelain stove, and even the portentous portrait of Hedda's father, General Gabler (a pointer which Meyerhold was, in fact, the first to discard). Using only seven simple rehearsal screens and a bare minimum of objects to denote the Tesman 'parlour', the director and his designer (Mago) transformed the entire stage space into an immense, dark red, velvetlike enclosure which evoked the prevailing mood of desolation and entrapment ('the odour of death' that Hedda tries to describe to Brack), rather than illustrating it in a photographic manner. 'He illuminated the drama in a light that was not of this world,' Siegfried Melchinger wrote in an influential and widely read review that appeared in *Theater heute*. 'His inspiration transformed the mathematical reality of the play into the workings of a dream, over whose outcome one has no control.'[13] As this critic and others recognized, meanwhile, Bergman's various technical strategies were all means to a single end, which was the close-up exposure of the inner essence of Hedda's situation. Even when not directly involved in the action, she remained a visible, restless, solitary presence, isolated but never private, on her own side of a movable middle divider that bisected the stage into two equal and adjacent spheres of simultaneous action. To the left, remorselessly exposed to view, one saw the unseen 'inner room' of Ibsen's stage directions, the physical and psychic retreat where Hedda's piano and her father's pistols are kept. Never allowed to disappear from sight in this version, she stood trapped before the audience, compelled to watch her own innermost spiritual agony dragged into the spotlight of public scrutiny. 'One might have thought that Hedda was spying,' Melchinger observed, 'but the impression produced was rather that the stage spied on Hedda, that she was being dissected by it against her will.' Perceived in the eerie unreality of this airless, timeless red inferno, illuminated by a uniformly cold light that tampered with contours and erased any secure sense of spatial dimensionality, all the characters in the drama appeared like figures suspended in a void. The outside world, the world of reality, had no place whatsoever. 'It exists only as a quotation,' commented *Frankfurter Allgemeine* (18 April 1979) when Bergman later revived his *Hedda* (for the third time in his career) at the Residenztheater in Munich. 'It impinges on what happens, and it even has the power to affect events, but it has no real meaning.'

Like his other approaches to Ibsen over the years, Bergman's revival of

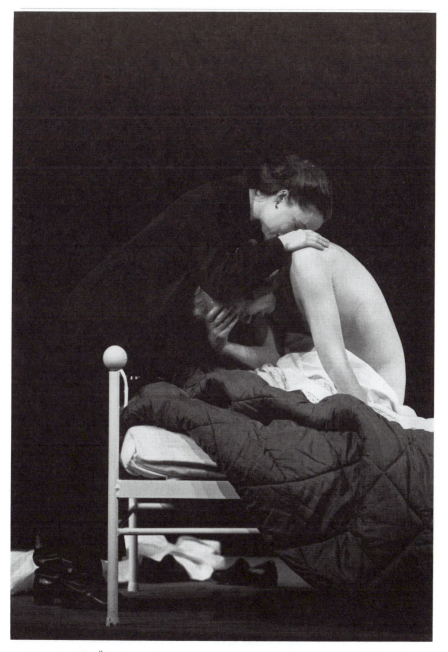

5   Nora (Pernilla Östergren) takes leave of Helmer (Per Mattsson) in Ingmar Bergman's
    revival of *A Doll's House* at the Royal Dramatic Theatre, Stockholm, 1989

A Doll's House at the Royal Dramatic Theatre in 1989 again stripped away the play's traditional period setting and realistic conventions in an effort to lay bare its inner essence – the 'despair, spiritual conflict, and dread' Ibsen describes in the memorandum he titled 'Notes for a Modern Tragedy'. In this production, however, Bergman adopted an even more overtly self-reflexive, metatheatrical style, which transposed the drama to a plane where the illusion of reality played, so to speak, no part at all and the demarcation between past and present vanished along with it. Glimpsed behind the action, enlarged projections of old photographs seemed to recollect and reconsider time past. On a sparsely furnished platform that seemed an island in a theatrical void, this Nora played out (or, perhaps, replayed) her life's struggle surrounded by the four silent, shadowy presences who populate and define her world. Around the periphery of the low platform, waiting for their cues to step in upon it as actors in Nora's drama, sat Helmer, Mrs Linde, Dr Rank and Krogstad. As in his Munich production of the same work at the Residenztheater eight years earlier, this visual device created an ironic double perspective that amplified the director's image of the play as a drama of destiny and entrapment, in which Nora is conscious from the outset of her frustration and her longing to break out of the unbreakable pattern of roles and masks and games in which she finds herself confined. In the Stockholm revision, meanwhile, Nora's final 'escape' – in this case out through the auditorium – became much more deeply ambiguous, juxtaposed as it was with the silent presence of little Hilde who, seen at the outset with her doll (another significant silent player), now stood unnoticed in the background, watching her mother make her exit from the time-stopped world of the play.

By the 1970s, the influence of Bergman's allusive, starkly dematerialized approach had begun to be felt widely in Europe, in performances of all of Ibsen's prose plays. Notably in England, however, the effect of this influence was largely negative, especially in the wake of the botched attempt in 1970 to reduplicate the stylized Bergman *Hedda* with an English cast better suited to the naturalistic mode. Hence, although a production such as the starkly simplified *John Gabriel Borkman* staged by Peter Hall's National Theatre company in 1975 was a decisive attempt at renewal, Hall's 'modified realism' (his term) was by no means the dominant trend. On the contrary, two post-Bergman revivals of *Hedda Gabler*, directed by Anthony Page at the Royal Court in 1972 and Trevor Nunn at the Aldwych in 1975, were embraced by the London critics for their return to the periodicity and psychological conventions usually associated with this play in the past. The Royal Court *Hedda*, 'adapted' for the occasion by playwright John Osborne, won particular praise in the *Guardian* (29 June 1972) for its 'un-

6 Gunhild Borkman (Wendy Hiller) confronts Fanny Wilton (Anna Carteret, left) as Erhart (Frank Grimes) looks on: Peter Hall's National Theatre production of *John Gabriel Borkman*, London, 1975

obtrusive', straightforward idiom, peppered with such 'splendid chips-off-the-old-Osborne' as Hedda's complaint about her husband's 'snorting around in libraries' and Tesman's declaration that he could never ask his wife to settle for 'a petty bourgeois pottage'.[14] In this same vein of subdued 'plain statement', the focus of interest in the Jonathan Miller revival of *Ghosts* at the Greenwich Theatre Festival in 1974 became Irene Worth's portrayal of Mrs Alving as a perfectly average, middle-class woman – in a performance in which, as the sun rose and Osvald's terrible end came on, the young man simply fell quietly asleep in his chair.

The only proper style for *Hedda Gabler* in the theatre, Charles Marowitz declared in his own indignant denunciation of Bergman's method, is 'the most diligent application of Stanislavski-based realism'.[15] In retrospect, this opinion seems less eccentric than its practical outcome, which was a free-wheeling expressionistic collage that juxtaposed familiar patches of Ibsen's text with invented scenes and graphically Freudian fantasy sequences (Hedda astride a gigantic phallic pistol, for instance, or caught up in the

7 Peer No. 8 (Bruno Ganz) meets a Strange Passenger (Klaus-Harald Kuhlmann, *right*) in
the last Act of Peter Stein's Schaubühne production of *Peer Gynt*, Berlin, 1971

sexual fun at Mademoiselle Diana's brothel). The intent of this 'free adaptation', which Marowitz first staged in Bergen during the Ibsen sesquicenten-
nial in 1978, was apparently to 'reveal' Hedda's psychosexual repressions –
notably, the Electra complex that has made her an emotional cripple in her
relations with men. In this respect, perhaps, the Stanislavski method's preoccupation with psychological motivation is not so remote an impetus after
all. The actual performance itself, however – played on a huge, white,
empty disc that symbolized the protagonist's inner life – focused on a
succession of contrived visual statements that left little room for the subtle-
ties and contradictions of naturalistic character analysis.

In its critical attitude toward this play ('The tragedy of Hedda Gabler is
that in the nineteenth century there was no such thing as xerox copiers'), the
Marowitz experiment falls squarely within a much broader movement of
Ibsen quotation and deconstruction that has, in recent years, formed the
most extreme antithesis to Bergman's (broadly speaking) existentialist
approach to the plays. In the work of such directors as Peter Stein and Peter
Zadek, we find the crises of Ibsen's characters presented not as images of
personal human suffering but as reflections of the false values of a corrupt
and corrupting bourgeois social system. Undoubtedly the most influential

exponent of this ideological school has been Stein himself, whose brilliantly executed transposition of *Peer Gynt* at his Schaubühne am Halleschen Ufer in Berlin in 1971 will unquestionably remain a milestone in the history of Ibsen performance. This massive spectacle, which divided Peer's life into eight segments, played by six different actors, was in every respect a denunciation of the play itself as an antiquated museum piece. 'Everything that is used, or let's rather say quoted, creates an illusion to a certain extent but it does so almost in passing,' the director explained at the time. 'We have to approach these things like pictures, objects and mummies which are displayed in museums.'[16] Stein's colourful pageant of nineteenth-century stage effects, which required two full evenings to perform, was thus a demonstration of the inherent obsolescence of the *petit bourgeois* myth of individualism underlying Peer's hopeless search for a 'true self'. 'This is the story of Peer and his bourgeois century: life lived at second hand, as a reproduction, a kitsch picture for a photograph album – a critical history of the human race,' declared *Frankfurter Allgemeine* (17 May 1972) in a review aptly headlined 'Picture Book of the Bourgeoisie'.

The core of Stein's approach was the ironic doubleness inherent in the concept of 'quotation' which his Schaubühne collective adopted from Brecht's theory of epic theatre (specifically, the statement in Brecht's 'Short Description of a New Technique of Acting' that the epic actor 'speaks his part not as if he were improvising it himself but like a quotation'.) Applied to *Peer Gynt*, the 'quoting' style meant the maintenance of a critical attitude toward the work and the events in it – such as Peer's entry into the troll kingdom, mounted on a stuffed pig on wheels and pushed by masked and singing trolls in shabby Victorian dress – without thereby dissipating a given moment's intrinsic imaginative appeal. Each of the eight 'chapters' into which this epic chronicle was divided was introduced by a brief adventure-story narrative, delivered over loudspeakers by an unseen master of ceremonies.[17] This 'serialization' of Peer's life history redirected the focus of attention from the inner struggles of the individual (the traditional view of the role in performance) to the social and economic circumstances that condition him at a particular stage. By breaking up the part and redistributing it among six actors (each perceptibly different in build and appearance), this deconstructive process served to render the title character itself a 'quotation', inviting the audience's critical scrutiny without precluding its emotional response. 'They act the role *and* criticize it,' Volker Canaris wrote in *Theater heute*. 'The bourgeois aesthetic of "embodying" a role has here been so perforated that it becomes a new style in itself, a critical dialectic, an aesthetic means of knowledge.' There was no 'distancing' involved in the individual actor's portrayal of Peer, this critic felt, 'no difference established between what is said and what is meant, between character and actor. Instead the character has at one and the same time the magic power of the story-teller who casts a spell over his listeners and the boastfulness of the charlatan whom no one believes.'[18] In this respect at least, Stein's approach reveals a striking sensitivity to that peculiar doubleness which is an essential facet of Peer's character as Ibsen conceived it – and, for that matter, as Richard Mansfield played it, with 'expertly simulated passion and suffering', at the beginning of this century.

It is tempting indeed to see the reconstituted *Peer Gynt* created by Ingmar Bergman at the Royal Dramatic Theatre in 1991 as a conscious rejoinder to the lengthy and elaborate critical quotation of this play by Stein. Using a superbly coordinated ensemble of thirty-five actors and extras, almost all of whom played at least two and usually three or more roles, the Bergman performance distilled Ibsen's sprawling dramatic poem into three tightly organized movements, with a total running time of just under four hours. Conceived by Bergman specifically for Dramaten's intimate, 160-seat studio theatre, the production utilized a spatial concept that directly reflected his interpretation of the play as an inner journey through what he called 'a world of Peer's imagination that we see created before us'. In essence, neither Peer nor the audience ever left the interior of Aase's rough wooden cottage, with its coloured windows stuffed with rags and its slightly skewed walls covered with faded flowered wallpaper. Within the fixed topography of this unchanging setting, which embraced the auditorium of the small theatre as well, change took place with the swiftness of a dreamer's or a poet's thought. A simple, totally flexible rectangular platform capable of being raised or lowered or tilted on edge became, at will, a precipitous cliff or a banquet table, the forbidding wall of a madhouse or the pitching and rolling deck of a ship in a storm. In this dream of life and passing time and death, anything was possible in the eager, irrepressible, childlike imagination of the Peer Gynt created by Börje Ahlstedt. The reality of his long journey – to Hægstad, to the Ronde, to Morocco, to Cairo and home again – was a purely theatrical reality, enacted on the small stage-upon-the-stage that changed colour for each new movement, from red to white to sombre black. The result was a drama of analogous situations, a system of mirrors in which each experience or encounter was reflected in continually changing and distorted guises. The configurations of characters Peer met on his way were always drastically different in appearance and yet somehow always the same, in a production in which the act of repetition became, as *Expressen* (28 April 1991) observed, 'the very core of Peer's life. He fleets from one fairy tale to the next, but the outcome is always the same . . . Over and over again he is compelled to endure his defeat and to deceive himself.'

8 Peer (Börje Ahlstedt) atop a disordered accumulation of his life's scrap: Ingmar Bergman's
revival of *Peer Gynt* at the Royal Dramatic Theatre, Stockholm, 1991

At the farthest end of the spectrum from Bergman's introspective and emotionally charged distillations of Ibsen has been the rowdy iconoclasm of Peter Zadek, one of the most consistently creative practitioners of the radical style adopted in Stein's *Peer Gynt*. Four years before that event, in fact, Zadek had already mounted an even more outspokenly critical 'quotation' of *A Doll's House* at the intimate Kammerspiele in Bremen, staged in what was scarcely a room or even a 'setting' at all – a door on either side, a veranda window as background, an old-fashioned sofa at the diagonal midpoint of the stage and virtually nothing more. The selective, sharply simplified nature of this spatial concept might, at first glance, have recalled Bergman's non-representationalism in *Hedda Gabler* – but here any resemblance ended. Zadek's objective was to establish a critical distance toward the play that openly questioned its underlying social assumptions and left, in the words of *Süddeutsche Zeitung* (28 February 1967), 'the naive psychology and the frequently banal verbal exchanges ruthlessly exposed'. In distinctly Brechtian style, this director not only repudiated the conventions of realistic illusion and atmospherics but also rearranged the text itself in epic manner. A disjunctive succession of individual scenes, set off from one another by blackouts, altered the flow of the action in order to compel the spectator to step back and think objectively. For Zadek, the key to *A Doll's House* was obviously not Nora's 'transformation' but the awakening of her social consciousness, demonstrated by her realization in the last scene that society can and must be changed. The pivotal force in his endeavour was the self-controlled, dispassionate Nora of Edith Clever – the same actress who subsequently appeared as a similarly tough-minded Mother Aase in the Schaubühne *Peer Gynt*.

The equally polemical, deliberately slow-paced quotation of *The Wild Duck* which Zadek directed at the Schauspielhaus in Hamburg in 1975 again invoked every conceivable stratagem to arouse the spectator's critical awareness. On a stage completely open to the fire walls, the machinery of the theatre was bared and scenic illusion was disrupted at every juncture in an effort to disclose the bankruptcy of the play's moral viewpoints. Bergman's production of this play in Stockholm three years earlier had taken the unusual step of placing the events in the Ekdal attic squarely before the audience, in order to deepen their emotional impact. By contrast, Zadek emulated the device of a visible attic for an entirely different purpose, as a means of revealing the Ekdals' 'private hunting preserve' as a signifier of bourgeois escapism. In general, this ironic quotation of the play used every available means to challenge the audience's conventional expectations. Projectors were occasionally trained on the spectators in an accusatory fashion; Gregers Werle stepped out of his role at times to address the audience

9 Halvard Solness (Hans Michael Rehberg), helped by Knut Brovik (Toni Berger) and watched by Hilde Wangel (Barbara Sukowa), prepares to climb his tower at the end of Peter Zadek's Residenztheater production of *The Master Builder*, Munich, 1983

directly; and even the practical Doctor Relling became a parody of a *raisonneur* who, after the intermission, carried on his angry exchanges with the misguided idealist from a seat in the auditorium. The overall result was a bitter social satire that continually teetered on the verge of travesty. At the end of the play, to drive home the negation of any trace of tragic catharsis, Zadek let his unusual *vox populi* remount the stage to lead the applause (and boos) and work the curtain for the first call.

Beyond Zadek, at the very periphery of what can still legitimately be called Ibsen performance, lie such purely idiosyncratic experiments as Marowitz's *Hedda* collage, or Charles Ludlam's performance of Hedda in drag at the American Ibsen Theatre in 1984, or the cacophonous 'meditation' on *When We Dead Awaken* conceived by Robert Wilson for the American Repertory Theatre in 1991. As for Zadek himself, meanwhile, his work has continued to hold indisputable significance in the history of Ibsen's plays in the modern theatre. At the Residenztheater in Munich in

1983, moreover, the style of his approach to *The Master Builder* appeared to critics startlingly different: 'Faithful to the text, perfect, beautiful, but in no way disturbing . . . He demonstrated here that what interested him most is "the smallest inner movement in the human being." '[19] In this new Ibsen work, Zadek abandoned shock tactics altogether to probe the paradoxes that grow, especially in the last plays, out of the individual's despair over human existence. In adopting a more ambiguous, less socially defined point of view toward this theme, 'the terror of an entire generation of subscribers' (as one Munich reviewer called him) seemed, in fact, to draw closer in spirit to Bergman's method, particularly as it manifested itself in the latter's production of *John Gabriel Borkman* on this same stage two years later. The basis for this stylistic *rapprochement* was, above all, the shared perception of disjuncture between the individual and his world that was felt in both these strongly anti-naturalistic performances.

In Zadek's case, the visual perspective itself actually shifted from the depiction of an external world to the suggestion of a much more obviously internal one. From a spacious and gloomy Victorian office–workroom for its first movement, the play was transposed to a stylized, semi-abstract living-room from the 1930s, midway in time between Ibsen's past and our present, and then to an open, timeless space overlooked by a threatening, ice-covered mountain-side, where no crowd and no brass band gathered to bear witness to the master builder's silent fall and Hilde's almost fanatical ecstasy. By comparison, the feeling of timelessness and dislocation was inescapable from the beginning of Bergman's *Borkman*, reinforced as it was by the deliberate disjuncture he established between the three-dimensionality of the actors and the obviously flattened perspective of the fragmentary, monochromatic 'settings' in which they moved. As a result, the true focus of the Bergman composition was – more undividedly than Zadek was prepared to make it – not society but the individual, not the ground of the composition but the figures in it, whose emotional turmoil was, in this case, literally brought closer to the viewer in what amounted to the theatrical equivalent of a cinematic close-up.

Ultimately, of course, no one director or performer or production ever provides a final 'answer' or expounds an ultimate 'solution' to the problem of bringing an Ibsen play to life for a contemporary audience. The relationship between author and audience continually changes and must continually be re-assembled in a new way by each successive generation. In itself, for example, the sheer variety of the productions that made up Nationaltheatret's first Ibsen Stage Festival in 1990 – which included among the offerings both Bergman's Swedish version of *A Doll's House* and John Barton's new adaptation of *Peer Gynt* for the Norwegian company – illustrated the breadth of the spectrum of responses and performance choices fostered by the challenge of the plays. From whatever angle one attempts to approach them in the theatre, however, the director or actor must invariably be brought back to the truth of Ibsen's own basic conviction about his art – a conviction embodied in a familiar remark of his about *Hedda Gabler*. 'My intention in this play has not really been to treat so-called social problems,' he wrote to his French translator. 'The main thing for me has been to depict human beings, human emotions, and human destinies against the background of certain prevailing social conditions and views.'[20] The contemporary social context to which the playwright refers here has long since become the historical past. The correspondence he perhaps intended between the destinies of his characters and their social reality now seems less immediate and far less important than other aspects of the plays. The *human* reality of Ibsen's characters and their emotional life remains undiminished in importance, meanwhile, and it is from this inner reality that any performance of his work, no matter how stylized or 'deconstructed', must ultimately derive its strength.

NOTES

1 Craig's programme note is reprinted in Denis Bablet, *Edward Gordon Craig* (London, 1966), pp. 87–8.

2 Julius Bab, *Das Theater der Gegenwart* (Leipzig, 1928), p. 126.

3 *Meyerhold on Theatre*, ed. and trans. Edward Braun (New York, 1969), pp. 29–30.

4 See Yartsev's notes in *Meyerhold on Theatre*, pp. 65–6.

5 Interview in *Berlingske Aftenavis* (Copenhagen) 27 October 1926; quoted in Frederick J. Marker and Lise-Lone Marker, *Edward Gordon Craig and 'The Pretenders': A Production Revisited* (Carbondale, 1981), p. 13.

6 Quoted in Bablet, *Edward Gordon Craig*, p. 88.

7 *Meyerhold on Theatre*, p. 25.

8 William Winter, *The Life and Art of Richard Mansfield, with Selections from his Letters* (New York, 1910), vol. II, p. 207.

9 Pär Lagerkvist, *Modern Theatre: Seven Plays and an Essay*, trans. Thomas R. Buckman (Lincoln, Nebr., 1966), p. 12.

10 Agne Beijer, *Teaterrecensioner 1925–1949* (Stockholm, 1954), p. 546.

11 Quoted in Walter Bilderback, 'Beyond Teacups and Wallpaper: The American Ibsen Theater,' *Theater*, 16 (Summer/Fall, 1985), p. 25.

12 Interview in Lise-Lone Marker and Frederick J. Marker, *Ingmar Bergman: Four Decades in the Theatre* (Cambridge, 1982), p. 222.

13 *Theater heute* 10 (1967), p. 8. Melchinger first saw the production when it was revived at Dramaten (and also played in Berlin) in 1967.

14 Osborne's capricious rewriting of *Hedda Gabler* was published by Faber and Faber in 1972.

15 Charles Marowitz, *Confessions of a Counterfeit Critic* (London, 1973), p. 170.

16 Interview with Bernard Dort in *Travail théâtral* (Lausanne, 1972), excerpted in Michael Patterson, *Peter Stein: Germany's Leading Theatre Director* (Cambridge, 1981), p. 74.

17 A full documentary and pictorial record of this production, including the text used, is found in *Peer Gynt: Ein Schauspiel aus dem neunzehnten Jahrhundert. Dokumentation der Schaubühnen-Inszenierung*, ed. Ellen Hammer, Karl-Ernst Herrmann and Botho Strauss (Berlin, 1971). A widely distributed videotape of the event was shown in German movie houses at the time.

18 *Theater heute*, 13 (1971), p. 32.

19 C. Bernd Sucher, *Theaterzauberer 2: von Bondy bis Zadek* (Munich, 1990), pp. 213–14; the Zadek quotation is from Mechthild Lange, *Peter Zadek* (Frankfurt, 1989), p. 62.

20 Letter to Count Moritz Prozor dated 4 December 1890.

Other books about Ibsen in performance

Friese, William, ed., *Ibsen auf der deutsche Bühne* (Tübingen, 1976).

Haakonsen, Daniel, *Henrik Ibsen, mennesket og kunstneren* (Oslo, 1981). For non-readers of Norwegian, the book contains a splendid pictorial record of contemporary productions.

Marker, Frederick J. and Lise-Lone Marker, *Ibsen's Lively Art: A Performance Study of the Major Plays* (Cambridge, 1989).

Nilsson, Niels Åke, *Ibsen in Russland* (Stockholm, 1958).

Schanke, Robert A., *Ibsen in America: A Century of Change* (Metuchen, N.J. and London, 1988).

Strømberg, Ulla and Jytte Wiingaard (eds.), *Den levende Ibsen: Analyser af udvalgte Ibsen-forestillinger 1973–78* (Copenhagen, 1978).

12

EGIL TÖRNQVIST

Ibsen on film and television

Next to Shakespeare, Ibsen is undoubtedly the world's most frequently screened playwright. There are to date more than fifty film versions of Ibsen plays, and probably about twice as many television versions.[1]

For obvious reasons, the earliest screened versions of Ibsen exist only in the medium of film; after 1950, however, when the first television broadcast of an Ibsen play took place, there was a distinct change of emphasis. Once the new medium had been introduced, the number of film productions dwindled quickly and television became the new partner to which the Ibsen play was wedded. In fact, most of the Ibsen films were produced during the 'international', silent, black-and-white era. With the arrival of the sound film around 1930 the number of film productions diminished.

Not surprisingly, the greatest number of screen versions concern *A Doll's House* and *Ghosts*, but many of the other social plays have also proved to be attractive to screen directors. As might be expected, little attention has been paid to the early plays and, as far as film is concerned, to the late ones.

The earliest films date back to 1911, when *Pillars of Society*, *A Doll's House*, *Ghosts* and *The Lady from the Sea* were made in the United States. In 1915 four new films were issued: three of them American (*The Pretenders*, *Peer Gynt*, *The Wild Duck*), and one Russian (*Brand*). (Four other films were soon to follow: *Terje Vigen* (Sweden, 1916), *Hedda Gabler* (USA, 1917), a further *Peer Gynt* (Germany, 1918) and *When We Dead Awaken* (Russia, 1918).

Of all these film adaptations only Victor Sjöström's *Terje Vigen* – in America entitled *A Man There Was* – has become something of a classic. Based on Ibsen's narrative poem from 1861, the film is an early example of what was to become the most characteristic contribution of the Swedish silent cinema to film history: the *plein air* photography, showing man struggling with the elements of nature. Here for the first time cinema manifested itself as a medium primarily concerned with man in his relationship to the surrounding environment.

During the thirties and early forties some of Ibsen's works were filmed in Germany, a dubious honour. For the rest there was little activity. In the fifties and sixties few Ibsen films, none of them of great significance, were launched.

The seventies brought new vitality. With the revival of the feminist movement, *A Doll's House* received great attention. Patrick Garland and Joseph Losey both produced a version of the play in 1973. Two years later Trevor Nunn presented his *Hedda*, while the Norwegian director Sverre Udnæs introduced yet another Ibsen woman to the big screen: *Lady Inger*. In Hans Werner Geissendörfer's German–Austrian version of *The Wild Duck* (1976), finally, a very young woman, Hedvig, is the focal figure.

If the debate in the seventies around woman's social position forms the background for these films, the threatening environmental problems in our time account for the revived interest in *An Enemy of the People*. Arthur Miller's adaptation of this play was the basis for George Shafer's very theatrical 1978 film version, divided into Acts and lacking exterior settings. Although it had as its stars Steve McQueen (made up to look like Ibsen) as Stockmann and Bibi Andersson as his wife, the film itself was a failure. Miller's adaptation – its setting now relocated to Maine, 1893 – again formed the basis for Jack O'Brian's American 1990 version. The well-known Indian director Satyajit Ray also tried his hand at this play in *Ganashatru* (1989) – again without conspicuous success. The setting this time is a contemporary Bengalese town, where the Hindu temple's holy water is found to be contaminated.

Turning to the televersions we must distinguish between: registrations of stage performances with or without an audience; adaptations of stage productions for television; and productions made directly for television. While the first category is nowadays rare, the second and third are both quite common. At times it can be difficult to make out whether one is dealing with an adaptation via a stage production or with an adaptation made directly for television. Yet the distinction is important, since it explains a number of formal differences. Both Arie Zinger's and Michael Gruner's West German versions of *Ghosts* (1985 and 1987 respectively) are in essence stage productions only minimally adapted for television. Zinger's comes in fact close to a straight registration: it opens with the rise of the curtain and presents a complete view of the sparsely furnished stage set. In both productions long shots are frequent, necessitated by the fact that the characters are often standing far apart – as they would be on the stage. Acting styles are theatrical rather than cinematic. The significance of the facial reactions of the characters is either lost when shown in long shot or seems exaggerated when shown in close-up. Badly fitted to the small screen, both performances are instructive examples of the dangers involved when mixing two rather different media.

By contrast, Magne Bleness's Norwegian and Elijah Moshinsky's British versions of *Ghosts* (from 1987 and 1986 respectively) both seem to have been positively adapted for television. Generally speaking, non-Scandinavian television productions have tended to take the form of adaptations of stage versions, whereas Scandinavian productions have been more usually purpose-made for television.

Although every transposition from book to screen signifies an adaptation from one medium to another, 'adaptation' is often used in a more specific sense as meaning a far-reaching rearrangement of the text of the play. When Henri Safran in his version of *The Wild Duck* (1983) relocates the action from the Norway of the 1880s to the Australia of the 1920s, we may speak of an adaptation in this stricter sense. The same goes for Fassbinder's West German version of *A Doll's House* (1974), significantly entitled *Nora Helmer*, where the rearrangement of the script offers a message very different from that carried by Ibsen's text. Fassbinder's Nora is a shrewd careerist who does not leave her home at the end but, on the contrary, seizes power in it. When this version was labelled 'a film by Rainer Werner Fassbinder', it was not so much a provocation as an honest declaration of the thematic distancing it represented from Ibsen's play.[2]

The fact that television was introduced in Britain at a very early stage explains why a large proportion of the television productions of Ibsen in the fifties tend to be British. The first Norwegian production (*Lady Inger*) was broadcast in 1961. After this date the number of Norwegian TV productions, as might be expected, outnumber those of other countries.

Transposing an Ibsen play from stage to screen necessarily involves a number of adjustments which have their origin in the differences between the media. In the theatre one has a fixed seat from which one is expected to be able to view the entire stage. When the curtain rises, the Helmers' living room is seen through the 'missing fourth wall', and throughout the performance the characters remain at roughly the same distance from the spectator. A screen version, by contrast, may well open with a shot of merely a part of the room or even of a small object in it. Unlike the situation in the theatre, we are for a while at a loss as to where we find ourselves. A *locus dramaticus*, Bazin points out, is in contradiction with the concept of the screen.[3]

In the theatre we normally have several characters in view and we have the freedom to choose on whom we wish to focus. In a film or television performance the camera, functioning as 'narrator', usually presents the characters by turns – often in the form of shot/reverse shot – forcing us to concentrate on one face and momentarily disregard another. Much of a television director's job consists in selecting whether the speaker, the listener or both should be on-screen. At times he may choose a frontal two-shot, having both characters face the spectator, one standing behind the other. By selecting a shot of this kind Arild Brinchmann, towards the end of his Norwegian *Hedda Gabler* (1975), could reveal to the spectator the differing reactions of both Hedda (Monna Tandberg) and, standing behind her, Tesman (Tor Stokke), while keeping each character ignorant of the other's facial expression.

The camera can also deal very emphatically with proxemics, i.e. spatial distances between the characters. By keeping Knut and Ragnar Brovik in the background and having Solness enter his office in the foreground, Michael Darlow in his televersion of *The Master Builder* (1987) stresses from the beginning the master–slave relation between Solness and his subordinates. The Broviks are literally kept small behind a giant Solness.

Proxemics can also refer to reflected distances. In Terje Mærli's Norwegian version of *The Master Builder* (1981), mirror scenes abound. Between a character's real self and his/her mirrored self another and more distant character is included. The device is highly effective. Apart from the narcissistic (even megalomaniac) implications and an indication of a divided ego, there is the suggestion that the distant figure is being squeezed between the two halves of this ego. And additionally there is the disturbing notion that we can never see ourselves 'genuinely', only as through a glass darkly.

Action occurring simultaneously in two different places is difficult to re-create on the stage. Not so on the screen. In his film version of *A Doll's House*, Garland cross-cuts between Nora and Helmer dancing together at the Stenborg fancy-dress ball and Mrs Linde visiting Krogstad in his simple home. In this way the contrast between the two relationships is under-scored. A different, quite common type of 'cross-cutting' is applied by Per Bronken in his Norwegian televersion of *The Lady from the Sea* (1979): here, static close-ups of Ellida (Liv Ullman) alternate with dynamic high-angle long shots of her and the restless Stranger (Thommy Berggren). The contrasting techniques, apart from suggesting two antithetic relationships (Ellida/the Stranger versus Ellida/Wangel), here help to clarify that the long-shot sequences, tantamount to subjective flashbacks, represent what is going through Ellida's mind.

Ibsen frequently divides his stage into two or three symbolically charged spaces: a front room, a back room and, often, a view of a background exterior. The big screen of the cinema, with its superior pictorial quality, can handle a tripartition of this kind but on the small screen what is 'upstage' will not be easily visible unless the camera is allowed to zoom in on it, a subjective device rarely resorted to. While the big screen lends itself to long-shots and mass scenes, the small screen is unsuitable for this type of shot/scene. To bring a crowd scene on to the small screen, a director would be forced to use long shots, which would impoverish the visibility.

Unlike a stage performance, a screen version usually utilizes only part of Ibsen's dialogue. If an Ibsen play runs to some two-and-a-half hours in the theatre, a television version of the same play is likely to last about an hour less. Only when a play is presented as a television series – as in the case of Bronken's *The League of Youth* (five parts, 1986–7) and Bo Widerberg's Swedish *Wild Duck* (three parts, 1989) – can Ibsen's dialogue be wholly retained. Although film versions may have about the same showing time as stage versions, drastic cuts are here even more the rule, since film is a much less verbal medium than television.

Generally speaking, one may distinguish three broad categories of signifiers (*signifiants*) of any stage or screen performance: cultural, medial (i.e. medium-conditioned) and directorial. The Christmas tree in *A Doll's House* may serve as a clarifying example. Here, the tree is a cultural signifier both in a spatial and in a temporal sense; spatially, since in non-Christian parts of the world it would not connote Christmas; temporally, since we do not respond any more to the fact that a Christmas tree in the 1870s was a distinct status symbol. As a medial signifier, the tree will appear differently on stage and screen: on stage it will constantly be in view and will be seen from about the same distance; on screen it will appear only incidentally and may be seen from various distances and angles. Precisely because of its continuing presence, on stage the Christmas tree will necessarily often appear non-expressive, even redundant, while its relative rarity on the screen will increase its significance whenever it is seen. As a directorial signifier, finally, the Christmas tree is already awarded specific significance in Ibsen's stage directions, which state in Act II: '*In the corner beside the piano stands the Christmas tree, stripped, bedraggled and with its candles burnt out.*'[4] Ibsen here operates as his own director. He describes where the Christmas tree at that particular moment is placed and what it looks like. In an actual performance this information will necessarily be supplemented, since a visual tree is very different from a verbal one. This will especially be the case in a screen version, where our relationship to the tree may become a very close one. When Ingmar Bergman in his 1989 stage version of *A Doll's House* decorated the tree with small Norwegian–Swedish flags, and thereby indicated that the action was taking place before 1905 when the Swedish–Norwegian union was dissolved, he was actually including an element better suited to the screen than to the stage.

The flags recall the cultural signifiers, which are of special interest in connection with the screen media, since one is here dealing with products often intended not only for a domestic but also for a foreign audience. Cultural signifiers actually play a much greater part than we normally realize. Since in Ibsen's case we are dealing with plays that are now about a hundred years old, there is necessarily a discrepancy between human conduct as depicted in them, mirroring that of Ibsen's period, and present-day behaviour. The question then arises: should a director adjust to the sender (Ibsen) or the receiver (the contemporary audience)? In Darlow's television versions of *The Master Builder* and *Little Eyolf* (1981) the erotic signifiers are quite modest compared to what we find in Mærli's and Eli Ryg's (1983) Norwegian television versions of the same plays. Darlow's Kaja kisses Solness's hand, while Mærli's Kaja very passionately kisses Solness's mouth. The difference may be due to the fact that we have here two different directors, each with his own individual psyche. It may reflect national differences – British puritanism versus Scandinavian unrestrained sensuality – both on the part of the director and the domestic audience. Or it may be a conscious choice, with Darlow settling for what he sees as credible behaviour around 1890, and Mærli for what seems natural to an audience today. Darlow is clearly running the risk that his Kaja/Solness relationship appears over-prudish to a present-day audience; on the other hand, Mærli's choice may give us the impression – possibly erroneous – that Solness and Kaja have a fully established liaison.

The situation is different with regard to *Little Eyolf*, for while Darlow here again sets the action in Ibsen's time, Ryg locates it in a modern, highly stylized environment. Considering this, a less formalized behaviour between the sexes is only what we would expect from Ryg's version. However, there are certain elements in the play which could not easily be updated and which therefore seem at odds with the modern setting. The contrast between rich and poor, which becomes particularly prominent at the end of the play when the opulent Rita and Allmers decide to devote themselves to charitable works, certainly applies less to present-day Norway than to that of a century ago. Similarly, Allmers's excuse that he married the wealthy Rita in order to help his young 'half-sister' Asta sounds rather hollow when placed in a present-day welfare-state context.

As for the spatial–cultural signifiers, Garland's rather theatrical *Doll's House* with its mingling of Norwegian connotations (it opens with a horse-drawn sleigh ride) and British ones (the singing of a Christmas carol) contrasts with Losey's cinematically authentic version of the same play, shot on location in Røros, Norway.

The two productions also point to another problem: how to handle the spatial unity of Ibsen's text in a medium resistant to such a unity. Garland, who opts for a theatrical solution, shows us little of the world outside the

Helmer apartment; and such an apartment in a film, Bazin assures us, feels even more cramped to an audience than a comparable room on the stage.[5] Losey, by contrast, who opts for a more cinematic solution, alternates between interiors and exteriors. The problem with this choice is that it does not fully accord with the spirit of the play. Ibsen's strict unity of place strengthens one's feeling that Nora is a prisoner in her husband's house. Her exit is given a sense of finality not least because it is the first time that we see her leave her doll's house. In Losey's film this essential aspect is destroyed.

Sound effects and music play a much more prominent part in screen versions than on stage. On the small screen especially, acoustic signifiers are at hand to replace visual ones. Instead of seeing a Norwegian fjord in the distance, which is not always easy to register on television, we may hear the crying of gulls – as in Ryg's *Little Eyolf*.

Alongside diegetic music, i.e. music naturally belonging to the situation (e.g. the tarantella in *A Doll's House* and Hjalmar Ekdal's flute playing in *The Wild Duck*), screen versions often have recourse to non-diegetic mood music. The 'flash-back' meetings between Ellida and the Stranger in Bronken's *Lady from the Sea* are made ominously pregnant by the musical accompaniment of Mahler's Symphony no. 9, not unlike the effect of Visconti's use of Mahler in *Death in Venice*. In Jonas Cornell's Swedish *Rosmersholm* (1984) Rosmer and Rebecca find their *Liebestod* to the accompaniment of music by Ravel. In Darlow's *Master Builder*, Hilde's and Solness's lyrical dreams about castles in the air are accompanied by a high soprano voice. One reason why the opening of Darlow's *Little Eyolf* appears more bleakly serene than Ryg's is that his images of a Norwegian fjord landscape are linked with Benjamin Britten's *Dawn*, the first sea interlude in *Peter Grimes*; violins and – in particular – a high flute contribute here to paint the mood. Ryg, by contrast, opens with disharmonic music in a minor key which presents a sombre undercurrent to the otherwise superficially friendly meeting between Asta and Rita.

Television versions nowadays frequently begin with a pre-title sequence. The basic reason for this is trivial. Unlike theatre and film, television is a private, continuous medium. As a consequence a transmitted teleplay has to compete with a number of surrounding factors: telephone, interference by family members, alternative TV programmes, etc. A pre-title sequence allows the spectator to miss the first couple of minutes of the transmission without missing the actual play. Although the reason for their existence is thus banal, pre-title sequences have a special potential in that they allow directors a greater amount of freedom than is often vouchsafed by the text of the plays alone.

The most common type of pre-title sequence incorporates the dramatization of one or more events in the past, events which in the analytical form of Ibsenist drama are merely related. Losey's *Doll's House*, for example, opens with a pre-title shot taking the audience back to the pre-scenic events of the play. A few opening shots establish that the period is the one defined by Ibsen's text: men and women (in long dresses!) are skating; there are horse-sleighs with bells. In a conversation between Nora (Jane Fonda) and Mrs Linde we learn that Nora is soon to be married to Torvald Helmer, whom she does not love, while Mrs Linde has in the past been forced to reject Krogstad, whom she loves, for a husband with a secure income. In other words: the woman joining a man is contrasted with the woman leaving one. Unlike Ibsen, Losey in this way interprets the past for us and makes us side with Mrs Linde rather than with Nora from the very beginning.

An unusually lengthy example of the pre-title sequence is to be seen in Safran's Australian adaptation of *The Wild Duck*. It opens with a picture of flying wild ducks; as one of them is shot, the image is frozen; then follows the title. We see the face of the marksman, Old Werle, here called George Wardle; then a shot of a swimming dog; the dog dives, picks up the duck under water and swims back with it in its mouth. The duck is not dead, only wounded. Wardle asks his servant Peters to wring its neck but Peters wants to spare the life of the duck, saying that he knows someone who might like to have it. We then see Old Ackland (Ekdal) go hunting in his attic. Peters arrives with his gift for Henrietta (Hedvig), who emphatically states that it is now *her* wild duck, etc.

The director has here pieced together information related in the play, added some scenes to establish time, place and (idyllic) mood and arranged his material in a relevant way. Wardle's real outdoor hunting, for example, is contrasted with the imaginary indoor pursuits of his former companion Ackland. What Ibsen serves us piecemeal via his characters – can we trust their versions? – is thus turned into a coherent, objective story.

A very different approach to the pre-title sequence is found in Waris Hussein's BBC *Hedda Gabler* (1972). The first shot shows Hedda (Janet Suzman), in dressing gown, her hair down, by the bedroom window, staring out, framed by the morning sunlight. Inside we become aware of a dark, vaguely outlined room. The camera pans with her as she moves into a red hallway. She looks one way but moves in the opposite direction. A little later we see her in her private room sitting beneath the portrait of her father. Another long shot shows her moving into the living room. Hussein then cuts to a close-up of Tesman, asleep in his bed. Hedda gets into her bed, takes a look at her husband, then turns her back to him. There is a close-up of Hedda, her head on the pillow, followed by a shot of a tricoloured (red, yellow, green) corner of the ceiling. After which the play proper begins with the arrival of Miss Tesman.

What is here brought into focus is not the significance of past events but rather Hedda's, the protagonist's, present state of mind. Her position by the window – a matter for repeated attention – is emblematic of her feeling of being imprisoned in a bourgeois way of life which she detests and of her longing to escape from it. Her basically passionate nature is echoed by the red of the hallway. Quite subtle is the implication that she wants to distance herself from her father yet cannot. Her aversion to Tesman, especially as a sexual partner, is clearly signalled; at the same time the close-up of the ceiling is a very marked low angle point-of-view shot, indicative of the discrepancy between Hedda's 'horizontal' existence and her 'vertical' desires.

Unlike Safran, who dramatizes events in the past, and Hussein, who dramatizes a state of mind, Mærli in his televersion of *The Master Builder* does both. In Ibsen's text Solness reveals to Hilde at a fairly late stage in their relationship that his success as a master builder is irrevocably linked to the demolition of Aline's family home and the devastation of their life together. Although he has not in any personal sense caused the fire that has laid their house in ashes, he has nevertheless secretly wished for it – enough, that is, to make him feel guilty. Mærli opens his teleplay not with an objective description of the fire but with a dream sequence. An initial close-up of Solness followed by a dissolve to the burning house informs us that *he* is the dreamer. People are running around the house trying to quench the fire. We hear a woman (Aline) screaming and the fateful sound of crows. Then follows a sequence of blue-toned shots: Solness in his bed watching himself standing close by (initiating the series of mirror sequences); a coffin being carried away; Aline in deep mourning; a wintry funeral procession; again a close-up of Solness; the title; a shot of Solness's office with his subordinates lined up around the room. This bluish sequence is followed by a shot in normal colour showing Solness waking up from his nightmare. In contrast to Ibsen, who only gradually exposes something of the reality of Solness's frailty of conscience, Mærli immediately informs us of his troubled state of mind. Although in this way some of the Ibsenist suspense evaporates, it might be argued that the extremely dynamic screen media can do without this kind of dramatic suspense.

The endings of Ibsen's plays have, rightly, attracted much interest. A screen director, utilizing the opportunities offered by his medium, can create endings differing radically from those feasible in stage versions. In Garland's *Doll's House*, Nora's (Claire Bloom's) exit is followed by a long-shot showing Helmer (Anthony Hopkins) walking back through the hall – a way of making him seem small and lonely – into the living-room, where he stops.

There is a slow zoom-in to a close-up of his face as he says, 'The miracle of miracles.' Then comes the sound of the street door slamming shut, crushing his hope. Fade-out and, as an ironical footnote, sweet, doll-like music, as from a musical-box – the kind of music that was heard at the beginning of the film.

When Losey's Helmer hears his ex-wife slam the street door shut, he lowers his head. There is a shot of the fatal letter-box, its 'door' ironically open, and a final exterior shot of the church of the doll town in the distance, swept in mist and snow. The chiming of the church bells mingles with the sombre brass music that was heard in the pre-title sequence of the film – two sounds expressing the power of the religious, bourgeois society of which Helmer and Nora have become victims.

Magne Bleness's blue-tinted *Ghosts* (1978)[6] ends with Mrs Alving (Henny Moan), in black, returning from the sunlit window in the background to Osvald (Bentein Baardson) sitting in the foreground as he asks for the sun, which we see reflected on his face. She half kneels to scrutinize his face – only to discover what *we* have already seen: that Osvald has indeed gone insane. Moshinsky, in his almost monochrome purplish blue setting, has mother and son seated close together already before Osvald (Kenneth Branagh) has his breakdown, Mrs Alving (Judi Dench) tenderly stroking her son's head as he leans it on her lap – a grouping suggesting both the past (Osvald as a little boy), the present (Osvald's desire to return to the womb) and the future (the *pietà* in store for them, once Mrs Alving fulfils her promise). When he asks for the sun, she raises up his head so that the beams of the rising sun can fall on his face – as though trying to give him a helping hand. As she utters her final 'no's', her sprawling fingers covering her face, the muted sombre bars of Schönberg's *Verklärte Nacht* (*Transfigured Night*) – what title could be more apt! – can be heard. Although the two versions are not radically different, Bleness retains a rather stagey approach to the ending, while Moshinsky, partly thanks to his superb actors, has transformed it into a magnificent piece of television drama, full of subtle nuances.

In Geissendörfer's, Safran's and Widerberg's *Wild Duck* the camera enters the attic, revealing the duck which Ibsen carefully keeps out of sight to enhance its symbolic value. Unlike Ibsen and Widerberg, Geissendörfer and Safran in addition show us Hedvig in her last moments. Geissendörfer's twelve-year-old girl stands with the wild duck in her arms, looking into the light seeping through the window above her. By this arrangement surrounded with a *gloria celestis*, Hedvig is seen in a cliché-ridden pose which agrees both with Hjalmar Ekdal's – the photographer's! – and with Gregers's wishful idea concerning Hedvig's death. Yet since the scene is shot not from their point of view but objectively, the effect of it is that the audience seem included in their 'life-lie'.[7] In Safran's version we see how Hedvig, while holding the wild duck to her breast, puts the pistol to *its* breast. As the director cuts to a close-up of Gina we hear the shot. When Gregory (Gregers) exclaims 'There's your proof!' we believe with him that Henrietta (Hedvig)has shot the duck. Yet in the next long shot we see, in slow motion, how the girl – just like the pre-title duck – falls down while the wild duck flies up. Did she intend to shoot the duck, herself or both? We do not know. In Widerberg's version, finally, there is no doubt that Hedvig has committed suicide. When the director cuts to Hedvig lying lifeless on the floor of the attic, we see the duck, hale and sound, in its basin next to her. A following close-up reveals a spot of blood by Hedvig's heart. With such objective proof, difficult to furnish in a stage version, Widerberg puts to shame Gregers's hope that Hedvig may have died accidentally.

Theatrical characteristics can sometimes be meaningfully combined with cinematic ones, as when Cornell, in *Rosmersholm*, has the camera for the first time leave the Rosmer interior at the end. Mrs Helseth's final line is followed by a dissolve to a shot of Rosmer and Rebecca embracing each other under water. Death signifies both the end of painful separateness and release from imprisoning life.

When Ibsen reveals two contrasting reactions at the end, a screen director may opt for a 'theatrical' solution and balance the two reactions or for a 'cinematic' one, focusing on one of them. Darlow's *Master Builder* finishes with a close-up of an excited Hilde looking upwards and, behind her, the back of a shadowy figure (Solness) tumbling down. By arranging the final (frozen) picture in this way the director makes us share Ragnar's rather than Hilde's vision. Unlike her we see Solness falling. The vision of the victorious master builder becomes exclusively Hilde's.

Mærli too shows an excited Hilde in close-up looking upwards. But in his version there is no tumbling Solness to be seen. Even Ragnar's 'Killed on the spot' is uttered off-screen – as though the idea cannot penetrate Hilde's mind. When the final shot is frozen we see half of Hilde's face, lit by the evening sun – a subtle indication that Solness (literally Sun-ness) has got under her skin.

There are innumerable problems involved in the transposition from book to screen – problems which are often only partly overcome. On the other hand, the protean and strongly emotive screen media have added new aspects to Ibsenist drama, aspects which cannot be disregarded by anyone who feels the need of keeping Ibsen in rapport with present-day audiences. For it is not, as we still tend to think, as readers of the drama texts or as spectators of stage performances that most people today get acquainted with Ibsen. Even a successful Ibsen production in Paris, London or New York will attract a far smaller – and socially much less varied – audience than a film or television version of the same play. For most people today an Ibsen play is neither book nor stage performance but screen adaptation. Also for this reason Ibsen scholars should pay due attention to what is happening in the post-Ibsen media.

NOTES

1 The figures for both film and television are, of course, approximate and concern mainly Europe and the USA. For details regarding film productions, see Karin Synnøve Hansen (ed.), *Henrik Ibsen, 1828–1978: A Filmography* (Oslo, 1978).
2 For an analysis of the teleplay, see Christian Braad Thomsen, '*Et Dukkehjem*. R. W. Fassbinder: *Nora Helmer*', in Ulla Strømberg and Jytte Wiingaard (eds.), *Den levende Ibsen: Analyser af udvalgte Ibsen-forestillinger 1973–1978* (Copenhagen, 1978), pp. 78–86.
3 André Bazin, *What Is Cinema?*, vol. I, trans. Hugh Gray (Berkeley, 1967) p. 105.
4 James McFarlane's translation [*v*, 143].
5 Bazin, *What is Cinema?*, vol. I p. 90.
6 For a discussion of this televersion, see Asbjørn Aarseth, '*Peer Gynt' and 'Ghosts': Text and Performance* (London, 1989), pp. 102–7.
7 This interpretation relies partly on that of Birgitta Steene in her 'Film as Theater: Geissendörfer's *The Wild Duck* (1976)', in Andrew S. Horton and Joan Magretta (eds.), *Modern European Filmmakers and the Art of Adaptation* (New York, 1981), p. 300.

Other sources relevant to this chapter include

Elghazali, Saad, 'Die Veränderungen vom Schauspiel zum Fernsehspiel', in his *Literatur als Fernsehspiel* (Hamburg, 1966).
Erenstein, R. L. (ed.), *Theatre and Television* (Amsterdam, 1988).
Törnqvist, Egil, *Transposing Drama: Studies in Representation* (London, 1991).
Waldmann, Werner and Rose, 'Theateradaption', in their *Einführung in die Analyse von Fernsehspielen* (Tübingen, 1980).

13

JOHN BARTON

On staging Ibsen

INTERVIEW BY JANET GARTON

JG: You have produced three Ibsen plays, one realistic, one historical and one poetic: *Pillars of the Community* with the Royal Shakespeare Company in 1977, *The Vikings at Helgeland* in Bergen in 1983, and *Peer Gynt* in Oslo in 1990. Why these three plays?

JB: It is a peculiar selection and it doesn't necessarily represent my interest in Ibsen. In general I think I tend to go for the flawed masterpiece or the early play or the undiscovered play, more often than not. So there is a certain common ground here, though it might not seem so. In the case of all the Ibsen plays I have done, either I was asked to or I chose to or I was required to adapt in some way, and this is something I always find myself drawn to. *Pillars of the Community* was the first major production outside Shakespeare that I had ever done at that time for the RSC. I pushed for it because I thought it was a potentially wonderful play. It is one of those plays that has to have a good group cast and there was a very good group available. I was also fascinated by all the problems of how to bring off the ending. I suppose on the surface it is like certain Elizabethan plays: it's plain sailing for four Acts and then goes crazy at the end. So there were resemblances.

JG: Why did the RSC decide to stage this play?

JB: It is part of their policy always to go for the neglected classics. This was an Ibsen play that had not been given a major production in England for a very long time.

JG: So when you say it was adapted, did you start with a translation that was already available and work on that? Or how did you go about adapting it?

JB: When I say I adapted it, in that instance I simply used some of the draft material from the earlier versions of the play in one or two places. I can't now remember what or why; but, as sometimes happens with certain play-wrights, I think it helped to make some things clearer or simpler.

JG: So you used nothing that Ibsen had not written at some time?

JB: No. This was therefore the *least* adapted of the three, but this element did come into it. But I always do this. When I did *The Three Sisters* I used one or two bits that are in Chekhov's draft and which had never been played. It was a wonderful bit. I always get a standard translation and then either a literal version or an advisor; and then I reword it as I want to or rewrite it myself.

JG: You say that you like working with plays that are flawed. Can you explain in what way you think this play is flawed?

JB: Well, if you read the play you find it's jolly hard to take the ending. It goes absolutely swimmingly until the last few pages and then everybody acknowledges there are problems. That is its reputation. But if you are going to do it in the theatre, you have to make interpretive decisions that are rather different from what one might make as a scholar in the study. If you are doing it in the theatre, you have to be pragmatic in terms of what will work with an audience, and also what the leading actor – in that case, Ian McKellan – thinks. So the solution is worked out between you.

JG: The question is whether Bernick – the character in question – comes over as a hypocrite at the end, or whether he is absolved?

JB: Yes, I seem to remember we played the ending itself completely straight, so there was a sort of wry ambiguity: you could see that Bernick knew that he was being hypocritical, but he meant it, as it were. Does that make sense? It is actually one of the most complicated of Ibsen's pre-plots, very confusing. Partly there was a kind of shared irony among the group listening to Bernick at the end, so that they knew what he was doing and he knew that they knew what he was doing, so there was a sort of admission. I do remember that in our production the last moments were peaceful and harmonious. Certainly we discussed it at great length and explored and tried many different things.

JG: Perhaps irony is the only way to do the ending? It's difficult to do it straight-faced, isn't it?

JB: Yes, but it's the *kind* of irony that matters. And as Ibsen is one of the very greatest ironic writers, it is not too difficult in his case. But I don't think that it's the dramatist's irony; I think we did it as Bernick's irony about himself, and an irony that was understood in the room around him. I think therefore we did find a theatrical solution.

JG: You said earlier that you have produced a good deal of Shakespeare. Indeed mainly Shakespeare, perhaps? Did you find that useful in approach-ing Ibsen?

JB: Yes. I think there are two or three very close resemblances. The most obvious is that they are both brilliant story-tellers; and they are both dramatists who make the fullest use of irony. In the theatre the suspense of the unfolding story, the discoveries, the shocks – they both deal in shocks – at bottom these are very similar. There is also much more comedy in both of them than people often think. Ibsen is as much a comic writer as a tragic writer. Black comedy it may be, dark comedy and ironic. But I think one of the most brilliant things about Ibsen is his comic sense – it is terrific, absolutely stunning. The problem with him in the theatre is the same as with Chekhov: theatre tradition has tended to push both of them towards the tragic. As we all know, Chekhov specifically called his plays comedies and he argued with Stanislavski about this. Ibsen's case was somewhat different: he was picked up very cosily by Shaw in England in the early days, and *heavy* Ibsen production was the way it all began. Now all actors acknowledge he has a comedic power, but somehow the dark side takes over as well.

JG: I think it is not so obvious when one reads the text as it is when one sees it on stage. That's when the comedy comes out. I am always having to point out to my students the funny parts. They sit and read it with straight faces.

JB: I think Pastor Manders is one of the funniest parts in drama.

JG: Yes, wonderful.

JB: I like *Pillars of the Community* a lot. It was at that point I came nearest to satisfying my urge to do a Chekhov, because there is something Chekhovian about bits of it. We wanted to show people that they had been too dismissive of it – it is a very good play.

JG: I would now like to ask you about your next two Ibsen productions. *The Vikings* you did at Bergen in 1983; and then you did *Peer Gynt* in Oslo in 1990. So both of these plays you have produced in Norway and in Norwegian. Did this create enormous difficulties: producing them in another language?

JB: I don't think in the end it did. I had never done it before, and to begin with I was terrified. But I think at bottom it didn't, mainly because of the very good English which the cast spoke.

JG: But it is not only a matter of communication is it? Isn't it a matter of understanding how the actors are interpreting the text, and then directing them in how to do it?

JB: Yes, the problem I found with both plays was in knowing where I was. But once I had got the story clear from the staging and from the actors and their intentions and their interplay, I found I could pick it up quickly. Long speeches were difficult; I could never be quite certain what point had been reached. One reason why my *Peer Gynt* worked well in Norway was apparently that people were saying 'I have never before been so clear about the story' – that was because I had to make it clear to myself in order to direct it. I experienced something of the same thing when I was doing *The Vikings*: here I did put it into verse, short verse lines, and this made it easier to follow.

JG: What sort of verse was *Vikings* in when you had finished with it? Did it rhyme?

JB: No, it was a verse I used on *The Greeks*, the three stress line to make it as simple as possible. And then my collaborator translated it into the same verse form, so I knew where I was.

JG: So you started with an English prose text and put that into verse?

JB: Well, entirely at their suggestion, we did a very odd thing. The idea was that I should first do a version in English – modernize the play, take out the melodramatic, archaic bits, and so on. Then Tom Remlov, who is dramaturg at Bergen, was to put it into modern Norwegian, because *they* claimed that the original text was so archaic as to be almost unintelligible. I took the opportunity to reinterpret it to some degree, rewrote bits, cut a lot, put stuff in. I made it more ironic and the characters more self-aware, which probably made it more into a slightly later Ibsen. We never published it, but it was a great success at the time. I mention this because much the same thing came up again when I later did *Peer Gynt*. I started off with a double parallel text: I had the Christopher Fry version from the McFarlane edition and I had Rolf Fjelde's American version. You can't *not* adapt *Peer Gynt*; so I cut it very carefully and again I used some of the draft material. There was a frightfully important scene (in my view) which helps it – the scene when Solveig comes up to the mountains and her father says Peer can marry her – which everybody assured me was very roughly written. But the actors and the dramaturg did do a lot to tighten up the wording.

JG: Did you re-arrange the order of the scenes at all?

JB: Yes, I did at that particular point. It was also because Aase and Solveig were doubling, and it was to make the double work. I also did *every* scene, even though it might be brief.

JG: Act IV is often considered a big problem in *Peer Gynt*. It is sometimes left out altogether.

JB: It *is* a big problem in that it is not so good as the others. I wanted to make it work, because there are some very funny things in it; but I did cut it very heavily. One scene in particular is a real killer: the opening scene with the businessmen and the capitalists. When we revived the production the following year, I cut even more of it – to everybody's relief.

JG: Of the two productions, it is said that the 1990 version was more serious, much more tragic, whereas the second version the following year

10 John Barton's production of *Peer Gynt* at Nationaltheatret, Oslo, 1990

was funnier, faster, racier, sexier and less moving in a way. Was that a deliberate change, or was it partly the result of a different cast?

JB: It was mainly that the second time round I found comedy in it which I hadn't seen before and which I felt we should bring out. But I don't think I set out to make it deliberately funnier.

JG: *Peer Gynt* poses more problems than later Ibsen in areas like stage sets and casting. It moves all around the place, it has an enormous cast. You solved the casting by a lot of doubling up, didn't you?

JB: Well, that was the other thing. I would never in a thousand years do it in a big theatre. You have got a play which Ibsen didn't write for the stage – doesn't he call it a dramatic poem? – but he allowed it to be performed because it was in the nineteenth century. They did a slap-up thing and this became the tradition. But that wasn't how he conceived it. I don't think this kind of production is still do-able. There is the setting – the mountains, the desert and all that – and this just gets on top of the poetic language as can happen with a Shakespeare play. It has got to be the actor and the text in the right ambience rather than a great epic setting.

JG: You would not attempt to produce it realistically?

JB: Absolutely not. It would be a killer. The great beauty of doing it in a small place was that I was able to do it in the round, which takes away the problems. You have no elaborate set and you can release a poetic play much more easily than you can in a big theatre.

11   Tone Danielsen as Aase in John Barton's production of *Peer Gynt*, Oslo, 1990

JG: Can you say a bit more about how Shakespearean experiences influenced you?

JB: Shakespeare cares an awful lot about music and in some plays it takes a major part. And I care even more – to me the music is in the end more important than the set in Shakespeare. One has to get the music right. Not necessarily in every case; but, for me, in most cases the music works the magic more powerfully than ever the set can do. I felt this was also obviously so with *Peer Gynt*.

JG: What music did you use for *Peer Gynt*? Did you use any one particular composer?

JB: I didn't use any of the traditional scores. Our musical director, Per Christian Revholt, arranged and himself played the music for the play. When he came over to England to discuss the production, he brought masses of Norwegian folk songs, nursery rhymes, opera songs so that I could get the feel of Norwegian folk music. In the end we used seven or eight tunes only in the whole thing and they were all Norwegian except for one: the famous English one 'The Sally Gardens'. We had it on tape in a Norwegian version, a brilliant rendering, on a synthesizer and high flute which absolutely sounded as if it was being played or sung at the top of a mountain in the snow.

JG: Why did you cast the same actress as Aase and Solveig?

JB: Because it makes it a much better part. Solveig is such a drip and tiny and was one part that Ibsen didn't bother with. It seemed clear that Ibsen meant her to be central to the play, seeing that he ends the action with her. But nobody will persuade a major actress to play that part if there is nothing there to play. So I put in the scene in the mountains which is a good scene, and putting it together also made it theatrically much more exciting and made it possible to double the rest. And I assumed that it must have been done before.

JG: I thought perhaps you were trying to say something about Peer's mother fixation by using the same actress?

JB: Well, perhaps it does say something about that, too. But I thought of it more theatrically than psychologically. Which brings me back to the main problem: how to do the poem with a small cast in a small theatre? I thought it was more powerful comedically than people had told me. I couldn't see that it was a tragedy, because it was about a man with self-delusion, evading the truth. I couldn't see that it shouldn't be comedic. I thought that the right theatre way was to think of it as if Ibsen had let his hair down to write this extraordinary thing; and a theatre production ought to reflect this.

JG: Can we talk a little bit about *The Vikings* which you rather hopped over. That's a play that is very rarely performed. You spoke of that too as 'a flawed masterpiece'.

JB: It is basically turgid and melodramatic, particularly Sigurd and Gunnar are pretty heavy going, though Hjørdis is a superb part. Dagny is under-written; and in my version I built her up. Ornulf is very good, but it's as though brilliant bits of Ibsen break through something that is heavy and not his touch.

JG: He was trying to write nationalistic romantic drama?

JB: Yes, he was caught in the nineteenth century and the nationalism of the time; but he broke out of it. This is why I judged it to be a flawed masterpiece. There is much in it that is good; but a lot of the time it is pretty intolerable. I gave Sigurd a greater sense of self-awareness and irony, if I remember; and Dagny I built up rather more against Hjørdis.

JG: How did you stage it? Did you do it realistically?

JB: Again it was in the studio theatre. We set it in the snow. We had a lot of snow. All you need is snow in the first Act, and a long table with benches and stools in the second Act, and a tomb for the last Act. It is a good studio theatre play: it is not a large cast, it has a powerful argument, it doesn't have big scenic demands, but I don't think it would work in a big theatre.

JG: *The Vikings* on the surface seems rather more like Shakespeare than a lot of Ibsen, being historical, costume drama. Did that affect you when you produced it?

JB: I would want to excise from my mind the concept of historical costume drama. It's a phrase of thirty years ago. I look for a different wording: I use the words 'epic' or 'chamber' for two basic kinds of play. With Shakespeare we say that there are certain plays that are more 'chamber' and certain plays that are more 'epic'. The paradox, however, is that there are one or two that seem to be 'chamber' but which work better as 'epic' in the theatre; and some 'epic' ones which work better as 'chamber'. I think that's probably true of Ibsen, too. I think it has to do with the space. It's not about costume. It's not about settings primarily. It's about going into a small space that sets its rules and limits and opportunities, and therefore also the style. Then one starts to think about how to costume it.

JG: I asked you earlier if your experience of Shakespeare affected the way you approached Ibsen. What about the other way round? Has producing Ibsen given you fresh insight into other writers? Is that a difficult question?

JB: No, I think I would slightly dodge it by saying that a handful of one's favourite greatest dramatists all cross-fertilize each other. Chekhovian moments certainly come into Shakespeare. It's all around European drama. It has a knock-on effect, like Shakespeare's influence on Schiller. When directing, one is always aware of something or other coming from another dramatist that's relevant: Brecht or – it could be almost anyone.

JG: There were bits of *Peer Gynt* that reminded me of Brecht, the way you staged it.

JB: Well, that's interesting because certainly I don't consciously remember doing that.

JG: Do you find, in the light of your experience in Bergen and in Oslo, that the actual theatre space affects the way in which you visualize a play?

JB: If I am asked to do a play, the first thing I want to do is to go round the particular space in which it is to be played; and then smell it out and think how I am going to use it before I decide what designs should be used. That is answer number one. But answer number two is that dramatists use a stock of theatre devices, the most obvious in the case of Ibsen is that he lived in an age when it was fashionable to shoot yourself with a revolver, so there is a lot of that. But that is a device, just as poison is for an Elizabethan. And in that sense they all do overlap, and every now and then somebody articulates it into a philosophy, whether it's Brecht or Stanislavski or whoever. But that's a relatively modern phenomenon. In the Elizabethan age or in Greek theatre they had certain bits of equipment only, which they used again and again; and therefore the dramatist embraces them and they keep turning up. Now Ibsen had an early period when he was into nationalist historical material; then he was in the period of naturalism and he seized on it. What I always say about Ibsen, and I suppose I'd stress it if I did one of the other plays, is that that's so obvious that the naturalistic takes care of itself. Surely what you'd go for is the mythical resonance as in *The Wild Duck* or *Rosmersholm*. There is myth behind them all. The fact that they are poetic plays using naturalism as the form in which to work doesn't stop them being in a sense poetic plays. And he *was* a poet. That's how I see Ibsen. Just as Shakespeare, who was a great poet but who nevertheless writes naturalistically and who in his tavern scenes isn't always poetic. You can be naturalistic as Shakespeare sometimes was, you can be poetic, you can be Brechtian, you can be black, you can be ironic . . .

JG: But Ibsen was trying to make his actors and directors do things that they didn't traditionally do, wasn't he? He was actually trying to change the way . . .

JB: Yes, he was reacting against a tradition: just as Chekhov unsuccessfully was trying to, or Brecht did. It usually has to do with reacting against something. I've only done three early plays by Ibsen, and I would like to do more. I would quite like to have a go at *Love's Comedy* sometime because I think that's rather good. You see, what's peculiar about that play (which is from 1862 or so) is that you read it and you think 'Shaw'. As though he was writing Shaw before Shaw. It's extraordinary. It's quite different. It's light-hearted, very witty, intelligent. I think my feeling is that he could have done anything.

JG: Are there none of the later plays that you would like to work on? None of them that tempt you to produce them? Or supposing you were given a free choice? If a theatre said, 'Do an Ibsen, any one you like . . .'

JB: Well, as I said, I would seriously like to do *Love's Comedy* because it's one that is rarely done, and it actually seems to me – though I've never talked to anyone about it – to be coherent and of a piece and funny and witty and could come alive very well on the stage.

JG: What about that other enormous play *Brand*. Does that tempt you?

JB: No, I'm not mad about *Brand*. I admire *Brand* but it does go *on*. I feel like saying, 'Excuse me, Ibsen, but you've made your point.' It has some very good things in it. I have seen it two or three times, and I am always impressed by it, but it doesn't seize me. Of the other ones, maybe *The Wild Duck*. They are all wonderful, but the trouble about them is that one's generally seen them bloody well done at some point. And if you've seen a play extremely well done and you know you couldn't do it better or get a better cast, you wipe it off your list. You tend to be attracted by ones where you think something's been missed, or where there is perhaps a different way of doing it. I have in fact seen most of the major Ibsens at some time or other very well done.

JG: What about the last ones like *Little Eyolf* or *When We Dead Awaken*?

JB: Well, I don't know how I'd do *When We Dead Awaken*. I'm open to correction, but people tell me it's a wonderful work, but I can't see it myself. *Little Eyolf*, yes I like *Little Eyolf*. No, I'm gripped by them and when I see them I think: 'My God, this is a wonderful writer, bloody good.' It doesn't necessarily mean however that I want to do it. *Hedda Gabler* – I've seen many *Hedda Gabler*s and very good ones. I wouldn't resist doing it if I had to, but I don't know if I'd choose to. I'd rather choose to do something which I've never seen work or which I have a special view of. And if a play declares itself – it's funny to say that about Ibsen because there's so much argument about interpretation – but however ambiguous *Hedda Gabler* is, you *know* what it's about. So I don't quite see why I would want to do it.

JG: Is there any chance of your going back to Norway to do something else?

JB: I would like to do something again there because I like the actors so much. But I wouldn't want it to be too soon, as I have spent a lot of time there in the last two years. One of the important things we haven't talked about, but which I think ought to be said, is how Norwegian Ibsen is. I think that Ibsen – because he travelled and was well read and was pretty cosmopolitan – chose to write about that society as his medium. I think of him as homing in on and using that, rather than the way people tend to look at him: as a social critic dramatist who wrote all those plays exposing the hypocrisy of his own society, when we have got this great corpus of earlier plays that don't do anything of the sort. It was as if he had come back, saw and decided to do it. But what I'm talking about I suppose is the totality of Ibsen. Why I'm interested in the early plays is because I take the great plays for granted as wonderful; but I think we misread Ibsen if we forget that he wrote an awful lot of things before he got to them. I think that they partly explain the sense of mischief that's in the man, the humour, the comedy; but naturally if he is writing about that society, he got caught by his own society. You see I don't think that they are that dependent on a Norwegian sensibility because the plots and situations in all of them could apply anywhere else and indeed do. Which is why people can latch on to the plays so powerfully.

14

ARTHUR MILLER

Ibsen and the drama of today

[In his Introduction to the 1957 edition of his *Collected Plays*, Arthur Miller singled out certain aspects of Ibsen's work for comment:

> There is one element in Ibsen's method which I do not think ought to be overlooked, let alone dismissed as it so often is nowadays. If his plays, and his method, do nothing else they reveal the evolutionary quality of life. One is constantly aware, in watching his plays, of process, change, development. I think too many modern plays assume, so to speak, that their duty is merely to show the present countenance rather than to account for what happens. It is therefore wrong to imagine that because his first and sometimes his second acts devote so much time to a studied revelation of antecedent material, his view is static compared to our own. In truth, it is profoundly dynamic, for that enormous past was always heavily documented to the end that the present be comprehended with wholeness, as a moment in a flow of time, and not – as with so many modern plays – as a situation without roots. Indeed, even though I can myself reject other aspects of his work, it nevertheless presents barely and unadorned what I believe is the biggest single dramatic problem, namely, how to dramatize what has gone before. I say this not merely out of technical interest, but because dramatic characters, and the drama itself, can never hope to attain a maximum degree of consciousness unless they contain a viable unveiling of the contrast between past and present, and an awareness of the process by which the present has become what it is. And I say this, finally, because I take it as a truth that the end of drama is the creation of a higher consciousness and not merely a subjective attack upon the audience's nerves and feelings. What is precious in the Ibsen method is its insistence upon valid causation, and this cannot be dismissed as a wooden notion.
>
> This is the 'real' in Ibsen's realism for me, for he was, after all, as much a mystic as a realist. Which is simply to say that while there are mysteries in life which no amount of analyzing will reduce to reason, it is perfectly realistic to admit and even to proclaim that hiatus as a truth. But the problem is not to make complex what is essentially explainable; it is to make understandable what is complex without distorting and oversimplifying what cannot be

explained. I think many of his devices are, in fact, quite arbitrary; that he betrays a Germanic ponderousness at times and a tendency to overprove what is quite clear in the first place. But we could do with more of his basic intention, which was to assert nothing he had not proved, and to cling always to the marvellous spectacle of life forcing one event out of the jaws of the preceding one and to reveal its elemental consistencies with surprise. In other words, I contrast his realism not with the lyrical, which I prize, but with sentimentality, which is always a leak in the dramatic dike. He sought to make a play as weighty and living a fact as the discovery of the steam engine or algebra. This can be scoffed away only at a price, and the price is a living drama.

Some thirty-five years after these words were written, Arthur Miller once again turned to the question of how one might assess Ibsen's influence today.]

I am not scholar enough – or journalist either – to be able to say with any real certainty what Ibsen's influence is today. I have only impressions, which may or may not be accurate.

I don't believe that many of today's playwrights look to his methods as models, but his standing as a modern has nevertheless improved, I think, over the past thirty or forty years. When I began writing plays in the late thirties he was a favourite of the Left for his radical politics and rebellious mind. His work, however, not often performed, was frequently regarded as quaintly methodical onion-peeling. If you had the patience to labour through it an Ibsen play was more like argument in a legal case than an entertainment. Such was the prejudice and ignorance of the time, his most important lack was thought to be the poetic spirit; it was fashionable, as it still is in some places today, to call him more of a carpenter than the visionary architect that Shaw, among others, thought him to be. What the young avant-garde wanted in the thirties, positioned as ever against clunky Broadway realism, was the lyrical voice. Clifford Odets and Sean O'Casey specifically, were the more or less Marxist prophets while Saroyan, a premature or closet absurdist, sang basically for his supper. In the Broadway/ West End mainstream Maxwell Anderson and Christopher Fry were trying to wring popular drama from unconventional word usage, reviving even Elizabethan iambics. These were very different writers but they were all attempting to sing the language on the stage, as Yeats had done for a more recondite audience and Eliot, too. All of these were self-conscious artists rather than stage shopsmiths but they would all have no doubt thought that Ibsen's time had passed.

Ibsen's language, lyrical as it may sound in Scandinavia, does not sing in translation, although his ideas often do. Of course they were only Ibsen's realistic social plays that were produced but these became his stamp, his mysticism having been more or less overlooked and his metaphysical side likewise. Probably his more social plays, like the genre itself, are fundamentally optimistic – demanding change, which is itself an upbeat notion and therefore easy to grasp, while his deepest personal thought is the opposite; symbolist, mythic, muffled in pessimism as it surveys the changeless sea, the sky, ageing, cowardice, the classic brick walls against which philosophy has always broken its head.

It is the quasi-journalistic element therefore which came down to later generations, at least in America. He seemed to write about 'issues', rather than circumstance. Especially in the Leftist tide of the thirties his stance was translated into an anti-capitalist militancy, but occasionally his apparent elitism seemed relevant to Fascism. For example, a small controversy developed over whether *An Enemy of the People* had a Fascistic tendency with its admittedly confusing claims for an elite of the intellect which must be trusted to lead ordinary folk. Nowadays the wheel has turned once more and probably something similar is happening now that political correctness is (again) in vogue. But *An Enemy of the People*, it seems to me, is really about Ibsen's belief that there is such a thing as a truth and that it bears something like holiness within it, regardless of the cost its discovery at any one moment entails. And the job of the elite is to guard and explain that holiness without compromise or stint.

For myself, I was deeply stirred by his indignation at the social lies of his time, but it was in his structures that I was thrilled to find his poetry. His plays were models of a stringent economy of means to create immense symphonic images of tragic proportions. It wasn't that things fit together but that *everything* fit together, like a natural organism, a human being, for example, or a rose. His works had an organic intensity making them, or most of them, undeniable. To me he was a reincarnation of the Greek dramatic spirit, especially its obsessive fascination with past transgressions as the seeds of current catastrophe. In this slow unfolding was wonder, even god. Past and present were drawn into a single continuity, and thus a secret moral order was being limned. He and the Greeks were related also through their powerful integrative impulse which, at least in theory, could make possible a total picture of a human being – character sprang from action, and like a spiritual CAT scan the drama could conceivably offer up a human being seen from within and without at the same time. (In fact, my *Death of a Salesman* would proceed in that fashion.) Present dilemma was simply the face that the past had left visible. Every catastrophe was the story of how the birds came home to roost, and I still believe that a play without a past is a mere shadow of a play, just as a man or woman whose past is largely blank or ineptly drawn is merely a suggestion of a man or a woman, and a trivialization to boot.

I don't know what exactly has happened to the concept of the past in contemporary dramaturgy but it is rarely there any more. Things happen, God knows why. Maybe we are just too tired of thinking, or maybe meaning itself has become an excrescence. But most likely it is that we have too often been wrong about what important things mean.

Perhaps it comes down to our loss of confidence in our ability to lay a finger on the inevitable in life; in the name of freedom and poetry it is now customary to declare, in effect, that our existence is itself a surprise and that surprise is the overwhelmingly central principle of life. Or maybe we are just surfeited with entertainment and prefer to lie back and let our brains enjoy a much needed rest.

The triumph of the past-less art is of course the film. A film persona requires no past or any other proof of his existence; he need only be photographed and he is palpably *there*.

The past keeps coming back to our art, however, if only in the parodistic form of the detective or crime story, probably our most popular fictional entertainment. The crime exists, or is about to happen and we have to move backwards to find out whose general character fits the crime, who has dropped hints of his dire tendency, and so forth. It is the tragic event scrubbed clean of its visionary moral values, its sole job being the engendering of anxiety and fear. (Detective fiction also reassures us about the stability of our civilization, but that's another story.)

The so-called absurd theatre, in a different way, also helped make any obsession with the past seem quaint, and Ibsen with it. The proof of a character's existence was simply his awareness of his ironical situation, that was all and that was enough. Character itself, which surely must mean individuation, smacked of realism, and in its stead were interchangeable stickmen whose individuation lay in their varying attitudes and remarks about the determining force, the situation. Without a past the present and its anxieties was all that was left to talk about. And the situation of the stickman is of course so utterly overwhelming – war, or concentration camps, or economic disaster – that what individually he may have had, his will or lack of will, his self-doubt or assurance, his faith or cynicism is squashed out, leaving only the irony of humans continuing to exist at all.

So that the quality we instantly recognized as supremely human was not characterological definition, which requires a history, but its very absence; whatever his personality, it is without significance because it doesn't affect history – that is, his kindness, his dreams of a different kind of life, his love, his devotion to duty or to another human being simply do not matter as he is marched towards the flames. It may be the Holocaust clinched the case for reducing personality to a laughable affectation. I am inclined to believe this to be so, even for people who never think about the events in Eastern Europe directly. The Holocaust – the story of a great nation turned criminal on a vast scale – implicitly defeated us, broke confidence in our claims to being irrevocably in the camp of what was once securely called humanity, and left us with absurdity as the defining human essence.

Again, the concept of a gradually in-gathering, swelling, evidenciary, revelatory explosion is now reserved for thrillers, by and large; but instead of insights we have clues, mechanically dropped most of the time, to both lead us on and astray. We are given, if you will, the skeleton of the Ibsen form without the soul or the flesh.

The revolt – or rather the loss of interest in what is commonly thought of as Ibsenism – also imagines itself to be a revolt against the well-made play, quite as though Ibsen was not himself the first to attack that kind of play. Instead of being well-made his plays are true. That is the difference. They follow the psycho-moral dilemma, not the plot. But we have arrived at a point where, as indicated, the very notion of inevitability is itself highly suspect – in short, no-one can know why great events happen let alone why the shifts and changes in human attitudes take place. Under the rubric of a new freedom and a deeper wisdom we have turned against the rational, claiming the delightful licence to simply express feeling and impressions, the more randomly the better to create surprise, the ultimate aesthetic value.

In short, Strindberg has won the philosophical battle with Ibsen and Ibsenism. The poet of instinct and the impromptu, of the paradoxical surprise, his mission is not to save anyone or a society, but simply to rip the habit of hypocrisy from the human heart and cant from the life of the mind. He is the destroying rebel chopping off the ever-growing heads of a thousand-armed dragon, a pessimistic labour to be sure. Ibsen, quite otherwise, is the revolutionary groping for a new system, an optimistic business, for when the old is destroyed the new construct implies rational decisions, and above all hope.

And who can gainsay Strindberg any more? Apart from the Holocaust are we not witnesses to the implosion of the Soviet Union, the most 'rationally' run society, falling in upon itself, a fraud and a farce? And what has survived but old chaotic, irrational capitalism, blinding itself to its poor behind the glaring lights of its packed store windows, and hiding its spiritual starvation under the shiny bonnets of its marvellous cars? How to rationally account for *this* surprise – the victory of the decadent doomed and the disgrace of the historically 'inevitable victors', the 'new men' who stand revealed as medieval fief-holders when they were not actual gangsters and killers of the dream?

Compare this awesome moral chaos, this wracking collapse of the comfortably predictable, with Ibsen's methodical unravelling of motives and the interplay of social and psychological causation, all of it speaking of rational control! They cannot jibe, our reality and his. So he must seem outmoded, a picturesque mind out of a more orderly time.

Perhaps that is why he seems to be coming back, at least his prestige as a modern if not precisely his methods. For while it is purely a sense of the new mood on my part, it does seem that the taste for 'real plays' rather than only fun effusions has begun to stir again. Of course there are still old-fashioned critics who think that anything that has a beginning and end is out of date, but there are young playwrights who would disagree and are looking to life rather than the theatre for their inspiration, and life of course includes not only surprise but the consequences flowing from our actions or structure, in other words.

Perhaps I ought to add here that in these past dozen years my most Ibsen-influenced play, *All My Sons*, written nearly fifty years ago, is more and more frequently and more widely produced now and the reviewers no longer feel obliged to dismiss its structure as not-modern. I have had to wonder whether this is partly due to the number of investigations of official malfeasance in the papers all the time, and the spectacle of men of stature and social influence being brought down practically every week by revelations excavated from the hidden past. From the heights of Wall Street, the Pentagon, the White House, big business, the same lesson seems to fly out at us – the past lives! As does Ibsen, the master of the explosive force when it bombs in the present, and above all, with the soul-rot that comes of the hypocrisy of its denial.

Needless to say, I have not attempted in this short note to deal with Ibsen as poet and creator of mythic plays, beginning with the opening of his career. For one thing, those plays remain to be interpreted for modern audiences, their mythology having little obvious meaning for most people outside Scandinavia.

15

ERROL DURBACH

A century of Ibsen criticism

MARXISM, PROPAGANDA AND SHAW: VARIETIES OF IBSENITE CRITICISM

'I feel I must do something to make people understand our Ibsen a little more than they do,' wrote Eleanor Marx to Havelock Ellis in late December 1885.[1] So invitations went out to a 'few people worth reading *Nora* to'; and on 15 January 1886, in their flat in Great Russell Street, Karl Marx's youngest daughter and her common-law husband, Edward Aveling, played host to one of the first readings in England of an Ibsen play – *A Doll's House* in the Henrietta Frances Lord translation. Bernard Shaw was a favoured invitee, playing the part of Krogstad to the Mrs Linde of William Morris's daughter, May. And the evening turned out to be an auspicious one for 'Ibsenism', a meeting point for the plethora of '-isms' – Marxism, Socialism and Fabianism – that hailed Ibsen as a spokesman of their cause.

Before the Great Russell Street soirée, Ibsen had been the subject of articles by proselytizing but generally apolitical English Scandinavianists, like Edmund Gosse, who were intent on making him known beyond the boundaries of Norway. Now Aveling was giving rabble-rousing papers on *Ghosts* and stirring up debate in the Playgoers' Club at which (writes Shaw) 'Mrs Aveling and I, being of course seasoned socialist mob orators, were much in the position of a pair of terriers dropped into a pit of rats.'[2] Eleanor Marx was spreading the Ibsenist gospel beyond the confines of Bloomsbury to the working-class districts of London and the Midlands. Shaw was developing his groundbreaking Fabian Lecture on Ibsen in 1890 (revised into the even more acclaimed *Quintessence of Ibsenism* one year later). And a third devoted Ibsenite was busily mounting his polemically vigorous pro-Ibsen campaign – William Archer: translator, apologist, reviewer, and director. I want briefly to review these three distinctly different forms of early Ibsenism as representative critical attitudes from the 1870s to the First World War.

Eleanor Marx is best known as one of the early translators of Ibsen plays;

but her significance to the history of criticism is rather that of an Ibsenite propagandist in the 1880s, when the spiritual fervour of British Socialism heard its ideology echoed in the theatre of the European avant-garde. *A Doll's House* clearly provided corroborative evidence for her politics, and it is fascinating to watch a sensibility shaped by Marxist doctrine and by the major Socialist publications of the decade incorporating Ibsen into the movement and pressing him into alliance.

On the night of the *Doll's House* reading in January 1886, Eleanor Marx and Edward Aveling played the roles of Nora and Torvald convinced that Ibsen's 'miracle of miracles' had already happened in their domestic Eden. In that same month they had jointly published an article in *The Westminster Review* entitled 'The Woman Question: From a Socialist Point of View',[3] in which they argue (quoting from Ibsen's play) that without the larger Socialist revolution women never will be free. For Eleanor, the 'miracle' was Marxist change with its promise of economic and intellectual emancipation for women and workers alike; and Nora's domestic predicament read as a metaphor for the exploitation and oppression of labour, where 'women are the creatures of an organized tyranny of men, as the workers are the creatures of an organized tyranny of idlers' (p. 211). But come the revolution, men and women would be joined in free contract, mind to mind, as a whole and harmonious entity. This is the miracle that she clung to as a living reality in her Bloomsbury doll's house.

In fact, Edward Aveling proved to be a promiscuous bigamist and embezzler of party funds. His conduct made a mockery of her Ibsenism to the point where she was to claim that 'even Ibsen has failed us.'[4] If, like a good Socialist, she had gone to *A Doll's House* to affirm the Marxist hope that cultural change and self-transformation were the happy consequence of subverting the social system, then Ibsen might indeed have betrayed her hopes and aspirations. What her Ibsenism had failed to note in the play was Ibsen's belief that spiritual revolution is prior to social change, and that there is only a tenuous hope for miracle in a world where evil may be endemic to human nature. In March 1898, unable to tolerate the doll's house world of emotional cruelty and infidelity any longer, she robed herself in a white garment, and swallowed a quantity of Prussic acid that she had ordered as 'rat-poison' from the chemist – and probably signed for in the very presence of Edward Aveling.[5]

Eleanor Marx's reading of *A Doll's House* is one of the earliest Marxist critiques of Ibsen as the prophet of change in an imploding bourgeois dispensation; and it must serve here as a paradigm, however fallible, of a critical argument prevalent in post-war Europe but never rigorously pursued in English criticism.[6] More relevant to contemporary approaches, Eleanor

Marx is first among Ibsen's feminist critics and progenitor of a movement that gained momentum in the 1970s with Kate Millett's image of Nora as 'the true insurrectionary of the sexual revolution'.[7] But unlike Bourgeois Feminists who argue that Nora's dilemma may be resolved by sex-equality in which women will attain to political, economic and social parity with men,[8] and unlike more Radical Feminists who locate the problem in the eternal conflict between male and female forces,[9] Eleanor Marx's Socialist Feminism argued that the struggle is primarily class-based, not gender-based, and that sectarian interests must resolve themselves in the greater revolutionary action. It is an argument that persists most forcefully in the work of contemporary Socialist Feminists like Caryl Churchill, whose *Top Girls* might have included Eleanor Marx among their number.

William Archer's brand of 'Ibsenism' is roguishly captured in Max Beerbohm's famous caricature in *The Poet's Corner* where a sycophantic Archer, on his knees before a bristling and irritated Ibsen, kisses the Master's boot. The image suggests a mindless adoration and, despite revisionist assessments of Archer as a prophet of the New Drama,[10] there remains the nagging doubt that he was blind to radical 'newness' when it appeared in the incipient Expressionism of the late Ibsen. As the champion of a fundamentally well-made form of Realism, he gazed in bewilderment at *When We Dead Awaken* and accounted for Ibsen's modernist masterpiece as a pathological symptom of terminal mental breakdown.[11] Rigorously dissociating 'poetry' from 'philosophy', Archer poured his considerable polemical energy into arguing that Ibsen was pure imagination devoid of thought, and not the intellectual of Shaw's *Quintessence*. In a public lecture entitled 'The True Greatness of Ibsen' and delivered at University College, London, in 1919, Archer's final pronouncement was that 'as works of reflection [Ibsen's plays] may be mediocre, but as works of the imagination they are superb'.[12] It is a statement that might well belong in Archer's own Schimpf-Lexicon of fatuous judgments on Ibsen's achievement.

The great strength of this Ibsenite surely lay in his militantly defensive stance: subverting Ibsen's detractors by publishing their hysterical gibberings, or battling against their vituperation with strenuous denials and vehement assertions.[13] But as a proselyte, spreading the gospel of Ibsen, his evangelism tends towards rhetorical flights of impressionistic enthusiasm, scrupulously avoiding the sort of interpretation that might reveal ideas and so betray the Master. In the final analysis, his Ibsen campaign represents the triumph of persistence and volume over prophetic insight or critical vision. He published over 200 articles and reviews on Ibsen from 1889–1919 – quite apart from editing, translating, and introducing the first collection of Ibsen's works in English. Without his discipleship, Ibsen's 'naturalization' in

England might have been less assured. Shaw was not as voluminous; the Socialists were misdirected in politicizing the plays; and no other translator of the period was as assiduous in the production of Ibsen's plays in the London theatres. But William Archer's peculiar brand of Ibsenism, so clearly defined in the University College lecture, finally corroborates the posture of uncritical adulation exaggerated in Beerbohm's cartoon: 'To this day,' he declares, 'there are many people who understand Ibsen better than I do – and sometimes, I suspect, better than Henrik Ibsen did – but there is no one in England or anywhere who enjoys him more than I do.'[14]

One critic who understood Ibsen considerably better than Archer was Bernard Shaw. But if Archer's vision of Ibsen was afflicted with blind spots, Shaw's was paradoxically compromised by its perfect clarity – by a moral decisiveness where Ibsen is slightly out of focus, and by unequivocal assertiveness where Ibsen is tentative and ironic. *His* Ibsen, unlike Eleanor Marx's, is no social reformer but a practical Shavian realist, intolerant of idealism and resolutely opposed to its cost in human sacrifice. It is with superb confidence, for instance, that Shaw can dismiss Brand – one of Ibsen's most ambivalent idealists – as a saint who dies 'having caused more intense suffering by his saintliness than the most talented sinner could possibly have done with twice his opportunities.'[15] But it is too simple to dismiss Ibsen's romantic idealists as destructive villains, especially when the defining effect of his plays is to leave us stripped of Shavian certainty about human motive, and challenged to search for focus in an astigmatic universe.

In his section of *The Quintessence of Ibsenism* on 'The Lesson of the Plays,' Shaw defines his Ibsenism in the most undogmatic and open manner possible, 'merely reminding those who may think that I have forgotten to reduce Ibsenism to a formula for them, that its quintessence is that there is no formula'.[16] This is witty, but not altogether true. Shaw's Ibsenism is compounded of several factors: an anti-idealistic bias, his enthusiastic conscription of Ibsen in a campaign to fight the moribund theatre of Scribe and Sardou with a new subversive drama, a celebration of Ibsen's technical revolution which generates discussion and debate through unsettled and conflicting ideas, and Ibsen's innovation of a new genre of tragedy-without-tears to salvage theatre from the tears-without-tragedy that had deluged the stages of melodrama and the *pièce bien faite*. His Ibsen is a superb technician, an intellectual dialectician, and a modern realist whose meaningful credibility challenges the sufficiency of Shakespeare as pre-eminent among world dramatists:

> Ibsen supplies the want left by Shakespear. He gives us not only ourselves, but ourselves in our own situations. The things that happen to his stage

figures are things that happen to us. One consequence is that his plays are much more important to us than Shakespear's. Another is that they are capable both of hurting us cruelly and of filling us with excited hopes of escape from idealistic tyrannies, and with visions of intenser life in the future.[17]

This is Shaw at his best: provocative, audacious, polemical. But in spite of his ability to move beyond the realistic surfaces of Ibsen's drama and detect a visionary aesthetic behind the everyday situation, his admiration of Ibsen is directed primarily towards the mimetic – modern men and women in recognizable contemporary situations. His Ibsen remains a theatrical realist who holds the mirror up to society and shows the age its moral form and anti-idealistic pressure. It will take a quantum leap into Modernism to shift the dramatic paradigm and penetrate beneath the realism into the luminously transparent depths behind the solid quotidian surfaces.

JOYCE AND THE SYMBOLISTS: VARIETIES OF MODERNIST CRITICISM

'A room is to him a room,' wrote Virginia Woolf of Ibsen, 'a writing table a writing table, and a waste paper basket, a waste paper basket. At the same time, the paraphernalia of reality have at certain times to become the veil through which we see infinity.'[18] For the Modernist writers, Ibsen's achievement lay in his transformation of the stage from mirror into lamp, from a world that merely reflects bourgeois existence into a revelation of the invisible forces behind the phenomenal world. Virginia Woolf's image of the infinite reaches and the suddenly lighted depths in Ibsen's realistic world had, of course, been anticipated fifty years before by Henry James's articles in the 1890s. Writing of *Hedda Gabler*, he detected a condition beneath the action, an *état d'âme*[19] – what the contemporary Norwegian novelist, Knut Hamsun, referred to as *det ubevidste sjæleliv*: the unconscious life of the soul. The 'mere dead rattle of the surface of life', in James's reading of the plays, is the entrée not only into the anguished life of the individual, but into the history of the human spirit; and the merging of reality into symbols hints at an 'Ibsen within an Ibsen', an idea which suffuses the whole and yet eludes precise articulation.[20]

This is the mystic dramatist of the Symbolist avant-garde, the 'new' Ibsen of Lugné-Poë's Théâtre de l'Oeuvre, with its non-illusionist theatre style and its search for that intense interior meaning still celebrated in Roy Fuller's poem half a century later. In Lugné-Poë's *Master Builder*, as in Fuller's reading of the symbol,

The tower is not ideals
Nor sex but one of those
Emblems without a key:
. . .
Ibsen revealed that the symbol had a past,
That crude interpretation could be stripped
Of rings of time, to find
Inside the foliate five
Acts the small pulsing germ.[21]

But the most influential Modernist crusader against crude interpretation was the young James Joyce who, in 1900, reviewed *When We Dead Awaken* for the *Fortnightly Review*.[22] Intending to rescue Ibsen from critical denunciation as either a muck-ferreting dog or an incomprehensible mystic, Joyce also pre-empted Archer's outmoded demands for the possible and conceivable by arguing for Ibsen's emancipation of the drama (as he and, later, Virginia Woolf were to release the novel) from evaluative criteria of mimetic verisimilitude.

Like Henry James, Joyce recognized in Ibsen a drama of 'soul-crisis', the revelation of a vast 'life in life' within the tightly compressed form, and a sounding of 'unfathomable depths' in the intensely spiritual life of his women. Instead of a drama of action or incident or character, he offers us a theatre of momentous epiphany, a perception of some illuminating truth arising out of dialectical conflict that renders criticism itself impertinent. 'Appreciation, hearkening,' he writes, 'is the only true criticism' – and this form of criticism is possible only in the theatre, in the living response of audience to the flux of performance, to the rush of time that frustrates attempts to verify ideas or codify thought or resolve problems:

> At some chance expression the mind is tortured with some question, and in a flash long reaches of life are opened up in vista, yet the vision is momentary unless we stay to ponder on it. It is just to prevent excessive pondering that Ibsen requires to be acted. Finally, it is foolish to expect that a problem, which has occupied Ibsen for nearly three years, will unroll smoothly before our eyes on a first or second reading. So it is better to leave the drama to plead for itself.

Taken literally, such admonition would render this chapter and the following century of Ibsen criticism entirely irrelevant. But Joyce's emphatic insistence on the visionary moment, on the glancing pain of disturbing inquiry, and on the necessary frustration of the audience's expectations of easy verification, lies at the very heart of his theatre aesthetics. Ultimately, in his view and Virginia Woolf's, the final epiphany of a play like *Ghosts* – that complex visual image of ice burning and fire congealing – becomes another veil through which we see an infinity that eludes selective interpretation.

The Modernist critics may seem irritatingly vague and impressionistic in their detection of an 'Ibsen within an Ibsen' and a Chinese puzzle-box of emblems without keys. But they bring to Ibsen criticism a vision that pierces the bourgeois solidity of the Ibsen world, a sensitive ear that hears the unspoken or hidden utterance, and a deeply intuitive sense of a subtext beneath the text. They encourage us, as James McFarlane puts it, 'to look not at what is positive and obtrusive but at what is (so to speak) conspicuously unobtrusive and even assertively negative'.[23] They reject the notion of a *quintessence* of Ibsenism as a reduction of complexity and ambiguity to a trivial nugget of extractable truth. And they expose the fallibility of forcing an answer without knowing what sort of question to ask.

Arising out of the Modernist fascination with 'soul-crises', 'unfathomable depths' and '*sjæleliv*', moreover, there is an implicit search for a language – as there is in Ibsen's plays – to describe the subconscious and find a methodology for dealing with the 'life in life' and the text beneath the text which is its history. It seems inevitable that, within a few years of Ibsen's death, his drama should have cropped up in the consulting rooms of Vienna as an analogue of the 'analytic method' described by Joyce in his article on *When We Dead Awaken*.

FREUD AND THE ANALYSTS: SUBTEXTUAL CRITICISM

In 1909 Sigmund Freud records the case-history now known as 'The Rat Man', a study in obsessional neurosis that, in spite of the wealth of accumulated material, seems to resist all diagnosis – 'until one day the Rat-Wife in Ibsen's *Little Eyolf* came up in the analysis, and it became impossible to escape the inference that in many of the shapes assumed by his obsessional deliria rats had another meaning still – namely, that of *children*'.[24] This is an early instance of Ibsen's use by the Viennese School as both clinical resource and humanistic evidence for psychoanalytic theory. Otto Rank would draw upon Ibsen a few years later in his study of *Das Inzest-Motiv in Dichtung und Sage* (1912); and Freud, in turn, would transform Rank's clinical theorizing into a hermeneutic methodology with profound implications for critical approaches to Ibsen. In his psychoanalytic study of *Rosmersholm* in 1916 Freud accords to Ibsen the canonic status of classical authority formerly attributed to Sophocles and Shakespeare; and in his response to a profoundly 'subterranean' concealment of motive in Rebecca West, his techniques of excavation and extrapolation offer the first significant application of the analytic method to an Ibsen play.

Freud's study of 'Those Wrecked by Success'[25] acknowledges the 'unfathomable depths' that the Modernists detected, and then proceeds to plumb them. What piques his curiosity is a syndrome, often observed in clinical practice, where a woman who has been single-mindedly striving for success suddenly collapses on attaining it. He first turns to an analysis of Lady Macbeth's strange illness in which callousness changes into penitence, and then withdraws baffled by layers of obscurity unavailable to psychoanalysis. Rebecca West is a more suitable subject – if only because Ibsen's 'conscious creative combination arose logically from unconscious premises' (p. 329), and because the semiotics of his theatre, its gestural/behavioural style, serves to 'articulate' the motives concealed within the oblique confessional mode of the dialogue.

The question Freud asks of Rebecca goes to the very heart of the play: why does this fearless woman, after ruthlessly disposing of Rosmer's burdensome wife, scream with joy when he eventually proposes marriage to her – and then, in the same breath, threaten suicide if he persists in his suit? Rebecca offers her own explanations. But Freud is wise to her confessional strategy: she deals, he points out, in half-truths that protect the unspeakable other half, exposing one motive to conceal another in a language precariously poised between intentional and unconscious lying. In his analysis of her enigmatic behaviour, Freud infers from the meticulously inserted hints in Ibsen's text a trauma in Rebecca's life, buried and unacknowledged by the conscious mind, that permeates her existence and renders her triumph ineffective even before she grasps the source of her disabling guilt. It arises from a never-mentioned incestuous coupling with her putative stepfather who, as the fog of guilt and self-reproach intensifies, rises to consciousness as her blood father. 'She stood,' writes Freud, 'under the domination of the Oedipus Complex, even though she did not know that the universal phantasy had in her case become a reality' (p. 330). And now, the trauma is about to be replicated in the new reality of her relationship with Rosmer.

We may not agree with Freud's specific diagnosis, or the implications of treating Ibsen's characters as clinical case-studies in neurosis. But it is virtually impossible, after Freud, to read Ibsen without scrutinizing the unspoken motives operating beneath the stated motives in the text, without recognizing the evolving moral consciousness driving his characters through the journey of the play, and without acknowledging the force of conscience as a tragic impulse in Ibsen's bourgeois civilization. Above all, his meticulous attention to detail and his need to *understand* the text as a conscious and logical construct of the artistic imagination has passed, directly or indirectly, into the methodology of a number of critical schools: Hermeneutics, which stresses meaning and textual interpretation; New Criticism, which applies the techniques of close reading to texts as autonomous constructs; and the many branches of post-Freudian psychoanalytical criticism that read the text as a dream-image of subconscious processes.

There is, however, an explicit acknowledgment in Freud's study of Rebecca West that calls in question the fundamental assumptions of pure psychoanalytic methodology – the danger of treating the character 'as if she were a living person and not a creation of Ibsen's imagination' and the consequent reduction and underrating of Ibsen's 'critical intelligence' (p. 329). When Hans Hiebel writes his chapter on Hedda Gabler as 'Bruchstück einer Hysterie-Analyse',[26] or James Hurt describes her as 'a thoroughly schizoid personality, driven by the terror of ego-loss back into an inner world',[27] or Hermann Weigand manipulates the text of The Master Builder to psychoanalyse Ibsen himself,[28] the clinical vocabulary alone should alert the reader to the fallacies inherent in a methodology misapplied. Is the meaning of The Master Builder exhausted by a biographical exposé of the author? Is it enough for the critic to account for Hedda as a hysteric or schizophrenic, without correlating the psychic history of the human spirit with the history of civilization which is the play's overarching concern? There is a great deal of brilliant psychoanalytic criticism – Weigand at his best is among the greatest – but, divorced from the textual strategies of the New Critics, it denies the essential link that Freud detected between Ibsen's creative consciousness and his logical mining of unconscious premise.

'THE POET IN THE THEATRE': TEXTUAL CRITICISM

Subtext and the unspoken: these are the areas in which Freud detected Ibsen's distinctive genius. But what of the *spoken* text? What of those contemporary plays where the poetry of Brand and Peer Gynt has been deliberately submerged beneath colloquial discourse in bourgeois parlours? Early twentieth-century dramatists, actively in search of a new stage-language, vehemently rejected the middle-period Ibsen as a drab realist responsible for driving poetic speech from the theatre. Yeats wrinkled his nose at the stale odour of his spilt poetry and denounced that 'horrible generation that in childhood sucked Ibsen from Archer's hygienic bottle',[29] and Synge dismissed his work as 'joyless and pallid.'[30] Others, like Yeats's compatriot Edward Martyn, certainly heard 'exquisite music' in Ibsen – but only in the late symbolic drama 'where subtle mental poetry finds expression in the most direct realism of speech' and where symphonic effects derive from ideas growing naturally from ideas.[31] But the realistic plays, so beloved of the Ibsenites and the analysts, seemed hopeless material for the textual critics with their own aesthetic criteria of the 'poetic' derived, largely, from the richly metaphoric language of Shakespearean blank verse.

Edward Martyn's notion of 'mental poetry', however, provides a clue to the anomalous aesthetic of Ibsen's prose-poetry. He draws attention to a language of intellectual concepts that, reiterated in the drama and linked with other idea-systems, form harmonious patterns in the dramatic structure, rather like dominant chords resonating in a musical composition to create the governing symphonic idea. It is a definition of dramatic poetry linking Ibsen not to Shakespeare, with his neologistic vocabulary and his highly imagistic language, but to Racine, the master of minimalism, whose language is scaled down to an irreducible sufficiency of terms where each concept grows from context to context until the colloquial phrase begins to resonate with the dynamic power of a poem. The very notion of dramatic poetry, as Ibsen had insisted, would have to shift in order to accommodate his achievement.[32] And so it has. The last half-century of textual criticism has firmly established Ibsen as a *theatre-poet* extending the resources of language through stagecraft, through the semiotics of gesture, and through performance. Nora *dances* meaning into existence in *A Doll's House*. The unutterable, seeking expression through the attenuated phrases of spilt poetry, finds complete articulation through a theatrical language as old as the Greeks.

In Halvdan Koht's *Life of Ibsen*,[33] he is first and foremost a 'dramatic poet', defining his function in a famous epigrammatic verse:

At *digte* – det er at holde   *Poetry* – that is to hold
dommedag over sig selv.   doomsday judgment over ourselves.

But the danger of this approach is that it encourages a tendentious correlation of the literature with the life. This is the fallacy clearly recognized by the New Critics of the 1930s who were determined to treat the poem as an autonomous work of art, no longer synonymous with its author's biography or his intention. In the United States, the New school defined itself as a form of criticism 'constantly returning to the object and constantly refining itself by fresh appeals to intuition and perception';[34] and in England, the New exegetical method of F. R. Leavis would soon be applied not only to Shakespeare's poetic drama but to Ibsen who, in James McFarlane's phrase, was to become 'naturalized by syllabus' in the English universities.

Muriel Bradbrook's *Ibsen the Norwegian* (1946), in its application of a poetic methodology to Ibsen's prose, constantly reminds us of a crucial point: that the plays are 'crystallized' out of a body of poetry already finely crafted, and that their integrity of vision derives from the same source of poetic imagination. *The Master Builder*, she argues, is a dramatic extension of the desiccated and calamitous condition of the fire-ravaged couple of 'De sad der, de to – ', a poem written seven years before in which the conflagration of faith and joy anticipates the burned-up condition of the later drama.[35] In this way, spare and laminated speech re-echoes a language already redolent with inference, and drives towards its restatement in crises of action and complex theatre images – as in the dénouement of *Ghosts* where the burst of sunlight reveals a desolate landscape of ice-peaks and waste. Behind the spectacle there resonates the chilling paradox of a poem written in 1863: 'Lysræd' (Lightfear), a neologism as remarkable as any of Shakespeare's in revealing the devastating experience of illuminated consciousness in Ibsen's play.

John Northam, in *Ibsen's Dramatic Method* (1953) extended this mode of critical inquiry beyond language into an early form of theatre semiotics. Working with signs and symbols often hidden from the reader in stage-directions – the *unspoken* information projected through costume, set-design, decor, properties, lighting – he correlates the suggestive visual detail of the drama with the poetic word and its aura of often ambiguous meaning.[36] Drama, he goes on to argue, is also revealed through significant juxtaposition and parallel, through structurally balanced events, and through a system of visual dialectics where meaning is generated – as in the opposition of Hedda Gabler and Thea Elvsted – by the strong physical distinctions between the two women. Implicit in John Northam's critical practice is the necessity for Ibsen's reader to become his own *director* by responding to the totality of verbal and visual metaphors as interpenetrating and reinforcing strategies of dramatic meaning.

Others have written brilliantly of Ibsen's poetry – Eric Bentley comes to mind, with his ingenious suggestion that Ibsen deliberately invents a form of 'anti-poetry', an 'anti-eloquence' that impresses itself upon us as another kind of art where action itself becomes articulate, where words are finally performed.[37] One textual critic, in particular, has illuminated Ibsen's rhetorical strategies as lived-through dramatic experiences (*det gjennemlevede*) in which literal utterance becomes the vehicle for spiritual revelation: Inga-Stina Ewbank, for whom Ibsen is both Norwegian poet and Universal poet, whose dramatic landscapes are both real and mountains of the mind. Her illustrative argument, spread over a collection of elegant articles, is easily damaged by reduction; and her titles must speak for themselves: 'Ibsen's Dramatic Language as a Link between his "Realism" and his "Symbolism"', 'Ibsen and "The Far More Difficult Art" of Prose', 'Ibsen and the Language of Women'.[38] Her emphasis, clearly stated in the second of these papers, is everywhere apparent in her writing; and I turn to it to restate the basic critical premise of this subsection:

I also think that [Ibsen's] extraordinary power, as a poet of the theatre, of creating in each play a subtext – a tissue of non-verbal interconnections – has sometimes unduly distracted our attention from the language of the play itself. Therefore – though I am aware that any distinction between text and subtext in Ibsen is ultimately artificial – I am concerned in this paper with the verbal tissue: with the function of Ibsen's prose in re-creating and communicating 'det gjennemlevede'.

IBSEN AND THE HISTORY OF IDEAS: SUPERTEXTUAL CRITICISM

Text conjoined to subtext, in Inga-Stina Ewbank's critical analysis of Ibsen's language, ultimately recreates a governing mood-image as the play's deep structure – a *Weltanschauung* lived through as experiential reality and tested upon pulse and heart and spiritual perception. Reacting against this approach, there are those critics who conjoin text to 'supertext' and insist upon intellectual process and philosophical idea as the deep structure of the drama – a *Weltanschauung* experienced in the dialectical tensions within reality and tested upon the plane of universal reason. As a revisionist movement, the Supertextual approach has finally put paid to the William Archer–H. L. Mencken contention that Ibsen's ideas, if he harboured any at all, were such 'as even a Harvard professor might evolve without bursting his brain';[39] and it has restored Ibsen to the context of European thought where he assumes his place among the philosopher–sages of his age: tragic theorists like Schopenhauer and Nietzsche; proto-Existentialists like Kant and Kierkegaard; cultural evolutionists like Hebbel and Hegel; and Romantic prophets like Goethe and Blake.

I have taken the notion of 'Supertextual' criticism from Brian Johnston whose *Text and Supertext in Ibsen's Drama* (1989) constitutes the latest hammerblow in an argument consistently developed over the past twenty years. The notion that Ibsen's plays leap fully formed from a hyperborean desert had already been challenged in Brian Downs's study, *Ibsen: The Intellectual Background* (1946). What is new in Johnston's Supertextual methodology is the comprehensive nature of its scope and its profound application of Hegelian dialectical theory to Ibsen's world-historical drama.[40]

Brian Johnston's basic premise, as it had been for G. Wilson Knight in his book on *Ibsen* (1962), is Ibsen's own injunction that 'only by comprehending and making one's own my entire production as a related continuous whole, will one receive the intended, striking impression of the various parts.'[41] It is Johnston's contention, rigorously argued in three major books, that Ibsen's twelve-play cycle from *Pillars of Society* to *When We Dead Awaken* unfolds in a meticulously planned sequence that recapitulates, by direct analogy, the evolution of human consciousness described in Hegel's *The Phenomenology of Mind* (1807).[42] Like Wilson Knight, moreover, he emphasizes the centrality to Ibsen's drama of *Emperor and Galilean* (1873) as a Hegelian paradigm of dialectical patterning: a collision of ideas in a process of continuous historical transformation, and a concomitant vision of human civilization evolving towards a Hegelian *Aufhebung* where cultural forces in mighty opposition absorb each other in a 'Third Empire' of the spirit.

It is an argument that expands the intellectual horizons of Ibsen's drama even as it shrivels character by depriving it of passionate vitality and human fallibility. In Johnston's view, the Supertextual protagonist must extend to match the immensity of Ibsen's intellectual intention, instead of descending towards a reductive subtextual or psychological order of explanation. There can be no Freudian 'inwardness', no Stanislavskian source of 'motivation' in this Theatre of Ideas. Nor is the Ibsen character subject to the audience's moral approval or evaluative judgement. 'The only life they possess,' as Johnston insists, 'is what we are able imaginatively to give them. They therefore are as great or as petty, as significant or as trivial, as we are capable of perceiving. If, as William Blake reminded us, the Idiot and the Wise Man do not see the same tree, they also do not see the same *Hedda Gabler, Little Eyolf*, or *John Gabriel Borkman*.'[43]

In my own work on Ibsen,[44] I risk such censure by detecting a grievous pettiness within the self-assumed greatness of Hedda or John Gabriel Borkman, a phenomenology of passion beneath the phenomenology of mind, and a sense of paradox and irony which calls in question the sufficiency of Hegelian absolutes. In *Ibsen the Romantic* (1982), my Supertext derives from the history of Romanticism itself – its redefinition of Man as a creature of infinite potential, its relocation of God as a force within human consciousness – and the myths and intellectual structures that project this image in a transformed theatre. But the price for assuming Godhead, in Ibsen's all-too-mortal realm, is paid for in dreadful anxiety and moral doubt; and the romantic assumption of freedom from old systems and orthodox beliefs is inevitably countermanded by forces '*i hjertets og hjernens hvælv*', 'in the depths of heart and mind' – the fear of death and sexuality, and the desperate attempt to fabricate symbols of permanence in a mutable and perishable existence. Supertextual concept, as I understand it, is of necessity linked to subtextual dread; and the 'Idea', whether a Third Empire of the spirit, or a mythically reconstructed Paradise, is often a consequence of the protagonist's deeply subjective striving after romantic impossibility.

How are we to reconcile superhuman potential and mortal fallibility, the romantic assertion of personal significance with the very real limitations imposed upon us by personal insufficiency? These are the questions Ibsen dramatizes in an 'open vision'[45] that can contemplate supertextual idea and its subtextual contradiction in a single visionary moment. Ibsen's concerns are ultimately existential: the problem of realigning 'essence' with 'existence' – or, in Kierkegaardian terms, the 'teleological' with the 'ethical', the divine imperative with the moral promises that bind us to the earth.

For another school of critics, Ibsen is Kierkegaard's poet, sharing with the Danish philosopher a range of philosophical premises and concepts relating to the existential bases of selfhood. In an article on *Peer Gynt*, Rolf Fjelde situates Ibsen on the cusp of nineteenth-century speculative philosophy as it modulates from an essentialist/Hegelian vision of self-realization towards an existential/Kierkegaardian worldview. In Kierkegaardian terms, he writes,

> Hegel is guilty of reducing the rich panoply of actual existence to a system of ideas or logical essences, and then proclaiming these essences as sole reality. But in point of fact, Kierkegaard observes, existence precedes and includes essence, which is only a barren field of concepts, a Begriffenfeld. The problem of how to realize the self – the theme of Peer Gynt – thus involves not the recognition of an essence, a soul given once and forever, but instead a contingent relationship of choosing oneself continually, day by day, experience to experience, through an existential act of self-determining will.[46]

Becoming oneself through decision, action and a 'leap of irrevocable choice' – these are the Kierkegaardian ideas in Ibsen that challenge the Hegelian quest towards perfectibility of spirit. But Ibsen's radical scepticism, in the final analysis, challenges even Kierkegaard's ultimate acquiescence in God's will as an absolute priority, or his 'absurd' belief in miracle.[47] The 'miraculous' in a play like *A Doll's House*, is synonymous with neither divine intervention nor the discovery of selfhood as some essential abstraction. Selfhood chooses its own vital existence; and the free and autonomous self must assume responsibility for choices made with tragic consequences for the life of illusory ideas. Where nineteenth-century Hegelian Romanticism ends, twentieth-century Sartrean Existentialism begins.

IBSEN ON STAGE: PERFORMANCE CRITICISM SUBTEXT OR SUPERTEXT?

To the professional actor who must play the part, this critical contention is largely irrelevant. 'You cannot act concepts or abstractions or theories,' writes Janet Suzman. 'Freud may well have been right about Rebecca West's Oedipus complex, but you can't act an Oedipus complex'[48] – a reminder that Ibsen exists in two distinct domains which all too seldom invigorate each other: on the page and on the stage, in scholarly contemplation and in the theatre where the drama's complex meanings evolve through what Jonathan Miller calls 'subsequent performances'[49] in which drama accrues a significance possibly unforeseen in its own age. The function of the performance critic is to record and evaluate each innovative staging of the text.

In accounting for the power of the plays as theatre pieces, critics like Rolf Fjelde, Freddie Rokem and Inga-Stina Ewbank[50] trace the history of Ibsen's stage as a metaphor that reconstructs, scenographically, the cosmic immensity of classical theatre-spaces: the Aeschylean theatre, shaped in the image of Ionian cosmography; the medieval theatre with its eschatological scenery of Hell-Mouth and Heaven; Shakespeare's microcosmic Globe with its overhanging tapestry of sun and stars. How, they ask, does Ibsen's bourgeois parlour become a comparable Everywhere? How do the Gods of ancient tragedy inhabit the illusionist conventions of Ibsen's proscenium-arch theatre? How does Ibsen's vertical geography of mountain-peak and sea-depths reconstruct a new cosmology for the modern mind?

As a record of what Jonathan Miller calls the play's 'emergent evolution' – in which contemporary meaning flows from the re-enactment of canonical texts – performance criticism also endorses Henry James's image of Ibsen as a barometer of the intellectual weather, a chronicle of changing theatrical style and audience taste captured in the variable meanings crafted by generations of actors, designers and directors. The basic premise of this approach is provided by its foremost North American exponents, Frederick and Lise-Lone Marker in their book on *Ibsen's Lively Art* (1981): 'Each succeeding generation seems to discover – or rediscover – elements in his work that renew the dialogue in which the past and the present continue to meet. Theatrical performance is the true meeting place where these elements in a dramatist's work are tested.'[51] We learn from the Markers, Fritz Paul and others, how in the first decade of the century the *auteurist* generation of Meyerhold and Reinhardt challenged the adequacy of what they considered to be the obsolescent realism of Ibsen's stage and created a Director's Theatre of deconstructed, highly atmospheric and anti-illusionist productions; how, sixty years later, Europe discovered the 'post-modern' Ibsen of Peter Stein's *Peer Gynt* collage in which text becomes the pretext for an eclectic amalgam of avant-garde directorial styles from Craig to Artaud and Beckett;[52] how the American Ibsen Theatre in Pittsburgh rediscovered a theatricalist style for supertextualizing Ibsen in the 1980s; and how Ingmar Bergman has evolved an Expressionist Strindbergian chamber-style for subtextualizing the inner life of Hedda Gabler. Just as we cannot step into the same river twice, so the living record of theatre-art reveals a new Nora and another Hedda each time a great actress creates life out of the shadow lands of the text and speaks to her own time of the timelessness of Ibsen's visionary imagination.

A SMÖRGÅSBORD OF 'CONTEMPORARY APPROACHES TO IBSEN'

The 'Contemporary Approaches' in this subtitle refers to a series of volumes initiated by Daniel Haakonsen in 1965 as the proceedings of the First International Ibsen Seminar in Oslo. In that same year Rolf Fjelde, Ibsen's distinguished American translator, edited an important volume of essays[53] in which he evaluated modern critical approaches to 'radical truth' as the goal and centre of Ibsen's dramatic achievement; and Einar Haugen published his great *Norwegian English Dictionary*.[54] The British pillar of modern Ibsen criticism, James McFarlane, had already initiated his magisterial Oxford edition of Ibsen's plays as an indispensable resource for scholarship. Over the past quarter century, the Ibsen Seminar has continued to meet in a variety of national and international locations – Cambridge, Bergen, Skien, Munich, New Haven; the *Oxford Ibsen* has been completed; the Ibsen Society of America (ISA), inaugurated in 1978, continues to flourish; and 1990 marked the First International Ibsen Stage Festival in Oslo, with its critical Symposium on the plays performed.

Contemporary Approaches to Ibsen is now published every second year; the Ibsen Newsletter for the ISA is a vital commentary on contemporary scholarship and performance; and the publication of scores of articles and several books on Ibsen each year makes a neat pigeonholing of approaches as impossible as a comprehensive survey of modern eclectic criticism. I intend no disrespect in my reference to a smörgåsbord. There is a veritable feast of contemporary Ibsen scholarship – mythic, comparative, thematic, feminist – and I would like to end with a roll-call of approaches to Ibsen that have eluded this survey but remain crucial to any comprehensive critical assessment of his Protean genius: Michael Meyer's biographical Ibsen; Robert Brustein's theatre rebel; Erik Christensen's anarchist; George Steiner's innovative tragedian *manqué*; Orley Holtan's mythopoeic mystic; Charles Lyons's Laingian analyst of divided consciousness; Daniel Haakonsen's humanist artist.[55] The list is extensive and inevitably out-of-date, with each new addition merely confirming Shaw's view that the quintessence of Ibsenism is a paradoxical *absence* of quintessence – a rejection of formulae that claim to be keys to total comprehension, and a refusal of the material to be narrowed down to a singleness of critical purpose.

NOTES

1 Quoted in Yvonne Kapp, *Eleanor Marx*, vol. II (London, 1976), p. 103. See also Ian Britain, 'A Transplanted Doll's House: Ibsenism, Feminism and Socialism in Late-Victorian and Edwardian England,' in Ian Donaldson (ed.), *Transformations in Modern European Drama* (London, 1983), p. 17.
2 Bernard Shaw, *Collected Letters, 1874–1897*, ed. Dan H. Laurence (New York, 1965), p. 288.
3 *The Westminster Review*, n.s. 69, 1, January 1886.
4 Ronald Florence, *Marx's Daughters* (New York, 1975), p. 58.
5 See Chushichi Tsuzuki, *The Life of Eleanor Marx, 1855–1898: A Socialist Tragedy* (Oxford, 1967).
6 Modern Marxist critics include Horst Bien, *Henrik Ibsens Realismus* (Berlin, 1970) and Peter Szondi, *Theorie des modernen Dramas* (Frankfurt/Main, 1959).
7 Kate Millett, *Sexual Politics* (New York, 1970), p. 115.
8 See Sandra Saari, 'Female Become Human: Nora Transformed', *Contemporary Approaches to Ibsen*, vol. VI, ed. Bjørn Hemmer and Vigdis Ystad (Oslo, 1988), pp. 41–55.
9 See Joan Templeton, 'The *Doll House* Backlash: Criticism, Feminism, and Ibsen,' *PMLA*, 104 (1989),28–40.
10 See Thomas Postlewait, *Prophet of the New Drama: William Archer and the Ibsen Campaign* (Westport, Conn., 1986).
11 *William Archer on Ibsen: The Major Essays, 1889–1919*, ed. Thomas Postlewait (Westport, Conn., 1984).
12 Ibid., p. 162
13 See, especially, 'The Mausoleum of Ibsen', *Major Essays*, pp. 35–52.
14 Ibid., p. 164.
15 Shaw, 'Brand, 1866,' in *Shaw and Ibsen: Bernard Shaw's 'The Quintessence of Ibsenism' and Related Writings*, ed. J. L. Wisenthal (Toronto, 1970), p. 133.
16 Ibid., p. 201.
17 Ibid., p. 218.
18 Virginia Woolf, *The Death of the Moth* (London, 1942), p. 108.
19 'On the Occasion of *Hedda Gabler*,' *New Review*, June 1891, reprinted in James McFarlane (ed.), *Henrik Ibsen*, Penguin Critical Anthologies (Harmondsworth, 1970), pp. 130 ff.
20 'On the Occasion of *The Master Builder*,' *Pall Mall Gazette*, February 1893, reprinted in *Henrik Ibsen*, ed. McFarlane, pp. 149–50.
21 Roy Fuller, 'Ibsen' (1954), reprinted in *Henrik Ibsen*, ed. McFarlane, p. 272.
22 'When We Dead Awaken,' *Fortnightly Review*, 73 (1900), reprinted in *Henrik Ibsen*, ed. McFarlane, pp. 172–8.
23 J. W. McFarlane, *Ibsen and the Temper of Norwegian Literature* (London, 1960), pp. 62–3.7
24 'Notes Upon a Case of Obsessional Neurosis' (1909), *The Standard Edition of the Complete Psychological Works of Sigmund Freud*, trans. and ed. James Strachey, vol. X (London, 1964), p. 215.
25 'Some Character-Types Met With in Psycho-Analytic Work' (1916), *The Standard Edition*, vol. XIV, pp. 324 ff. This analysis is more easily available in *Henrik Ibsen*, ed. McFarlane, pp. 392 ff.

26 Hans H. Hiebel, *Henrik Ibsens psycho-analytische Dramen* (Munich, 1990).

27 *Catiline's Dream* (Urbana, Ill., 1972), p. 150.

28 *The Modern Ibsen: A Reconsideration* (New York, 1925).

29 W. B. Yeats, *A Vision* (New York, 1966), p. 35.

30 J. M. Synge, 'Preface,' *The Playboy of the Western World* in J. M. Synge's *Plays, Poems, and Prose* (London, 1959), p. 108.

31 See Denis Gwynn, *Edward Martyn and the Irish Revival* (London, 1930), p. 142.

32 'My work is poetry; and if it isn't, it shall become it. The concept of poetry ... will come to conform to thework.' Ibsen, in a letter to Bjørnson, December 1867 [*iii*, 488].

33 Halvdan Koht, *Life of Ibsen*, trans. and ed. Einar Haugen and A. E. Santaniello (New York, 1971), p. 17.

34 Cleanth Brooks and Robert Penn Warren, 'Letter to the Teacher (1938)', *Understanding Poetry* (New York, 1959), p. xxiii.

35 Muriel Bradbrook, *Ibsen the Norwegian: A Revaluation*, new edition (Hamden, Conn., 1969), p. 3.

36 John Northam, *Ibsen's Dramatic Method: A Study of the Prose Dramas* (London, 1953), p. 13.

37 Eric Bentley, *The Life of the Drama* (New York, 1965), pp. 96–8.

38 See, respectively, *Contemporary Approaches to Ibsen*, vol. I, ed. Daniel Haakonsen (Oslo, 1966), pp. 96–123; *Contemporary Approaches to Ibsen*, vol. II, ed. Daniel Haakonsen (Oslo, 1971), pp. 60–83; and *Women Writing and Writing about Women*, ed. Mary Jacobus (London, 1979), pp. 114–32.

39 H. L. Mencken, *Eleven Plays of Ibsen* (1935), reprinted in *Henrik Ibsen*, ed. McFarlane, p. 238.

40 Brian Johnston, *Text and Supertext in Ibsen's Drama* (University Park, Penn., 1989).

41 Quoted as an epigraph in Wilson Knight, *Ibsen* (Edinburgh, 1962).

42 Brian Johnston, *The Ibsen Cycle* (Boston, 1975) and *Towards the Third Empire* (Minneapolis, 1980).

43 *Text and Supertext*, pp. 72–3.

44 Errol Durbach, *'Ibsen the Romantic': Analogues of Paradise in the Later Plays* (London, 1982).

45 See John Chamberlain, *Ibsen: The Open Vision* (London, 1982).

46 Rolf Fjelde, 'Peer Gynt, Naturalism, and the Dissolving Self,' *The Drama Review*, 13:2 (Winter, 1968), 37.

47 For a recent interpretation of Ibsen as Kierkegaard's poet, see Richard Hornby, *Patterns in Ibsen's Middle Plays* (Lewisburg, Penn., 1981).

48 Janet Suzman, '*Hedda Gabler*: The Play in Performance,' *Ibsen and the Theatre*, ed. E. Durbach (London, 1980), p. 83.

49 Jonathan Miller, *Subsequent Performances* (London, 1986).

50 See Rolf Fjelde, 'The Dimensions of Ibsen's Dramatic World,' *Contemporary Approaches to Ibsen*, vol. II, ed. D. Haakonsen (Oslo, 1971), pp. 161–80; Freddie Rokem, *Theatrical Space in Ibsen, Chekhov and Strindberg: Public Forms of Privacy* (Ann Arbor, Mich., 1986); Inga-Stina Ewbank, 'Ibsen on the English Stage,' *Ibsen and the Theatre*, ed. E. Durbach (London, 1980), pp. 27–48.

51 *Ibsen's Lively Art* (Cambridge, 1989), p. ix.

52 See Frederick J. Marker and Lise-Lone Marker, 'Ibsen and the Director: From

Traditionalism to Travesty in Recent European Theatre', and Fritz Paul, 'Text – Translation – Performance. Some Observations on Placing Peter Stein's Berlin Production of *Peer Gynt* (1971) within Theatre History', *Contemporary Approaches to Ibsen*, vol. VII, ed. Bjørn Hemmer and Vigdis Ystad (Oslo, 1991). The papers published in this volume deal extensively with 'Ibsen in Performance'.

53 Rolf Fjelde (ed.), *Ibsen: A Collection of Critical Essays,* in the Twentieth Century Views series (Englewood Cliffs, N.J., 1965).

54 *Norwegian English Dictionary* (Oslo and Madison, 1965).

55 Meyer, *Ibsen: A Biography* (London, 1971); Brustein, *The Theater of Revolt* (Boston, 1964); Christensen, *Henrik Ibsens anarkisme* (Copenhagen, 1985); Steiner, *The Death of Tragedy* (London, 1961); Holtan, *Mythic Patterns in Ibsen's Last Plays* (Minneapolis, 1970); Lyons, *Henrik Ibsen: The Divided Consciousness* (Carbondale, 1972); Haakonsen, *Henrik Ibsen: Mennesket og Kunstneren* (Oslo, 1981).

Works of reference

The single most comprehensive reference work for the English-speaking student of Ibsen's plays is the eight-volume *The Oxford Ibsen* (1960–77). Edited by James McFarlane, the set comprises translations by McFarlane and others of all of Ibsen's plays, based on the Norwegian texts in the standard edition: Henrik Ibsen, *Samlede Verker*, Hundreårsutgave, Oslo, 1928–57 (Henrik Ibsen, *Collected Works*, Centenary Edition), and includes translations of extant drafts, fragments and the 'Epic Brand'. As well, each volume begins with a lengthy, authoritative critical essay by McFarlane, situating its plays in Ibsen's life and times and setting out significant lines of interpretive inquiry. Each volume concludes with appendices and a selected bibliography. The appendices include for each of the plays in that volume: discussions of dates of composition; draft manuscripts; some relevant comments by Ibsen and his contemporaries; and contemporary reception of book sales and play productions. The bibliography (volume I contains a Select Bibliography of Ibsen 1850–1857 and volume VIII contains the most current, 1977) includes selected lists of: bibliographies; biographies; collected editions of translations into English of the plays and of letters, articles and speeches; and works of criticism – a chronological listing of general Ibsen studies in English and a listing of additional studies of the plays in the given volume in English and other languages. Volume I contains two biographical appendices: 'Ibsen in Christiania 1850–1851' and 'Ibsen and the Bergen Theatre 1851–1857'; volume VII contains one: 'Ibsen 1888–1892: Life and Art.' For the modern plays, beginning with volume V, an additional appendix lists principal London stage productions, BBC radio productions, and television productions in Britain; for the plays in the given volume, the cast is named. *The Oxford Ibsen* also includes translations of those of Ibsen's poems directly relevant to the plays.

If *The Oxford Ibsen* is the best-equipped English-language vehicle for embarking on research, then the on-going *Ibsenårbok[en]* (*[The] Ibsen Yearbook*) / *Contemporary Approaches to Ibsen* affords the most detailed, continuously updated map of the territory. Beginning in 1952, this series provides extensive, international bibliographic coverage and a collection of articles and commentaries in various languages. The five volumes of the yearbook containing reports from the International Ibsen Seminar – 1965–6, 1970–1, 1975–6, 1978, 1983–4 – are entitled *Contemporary Approaches to Ibsen*. Beginning with the sixth volume of *Contemporary Approaches to Ibsen* (1988), the *Ibsenårbok[en]* is wholly subsumed under the more descriptive English title, the frequency is biennial, and the language of publication is English. Following the new editorial policy, *Contemporary Approaches to Ibsen*, vol. VII (1991) includes selected papers from the 1989 Sixth International Ibsen Seminar, other articles of new research, an important earlier Norwegian article not previously available in English, and two book reviews. The 'Ibsen Bibliography 1987–1990' in vol. VII contains references not only to books and articles but also to book reviews, Nordic newspaper articles and reviews, *Times Literary Supplement* reviews, and so forth. The new *Contemporary Approaches to Ibsen* provides the most current and comprehensive information available on international Ibsen scholarship.

A third important reference source of a very different sort is *Ibsen News and Comment: Journal of the Ibsen Year in America*. The contents of this slim annual of the Ibsen Society of America include editorials and other essays, reports on presentations at the Society's twice-yearly meetings, interviews highlighting important perspectives on Ibsen and book reviews. Three other features deserve special mention because of their unusual research value. The first, 'Articles on Ibsen', reviews the previous year's more important articles and essays, providing an overview, significant highlights and a brief comparative analysis. The second, 'Ibsen on Stage', begins in volume 1 (Spring 1980) as a collection of reviews of Ibsen productions, but with volume 12 (1991) undergoes a significant change. The pieces now focus primarily on those innovative or potentially instructive elements of a production that may contain new critical insights for theatre artists and Ibsen scholars. Finally, 'Membership News' lists members' works recently produced or published and work in progress. Since the Ibsen Society of America includes both Ibsen scholars and theatre practitioners (directors, actors, set designers, dramaturgs and so forth), this compilation provides the best available cross-section of what is occurring currently in Ibsen scholarship and theatre production in Canada and the United States.

In the categories that follow, the major principle of selection has been to include those books whose sole topic is Ibsen and which a good self-respecting British or American undergraduate library would be likely to have to support the English-speaking student of Ibsen.

BIBLIOGRAPHIES

In addition to the bibliographic sources listed in the eight volumes of *The Oxford Ibsen* and those in the successive numbers of *Contemporary Approaches to Ibsen*, the Modern Language Association's *MLA International Bibliography* is a useful source for consultation. Because an item is listed only once in the classified sections in the post-1980 *MLA Bibliography*, a complete search for Ibsen citations requires three points of consultation for each year: the volume II, Classified Listings (Norwegian Literature/1800–1988, Ibsen, Henrik); and the Subject and Author Indexes (Subject Index, Ibsen, Henrik) for both volume I and volume II. The annual bibliographies in periodicals such as *Modern Drama* are useful because they have more currency than is afforded by the year's publication delay of the *MLA Bibliography*. In addition, most of the more recent books listed below contain selected bibliographies.

BIOGRAPHY, LIFE AND TIMES, THE MAN AND HIS WORK

Three biographies available in English can serve as the starting point: the contemporaneous biography by Henrik Jæger, *Henrik Ibsen: A Critical Biography* (2nd rev. and augmented edn, 1901, reprinted 1972); Halvdan Koht's historical and psychological *Life of Ibsen* (1971, trans. from the 2nd rev. Norwegian edn 1954); and Michael Meyer's focus on everyday life and the artist in society in *Ibsen: A Biography* (3 vols. 1967–70, publ. as one vol. 1971). To these might be added a fourth scheduled for translation and publication in the mid-1990s: Daniel Haakonsen, *Henrik Ibsen: mennesket og kunstneren* (1981; The Man and the Artist), a biographical and critical analysis superbly illustrated with scenes connected with Ibsen's life and travels and with photographs of Ibsen productions around the world.

Another six books provide a family background and an intellectual and cultural setting. Ibsen's daughter-in-law Bergliot writes *The Three Ibsens: Memories of Henrik Ibsen, Suzannah Ibsen and Sigurd Ibsen* (1951, trans. from the 1949 Norwegian publ.); Edmund Gosse, *Northern Studies* (1890, reissued 1970); Georg Brandes, *Henrik Ibsen, A Critical Study* (1899, repr. 1964); Brian W. Downs, *Ibsen: The Intellectual Background* (1946) and *Modern Norwegian Literature 1860–1918* (1966); and James McFarlane, *Ibsen and the Temper of Norwegian Literature* (1960).

Two very different works provide a further sense of the intellectual response during Ibsen's lifetime. From her position as his contemporary, the European intellectual and free-thinker Lou Salomé responds to and interprets Ibsen's portrayal of women in *Ibsen's Heroines*, (1892, trans. 1985). In America, Hjalmar Hjorth Boyesen is one of the first defenders of Ibsen in *A Commentary on the Works of Henrik Ibsen* (1894, reissued 1973).

The remaining biographical–critical works can be divided into those from the first half of this century: Janko Lavrin, *Ibsen and his Creation: A Psycho-Critical Study* (1921); A. E. Zucker, *Ibsen: The Master Builder* (1929); Theodore Jorgenson, *Henrik Ibsen: Life and Drama* (1945); and M. C. Bradbrook's emphasis of the poetry of the theatre in *Ibsen the Norwegian: A Revaluation* (1946, new edn with new final chapter and translation of twelve poems, 1966). The second group begins with the 1960s: Hans Heiberg, *Ibsen: A Portrait of the Artist* (1969, trans. from the Norwegian edn of 1967); Harold Clurman, *Ibsen* (1977); Edvard Beyer, *Ibsen: The Man and His Work* (trans. 1978); Einar Haugen, *Ibsen's Drama: Author to Audience* (1979); and David Thomas, *Henrik Ibsen* (1983). Clurman, Haugen and Thomas include discussions of Ibsen on stage.

TRANSLATIONS

For an interpretation of the concept of translation, its limits and its capabilities, James McFarlane's essay, 'Modes of Translation', in *Ibsen and Meaning: Studies, Essays and Prefaces 1953–87* (1989) is a model discussion.

Because it is particularly important that the dialogue in Ibsen's realistic plays be rendered in a language that sounds natural to the listener's ear, and because the differences between British English and American English are often precisely those affecting this quality, care should be taken to note the language of the translator. British English translators include William Archer, Una Ellis-Fermor, Peter Watts, Michael Meyer and James McFarlane. American English translators include Rolf Fjelde and Eva Le Gallienne; of these two, Fjelde is the more faithful on several counts.

A detailed list of play translations into English listed according to collected editions is given on pages 384–5 of volume VIII of *The Oxford Ibsen*. A detailed list of translations listed according to play titles is given on pages 166–8 of Einar Haugen's *Ibsen's Drama: Author to Audience*. Two more recent publications of the earlier drama are Rolf Fjelde's revised verse translation of *Peer Gynt* (1980) and Thomas Van Laan's verse translation of the 1850 and the 1875 editions of *Catiline* in *'Catiline' and 'The Burial Mound'* (1991).

Ibsen's *Poems* and *Selected Poems 1848–1872* are available in John Northam's finely translated versions, *Ibsen's Poems* (1986). Evert Sprinchorn's thoughtful collection and translation of selected letters and speeches, *Ibsen: Letters and Speeches* (1964), continues to serve most admirably.

CONCORDANCE, DICTIONARIES, GUIDES

After nearly fifteen years of work, the first phase of the Bergen Ibsen project, under the general editorship of Harald Noreng, was completed in 1992 with the *Ibsen Concordance*. The complete electronic version, available from the Norwegian Computing Centre for the Humanities in Bergen, Norway, is also likely to become available on floppy disk. The abbreviated print version (some 3,200 pages) contains about 40 per cent of the 676,136 words in Ibsen's 26 plays, collected poems, and collection of supplementary texts. Since the context is provided for each instance of a word, the *Ibsen Concordance* is in essence a dictionary of quotations. The much briefer (475 pages) *Henrik Ibsens Ordskatt: Vokabular over hans diktning* (1987), edited by Harald Noreng, Knut Hofland and Kristin Natvig, is a listing of Ibsen's vocabulary with each word's frequency in each play, the poems and the supplementary texts. Among the statistical displays in this volume are tables of each play's frequency of parts of speech and verb forms, further divided into two types of stage directions and into three types of dialogue: male, female and undetermined. The primary text basis for the Bergen Ibsen project is the Centenary Edition (1928–57) of Ibsen's collected works. For the most part, the utility of the concordance materials is in direct proportion to the user's ability to read Ibsen's Norwegian.

The projected second phase of the Bergen Ibsen project is a hypermedia edition of Ibsen material which, using the enhanced Ibsen text, would add related texts, pictures, sound, and video sequences. This would enable the inclusion and cross-referencing of influences and sources, criticism, contemporary reactions, theatre material showing various interpretations, and so forth. The first step is a prototype hypermedia edition of one or two Ibsen plays.

The older *Ibsen-Ordbok* (1958), a separate printing of volume XXI of the Centenary Edition, is an alphabetic vocabulary listing with context. This volume is of limited usefulness to the reader of Ibsen's Norwegian because the referencing is by no means complete. Likewise, lack of appropriate completeness, compounded by some problems of inaccuracy, reductive analysis and eccentric valuing of items, detracts from the over-all reference value of George B. Bryan's *An Ibsen Companion: A Dictionary-Guide to the Life, Works, and Critical Reception of Henrik Ibsen* (1984). The two short general guides – Michael Meyer, *Ibsen on File* (1985) and Yvonne Shafer, *Henrik Ibsen: Life, Work, and Criticism* (1985) – share some of these same problems.

WORKS OF CRITICAL INTERPRETATION

One of the best general starting points for critical interpretation is John Northam's pioneering analysis of Ibsen's dramatic language and visual imagery on stage, *Ibsen's Dramatic Method: A Study of the Prose Dramas* (1953, 1971), and his analysis of the poetic character of the plays in *Ibsen: A Critical Study* (1973). P. D. F. Tennant's analysis of the plays' formal structures, *Ibsen's Dramatic Technique* (1948, repr. 1965), provides a good next step. The third step, into a powerfully rendered argument about the nature and meaning of Ibsen's plays, leads to Errol Durbach and '*Ibsen the Romantic': Analogues of Paradise in the Later Plays* (1982), an analysis of the simultaneity of romantic and counter-romantic attitudes in Ibsen that shapes his protagonists' searches for redemption from meaninglessness and renders them representative of a pervasive European mood. And finally, James McFarlane in *Ibsen and Meaning: Studies, Essays and Prefaces 1953–87* (1989), gathers the eight introductions from *The Oxford Ibsen* together with six other essays to make a volume which provides for Ibsen's career as a whole and for each of the plays, an immensely rich and detailed analysis and series of interpretations.

Four collections of essays provide access to very different sorts of important critical materials, some of which are otherwise difficult to obtain. James McFarlane edits two of these: *Discussions of Henrik Ibsen* (1962) and *Henrik Ibsen: A Critical Anthology* (1970). Rolf Fjelde edits *Ibsen: A Collection of Critical Essays* (1965) and Charles R. Lyons edits *Critical Essays on Henrik Ibsen* (1987).

Two publishing series have focused on Ibsen's most famous modern plays. The Modern Language Association's series, 'Approaches to Teaching Masterpieces of World Literature', has a volume on *A Doll House*. Yvonne Shafer edits *Approaches to Teaching Ibsen's 'A Doll House'* (1985), which as the title suggests is an anthology of articles and materials designed to describe and assist teaching the play at the college level. Twayne's Masterwork Studies has volumes on *A Doll House* and *Hedda Gabler*. Errol Durbach in '*A Doll's House': Ibsen's Myth of Transformation* (1991) first elaborates the literary and historical context of the play and then develops a sustained, compelling interpretation by considering translation, visual metaphors and performance, form and genre, dramatic structure and techniques, and thematic issues related to the redefinition and transformation of self. Charles R. Lyons in '*Hedda Gabler': Gender, Role, and World* (published 1990, copyright 1991) develops the literary and historical context of the play and then addresses the play as a mimesis of human behaviour in a historical moment and as a created aesthetic structure, arguing for a response that incorporates both representation and schematization.

Earlier Ibsen critics whose interpretive insights are still very significant to the contemporary reader are: Hermann J. Weigand, *The Modern Ibsen: A Reconsideration* (1925, repr. 1960); Brian W. Downs, *A Study of Six Plays by Ibsen* (1950); F. L. Lucas, *The Drama of Ibsen and Strindberg* (1962); and G. Wilson Knight, *Ibsen* (1962).

The 1970s saw a resurgence of Ibsen critics with various allegiances to 'external codes'. Orley I. Holtan uses mythology to shape his reading in *Mythic Patterns in Ibsen's Last Plays* (1970); Charles R. Lyons uses a phenomenological approach in *Henrik Ibsen: The Divided Consciousness* (1972); Hans Georg Meyer uses German and Danish philosophy in *Henrik Ibsen* (trans. 1972); James Hurt adopts a psychoanalytic approach in *Catiline's Dream: An Essay on Ibsen's Plays* (1972). Brian Johnston employs Hegel's phenomenological structure in *The Ibsen Cycle: The Design of the Plays from 'Pillars of Society' to 'When We Dead Awaken'* (1975) and in his two subsequent volumes, *To the Third Empire: Ibsen's Early Drama* (1980) and *Text and Supertext in Ibsen's Drama* (1989). Richard Hornby uses structuralism in *Patterns in Ibsen's Middle Plays* (1981). However, Ronald Gray in *Ibsen – A Dissenting View: A Study of the Last Twelve Plays* (1977) argues that the values ascribed to Ibsen's drama are for the greater part external to the plays themselves.

Other recent critical scholarship has varying viewpoints. John S. Chamberlain explores Ibsen's radical ambiguity in *Ibsen: The Open Vision* (1982). Per Schelde Jacobsen uses semiotics to analyse folk ballads and Barbara Fass Leavy uses folklore to analyse the plays in *Ibsen's Forsaken Merman: Folklore in the Late Plays* (1988). Robin Young argues that the disinherited child is present in the adult in *Time's Disinherited Children: Childhood, Regression and Sacrifice in the Plays of Henrik Ibsen* (1989). Bruce G. Shapiro's title suggests his thesis: *Divine Madness and the Absurd Paradox: Ibsen's 'Peer Gynt' and the Philosophy of Kierkegaard* (1990). Naomi Lebowitz analyses Ibsen's protagonist's ironic climb from the small, flawed inhabited world toward the Great World in *Ibsen and the Great World* (1990).

THEATRE HISTORY, PRODUCTION, RECEPTION, REVIEWS

The most useful beginnings of an inquiry into Ibsen productions and reception in England are the appendices in the appropriate volumes of Mc-

Farlane, *The Oxford Ibsen* (1960–77). Listed are principal London stage productions, BBC radio productions, and television productions in Britain, together with some early reviews and commentary. The starting point for a similar inquiry for the United States is the appendix in Rolf Fjelde's volume of selected translations *Ibsen: The Complete Major Prose Plays* (1978); entitled 'Ibsen in the American Theater: An Abbreviated Stage History of the Major Prose Plays' it lists production information and cast.

Several books treat Ibsen on the English stage and his reception by his contemporaries and near-contemporaries. Michael Egan (ed.), *Ibsen: The Critical Heritage* (1972) is a collection of critical reviews of Ibsen productions between 1872 and 1906. J. L. Wisenthal (ed.), *Shaw and Ibsen: Bernard Shaw's 'The Quintessence of Ibsenism' and Related Writings* (1979) brings together Shaw's major commentary and several shorter pieces on Ibsen. Keith May elaborates that connection in *Ibsen and Shaw* (1985). Thomas Postlewait edits *William Archer on Ibsen: The Major Essays, 1889–1919* (1984) and subsequently provides a comprehensive analysis of the 'Ibsen Campaign' in his *Prophet of the New Drama: William Archer and the Ibsen Campaign* (1986). Gretchen Ackerman elaborates the theatrical account in *Ibsen and the English Stage: 1889–1903* (1987).

Though similarly detailed critical analyses of Ibsen's impact on the theatre in the United States have not yet been published, Robert Schanke in *Ibsen in America: A Century of Change* (1988) places Ibsen productions from 1882 to 1982 in an American cultural setting and collects essays and interviews by well-known Ibsen actresses. James Salem's *A Guide to Critical Reviews: Part III: Foreign Drama, 1909–1977* (2nd edn 1979), a work of more general reference, gives a listing of Ibsen plays mounted on the New York Stage (Broadway, Off Broadway, and Off Off Broadway) and their reviews in American and Canadian periodicals and in the *New York Times*. The compilation of numbers of New York productions for 1909–77 indicates that the three predominantly popular foreign playwrights were Shaw (190), Ibsen (112), and Chekhov (110).

Among the most provocative books on Ibsen's relation to theatre and performance, *Ibsen and the Theatre* (1980), edited by Errol Durbach, provides nine quite different approaches, while Frederick J. Marker and Lise-Lone Marker's *Ibsen's Lively Art: A Performance Study of the Major Plays* (1989) sustains a uniform one, as does their earlier *Edward Gordon Craig and 'The Pretenders': A Production Revisited* (1981). Other books to be mentioned are Asbjørn Aarseth's slim volume in an undergraduate series, *'Peer Gynt' and 'Ghosts': Text and Performance* (1989); Freddie Rokem's treatment of the semiotics of visual elements in *Theatrical Space in Ibsen,*

Chekhov and Strindberg: Public Forms of Privacy (1986); and Jane Ellert Tammany's loosely juxtaposed presentation of Ibsen and Kierkegaard in *Henrik Ibsen's Theatre Aesthetic and Dramatic Art* (1980).

Approaching Ibsen from the viewpoint of leading actresses provides another important theatrical perspective. Among early volumes are Jeanette Lee's *The Ibsen Secret: A Key to the Prose Dramas of Henrik Ibsen* (1907) and Elizabeth Robins's *Ibsen and the Actress* (1928). Two biographies of Eleonora Duse are also important in this respect: Eva Le Gallienne, *The Mystic in the Theatre: Eleonora Duse* (1973) and William Weaver, *Duse: A Biography* (1984). 'Part Two: Actresses on Ibsen' in Schanke's *Ibsen in America: A Century of Change* and his bibliography provide further resources.

Henrik Ibsen, 1828–1978: A Filmography (1978), compiled by Karin Synnøve Hansen on behalf of the Norwegian Film Institute, is a pamphlet that lists some film versions of Ibsen plays, giving country, language, date and some production credits. The countries represented are Norway, Sweden, Germany, Russia, USA, England, Argentina, Italy and Austria. Hardly definitive, it is, however, the only filmography available.

INDEX

Within this general index there are two specialized and comprehensive sub-headings: the one is 'Works' covering Ibsen's dramatic and non-dramatic works by their English titles; the other is 'Characters', which registers the characters in those works by name in their English form. The reader who wishes to establish the Norwegian titles of the major works is referred to pp. xxi–xxvi. Alphabetization is by English dictionary conventions, i.e. 'å' is sorted as 'a', 'æ' as 'ae', 'ø' as 'o', etc.